Student Affairs:
A Profession's Heritage

EDITORS

Gerald L. Saddlemire & Audrey L. Rentz
Department of College Student Personnel
Bowling Green State University

AMERICAN COLLEGE PERSONNEL ASSOCIATION
MEDIA PUBLICATION NO. 40

ACPA is a division of the
American Association for Counseling and Development

Library of Congress Cataloging-in-Publication Data
Main entry under title:

Readings in college student personnel.

  (Media publication; no. 40)
  Bibliography: p.
  1. Personnel service in higher education—United
States—History—20th century—Sources
I. Saddlemire, Gerald L. II. Rentz, Audrey L.
III. Series: ACPA media publication; no 40
LB2343.R391983   378'.194   83-6045
ISBN 0-8093-9910-5

Second Printing

Printed in the United States of America.

Materials reprinted by permission.

iii

The American College Personnel Association is a division of the American Association for Counseling and Development dedicated to serving students through professional programs for educators committed to student development. The Association unites the functions, services and programs of college and university student affairs professionals which include areas such as admissions, financial aid, counseling, career services, commuter programs, residence life, activities and health services. As the largest national professional organization of student affairs professionals with over 7,000 members, ACPA conducts ongoing professional development activities for members, provides the vehicle for profession-related social and political action, encourages human development and determines and maintains ethical standards in the profession.

The American College Personnel Association does not discriminate on the basis of race, color, national origin, religion, sex, age, affectional/preference, or disability in any of its policies, procedures or practices. This non-discrimination policy covers membership and access to association programs and activities including but not limited to National Conventions, placement services, publications, educational services and employment.

Also by ACPA Media

Alcohol Programming for Higher Education	James C. Dean & William A. Bryan
Creating Community in Residence Halls: A Workbook for Definition, Design & Delivery	Ken Ender, Nancy Kane, Phyllis Mable & Meredith Strohm
The Eighties: Challenges for Fraternities and Sororities	William A. Bryan & Robert A. Schwartz
Evaluation in Student Affairs	George D. Kuh, Ed.
A Guidebook for the Successful Job Search in Student Development	Tom Bachhuber
A Handbook for Student Group Advisers	John Schuh, Ed.
A Leaders Guide to the Successful Job Search in Student Development	Wendy Settle & Eric Schlesinger
Personal Education & Community	David A. DeCoster & Phyllis Mable, Eds.
Residence Education: A Career Beginning or A Career Path	Edward L. Reynolds, Jr., Susan Bowling Komives & Phyllis Mable
The Student Affairs Profession: A Selected Biography	Beverly A. Belson & Louis C. Stamatakos
Student Development in Higher Education: Theories, Practices & Future Directions	Don G. Creamer, Ed.
Student Leadership Programs in Higher Education	Dennis C. Roberts, Ed.
Thus We Spoke: ACPA-NAWDAC 1958–1975	Beverly A. Belson & Laurine E. Fitzgerald
Up the Ladder: Women Professionals & Clients in College Student Personnel	Beverly Prosser Gelwick, Ed.

Assessing Intellectual Development: M. Baxter-Magolda
The Link Between Theory and W. D. Porterfield
Practice

Available From:
Order Services Department
American Association for Counseling and Development
5999 Stevenson Avenue
Alexandria, VA 23304

Contents

Foreword

When student affairs practitioners, preparation program faculty and students and higher education scholars seek literature that contains the basic assumptions, concepts and rationales for the student personnel/development profession, they find some articles out of print and others difficult to locate because of limited distribution. This book gathers together materials with the following purposes:

1. To preserve and make available articles reflecting the significant contributions made by early writers during the initial stages of the profession generally referred to as college student personnel.

2. To preserve and make available significant documents/statements issued by professional associations concerned with the college student personnel field.

3. To present the above literature in the style of a collection of readings to be used in graduate seminars.

4. To make readings available for the professional practitioner who is interested in learning about the contributions made by specific authors and commissions and/or committees to the development of college student personnel.

5. To identify early contributors and representative papers that help us understand the evolution of our profession. Some practitioners have entered the profession without being introduced to the profession's heritage or may have come to the field by way of other specialty graduate degree programs.

The editors appreciate the suggestions made by fifty-five graduate program directors suggesting the materials that should be included in this collection of readings. Arbitrary choices had to be made among articles that had value so that the book would not exceed reasonable length. It was gratifying to note the quality of the literature, but frustrating to exclude articles that merit our attention when we examine our heritage. Bibliographies and references may help those who wish to look further for other works important to our profession.

Gerald L. Saddlemire
Audrey L. Rentz

I

The Early Years

One measure of the maturity of the student affairs profession is the body of literature that describes its origin, its growth and the concepts central to its role in higher education. Until recently, the senior members of the profession had personally experienced and examined many of the documents at the time they were published or they were introduced to the early documents as a part of their advanced degree work. Since this is no longer possible, graduate students and younger practitioners must become familiar with the heritage of the profession by a systematic examination of representative articles as reproduced in this book. Our current identity, basic assumptions, roles and responsibilities can be traced to statements made in the early part of this century when the number of student affairs practitioners was finally large enough to encourage early authors to describe and justify personnel work.

In the late 19th century there had been several pioneer deans who were celebrated for their historical significance, but the literature describing their contributions to the field was not available until the early twentieth century.

In Part One: The Early Years, seven articles are included to illustrate both the early efforts to define and justify the field as well as to identify the individuals who had the courage and vision to publish articles describing the role of student personnel work in higher education.

One of the first persons to suggest the need for what was to become a student affairs department was C. S. Yoakum, who argued in 1919 that an important lesson learned in the War Department in World War I was the need to have a personnel bureau as part of (educational) institutions. He says that such a bureau needs to collect and codify accu-

1

rate data on each student, collect and classify vocational information, present occupational information to the student, and establish cumulative student records. Yoakum, a major in the Sanitary Corps USA when he wrote this article, also describes the specialized knowledge needed among the personnel staffing this bureau.

Robert C. Clothier, Chairman of the Committee on Personnel Principles and Functions, submitted a report in 1931 that responded to the charge from the Executive Committee of the American College Personnel Association to develop a statement of principles, functions and accrediting methods for student personnel work. It will be interesting to those now preparing standards for accreditation agencies to read this early comment about the accreditation process. The statement of principles and the list of functions were the basis for the A.C.E. *Student Personnel Point of View* (Commission statement) issued just six years later in 1937.

Esther Lloyd-Jones, in 1934, examines the definitions of student personnel work and concludes that a distinction must be made between student personnel work and student personnel administration. She argues for coordinating, organizing and administering as necessary duties in the student personnel field. Her commitment to the administrator role is reflected in the name given to the graduate department Student Personnel Administration at Teachers College, Columbia, one of the early graduate programs responsible for preparing student affairs professionals.

The length of the article by Cowley and Waller made it necessary to edit some portions of the manuscript while retaining the essential message. A call is made for the systematic study of student life by the behavioral scientist. This article is strengthened by including a number of examples of student behavior that, upon analysis, provide a better understanding of student life. Sociologists, social psychologists and cultural anthropologists were invited to examine the environmental pressures of the campus. Here is an early indication of the central role of the behavioral scientist in student personnel work.

In 1936 Bradshaw deals with the aims of educational personnel work at the college and university level. He summarizes the statements on core functions made by earlier authors and then presents his own convictions regarding trends and basic assumptions.

Any study of the widely used definitions of personnel work will depend heavily on Cowley's effort to clarify the nature of student personnel work. He distinguishes between "guidance" and "personnel work," a debate that still can be heard among professionals. Cowley's attempt to identify the nature of student personnel work leads him to call for representatives of all college personnel groups to come together for a definitive discussion of the nature of their common task.

Such a group did come together under the auspices of the American Council on Education and issued the widely acclaimed *Student Personnel Point of View* in 1937. Chaired by E. G. Williamson, this committee of faculty and administrators developed a statement about the field that reflected a consensus of the philosophy, services, administrative relationships and a call for national leadership to undertake activities identified as essential to the future of student personnel work (e.g., position papers, research). It should be noted that this document was the first prepared by a cross section of educators who could speak authoritatively for the entire field.

Plan for a Personnel Bureau in Educational Institutions

C. S. Yoakum

Personnel problems connected with the formation of the United States Army brought into high relief certain difficulties that institutions dealing with the training and education of young men and women had vaguely felt. A few institutions had attempted to set into operation methods aimed at the solution of these questions. The systematic and persistent exploration of the difficulties and their solution were forced upon the War Department. Its rapid and unprecedented expansion gave clear definition to many unsettled personnel problems. It found the source of supply unanalyzed and its own needs but vaguely in mind. Large numbers of specialists were suddenly demanded. Experience quickly demonstrated that personal qualities were extremely important assets in war. It became necessary to specify in detail the personal, educational and technical requirements for each important task. To insure proper qualifications, specially devised tests proved necessary. The increased size of the army forced it to maintain complete and detailed systems of personnel records and to devise special "follow-up" methods.

Army experience can be duplicated in the experience of our educational institutions. We believe that the pressure of war has produced a clearer conception of the problems involved in training and placement. It has emphasized the advantages of carefully systematized procedure in discovering needed qualities of human nature, and the importance of freeing estimates of persons, as much as possible, from the errors of personal bias and incidental acquaintance. Vague memories of so-and-so's personality and qualifications broke down utterly as a means of building up an army.

This article proposes the general outline of a plan for a personnel bureau. The principal features of such a bureau can be put into operation in any educational institution, large or small. The plan considers

4

the study of student personnel as fundamental in any institution that believes its function is connected in any way with the well-being of its patrons and with the success of its graduates in their chosen professions. It also contains the implication that such an institution must keep fuller and more definite records of success and failure, of personalities and of the results of its training and teaching. The essential functions of such a bureau, or committee, are four. Modifications of the plan will emphasize one or the other of these functions, according to local conditions, the specific aims of the institution or the personnel of the bureau itself; subdivision of functions will increase with the growth of the bureau and the financial and moral encouragement given it.

The primary functions of the bureau are, to obtain accurate data on each student, to codify the requirements of different professions, to supervise the use of tests and to provide means whereby each student may become acquainted with his abilities and the requirements of the occupations in which he is interested. Properly to perform these functions as complete an inventory of the human material passing through the institution as is possible must be made in permanent form. Second, the files of this bureau must contain a similar inventory of the important vocations. Third, the bureau will provide the responsible agencies for bringing to the student seeking a life occupation all its systematic material on the opportunities and requirements necessary to attain a certain degree of success in those vocations open to him. Fourth, the bureau will proceed on the assumption that all of these problems can be investigated in a scientific manner and will initiate and encourage research in this field.

The essentials of the inventory of human material can be placed on a single card—the personal history card or qualification card. This qualification card will contain facts concerning the previous history of the individual. This previous history should contain items concerning his social and school life pertinent to the purpose of such an inventory. The card will also be a permanent record of his educational career. It is not necessary to summarize in detail the items involved in such a record. Ratings which will consist of elementary school grades, marks in college or technical school studies and the results of specially devised rating plans will also be recorded on this card. It is further expected that on the student's qualification card space be left for recording the results of intelligence tests and of other tests important in determining the qualifications of the individual. Recent determinations of the usefulness of such intelligence ratings and specialized tests make it probable that in the future no institution will be without such information concerning its student body.

The information desired as a part of the student's permanent record may be obtained in several well-known ways; though at present none of these is satisfactory. Extremely valuable estimates of the individual's qualifications and qualities of mind and person may nevertheless be obtained by careful interviewing when he reports for entrance to the college or other educational institution. Such estimates as the student himself gives at this interview can be supplemented and checked by carefully prepared letters of inquiry to persons who have known him in his previous school work and outside activities. Additional ratings and estimates on personal qualities and on special aptitudes should be obtained at least yearly from his instructors and fellow students. These estimates properly tabulated and combined with the objective ratings obtained from the tests give the foundation for tentative judgments of the student's ability and probable future career.

The second function of this bureau is the collection and classification of vocational information. This should include carefully obtained opinions on the qualities necessary for success in each of the vocations studied. Each vocation should be carefully studied from the point of view of the range of mental capacity that will stand a satisfactory chance for success. A card for a vocation should also indicate minimum and maximum educational qualifications so far as they can be returned. Such a record must also specify the need for any special ability if such is an essential. When properly completed the specifications for any vocation will also include a statement of the more essential qualities necessary for success in that vocation. It is not too much to believe that sometime in the future these may be given their proper weighting in a great many vocations. Bibliographies pertaining to special fields can also be made available to students through the bureau.

Again much careful investigation is necessary. This part of the work of the bureau must begin at the beginning. The utter lack of agreement on the qualities that produce success and satisfaction in life is easily demonstrated. Whether this failure to agree is a matter of permanent differences indicating many roads to success or satisfaction, or is rather one in which a limited number of qualities receive different weights un-

der definitely describable conditions, is surely a problem worth experimentation. Minimal requirements of education and training can undoubtedly be specified and standardized.

The third important function of this personal bureau will be to bring
to the student seeking a life vocation all material collected on vocations. By proper methods of cataloguing this material can be readily
presented to the student. In this conference section of the bureau,
problems concerning his college advancement may also be taken up
with the student. It is, of course, here that the importance of the objective tests can most readily be seen. The collection and recording of the
information as described above will be of extreme advantage to the
dean, and to others whose duty it is to discuss with the student his place
in the school work and his success in advanced studies.

Properly to develop the fourth function, it is important that a single
responsible agency have charge of general intelligence tests and other
forms of testing used. This agency should not be within any single
school or department of the institution. The value of modern group
and individual examinations of relative intelligence is now thoroughly
established. The plan proposed aims to make these an integral part of
the personnel inventory. The satisfactory development of their values
rests on the scientific care and common-sense skill with which they are
used. Their proper use is obviously in connection with the two inventories above described. So used they will undoubtedly prove invaluable
aids in personnel interviews with students.

The importance of following up the use of tests is, of course, patent.
The correlations desired are essential in estimating the significance of
tests, the prophetic value of personal data and the weightings for vocational qualifications. Constant revision, retrial and experimentation
are implied in this fourth function of the bureau.

The personnel of such a bureau should be carefully selected. During
the first years of its operation and in preparing the final form of organization, its work should be supervised by a general committee. Immediate responsibility for the bureau should be in the hands of a smaller
group of men who have shown themselves to be particularly interested
in human qualities and their development. If properly managed, it will
require part time from at least three men of professional rank. The
chairman of this smaller group should be responsible for the general organization of the plan and its coordination with other university activi-

ties. The second member of the sub-committee should be a specialist who is thoroughly acquainted with business methods and vocational specifications. The third member should have special qualities fitting him for personal contact with the student and for the *unbiased* presentation of the requirements of different vocations. The direct management of the affairs of the bureau should be in the hands of a secretary, who should have at least the rank of an assistant professor. It is probable that practically full time will be required of this man, and in the current management of such a bureau he doubtless will be the important active member of it.

The proposed bureau does not present a scheme for vocational guidance. If an institution or a dean feels that it or he can properly carry the responsibility, the bureau provides the only safe procedure for obtaining guidance in passing out such advice. We believe rather that an institution owes it to its student body to provide systematically prepared information about life and its business. Further, if the study of human qualities is to be removed from the realm of palmistry and "get rich quick" schemes, systematized research must provide the means. Persistent and organized research of this type must be done in permanent institutions that will provide continuous and accessible records. Several years of cooperative research among widely distributed institutions might even produce principles for vocational guidance.

College Personnel Principles and Functions

Robert C. Clothier

From the Executive Committee of the Association, the Committee on Personnel Principles and Functions has received instructions:

1. To prepare a statement of *principles* which the Association might propose as the basis of establishing personnel work in the colleges;
2. To prepare a *statement of functions* and techniques recommended;
3. To prepare a statement of the *methods of accrediting* various college personnel bureaus or departments.

Your Committee feels that the discharge of this commission is not something which can be accomplished overnight, if in fact it can be accomplished at all. The developing of a statement of principles, of functions and of accrediting methods must be an evolutionary process which must take into consideration the experience and point of view of many persons working in the field and of many institutions of differing size, nature, scope and purpose.

This report attempts to set forth a point of departure in this evolutionary process. We begin by presenting (a) certain definitions of terms. This introductory part is followed, in order, by (b) a statement of principles, (c) a statement of functions, (d) a statement relative to methods of accrediting, and (e) conclusion.

(A) Definition of Terms

It seems to us that the first step in this evolutionary process must be an attempt to define terms. There is urgent need for such definition. Even the term "personnel work" is interpreted in different ways. To some of us it is broad in its meaning, involving all those aspects of col-

9

lege work which affect the student as an individual. To others it denotes certain specific functions. The former concept is unsatisfactory to some persons because, in its general nature, it seems to lack specific meaning; the latter is equally unsatisfactory to others because it seems incomplete.

As a point of departure we recommend as a definition of personnel work the following:

Personnel work in a college or university is the systematic bringing to bear on the individual student all those influences, of whatever nature, which will stimulate him and assist him, through his own efforts, to develop in body, mind and character to the limit of his individual capacity for growth, and helping him to apply his powers so developed most effectively to the work of the world.

One of the key words in this definition is the word "individual." The implication of this word involves the recognition of the entire principle of individual differences. Personnel work, consequently, accepts as one of its fundamental principles that students differ one from the other, not only in the mere physical characteristics which are obvious, but in all those relatively intangible characteristics of mind, emotion and character which affect so greatly their performance of different kinds of work and their reactions to different stimuli. By way of illustration, it recognizes that one student may perform with ease a task which another may perform only with the greatest difficulty; may respond with enthusiasm to a factor of environment which might leave another cold or even antagonistic; may possess a sense of right and wrong, of moral obligation, of courage, of determination which another may lack entirely. The individual's equipment in such terms as these must be known, understood and considered in planning his work and in directing him in its execution, if the college is to be fully successful in his education.

It is obvious that knowing and steering the student thus cannot be isolated in any one department. Personnel work cannot be departmentalized, except for certain specific functions which will be discussed later. Rather personnel work must be a leaven throughout the whole college and these influences, of which we speak in our definition, must be brought to bear on the student by all who come in contact with him—by professor, instructor, dean, registrar, adviser, coach, proctor, yes even janitor. It's not the official status that makes the good person-nel man, it's the sincerity and intelligence of his interest in the student.

This statement of the nature and scope of personnel work naturally raises the question: What is the official status of personnel work in a college?

In other words personnel work in a college consists in promoting a point of view on the part of administrators and instructors which is fa-vorable to the consideration of the student as an individual and in maintaining such services, outside the purely academic functions, as contribute to the individual student's success at college (e.g., personal and vocational guidance, health, mental hygiene, financial counseling and assistance, housing, placement).

Although personnel work is conducted in different ways in different institutions, it is generally directed through a department generally known as the Personnel Department. A definition might be expressed as follows:

The Personnel Department is that department of the administration or that group of persons in which initiative and responsibility for the personnel work of the college is vested.

This department may have different titles in different institutions, different powers, different responsibilities, according to the type of organization and nature of work in those institutions but its field and purpose is to promote throughout the college the sympathetic and thor-ough consideration of the student as an individual.

Except for such functions as exist as line functions within the Person-nel Department (such as, for instance, personnel counselling, voca-tional guidance and placement), the Personnel Department usually functions without authority in promoting the personnel point of view throughout the organization, through developing a cooperative work-ing relationship with administrators, educational heads, members of faculties and others based on service rendered. The possession of ad-ministrative authority is regarded as a very questionable advantage as a personnel point of view cannot be legislated into existence; administra-tors and teachers will entertain it in their relations with students only if they believe in it and no amount of legislation can effect it otherwise.

The directing head of the Personnel Department, or where no formal personnel department exists, that officer or executive who by virtue of his position or his interest assumes responsibility for the personnel work in a college, is known as the Personnel Director, or other equivalent title. He reports directly to the president, or administrative head of the college, whom he represents in this work. Stated as a definition:

The Personnel Director is that official or executive, reporting directly to the administrative head of the college, who assumes initiative and responsibility for the development of the personnel program of the institution. As a staff officer he cooperates with other administrative and educational heads in promoting the interests of the individual student in all his college relationships both inside and outside the classroom. As a line officer he assumes direction of those personnel functions which administratively lie within the jurisdiction of the personnel department.

Our definition of personnel work includes the phrase "and helping him (the student) to apply his powers so developed most effectively to the work of the world." In short personnel work necessarily includes the functions of *vocational guidance* and *placement*. It seems appropriate, at this point, to set forth two additional definitions.

Vocational guidance is that service which the college renders to the individual student which serves to assist him in evaluating his own aptitudes and interests, to acquire knowledge about many fields of work and the requirements for success in those fields, and to decide wisely in which field of endeavor he will most likely find success and satisfaction.

And

Placement is that service which the college renders to the individual student which enables him to learn of opportunities in the field of his selection and to secure that position in which he will most likely find success and satisfaction.

(B) Principles

In these several definitions certain principles have been set forth. At the risk of repetition, we present here a general statement of principles:

1. Every student differs from every other student in aptitudes, inher-

ited or acquired—those powers of hand and brain which are his tools of workmanship; in interests, those impulses and motives which stimulate or inhibit the exercise of those powers under different circumstances and at different kinds of work; in character traits—integrity, perseverance, etc. The college must know these qualifications so far as it is possible to do so and must utilize that knowledge in planning his college course, both within and without the curriculum, in stimulating him to pursue it, and in guiding him afterward to his vocational opportunity.

2. Every agency within the college should consider these differences between students—the administrative officials; the educational, personal and vocational counsellors; the members of the teaching staffs and others who come in contact with the students as individuals.

3. The Personnel Department, under the Personnel Director, is responsible for the development of this point of view throughout the organization. In promoting it, the Personnel Department will work through the administrative heads of schools and departments and through their associates and subordinates. The relationship is ordinarily an informal and personal one, without authority.

4. Each college should provide adequate facilities—in terms both of procedures and equipment—for the maintenance of harmonious and effective relationships among students, faculty members and administrative officials.

5. Each college should select its students with proper knowledge of their qualifications and with due regard to their fitness. This is a function in which the Personnel Department cannot fail to have an active interest.

6. Supplementing the teaching work of the members of the faculties, the college should make provision for the counselling of students on educational, personal and vocational matters. In each instance the counselling should be based upon a critical evaluation of the student's aptitudes and interests and of all other factors present in the situation. Good counselling provides for the student to reach his own decision in any uncertainty with the counsellor's assistance, rather than for him to accept the counsellor's decision.

7. The college should provide a plan for the continuing orientation of its students as they embark upon each new phase of their college life—from the secondary school senior entering the junior college to the college graduate embarking upon his life work.

8. The college must assume its share of responsibility for the physical health of the students, as their physical health is of paramount importance, not only for its own sake, but because of its effect upon their success in their college work. This function is usually exercised by a department of student health, consisting of one or more physicians according to the size and nature of the college.

9. The college must assume its share of responsibility for the mental health of its students for the same reasons as apply to their physical health, and must maintain a mental hygiene service as a part of, or parallel to, its physical health service.

10. The student's physical environment, including his living environment, has a real effect upon his morale and upon his success in his work. In still other ways it has its effect upon the student's personality development. It is the responsibility of the college to provide adequate housing facilities for its students.

11. The college should assist those students whose collegiate progress is threatened by financial anxieties to secure part-time employment; it should provide loan funds which can be made available, in emergency, to responsible students on a definite refund basis; it should provide scholarships to deserving and needy students.

12. The so-called extra-curricular activities should be recognized as potential agencies of character development and should be encouraged and directed by the college but without impairing the student's initiative, leadership, organizing ability and sense of responsibility. They should be integrated so far as possible with the work of the curriculum.

13. Adequate records are essential to good personnel work. The personnel records of a college should (so far as possible) be brought together in one place so that personnel officers, deans, instructors— anyone interested in a student's progress—may find there a complete, cumulative record of his history, background, scholastic and extra-scholastic activities, personal qualification, physical and mental ratings, interests, objectives, etc., in order that projected action may in each instance be taken with due regard to all the facts.

14. The college must recognize that research is an integral part of its personnel work and must make adequate provision, in staff and equipment, for it.

15. The college should make available to the student full information about the nature, opportunity and requirements of different voca-

tions and should help him evaluate his own aptitudes and interests in the light of such information in an attempt to decide wisely what vocation to take up upon graduation. In each case the student should make the decision.

16. The college should establish contacts with as many employers as possible in fields of vocational activity in order to help its students, upon graduation, "to apply their powers most effectively to the work of the world." In each instance the student should "place" himself. The college should follow-up the students so assisted to make sure their powers *are* applied effectively, and aid those who are misplaced to find their proper places.

(C) *Functions*

A consideration of these principles emphasizes the point of view that in personnel work we are interested in the individual student's development, not in any one phase of his program such as scholarship, intellect, leadership, but from the aspect of his whole personality. We are concerned with all those methods and the procedures which bring influences to bear upon him "of whatever nature." And this brings us to the question of functions.

It is impossible for any agency, such as the National Association of Placement and Personnel Officers, to prepare a list of personnel functions with any expectation that such a list will satisfy conditions on all campuses. On one campus, certain functions will be found essential, on another unimportant. Where a restricted interpretation of personnel work is accepted, many of the functions which are listed in this section will appear irrelevant. Where personnel work is interpreted broadly in the sense of our original definition, it is apparent that all these functions should be considered.

Certain of these functions will fall under the administrative jurisdiction of the personnel department, over which the Personnel Director has a direct line of control. Others will fall under the administrative jurisdiction of other departments; these are the functions with which the Personnel Department has merely a staff relationship.

Whether the Personnel Department exercises a line or a staff influence over a given function depends upon the set-up in that particular college.

1. Selection of students. Debarment of applicants whose likelihood of success in college is negligible. Direction of others to those schools and courses in which they will most likely find success.

2. Selection of instructors. The personnel situation in a college is vitally affected by the type of instructors engaged. Those incapable of taking a sincere and intelligent interest in the individual student should be debarred.

3. Orientation of students. Adoption of procedures which serve to integrate the student with his new environment and offset those negative influences, arising from unfamiliarity with new personalities and procedures, which tend to retard a student in his work.

4. Educational guidance. Adoption of procedures which will serve to assist the student select those curricula and course of study which will best serve his cultural and vocational objectives.

5. Personal Counselling. Adoption of procedures which serve to assist the student solve those problems of a social or personal nature which, unsolved, tend to impede him in his work.

6. Scholastic motivation. Discovery and development of incentives, through personal conference or otherwise, which will stimulate the individual student to succeed best in his work.

7. Housing Service. Assuring the student a housing environment which will make for morale and effective work.

8. Financial assistance for needy students, in the form of part-time employment made available through an employment bureau or through loans or scholarships.

9. Supervision and direction of extra-curricular activities, including athletics and fraternities.

10. Supervision of student health, through control of environment and through individual examination and treatment where necessary.

11. Mental hygiene. Maintenance of staff of counsellors and psychiatrists equipped to help all students attain as favorable mental attitude toward their work as possible and to treat those who are badly adjusted or mentally ill.

12. Maintenance of adequate personnel records, furnishing full information about each student to instructors, advisers and others who have to do with him.

13. Research. A continuing study and investigation of factors in the personnel situation of the college.

14. Vocational guidance. Maintenance of an adequate infomational and advisory service to assist individual students to learn about different occupations, and to analyze their own powers, and to choose wisely their life careers.

15. Placement. Maintenance of a service to assist graduating students find positions for which they are qualified and in which they will most likely find success.

It is not the Committee's claim that this list of functions is final, nor complete. These fifteen functions are set forth as a point of departure in the discussion and are subject to review.

(D) Methods of Accrediting

Your Committee approaches the problem of devising methods of accrediting colleges according to the effectiveness of their personnel work with grave doubts as to the desirability and practicability of doing so.

In the first place, we do not believe that any organization such as ours has yet arrived at a sufficiently clear and definite set of standards by which to measure the effectiveness of personnel work in a college.

In the second place, we are dealing with values it is hard to measure because the effectiveness of personnel work in a college depends not so much on *what* is done as on *how* it is done. By way of illustration, a college which has no plan for vocational guidance may be guiding its pupils very effectively through informal methods and another with a vocational guidance plan well worked out on paper may, through the personal inadequacy of its counsellors, fall far short of real success.

The devising of methods of accrediting colleges according to the effectiveness of their personnel work must similarly be a matter of gradual development, rather than of abrupt legislation. Without any thought of accrediting, however, it is logical that a college should constantly take stock of its own situation in order to know what phases of its personnel work are being well done and which are not being well done. As a point of departure in such a self-analysis, your Committee proposes the following questions which the administrative official of a college might ask himself and his associates.

1. Does the college make a conscious attempt to determine the qualifications of applicants for admission, to debar those whose previous record and personal analysis indicate a likelihood of failure, to direct others to those schools and courses in which they will most likely find success?

2. Does the college, in selecting instructors, consider their point of view on personnel matters and the sincerity of their interest in course content?

3. Does the college have a well-defined, carefully worked-out plan for the orienting of its new students, for helping the student make a happy adjustment to each new phase of his college life?

4. Does the college have a well-defined, successfully-operating plan to guide its students wisely in organizing their college campaign and in selecting their curricula and courses of study?

5. Does the college have a well-defined, successfully-operating plan to guide and assist the student in solving social and personal problems?

6. Is the college as a whole inspired with the importance, not only of instructing the student, but of inspiring him to make the most of such instruction? Has it developed techniques of bringing definite incentives to bear on him?

7. Does the college provide for the adequate housing of its students?

8. Does the college coöperate effectively with the student in meeting his economic problems (a) by helping him obtain congenial and remunerative part-time employment, (b) by granting loans when necessary, (c) by granting scholarships to students of high potentiality?

9. Does the college regard extracurricular activities as supplementary agencies of education and character-development, and supervise them accordingly?

10. Does the college provide adequately for the physical health of the students through a medical department which studies each student as an individual and recommends specific treatment when necessary, either for prevention of disability or for cure; through continuous inspection of the student's environment from the sanitary point of view?

11. Does the college maintain a mental hygiene service through which students are kept in good mental health and those who are ill or seriously maladjusted are given restorative treatment?

12. Does the college maintain adequate personnel records in such a

way that all significant information about an individual student is made available to administrators and teachers, enabling them to deal with him more understandingly and more effectively?

13. Does the college recognize the significance of research in personnel work and provide adequately for its maintenance?

14. Does the college maintain a coöperative relationship with employers on an extensive scale through which its graduating seniors are assisted in obtaining permanent positions in their chosen fields of work?

15. Is there a personnel department under an officer reporting directly to the administrative head of the college whose responsibility it is to promote the development of such personnel activities as these, either indirectly as a staff function or directly as a line function, into a *coordinated personnel program?*

(E) Conclusion

The heart of personnel work lies in the genuine and intelligent interest of instructors and others in the individual student. Its ends are well served if the instructor thinks of his subject as a means of teaching the student, poorly served if he thinks of the student as a means of teaching his subject. Its purposes are advanced if those services outside the classroom which remove obstacles and help him make the most of his college career are well-organized and operating effectively, retarded if they are not.

Sometimes personnel work is organized under a centralized control and this type of organization has certain advantages. More generally it is decentralized, each department and each individual assuming responsibility for his part of the work. When the work is decentralized in this way, provision should be made—as herein set forth—for the coördination of these independent but related functions through a Personnel Director, or other person or groups of persons, who can visualize the situation as a whole and contribute initiative and assistance where needed.

In closing we recommend that the Association regard this report as the point of departure in a continuing study of principles and functions, that our objectives may become clearer and clearer and our procedures more and more effective. There will be advantage in making haste slowly.

The Committee on Principles and Functions: Robert C. Clothier, *Chairman*, Mabelle B. Blake, Earl W. Anderson, N. M. McKnight, Grace E. Manson.

Personnel Administration

Esther Lloyd-Jones

Student-Personnel work is in the stage where it is being talked about with sublime assurance by individuals who hold widely differing points of view as to what it really is; but a number of individuals possessed of wide theoretical background and sound experience have most helpfully defined and delimited the field. President Hopkins' classic definition of personnel work is, "Work having to do specifically with individuals." Dean Hawkes limited this broad definition to, "Work for the individual student which is being done outside the classroom." The definition of President Clothier and his Committee on Principles and Functions of the American College Personnel Association once more broadened the scope of personnel work at the same time that it made it more specific:

Personnel work in a college or university is the systematic bringing to bear on the individual student all those influences, of whatever nature, which will stimulate him and assist him, through his own efforts to develop in body, mind, and character to the limit of his individual capacity for growth, and helping him to apply his powers so developed most effectively to the work of the world.

The latest of these four definitions is that of Cowley, who, agreeing with Dean Hawkes, says that student-personnel administration is, "The administration of all university-student relationships aside from formal instruction."

There is by no means universal acceptance of any of these definitions. There does seem to be, however, fairly general agreement as to the functions that personnel work includes. These are: administration of admissions, including selection and pre-college guidance; orientation of students; educational guidance, including the use of such instruments as objective tests; personal counseling, whether classified as psychological, religious, ethical, vocational, or personal; administration of

21

the social program; supervision and direction of extra-curricular activities, including athletics and fraternities; administration of housing; administration of financial aid and part-time employment; supervision of student health; provision for a mental-hygiene program; maintenance and administration of adequate personnel records; placement; and research.

It is important to describe more clearly what student-personnel administration is, what its relation is to general administration, and what its relation is to the various personnel services. In the first place, student-personnel administration and student-personnel work are not synonymous. Any of the "personnel services" included in student-personnel administration are "personnel work," but the co-ordination of student-personnel services into a total program and the supplementing of those existent personnel services by other necessary services is student-personnel administration. With this distinction in mind, President Hopkins' definition is seen to be one of personnel work; Dean Hawkes's, also, is a definition of personnel work. On the other hand, President Clothier's is an excellent definition of personnel administration, although he says it is one of personnel work. Cowley's definition is clearly one of personnel administration, and he so states it.

It is necessary for me in this connection to revise my own earlier definition of personnel work also: "Personnel administration"—not, as I formerly said, "personnel work"—"is the co-ordination and concentration of all the resources of the institution together with the information afforded by scientific investigations for the purpose of furthering the best interests of each individual in all of his aspects."[1]

Student-personnel administration is one of the three main divisions of educational administration. The others are instructional administration and operational administration. Student-personnel administration, unlike specific personnel service, is essentially a function of administration and resides originally and ultimately in the administrative head of an institution. It is generally delegated by the president or principal to a specialist in student-personnel administration, usually called by some such title as director of personnel, dean of men or dean of women, adviser of boys or girls, and the like. It is split off from general

---

1. Lloyd-Jones, Esther. *Student Personnel Work.* New York: Harper and Brothers, 1929. p. 207.

administration when some such conditions as the following make it necessary: large numbers of students; pressure of total administration laid on the president or principal; lack of training on the part of the president or principal to perform the functions of personnel administration, so that elements of the program of student-personnel work are being neglected; and appreciation on the part of the general administration of the desirability of a good deal of time and skilled effort being given to this aspect of education.

Those who have attempted definitions of personnel work or administration have had some difficulty in distinguishing the personnel field from that of education itself. Hopkins specifically says, "He does not assume that it does differ from education itself." Clothier might well have said that his definition was one of education itself. Hawkes and Cowley, however, try to separate it from the classroom. Student-personnel administration can no more be set apart from the intimate processes of education, either in or out of the classroom, than can general administration. Its sole reason for effort is to advance in every way possible the best development of everyone with whom education is concerned.

When one recognizes some distinction between personnel work and personnel administration, it becomes clear that the teacher as a personnel worker is indispensable in any adequate system of personnel administration. The director of student-personnel administration or dean will succeed only to the extent that he promotes among the teaching faculty the personnel point of view and utilizes every bit of skill and wisdom the teacher may possess as a personnel worker in an ever evolving system of personnel administration.

There still exists, even in the minds of those professionally engaged in personnel work, considerable uncertainty as to what student-personnel administration is; consequently, there is still fogginess and confusion about the relationship between student-personnel administration and such personnel services as vocational guidance, psychological counseling, record-keeping, administration of extra-curricular activities, and placements. Some completely identify vocational guidance, placement, or research with student-personnel administration, fallaciously arguing that because student-personnel administration includes vocational guidance, vocational guidance is personnel administration.

The best philosophy of the administration of family life and that of student-personnel administration are identical. The finest kind of home life is not built through the exercise of despotism—not even of benevolent despotism on the part of some one member who is highly skilled; only through a truly creative group method in which each co-operates for the sake of the others' and his own happiness can individuals best develop. The greatest skill in achieving this type of relationship, in which all can thrive and be happy, consists in the ability to get spontaneous participation on the part of each member, as well as in the ability to supplement and co-ordinate individual efforts deftly and inconspicuously.

The stern, indomitable type of leadership found in typical matriarchies and patriarchies is recognized as inimical to the best development of personalities within the family group. While the dictator in government seems to be having his little moment again, dictators in the rôle of administrators of student personnel not only doom themselves to short tenure, but also greatly jeopardize the success of the work itself. A policy of "putting something over," of "making someone come to time," of "riding roughshod over the opposition," while temporarily intoxicating enough to make one feel the brilliant, irresistible leader, inevitably spells disaster to the professed purposes of personnel work and of sound education.

A home-maker does not do her duty completely when she fills the stomachs of her family three times a day with satisfying food. To the extent that she is intelligent and modern in her viewpoint, she utilizes eating for social values; she uses ceremony to achieve psychological satisfactions. The basic values guiding her everyday administration of the culinary side of household management are those having to do with health and physical development and social needs. The home-maker may use the specialized knowledge of dieticians, she may employ chefs in her kitchen, but, in general, the responsibility for administering the day-by-day program and having it carried out satisfactorily rests with her.

The director of student personnel in an educational institution may have a minimum of staff—perhaps only one cook, as he does in some small, poverty-stricken institutions—or he may have a splendid retinue of dieticians and cooking experts in charge of the cafeterias and dining rooms. To the extent that the experts utilize eating for education in

health and social values, the personnel administrator is fortunate; residual responsibility, however, falls to his office. He is also responsible
for co-ordinating this area for student life with all the other areas which
personnel administration includes within its scope.

The housing of a family is not merely a matter of having a safe shelter
from the elements. Even if a home-maker employs a staff of architects,
interior decorators, and landscape gardeners, there is still much that
someone must do to make functional living within that material setting
happy and attractive. Similarly, although the director of student personnel may not have more than a consultative relationship to the architect in the planning of a dormitory, his is the voice that must insist
that there is much that housing can contribute directly to aesthetic enjoyment, social education, recreation, health, and convenience; his is
the responsibility for seeing that the housing of the students does contribute these values to a maximum degree. He may be able to work directly with capable, personally selected heads of dormitories; he may
have to work with private householders who house the students in off-
campus residences. In either case, this function of personnel administration is co-ordinated through his office with other personnel functions, and residual responsibilities fall directly upon him.

The health program is one that is included within the personnel-
administration field. It, also, is one of the main responsibilities of the
home-maker. The intelligent home manager realizes that health is to a
very large extent a matter of hour-by-hour living. She realizes that it is
of the greatest importance to build health that will withstand unavoidable strain and stress; accordingly, she guides the program of the family
with this in mind. She believes in periodic health examinations for
every member of the family. When need arises, she uses the best medical specialists available; but the really constructive work comes in putting into actual effect the recommendations arising from the examinations and from the advice of the medical experts. Parents, if they are
wise, employ trained nurses and medical specialists in emergencies, but
they also exercise common sense and ordinary skill in caring for routine
scratches and minor injuries.

The director of student personnel recognizes the health program as
on of the fundamental responsibilities of an educational institution. He
will sacrifice other elements of a complete personnel program, if neces-

sary, for the sake of the health aspect. Dean Smiley has set down the health factors which the average college student needs in order that he may most successfully develop through his college years as:

1. Healthful living conditions including:
   Good food at a reasonable price
   Comfortable and healthy classrooms and quarters
2. Balanced activities including:
   A wisely chosen schedule of studies
   Suitable physical exercise
   Suitable social and recreational activities
3. Efficient health service including:
   A thorough physical examination periodically
   A periodic inventory of health habits
   Convenient medical consultation service
   Communicable disease control measures
   Infirmary care and laboratory service
4. Effective health and character training including:
   Training in elements of biology and bacteriology
   Training in the elements of human anatomy and physiology
   Training in personal hygiene and the elements of community hygiene
   Training in the elements of religion, ethics, and mental hygiene.[2]

From this outline it is apparent that a complete health program as viewed by a college health officer must be a co-operative enterprise. The school or college medical staff may have the vision and ability to achieve an integrated health program; to the extent that it can, and does, the director of student personnel can feel less direct responsibility for this aspect of the personnel program. His responsibility in this case would consist of co-operating at every point with the health officers, and in co-ordinating the total health program with the other aspects of a complete personnel program.

An intelligent family gives serious consideration to the vocational plans and adjustment of its members. Parents attempt to give the kind of character training that will make their children stable and productive members of economic groups; they attempt to build strong bodies

2. Smiley, Dean F. "Provision for the Health of Students," *Provision for the Individual in College Education*, W. S. Gray, editor. Chicago: University of Chicago Press, 1932. pp. 177–88.

and nerves to serve their children as participants in a working society; or they attempt to guide their interests and provide training that will enable them to be self-supporting in spite of some physical handicap; parents attempt to provide opportunities for education that will fit their children as well as may be for some profession or occupation. They use their own experience and that of friends in attempting to help their children decide the general vocational trend which they should adopt. In addition to all this, however, they will gratefully use the scientific information of a specialist in vocational guidance who can make a careful objective inventory of their children's abilities and disabilities and interests, provide sound and extensive information about vocations in our complex economic society, and give definite information about opportunities for employment.

Similarly, in a school or college, the director of personnel who can have within the institution an expert in vocational guidance and an expert in placement must gratefully utilize the valuable services which these experts can provide for the students. The task of "assisting the individual to choose an occupation, prepare for it, enter upon and progress in it" is one requiring expert knowledge and skills. It is also a task requiring a high degree of cooperation with the director of the health program, the director of the curriculum, and with many outside agencies. The relationship of the director of personnel, then, to the vocational-guidance program is that of co-ordinator, supplementer. He will integrate the valuable services of the director of vocational guidance, and the director of the appointment bureau with the total plan of personnel administration. In the event that the director of vocational guidance, the health officer, and the director of religion, each may conceive as one of his primary duties that of training students in the elements of ethics and mental hygiene, the director of student personnel will attempt to co-ordinate their efforts and make the total impact on the student as effective as the enthusiasm of these specialists makes possible.

In similar fashion, one could point out the relationship of the director of student personnel to other parts of the total personnel program and as the mental-hygiene program of the institution. Specialists and psychiatrists, if available, are exceedingly valuable, but mental hygiene actually comes about to a large extent through day-by-day living in an environment that is favorable to it.

One of the most important functions of personnel administration is that of co-ordinating information about each individual. The physician will collect much information about the student's health history, and will, for each year of his college life, summarize his health and physical status. The academic adviser will discover and record year after year facts of considerable importance about his academic interests, his successes and failures. There may be considerable overlapping between the facts gathered by the physical and the academic advisers. Other personnel workers, similarly, will possess specialized information about the student. The duty of the administrator of student personnel, however, is to take the contributions of each one who has information and insight concerning the young person, verify this information, supplement it, co-ordinate it, and record it cumulatively, and make it function as an important guide for his education.

The growth of personnel services in educational institutions since 1920 has been amazing; personnel experts of all sorts have been employed in rapidly increasing numbers. The relationship of all these specialists among themselves, and between them and the person responsible for the administration of personnel work, has been extremely indefinite and unsatisfactory in most instances. On the one hand, each personnel expert has felt a compulsion to encompass the whole field: psychiatrists, for instance, starting with their more immediate professional duties, soon see the necessity of relating their information to all other phases of personnel work; directors of vocational guidance soon see the value of directing aspects of the total personnel program other than the vocational guidance function; it is obvious that the health officers encompass a broad field. On the other hand, deans or directors of student-personnel administration have felt to some extent a sense of guilt if they were not equally skilled in all the personnel functions, if they were not competent medical officers as well as vocational-guidance experts, psychoanalysts, statisticians, dietitians, architects, and administrators.

We hope it is clear from this analysis that the specialist in any aspect of personnel work may have a distinct professional field within which he may render inestimable value, just as the pediatrist, while advising with regard to and directing the upbringing of a child, performs an expert service of inestimable value to the parents in their total plan for the welfare of the family. On the other hand, we have also tried to point out that the administrator of personnel work has a distinct func-

tion in co-ordinating the efforts of these specialists, supplementing
them in every way possible, and in making the total impact of the complete personnel program as beneficial to each individual student as it
can be.

We cannot assume, unfortunately, that all personnel directors, any
more than all home managers, are going to be burdened within the
next few years with an oversupply of expert help. Just as mothers are
going to have to get along without interior decorators and cooks, so
directors of student-personnel administration are going to have to do
their own directing of extra-curricular activities, and much of their own
counseling. The home manager will have to be adjustable enough, intelligent enough, and well enough trained to be able to keep her home
attractive and livable, even to the extent of doing her own scrubbing;
she must keep her family well fed, even to the extent of preparing the
vegetables and washing the dishes afterwards. The director of student-
personnel administration, likewise, must be adaptable enough, intelligent enough, and well enough trained to be able to supplement the
services of those few experts in personnel work who may be available.
It will be well for everyone entering the field of student-personnel administration, in addition to having thorough preparation in the field of
education and administration, to know something about organizing a
testing program, about administering a social program, and about the
principles of counseling, of making a case study, of vocational guidance, of statistics, and of record keeping.

A Study of Student Life

W. H. Cowley and Willard Waller

Obviously, it is not necessary to point out the importance of student life in the educational process. Sociologists do not need to be reminded that the sanctions and compulsions of college life influence every student on every campus. How vigorously the undergraduate may apply himself to his academic work, what friends of both sexes he may choose, what clothes he may wear, where and what he may eat—all these, and much besides, are largely determined for him by the social heritages of the groups and subgroups of which he is a part.

The sociologist, of course, has no interest in taking sides in any verbalistic evaluation of so-called "college atmosphere." He may well concern himself in his choice of research projects, however, with the judgments of these leading educators who have for many years watched students in their communal life together and who have been moved to strong favorable or critical utterances. Over a million undergraduates are today being subjected to the environmental pressures of student life. What these pressures are, whence they come, and how they operate should be thoroughly assessed. These influences present a rich and challenging field for sociological and anthropological study. It is the purpose of this paper not only to report what has been undertaken thus far, but also to petition the aid of other sociologists and anthropologists in the enterprise.

For pragmatic purposes the investigation has been called a study of student traditions. More correctly it might be labeled "a sociological study of student life."

The investigation seeks to examine the whole range of socially inherited behavior among college students. The phrase "student tradition" is employed only because much of the material for appraisal must of necessity be secured from undergraduate participant observers. We seek,

30

in brief, to review and analyze the cultural complexes and processes of American student life.

Clearly the influences which shape college life are much the same as those which play upon all other groups. In the first place, the college generation is but four years long in contrast with the much longer span of adult groups. Traditions age rapidly in the student world because of this telescoping of social processes, and thus the campus furnishes an experimental laboratory comparable to that of the biologist with his white rats, guinea pigs, and drosophila flies.

In the second place, the ancestors of each generation do not die and pass out of the picture. On the contrary, they are very much alive and vocal and must be reckoned with in the persons of alumni who return at frequent intervals to beat their tom-toms "lest the old traditions fail."

In the third place, the college community is a smaller and better defined unit than most groups available to the social scientist. The compact small college and even the more heterogeneous large university present a laboratory for sociological and anthropological investigation much more easily available for study than Middletown, the slums of the great cities, or the taxi dance halls of Chicago.

In order to achieve their objectives the investigators must bring together a great mass of descriptive material about college life. For this they must depend upon students who are at once participants and observers. To discover such students it is first necessary to enlist the co-operation of college teachers of sociology because they understand the problem. Thus far thirty-five sociologists in as many colleges have associated themselves with the undertaking, and the reports from their students are now being tabulated.

When all collectible data have been gathered and classified, they may be analyzed from several points of view. It is the responsibility of the investigators to discover well-defined patterns of human behavior, to refine and universalize them, and to formulate and publicize concepts in the interest of obtaining a better understanding of student life.

To begin with, the history of the college culture complex and of traditional patterns of student behavior may, without too much difficulty, be traced. Communities of students have for centuries been an important part of western European culture and have changed their forms and functions as that culture has evolved. There are, however, in the college world numerous examples of survivals of cultural lag. Town and gown riots are still with us, although it seems likely that they will never reach such violence as the fourteenth century riot at Oxford when 63 students were killed by the townsmen. Initiations, hazing, hell weeks, and the like obviously reach down from the past into the present day college. . . . The tearing down of goal posts after football victories and the wiggles of snake dancers have also a manifest relationship to the victory dances of warlike tribes.

These illustrations perhaps serve to indicate the abundance of material for the genetic study of student group life. This material must be unscrambled and unraveled in a hunt for specific origins. The presence of a given culture trait in the traditions of any student body indicates that it was either invented by the members of that group or borrowed from another group. It is possible, therefore, to approach student life as Wissler and Koreber have approached the culture of the American Indian, namely, in terms of invention and diffusion. The examples of these mechanisms at work in the American college strike one on every hand. When Harvard and Yale engaged in their first intercollegiate athletic contest (a crew race on Lake Winnipiseogee in 1852), other colleges soon followed their example. When Rutgers and Princeton played the first contest of intercollegiate football in the United States, the game spread rapidly and is now recognized as more of a national sport than baseball. In dramatics, in debating, in student publications, and in fact all down the line of extra-curricular activities invention and diffusion are continuously shaping and reshaping campus life. These not only thread through the much publicized sectors of student affairs, but also through the more intimate life of students.

Another example comes from women's colleges. Years ago someone at Vassar had the happy notion that commencement ceremonies would be made considerably more pretentious if the best looking girls in the sophomore class would parade carrying a daisy chain. This ceremony has become so well publicized that Vassar is better know to the layman because of its daisy chain than because of its School of Euthenics. In time other institutions took over the pageantry for themselves.

Because of the mentioned brevity of the college generations traditional practices change rapidly, and the investigators are discovering some difficulty in fitting together as complete a mosaic of the genetic factors involved in student traditions as they should like.

We are also interested in the processes of social control, that is to say, the whole set of interactions by means of which behavior norms are established and enforced. A large number of patterns from the past shape the behavior of college students. One student generation transmits them to the next, and they are unreflectively accepted and obeyed. This is control through indoctrination. Indoctrination is supplemented by other varieties of regulation: informal gossip; initiation practices and other mores of assimilation; ceremonies, which usually have definite and ascertainable functions; the coercions and selective mechanisms of activity groups such as fraternities, athletic teams, campus publications, and other extra-curricular activities. . . .

All of these varieties of social control, as well as several others, might be exemplified. Consider the Princeton honor system. At that university no proctors have been present at examinations since 1893, and cheating is all but non-existent because the student body governs its own behavior in examinations through its highly developed standard of honor. This is a clear-cut example of control through indoctrination.

Traditions operate not only in this area but in every other conceivable direction. Faculty and student relationships are in a large measure determined by custom. Even though a student may honestly desire to know his professors outside of class, at many institutions he may achieve a faculty friendship only at the risk of being labeled a "chiseler," a "sponger," or an "apple polisher."

Turning to the selection practices of student social groups many dramatic situations can easily be spotted, more especially among fraternities. A noted social psychological atomist has stated his belief that the fraternity does not mold personality but obtains its unanimity largely by selection. Incidents have come to light which clearly indicate that it both selects and molds. For example, a few years ago a brilliant Freshman matriculated at an eastern college, and because of his credentials one of the better fraternities immediately rushed him. It did not elect him, however, because of two personal characteristics which led the rushing committee to believe that he would turn out to be a flighty and, therefore, undesirable member. In the first place, he wore his curly hair much too long, and, in the second place, he shook hands with his right elbow so far in the air that they thought him an affected fop. Another less prominent group pledged him, and many were the regrets of the first fraternity when he turned out to be a track star and the valedictorian of his class. The second fraternity had been annoyed by these same superficial traits but rapidly brought him into line, making possible his subsequent success. One fraternity had exerted control by not electing him. The other had expressed its control by molding him to its model.

All social organizations, of course, have admissions barriers of one sort of another. The analysis of these selective patterns reveals how the control culture of the college intermeshes with that of American society. The social hierarchy of the campus parallels that of the world outside. The old-line fraternities, in general, almost universally discriminate against Jews and many of them against Catholics. A large number will not consider an individual who does not come from a monied family, and the preparatory school from which a student comes has much to do with the fraternities which seek him out.

Speaking of preparatory schools, Corliss Lamont in 1924 demonstrated that the large majority of campus positions at Harvard were held by the graduates of a few eastern preparatory schools: Groton, Exeter, Andover, and the Hill School. No matter what abilities an undergraduate might have, his chances of success in the campus life of Harvard, Lamont found, depended in large measure upon the school from which he had come.

A little historical perspective with regard to the relation of the class system on the campus to the class system of the world outside serves to develop tolerance. Class distinctions on the campus were once a great deal more in evidence than they are today. Students at Harvard College in Colonial days were seated in class according to the social positions of their fathers. An amusing story is told of the son of a shoemaker who innocently listed his father's occupation as "the bench." This the aristocratic president interpreted to mean that the student's father held a judgeship, and he seated the shoemaker's son at the head of the class.

The methods of big business are also pushing their way into student affairs. Within the past few years two large public relations organizations have undertaken to help fraternities choose their new members. They have devised an elaborate system of follow-up letters to the alumni asking for their recommendation of recent high-school graduates who might be rushed. They not only write and mail the letters but receive the answers, tabulate them, and in some cases even investigate the nominees. It is now possible for a rushing chairman whose fraternity subscribes to one of these services to do little more than insert a pledge button in the lapel of the Freshman who has been so carefully and thoroughly looked over by these experts.

These illustrations are only the most spectacular of a wide variety which demonstrate how adult culture complexes shape undergraduate life. That these influences work both ways is, of course, obvious, but as yet no comprehensive attempt has been made to canvass and plot them with any degree of completeness. To arrive at an understanding of these mechanisms becomes a natural and important objective of the present study.

This brief overview of social controls is perhaps sufficient to indicate its importance. We may turn, therefore, to the consideration of the social utility of the many varieties of student institutions. What, in general, one may query, are the functions of extra-curricular activities? On the one hand, many alumni and students, as everybody knows, think them much more valuable educationally than course work. On the other hand, an appreciable percentage of most faculties agree with Woodrow Wilson that these side shows have ruined the business of the big tent. Without taking sides in this now-and-then heated controversy, the investigators must sort out fact from verbiage and attempt to discover the functions of the wide assortment of campus activities.

In all this endeavor they must first of all go back several decades to the beginnings of extra-curricular life as we know it today. The fact must not be overlooked that non-academic organizations on the college campus arose to meet a very definite need. The college of the middle nineteenth century . . . possessed a solicity and compactness the like of which cannot be discovered even in the most self-contained small college of the 1930's. In those days every student took the same course as every other student, and an entering freshman class went together as a group through every class meeting from matriculation to graduation. Because the elective system had not yet appeared, the universally accepted classical curriculum gave undergraduates a common meeting ground and a common range of conversation. But the adoption of the elective system scuttled all this. The new method brought divergence of courses of study and intellectual and conversational isolation. The growth in numbers of student accelerated the disintegration.

At this point extra-curricular activities began to appear and to grow with great rapidity. The old and desirable solidarity had vanished, and gregarious youth sought a substitute, a ground on which to meet, to understand one another's conversation, and to feel a sense of oneness. Extra-curricular activities—especially athletics—furnished the necessary common denominator. All . . . could . . . (students) talk about the flying wedge, the new crew stroke, and yesterday's editorial about the importance of attending tonight's football rally.

If this is a sound analysis of the major reason for the rise of extra-curricular activities, it must be continuously borne in mind in appraising student affairs. Other factors have, of course, contributed to the widespread opinion that the campus has seemed to swallow up the classroom. Our fundamental point, however, is unchanged: the functions of all student organizations must be canvassed and evaluated in terms of fulfillment of human purposes.

A different type of functional approach is that which leads into the analysis of configurations of student culture. A number of anthropologists have put us greatly in their debt by insisting that cultural facts must not be wrested from their setting, but they must be studied in their total interrelatedness. Thus a given cultural fact externally the same may have one meaning in one culture and a totally different meaning in another. Ruth Benedict in her provocative discussion of "Configurations of Culture in North America" appearing in the *American Anthropologist* for January, 1933, has brilliantly analyzed the effect of these total configurations. Her point of view may be readily applied to the study of student life. What undergraduates mean to imply when they speak of the traditions of their campus is not that the details of their traditions are distinctive but that the configurations are different. Partly this is an optical illusion which results from the fact that they are participants in one group and view the behavior of other groups as outsiders, but unquestionably these are distinguishable patterns from campus to campus.

Among women's colleges the configurational pattern of the finishing school contrasts strikingly with that of the feminist school. Finishing schools emphasize social ease, familiarity with the amenities, and probably give their graduates some advantages over their sisters in competition for eligible mates and for social prestige in general. On the other hand, in the feminist school the revolt against male domination gives tone to their cultural complex and is aptly illustrated by the girls at one leading women's college who pride themselves upon not washing their necks and upon dressing in slovenly skirts, sweaters, and smocks.

Other configurations might be cited. Professional schools commonly take their accent from the occupational groups to which their students look forward. Where most students live in dormitories the student form of life differs from that in the so-called "trolley-car colleges." A common configuration is that of the small denominational college best exemplified by an Ohio institution which for the first time in its history permitted a dance to be held this year upon its campus.

The ramifications of these designs must be scrutinized in terms both of structure and of function. The study of configurations of student culture requires a combination of quantitative and case study methods. Institutions must be reviewed by size and complexity since the cultural processes of the large urban institution differ markedly from those of the small rural college. They must be similarly considered by age, by the socio-economic status of their clienteles, and by religious and political affiliations. Likewise coeducational institutions must be contrasted with men's and women's colleges, professional institutions compared with one another, and public and private institutions surveyed for their distinctive characteristics. Besides these there are other variables to be reckoned with. Student life differs from place to place depending upon the combinations and permutations of at least a half-score of factors. All need isolation and interpretation.

In view of all these considerations it perhaps becomes clear that educators must come more definitely to recognize that to the average undergraduate student life constitutes the real life of the college. From his first day as a Freshman to the last ceremony of commencement he is being fashioned by pressures which he understands little, but which he knows to be vital. Cardinal Newman even went so far as to adjudge the educational values of student give-and-take as above those of the classroom. Whether or not one agrees with him, there is no gainsaying the obvious fact that educators must actively and intelligently seek to understand and to capitalize the educational potentialities of college life.

It is no less clear, however, that such a study as this must constantly raise more questions than it can answer. We have seen that some features of college life are spread by diffusion, but to what extent can fundamental attitudes be diffused? Student tradition on American campuses is fundamentally conservative, and we explain this by saying that the college is an expression of American life. The universities of Europe, however, are centers of revolutionary sentiment. Why do these differences exist? To what extent is student tradition an independent variable in the life of the larger society? To what extent can faculties control and manipulate student tradition? The answer to these and similar questions is: We do not know.

If we are ever to have the answers, the sociologist must play a major role in framing them. He alone of all the academic family has the equipment that the undertaking requires: a set of conceptual tools with which to make social and cultural processes intelligible. Aside from the practical value of the findings in the educational programs of the college, the problem constitutes an unusually attractive field for sociological research. The material is highly accessible: the students are right at hand; the forces being studied shape and reshape themselves daily before the investigators' very eyes; the necessary documents can be secured for the asking; and the sociologist may carry on his studies without leaving his teaching job. The interested and even enthusiastic response of three dozen sociologists over the country for co-operative assistance in the present exploration has been most gratifying. Perhaps this paper will bring the participation of still a larger number.

The Scope and Aim of a Personnel Program

Francis F. Bradshaw

Since the scope of a program of any sort must be determined by its aim, or aims, I shall deal first and foremost with the aims of educational personnel work at the college and university level. These aims grow out of the general aims of American educational tradition, in accord with which the college is responsible for furnishing service to its students over and above classroom instruction. Arm-chair thinkers day-dream of a release from this responsibility in order that the faculty members may receive the total income of the institution for salaries and supplies and give in return scholarly lectures and occasional advice relative to their field of study. However, the student gets sick, has no money, goes slack because of vocational anxieties, encounters poor study conditions, becomes dissipated by unwholesome recreations, rebels against misunderstood university regulations, registers for the wrong level of French instruction, is harassed by debt, finds the moral and religious universe of his childhood too rudely shattered, or is home-sick or love-sick; and any of these may entirely negate the best of instruction. The American college has been sufficiently practical minded to realize that instruction itself demands allied services to the student. The student cannot be sent to college without bringing his body, emotional status, and moral make-up with him. Nor can his mind function without regard to the status of other aspects of his development. The practical wisdom of the American tradition seems incontrovertible. All theory of release from it seems to the writer to be 100 percent wishful thinking on the part of the faculty. And this conclusion is based not on the interests of parents, students, alumni, and trustees, but solely upon consideration of the teaching effectiveness of the institution—the interest of the faculty itself.

Until approximately 1900 the policy described above expressed itself mainly in two directions; namely, on the one hand many faculty meetings, faculty committee meetings, and faculty-student interviews devoted to the problems listed above; and, on the other hand, the gradual absorption of college presidents in such problems. Then, as the colleges grew in size and the faculty became increasingly unwilling to spend time on such matters not directly germane to their teaching and research, there have arisen additional administrative provisions, viz., academic deans, registrars, deans of men and women, student advisers, student associations (religious and secular), guidance bureaus, infirmaries and health officers, psychological consultants, psychiatric experts, etc.

In the beginning such administrative duties as dealt mainly with students were primarily regulatory and disciplinary. Gradually they became conceived of as prophylactic and morale building. In addition, they have come to be considered definitely and directly educational as dealing with the total needs of the total student personality. Finally, they have come to be thought of as mediating between general curricula or regulations on the one hand and the limitless individualities of motives, needs, and abilities on the other hand. In all this development, however, there has been no element of the program that could not *theoretically* justify itself in terms of service to the teaching faculty through release of the teaching staff from duties they were least interested in performing, and through delivering the student to the classroom in the optimum condition for profiting by instruction.

The foregoing running start from history is taken in order to afford for our discussion of aims and scope a standard for validating such aims. This standard would probably be acceptable to all if we define student personnel service as all the instructional service to students which demonstrably increases the effectiveness of instruction. When the personnel service introduces a placement test in French which reduces student mortality 25 per cent, such increased effectiveness is immediately obvious. More adequate admissions programs or sanitary inspection of student residences may have less obvious but equally real value to the instructional objectives of the institution.

There is one point in this historical summary that has been omitted—namely, the introduction of the term "personnel." Probably this term was not used in college circles until after 1917. The term has been used in many senses since that date. H. D. Kitson published in 1917 a monograph supplement of the *Psychological Review*, entitled "The Scientific Study of the College Student." The application of social case work methods, psychological techniques, and more refined statistical methods of handling data on large groups began to demand a new term for a new administrative point of view.

L. B. Hopkins, in a study of "Personnel Procedure in Education" (October, 1926, EDUCATIONAL RECORD), listed the functions of personnel work as including: Selective process, Freshman Week, psychological tests, placement tests, faculty advisers, other organized student interviews, health service, mental hygiene service, vocational information, employment and placement, discipline, curriculum improvement, selection of instructors, improvement of teaching methods, objective examinations, research concerning teaching, research concerning the individual, coordination of personnel services in the college and the whole institution, and coordination of outside agencies affecting students.

The general aim embracing the functions listed above Hopkins presented as follows:

The concept I have had before me has been that it means work having to do specifically with the individual. In education one might question how this differs from the concept of education itself. I do not assume that it does differ. However, other factors constantly force themselves on the minds of those responsible for administration. In industry, it would be fair to say that management must concern itself with raw materials and output, with buildings and equipment, and with innumerable other items. So also in education, the administration is beset with many serious problems and certain of these problems become so acute at times that there is danger that they may be met and solved without sufficient time for their ultimate effect upon the individual student. One of the functions, therefore, of personnel administration in education is to bring to bear upon any educational problem the point of view which concerns itself primarily with the individual. Thus, in this particular as in all others, personnel work should remain consistent with the theory and purpose of education by tending constantly to emphasize the problem that underlies all other problems of education; namely, how the institution may best serve the individual.

Esther Lloyd-Jones, in 1929, in her book, "Student Personnel Work at Northwestern," elaborated the position that educational personnel was a major division of university work equal in importance and unity to teaching and finance.

R. C. Clothier, as Chairman of a Committee on Policy and Procedures and Standards of the American College Personnel Association, included in his report in 1931 the following principles of educational personnel work:

1. Every student differs from every other student in aptitudes, inherited or acquired. . . . The college must know these qualifications so far as it is possible to do so and must utilize that knowledge in planning his college course, both within and without the curriculum. . . .

2. Every agency within the college should consider these differences between students. . . .

3. The Personnel Department, under the Personnel Director, is responsible for the development of this point of view throughout the organization. . . .

4. Each college should provide adequate facilities—in terms both of procedures and equipment—for the maintenance of harmonious and effective relationships among students, faculty members, and administrative officials. . . .

M. E. Townsend, in 1932, studying "The Administration of Student Personnel Services in Teaching Training Instutitions of the United States," describes the function of personnel as follows:

Personnel is a new term. On the other hand, the province of personnel is as old as the establishment of society itself. As the name itself indicates, personnel is concerned with those inquiries about and those relationships toward persons—as persons—carried on primarily for the purpose of insuring human effectiveness in productive work. It is, of course, interested in the skills, informations, and techniques already mentioned, but essentially with a view to establishing proper physical, mental, emotional, social, and ethical readiness within the human being who is to do the work, to the end that these factors may serve the worker in a positive, constructive manner in the pursuit of the activity. The personality pattern of the individual at work is its legitimate field.

President Townsend calls attention to the fact that the term "personnel" is so recent that with one unimportant exception it does not appear in the *Readers Guide* until the volume of 1919–1921. He says further:

. . . Just what forces combined to change the emphasis is industry and in all fields of vocation from the task to be done to the doer of the task, is not very difficult to discern. Until the first decade of the twentieth century psychology—one of the basic instruments of investigation in this field—was practically unprepared for the task. The rise of the testing movement, largely experimental and academic at first, provided practical means at hand for the further refinement of the techniques of research in the field of personality. And upon the accumulation of authentic and usable information about personality itself all of personnel as a scientific procedure depends. That one stands at present in possession of anything like a fully competent body of predictive or diagnostic procedures in this field is far from the truth. But important beginnings have undoubtedly been made . . . The interview, the case history, tests, measures of relationship between significant personal conditioners, the survey, the controlled experiment are familiar procedures, whether the personnel researcher is inquiring within the fields of the skilled trades, engineering, medicine, civil service, or teaching. The fact that personal factors affecting accomplishment are relatively more easily discernible, and bear a more direct relationship to output, in terms of goods produced or goods sold, has probably resulted in more investigation being carried forward within the general field of commerce and industry than within those fields of service where results are more intangible, and more complicated by delay of fruition, or by the operation of extraneous factors, as is the case with the professions.

Although "personnel" did not appear in the *Readers Guide* before 1919, W. H. Cowley, of Ohio State University, was able in 1932 to issue a volume entitled "The Personnel Bibliographical Index." To prepare the Index it was necessary to read 4,902 books, articles, monographs, and pamphlets, of which 2,183 are annotated and indexed in the resulting volume.

Dr. Cowley, who had just previously devoted considerable time to the development of techniques for making surveys of personnel work in universities, bases his volume upon five assumptions concerning the aims and scope. In abbreviated form these assumptions are as follows:

1. Student personnel administration is not analogous to industrial personnel administration. The accepted function of industry, perhaps incorrectly, is the production and the sale of goods and services. Individuals are contributors merely. In education, however, the individual takes the center of the stage. His training and development are the

raison d'etre of the college. All units of the college staff make their contribution toward the common end. The Personnel Division is one of
these units, performing its specialized services toward the education of
the student.

2. Personnel administration is one of four main divisions of university administration. As educators become interested in and cognizant of
the development of management techniques in industry, they are recognizing that college or university administration may be classified
functionally in at least four divisions: operational (or business) administration, instructional administration, research administration, and
personnel administration.

3. Recognizing student personnel administration as a major functional division of university administration, we may define it as the administration of all university-student relationships *aside from formal
instruction.* . . . These include counseling of various types, medical attention, supervision of extra-curricular activities, administration of
admissions, of intelligence-testing programs, of housing, and so forth.
Moreover, these functions group themselves together as thoroughly
different from formal instruction, and as a group they are generally
thought of as personnel services.

4. Ideally, every instructor is essentially a personnel officer, but he
must depend upon specialists to perform certain personnel services for
which he is untrained. In the best of possible colleges every instructor
would be individually interested in the students under his direction, but
he cannot treat them when they are ill, nor counsel them concerning
complex vocational problems, nor administer loans and scholarships,
nor direct intelligence-testing programs, nor undertake responsibility
for a number of other personnel services.

5. Student personnel administration divides itself logically into individualized services, administrative services, personnel research, and cooperative research services.

(*a*) Individualized personnel services include educational counseling, vocational counseling, personal adjustment counseling (namely,
social counseling, psychological counseling, and religious counseling),
discipline, placement both part-time and permanent, health counseling, and loans and scholarships. In all of these relationships the individual student has the center of the stage. The contact between the
personnel officer and the student is always a face-to-face and one-to-

one contact. It is seldom a group relationship. One may properly, therefore group these functions together and label them individualized personnel services.

(b) Administrative personnel services include admissions, freshman orientation, intelligence-testing programs, supervision of extra-
curricular activities, housing, personnel record-keeping, and supervision of social life. It may frequently happen, of course, that these
administrative personnel services may also be individualized personnel
services, but in general they are administered for groups of students
rather than for individuals. They are, therefore, set apart from the individualized services because of their distinctive and more or less impersonal emphasis.

(c) Personnel research takes in all types of investigations of individualized and administrative personnel problems. The effective administration of both individualized personnel services and administrative
personnel services requires continuous research in problems as diverse
as they are numerous. No ideal personnel program can be conducted
without research. The function is so important that it must be recognized as a major classification of personnel administration.

(d) Cooperative research services are those research services performed for departments of instruction. Although by definition a clear-
cut distinction is made between instructional administration and personnel administration, it frequently happens, and very likely must
continue to happen, that the personnel organization conducts research
for instructional departments in problems of two general types:

1. The measurement of students for sectioning on the basis of ability, for
honors courses, for the discovery of gifted students, for the prediction of scholarship, and for similar instructional purposes.

2. The development of techniques for probation courses, remedial instruction, how-to-study course, orientation courses, and the like.

Not only has this item of "personnel" appeared in *Readers Guides*,
indexes and research summaries, but it also has an important section of
the Manual of Accrediting Procedures of the North Central Association (1934). The Accrediting Committee proposes to examine the
adequacy of what it calls "Student Personnel Service," under which
heading it does not include "Admission and Orientation of Students,"

but does include "Student Records," "Counseling Procedures," "Extra-curricular Activities," "Loans, Scholarships and Grants-of-Aid," "Health Service," "Housing and Boarding of Students," "Placement Service," "Student Discipline," and "Administrative Arrangements Whereby the Various Types of Student Personnel Service Are Effectively Coordinated." Under this better heading the admission and registration of students is included in the group of functions to be effectively correlated.

I have called attention to these various statements just quoted in order to avoid settling down on any one point of view in regard to a movement still in its formative stages. I am willing, however, to record some convictions as to valuable trends within the movement. I am confident the following are clear gains and worthy of development at any institution:

1. The emphasis on the essentiality of certain services to students.

2. The grouping of these together to form a single general function calling for special staff with special qualifications, training, etc.

3. The realization of the existence of ultimate individual differences in student needs and aptitudes, and their radical importance for instruction and adjustment.

4. The adoption of scientific techniques in the study of individual problems and institutional processes.

5. The realization of the unity of student personality and the necessity of dealing with each student at each contact as a total person—and end in himself, and never a mere abstraction or a means to an end.

6. The necessity for continuous research and revision in the work of an educational institution instead of periodic and explosive re-planning, followed by periods of static and routine administration of unchanging plans.

Furthermore, I believe that this movement is thoroughly appropriate to the present nature of American civilization which is trying in all its institutions of government and business, as well as education, to substitute science for guess work, humanistic values for unrestricted institutionalism, and continuous development for cataclysmic alternations of repression and revolution. It is part and parcel of the unique effort to create a better relationship between individuals and institutions that is central in the American way of life.

The Nature of Student Personnel Work

W. H. Cowley

I. Introduction

This article represents an effort to clarify the nature of student personnel work. During the past forty years, and more particularly during the past two decades, a new group of educational officers have made their appearance upon American college campuses. Generally referred to as student personnel workers, they include among their numbers deans of men, deans of women, deans of freshmen, directors of admission, social directors, directors of student health services, student counselors, vocational counselors, psychological clinicians, directors of placement bureaus, directors of dormitories, and a variety of others.

These personnel workers have been appointed to perform a wide range of activities which have come to be regarded as educationally significant and indeed indispensable. Devoting their attention to the student as an individual rather than as a mind merely, they enhance and supplement the formal instructional programs of the college. They are interested in his emotional and social development, in his health, in his selection of courses as they relate to his personal objectives, in his place of residence, in his extra-curricular activities, in his financial needs, and in any number of other considerations which bear upon his education broadly considered.

The literature of student personnel services and their administration has been abundant in recent years. Most of what has been written, however, has been segmental rather than comprehensive. Few attempts have been made to view these services in the broad, to see the work of one personnel officer in relation to the work of his fellows, or to appraise the concepts common to them all. An essential unity underlies all the many types of personnel service fostered in the colleges, but this unity has seldom been stressed. Very properly personnel officers as individuals and as specialized groups have been absorbed in pioneering efforts to cultivate their own sectors of the terrain. They have had little leisure to discuss common objectives and common problems.

The pioneering days of the student personnel movement are rapidly passing, however, and the time seems to be ripe for a systematic discussion of what personnel people do, what they stand for, and how their activities fit into the educational programs of colleges and universities. In this article the writer seeks to do two things: first, to point out the inadequacy of several widely used definitions of personnel work; and second, to indicate and develop another which is implicit in the publications of several writers in the field and in recent developments at a number of universities.

II. The Prevailing Confusion

Speaking before a meeting of personnel [1] officers at Purdue University in October, 1929, President L. B. Hopkins of Wabash College expressed concern because "the word 'personnel' means one thing to some people and another thing to others" and particularly because "so many of our associates on the faculties of colleges and universities have no real understanding of what we are thinking or trying to do in . . . personnel work." [2]

If Mr. Hopkins were still writing and speaking about student personnel problems, he would more than likely express even greater concern today. The confusion and lack of understanding in 1936 are considerably greater than in 1929. The terms *personnel work, personnel administration, personnel services, personnel research,* and *personnel point of view* continue to be bandied about so variously and carelessly that faculty

1. Every time the word *personnel* is used in this discussion the qualifying word *student* is understood. It is perhaps unnecessary to observe that educational institutions have personnel problems relating to faculty members and to employees which are important but different from student personnel problems.

2. Hopkins, L. B., "Personnel Procedures in Education," *College Personnel Procedures,* Proceedings of Purdue-Wabash Conf. of College Personnel Officers, October, 1929. Bulletin No. 21 of Eng. Extension Depart. at Purdue, p. 43.

members cannot possibly be expected to know what personnel workers are about. Indeed, plenty of evidence exists to suggest that personnel people do not themselves know. At least, few personnel workers agree among themselves; and until they do, faculties and administrators will continue to be perplexed and apathetic if not unfriendly and even antagonistic.

Two years after Mr. Hopkins' Purdue address a committee of the American College Personnel Association, headed by Robert C. Clothier, who was soon to become the president of Rutgers University, called attention to the "urgent need for . . . definition." In their report they said in part:

Even the term "personnel work" is interpreted in different ways. To some of us it is broad in its meaning, involving all those aspects of college work which affect the student as an individual. To others it denotes certain specific functions. The former concept is unsatisfactory to some persons because, in its general nature, it seems to lack specific meaning; the latter is equally unsatisfactory to others because it seems incomplete.[3]

The Clothier committee set about defining the personnel field in an attempt to end the confusion to which they and Hopkins referred. That their discussions were unsatisfactory to some personnel people at least is demonstrated by the plea of A. B. Crawford, written several months after the appearance of the Clothier report.

Referring to personnel work as a "murky subject," Crawford suggested "that college personnel officers more broadly establish their position, purposes, and procedure" and "that as a body they prepare a statement of . . . the total scope and purpose of personnel work." He wrote in part as follows:

College personnel work has necessarily developed rapidly but unevenly. Pressure for immediate action has led to makeshift procedures, with resulting confusion and loss of perspective. . . . In this comparatively new field great advances

3. "College Personnel Principles and Functions." *The Personnel Journal*, Vol. X (June, 1931), p. 10. President Clothier's name is used because he served as chairman of the committee of the American College Personnel Association which made the report submitted in this article. The other members of the committee were Earl W. Anderson, Mabelle B. Blake, Grace Manson, and N. M. McKnight.

have already been made, but rather by the process of scurrying forward from one immediate objective to the next than in pursuit of comprehensive or far-sighted ends. The time therefore seems to have come for an estimate of the situation as a whole, for comparative study of its component parts and for trying to visualize their interrelations more clearly.[4]

Despite the Clothier and Crawford attempts at clarification, no generally accepted interpretation of the nature of personnel work has yet been stated. Instead the appearance of new books and articles have served to compound the confusion rather than to eliminate it. Bad as this may be for personnel people in their relationships with one another, much worse is its effect upon their programs. As Mr. Hopkins has pointed out, few faculty members and administrators understand what personnel workers are trying to do. Yet the need of such understanding cannot be too urgently stressed. If personnel services are to contribute to higher education as effectively as they properly should, the personnel point of view must pervade the thinking and influence the activities of all members of college and university staffs. This will never happen, however, until personnel people arrive at an understanding among themselves as to what they are trying to accomplish. To achieve such a common understanding requires a definition of the field which is logical, lucid, and generally acceptable.

III. Clarity of Definition the Basis of Understanding

In his book How We Think[5] John Dewey has devoted considerable space to an appraisal of the nature of understanding. He points out that "to understand is to grasp meanings"[6] and that "the process of arriving at . . . units of meaning (and of stating them when reached) is definition."[7] In brief, understanding follows from clarity of definition. If,

4. Crawford, A. B., "Educational Personnel Work." *The Personnel Journal*, Vol. X, No. 6 (April 1932), pp. 405–6.
5. Revised edition, D. C. Heath and Company, 1933.
6. *Ibid.*, p. 137.
7. *Ibid.*, p. 160.

therefore, personnel people are to understand one another and in turn be understood by their faculty and administrative associates, they must obviously give careful thought to defining their field of endeavor.

To date a good definition is no simple matter. Without going into an involved discussion of types of definitions and their characteristics it may be pointed out that a definition is "a declaration of intention to use a word or phrase as a substitute for another word or phrase."[8] For example, in Euclidean geometry it would be cumbersome to use the phrase "lines that do not intersect in a plane" every time such lines are encountered. The shorter expression "parallel lines" has therefore been substituted; and whenever one want to say "lines that do not intersect in a plane," he can say instead "parallel lines."

Anyone can, of course, manufacture as many definitions as he pleases. It is perfectly possible, for example, for an individual to define a chair as a thingamabob. He can go through life so designating every chair he encounters. No one can logically prove that a chair is not a thingamabob. The most that anyone can do is to indicate that such a definition has no utility, that people do not understand what he means. The only test of a definition, the logicians agree, is its utility, and utility is determined by practice. If people readily and regularly substitute one term for another, then the definition thus stated can be said to be useful.

To summarize: a definition is a substitution of a word or a phrase for another word or phrase, and that definition is useful which is generally acceptable. This statement may now be applied to several current definitions of personnel work.

IV. Definitions That Are Too Inclusive

The Hopkins-Clothier Definition: Perhaps the most widely accepted definition of personnel work is that which avers that personnel work and education are synonymous. This definition has been stated by L. B. Hopkins and by the committee of the American College Personnel

8. Eaton, Ralph M., *General Logic.* New York: Chas. Scribner's Sons, 1931, p. 295.

Association of which R. C. Clothier was chairman and to which reference has already been made.[9] As the most frequently quoted definition of the field, it should properly be appraised first.

In 1926, after a careful inspection of personnel practices in fourteen colleges and universities, Hopkins defined personnel work as "work having to do specifically with the individual."[10] He then observed that "one might question how this differs from the concept of education itself. I don't assume that it does differ." Clothier in 1931 presented a similar formulation in these words: personnel work is "the systematic bringing to bear on the individual student of all those influences, of whatever nature, which will stimulate him and assist him through his own efforts, to develop in body, mind, and character to the limit of his individual capacity for growth, and help him to apply his powers of developing more effectively to the world."[11] In 1935 he repeated this definition substantially and wrote that "very largely we might define education itself in such terms. If so, personnel work and education are the same thing—which, broadly speaking, is perfectly true."[12]

To say that "personnel work and education are the same thing" is just another way of saying that personnel work is education and that education is personnel work. On the face of it, this is not a useful definition of the personnel field. As indicated, a definition has utility only when one term of the statement can be substituted for the other term with general agreement among interested individuals. But can the term *personnel work* be consistently substituted for the term *education*? Obviously not. Learning the scientific method is admittedly education, but who is there who would say that learning the scientific method is personnel work? Similarly learning the principles of economics is education, but it certainly is not personnel work. Hence, although the Hopkins-Clothier statement (the two are so much alike that they can be considered as one) constitutes a definition, it has no utility as a definition of the personnel field.

9. *Op. cit.*

10. Hopkins, L. B., "Personnel Procedure In Education," Supplement to *The Educational Record*. No. 3, American Council on Education, Washington, D.C. (October, 1926), p. 50.

11. *Op. cit.*

12. Clothier, R. C., in the Foreword to *Individualizing Education*, by J. E. Walters. New York: John Wiley & Sons, Inc., 1935, pp. vii.

The Scott Definition: A second unacceptable definition is that of Walter Dill Scott which reads: "Personnel work is the systematic consideration of the individual, for the sake of the individual, and by specialists in that field."[13] If anything, this is even more inclusive than the definitions of Clothier and Hopkins. They label all education personnel work, but Scott outdoes them. He brings into the personnel fold dozens of varieties of experts from the pediatrician who directs the individual's weaning during his first months to the attorney who draws up his will upon his death bed. All these specialists patently consider the individual systematically "for the sake of the individual," but they would be surprised to discover that they are personnel workers. And, or course, they are not. To define personnel work so broadly is to render the term meaningless.

Personnel Work Is the Individualization of Education: Faced with this critique President Scott would very likely suggest that his words have been taken too literally and that his definition is not meant to be so broad as it reads. In all probability he would point out that what he really means by personnel work is the individualization of education. Hopkins[14] and Clothier[15] would more than likely make similar statements. All have generally been so interpreted. Walters, for example, has just published a book on personnel work and has called it *Individualizing Education*.[16] Strang in her book, *The Role of the Teacher in Personnel Work*[17] recognizes that the terms *personnel work* and the *individualizing of education* are frequently used interchangeably. Caliver[18] and numerous others have implied that they are one and the same concept. To these writers personnel work is the individualizing or personalizing of the educational process.

---

13. Scott, Walter D., in the Foreword to *Student Personnel Work at Northwestern University* by Esther McD. Lloyd-Jones, Ph.D. New York: Harper & Brothers, 1929, p. v.

14. Hopkins, L. B., *The Educational Record*, American Council on Education. Vol. 7, No. 3 (July, 1926), p. 174.

15. Clothier, Robert C., "College Personnel Principles and Functions." *The Personnel Journal*, Vol. X, No. 1 (June, 1931), p. 17.

16. *Op. cit.*

17. Strang, Ruth, *The Role of the Teacher in Personnel Work*. New York: Teachers College, Columbia University, 1935, p. 11, pp. 14–15.

18. Caliver, Ambrose, *A Personnel Study of Negro College Students*. Columbia Contributions to Education, Teachers College Series.

But this third definition is also too-inclusive and therefore undesirable. If every device to individualize education is personnel work, then most of the techniques to improve instruction developed during recent years must be so designated. These include the Harvard system of tutors, the preceptorial conferences at Princeton, the honors courses at Swarthmore and a hundred other institutions, the project and unit plans adopted by a number of academic departments in several colleges, the innumerable programs established the country over for gifted students, the grouping of classes according to ability, and such total programs as that of Bennington and Sarah Lawrence which stress individual instruction through the whole curriculum. Merely to list these curricular and instructional methods of personalizing education is enough to demonstrate they are beyond the scope of personnel work. According to the definition under discussion the Harvard, Princeton, Swarthmore, Bennington, and many other faculties, whether they know it or not, are personnel workers. Personnel work is individualizing education, therefore perforce, anyone who individualizes education is a personnel worker.

The flaw in such a concept is the same as that in the first definition discussed. A definition to be acceptable must delimit the field being defined. If it cannot be delimited, then nothing distinctive exists to define. Ergo, if there is nothing distinctive about personnel work, the term should be abandoned.

To abandon the concept is, of course, out of the question. It has an important place in education and must be protected from some of its friends who seem to want to smother it with generosity. Unfortunately the impression has grown that personnel workers want to encompass all education. The result has been that frequently they have met with antagonism and more frequently with deadlier indifference. Such faculty attitudes have been inevitable, and because of them personnel programs have in general marked time or actually lost ground.

This unhappy situation is not likely to change for the better until personnel people agree among themselves upon boundaries within which to operate. It cannot be reiterated too often that exact thinking requires exact limiting expression. The natural sciences, and the professions which have grown from them, have advanced so much more rapidly than the social sciences, and the professions dependent upon them, chiefly because of the exactness of their concepts. Social scientists—personnel workers among them—must strive for a similar precision.[19]

V. Definitions That Are Too Restrictive

Side by side with these all-inclusive definitions may be placed a number of too-restrictive definitions most of which are implicit in the literature rather than clearly stated. One must look for them in such passages as the following from a recent article by Cowdery:

A psychiatrist on the staff of a large eastern university—himself carrying on high-grade personnel work—was recently asked in conversation what is his relation to the Personnel Director of his institution. His reply was that there is no occasion for relations to or with the "personnel organization and its director." Pressed for an explanation of this reply, the psychiatrist pointed out that with them the personnel office carries on one primary activity—placement in jobs and followup of graduates.[20]

The psychiatrist referred to in this report obviously considers personnel work to be placement and graduate followup—nothing more. A number of other people similarly define the personnel field. For example, a bulletin appeared in 1931 entitled "Twenty-five Years of Personnel and Placement Work at the Carnegie Institute of Technology." Its thirty-one pages are devoted entirely to the placement activities of the Carnegie Bureau of Recommendations, and although in the introduction a word is said about vocational and educational guidance, one is given the impression that essentially personnel work at Carnegie means

19. A pertinent discussion of this point with particular reference to education may be found in R. O. Billett's volume, *Provision for Individual Differences, Marking, and Promotion*, U.S. Dept. of Interior, Office of Education, Bulletin, 1932, No. 17, Monog. No. 3, pp. 234–36.

20. Cowdery, Karl M., "The Guidance of Youth in the College." *Occupations*, Vol. 12 (Dec., 1933), p. 14.

only placement.[21] The same definition is in vogue at a number of other institutions.

A second narrow interpretation confines the scope of personnel activities to personnel research. This definition goes back to the years immediately following the war when the word *personnel* came into educational terminology for the first time. In those early days personnel work meant personnel research almost exclusively. Yoakum, for example, while still an army psychologist, proposed a plan, in the spring of 1919, for a college personnel bureau. He wrote:

> The primary functions of the bureau are to obtain accurate data on each student, to codify the requirements of different professions; to supervise the use of tests and to provide means whereby each student may become acquainted with his abilities and the requirements of the occupations in which he is interested. . . . The bureau will proceed on the assumption that all of these problems can be investigated in a scientific manner and will initiate and encourage research in this field.[22]

The Yoakum bureau was, obviously, essentially a research organization confining itself largely to vocational problems. A number of personnel departments were established after the Yoakum pattern or after others much like it. Some of these still continue to operate within the confines of their original commissions; others have extended their investigations to other types of student problems; and still others have added counseling and other activities to their research work.

To many people, however, personnel work is still considered to be nothing more than personnel research. In 1927 Howard R. Taylor of the University of Oregon wrote that "the task of a university personnel organization is . . . a threefold one." He proposed that these tasks are:

> (*a*) To evaluate the information already available concerning each student so that the collection and recording of non-essential or inaccurate information may be dispensed with.

21. This impression is borne out by the editorial campaign during 1934–35 of the student newspaper, *The Carnegie Tartan*, for the establishment of what the editors called a student personnel advisory service.

22. Yoakum, C. S. (Major, Sanitary Corps, U.S.A.). *School and Society*, Vol. IX, No. 228 (May 10, 1919), p. 559.

(*b*) To develop additional and better measures of such factors as are needed to give a fairly complete picture of each student as he differs from others. In this way he can be understood and advised wisely and accurately.

(*c*) To coordinate and translate these data so that they can be readily interpreted and widely used.[23]

Four years later Professor Lorin A. Thompson, Jr., of Ohio Wesleyan University, speaking before the National Association of Deans and Advisers of Men, similarly restricted personnel work to research. He said in part:

The personnel officer in any college, whether large or small, as I conceive it, should be a man who is technically trained in methods of research and methods of handling and dealing with all forms of collected data. His chief purpose should be that of studying the policies of the institution, collecting information and data, preparing reports and advising both faculty and administration concerning policies dealing with all phases of student life. In a very strict sense he should be an expert whose chief interest is in personnel research, rather than in the field of individual guidance.[24]

Without making a national canvass it is impossible to determine how many personnel people accept this limited notion of personnel work. Their numbers are very likely small, but that even a few define the personnel field in this narrow fashion is a fact to be reckoned with.

A third point of view restricts personnel work to counseling. Boucher, for example, devotes a chapter of his book *The Chicago College Plan*[24] to "Student Guidance and Personnel Work." In this chapter he discusses nothing but student counseling: Freshman Week counseling, educational counseling after Freshman Week, and vocational counsel-

23. Taylor, Howard R. *School and Society*, Vol. XXVI, No. 673 (Nov. 19, 1927), p. 654.

24. Thompson, Lorin A., Jr., "Relationship of the Dean of Men to the Personnel Officer in the Small College." *Secretarial Notes for the 13th Annual Conf. of the Nat'l Assn. of Deans and Advisers of Men.* April, 1931, p. 39.

25. Boucher, Chauncey Samuel, Ph.D., *The Chicago College Plan.* Chicago: The Univ. of Chicago Press, 1935, p. 151.

ing. As this chapter stands the reader must conclude that Boucher confines guidance and personnel work (he does not indicate if and how these two terms are different) to counseling in the three areas which he has discussed.

Jones considers personnel work in much the same light. He writes that "many colleges have organized personnel departments for the special purpose of assisting the individual student in his adjustment and in preventing failures. . . . Personnel directors arrange personal conferences with students who are in trouble of any kind, assist in improving study habits, and give very useful help of all kinds."[26] This is a broader statement than Boucher's, but it still confines personnel work to counseling. It is broader only in that Jones includes more types of counseling, i.e., "trouble of any kind" and "help of all kinds."

Several other narrow definitions might be cited, but the limitations of these three examples apply to all similar definitions. What, briefly, is wrong with statements of this sort? For some people it is sufficient to observe categorically that they are too restrictive. Others, however, will require demonstration that they actually are too restrictive.

The logical error involved in these narrow definitions is the fallacy of illicit simple conversion.[27] One cannot argue that because all Ohioans are Americans that all Americans are Ohioans. If anyone (taking the first of those three narrow statements) defines personnel work as placement, he implies that it is false to say that some personnel work is not placement. This affirmatively stated means that all personnel work is placement. perhaps a few individuals will make such an affirmation, but certainly no more than a few. Most personnel people will shy away from using *personnel work* and *placement* synonymously.

One may reasonably say that some personnel work is placement since the converse of such a statement reads that placement is a part of personnel work. Similarly one may acceptably observe that research is a part of personnel work and that counseling is a part of personnel work. It is fallacious, however, to say either that research is personnel work or that counseling is personnel work. To make such statements involves confusing the part with the whole.

    26. Jones, Arthur J., *Principles of Guidance*. New York: McGraw-Hill Book Co., Inc., 1930, p. 270.
    27. Eaton, *opus cit.*, p. 201.

VI. *"Guidance" and "Personnel Work" Not Synonymous Terms*

Frequently the word *guidance* is used synonymously with the phrase *personnel work*. Strang writes, for example, in the opening pages of her book *The Role of the Teacher in Personnel Work* [28] that "in this book *guidance* and *personnel work* will be used interchangeably"; Doermann in his book, *The Orientation of College Freshmen,* [29] footnotes *personnel service* with the observation that he uses the term "as designating the guidance organization"; and McConn [30] typifies a large number of people who use such expressions as "the personnel or guidance movement" indicating that they consider guidance and personnel work to be the same thing.

Exactly what these authors mean by guidance it is difficult to discover. They seem not to be aware that the guidance people on the lower educational levels (who coined the word in its technical sense) are divided into three camps which define *guidance* dissimilarly. Brewer of Harvard and Kitson of Columbia, as the most vocal representatives of two of these groups, have been wrangling in the journals for several years. Koos and Kefauver represent the third position which stand somewhere between those of Kitson and Brewer. If college personnel people are to use the word, they ought properly to indicate in which sense they employ it. Their positions cannot otherwise be intelligently understood.

Consider first the Brewer definition. By guidance Brewer means a complete philosophy of education. He writes that "a true education . . . means guidance" [31] and that guidance is "the heart of education." [32] His "general statement of whole process of guidance" includes the following agencies or media:

1. An organized, rich life of normal, interesting, and important *activities*, making up the juvenile community.

28. Strang, *op. cit.*
29. Doermann, Henry J., *The Orientation of College Freshmen*. Baltimore: Williams & Wilkins Co., 1926, p. 113.
30. "Fifty-seven Varieties of Guidance." *Bulletin of the American Association of Collegiate Registrars*, Vol. 3, No. 4 (April, 1928), p. 359.
31. Brewer, John M., *Education is Guidance*. New York: The Macmillan Co., 1932, pp. 2–3.
32. *Ibid.*, p. 23.

2. *Classes* and study groups for the discussion of the problems involved in these activities, for such information and technical knowledge as may be needed to develop an appropriate skill in them, and for the wise motivation and integration of all the activities of life.

3. *Counseling* in these activities, with fostering and friendly supervision, to develop wisdom in specific activities and to develop skill in planning, balancing, and integrating them.[33]

Brewer takes the position that these guidance media "should gradually supplant most of the present subjects of instruction"[34] to the end that guidance be recognized as the "chief function of school and college."[35] Succinctly expressed Brewer proposes that education and guidance are exactly the same thing—or ideally should be.

Such a conception of guidance is sufficient demonstration that personnel work and guidance (as Brewer defines it) are not synonymous. Brewer has defined guidance in exactly the same way that Hopkins and Clothier have defined personnel work, but their statements have been proved too inclusive. It follows, therefore, that Brewer's interpretation is also too broad to make guidance an acceptable definition of personnel work. Brewer, incidentally, recognizes the difference between the two terms and never uses them synonymously.[36]

Kitson's interpretation of the scope of guidance is as narrow as Brewer's is broad. In taking Brewer to task for his all-inclusive use of the word he writes that "the term 'guidance' appears to be about to swallow up all education and all types of life activity."[37] He therefore "proposes that the term 'general guidance' be abandoned—that the word 'guidance' be reserved to designate only vocational guidance, its point of origin."[38]

It should be made clear that Kitson does not take the position that the activities which Brewer and others lump under the term *guidance* is

33. *Op. cit.*, p. 111. Brewer includes a fourth factor in this general statement, but this is not reproduced here because it concerns the administration of guidance and is therefore not germane to this discussion of definitions.

34. *Op. cit.*, p. vii.

35. *Op. cit.*, p. 112.

36. *Op. cit.*, p. 23.

37. Kitson, Harry D., "Getting Rid of a Piece of Educational Rubbish." *Teachers College Record*, Vol. xxxvi, No. 1 (October, 1934), p. 30.

38. *Ibid.*, p. 33.

such a catch-all that it should be abandoned except when associated with the word *vocational* in the term *vocational guidance*. It is not within the scope of this article to discuss the merits of Kitson's proposal. All that is important here is to demonstrate that the term *guidance* (i.e., vocational guidance), as he uses it, has no utility as a definition of personnel work. Certainly few will agree that personnel work includes only vocational guidance. Thus the Kitson interpretation of the scope of guidance must be ruled out as a statement of the nature of personnel work. It falls clearly under the classification of too-restrictive definitions.

Koos and Kefauver accept neither the Brewer nor the Kitson idea of the nature of guidance. They suggest "a concept which is neither restricted to vocational guidance at one extreme nor extended to make guidance synonymous with all education at the other." [39] They criticize the Brewer position in these words:

Guidance is not the whole of education. The term should not even be regarded, as some seem to regard it, as a beneficent synonym for education. It represents one aspect only of the process of education, notwithstanding this is a momentous one. The scope of guidance cannot be understood to comprehend in any large measure the other processes or features of the school, such as teaching, supervision, curriculum-making, vocational training, or the extracurriculum. At the same time, as the illustrations given have indicated, there are vital points of contact that permit the guidance program to enhance the service of these features, or *vice versa*. The type of expansion of the concept that would include these other features of the school is sheer inflation. [40]

They criticize the Kitson position in these words:

Guidance in relation to vocation is only one portion of the whole program, although a most important one. The word "educational" is understood to comprehend preparation for vocation and to admit additional relationships, no less important than the vocational. [41]

39. *Op. cit.*, p. v.
40. Koos, Leonard V., and Kefauver, Grayson N., *Guidance in Secondary Schools.* New York: Macmillan, 1932, p. 19.
41. *Ibid.*, p. 15.

Guidance according to these authors includes three general functions: "(1) informing students concerning educational and vocational opportunities, (2) securing information concerning the student, (3) guiding the individual student." [42] Functions one and two are designated as preparatory to function three, [43] under which fourteen counseling problems are listed. All of these are educational and vocational, and thus one may conclude that by guidance Koos and Kefauver mean educational [44] and vocational guidance. These are of course important personnel functions, but few personnel workers have restricted the personnel field to these two activities. The Koos and Kefauver concept of guidance is therefore no more acceptable as a definition of personnel work than those of Brewer and Kitson.

It would be interesting, if space were available, to review the positions of Myers, Proctor, and several other guidance authorities. All are related, in the broad, to one of the three guidance definitions discussed. It can be concluded, therefore, that no definition which has as yet been stated makes guidance and personnel work synonymous.

VII. A Definition Implicit in the Literature and in Recent Practise

Up to this point in the discussion the writer has sought to do four things: (1) to indicate the confusion in the personnel field, (2) to suggest that the disorder will continue until a common understanding has been reached through a generally acceptable definition, (3) to demonstrate the most current definitions are either too inclusive or too restrictive, and (4) to point out that guidance and personnel work are not the same. The remaining pages are devoted to an attempt to develop what seems to the writer to be a more adequate definition of the personnel

42, *Ibid.*, p. v.

43. *Ibid.*, p. 403.

44. In the early pages of their book Koos and Kefauver include recreational, health, and civic-social-moral guidance; but they pay little attention to them from that point on. It seems fair to say, therefore, that *guidance* to these writers means educational and vocational guidance.

field. This definition, it will be indicated, is implied in the writings of a number of personnel people. It is also implicit in the organizational plans which have recently been adopted by several universities.

At the outset one must recognize the justice of Esther Lloyd-Jones' criticism[45] of the synonymous use of such terms as *personnel work, personnel services,* and *personnel administration.* She points out, and correctly, that although many individuals employ these terms interchangeably they do not mean the same thing. Before attempting to distinguish between them, however, it should be observed that they have something to do with the relationships between colleges and students. If the nature of these relationships can be determined, then the nature of personnel work can, perhaps, also be determined.

In general three different kinds of college-student relationships are recognizable: those that have to do with business arrangements, those that have to do with instruction, and those that have to do with extra-instructional activities. Under business relationships come the payment of fees, the renting of equipment and apparatus, the purchase of supplies, and a large number of other routine operations that have to do with *matèriel.* Under instructional relationships come all varieties of contacts having to do with the formal courses of the curriculum whether these be with individual students or with groups, library and laboratory work, and the determination by examination of the results of instruction.

Under extra-instructional relationship come a range of activities including among other admissions, student orientation to college life and work, housing, health, the securing of part-time employment and financial aid, social and extra-curricular programs, and many types of counseling upon such diverse problems as the course to be taken during a particular term, the way to develop one's social intelligence, and what to do about homesickness or lovesickness.

In the nineteenth century college faculty members engaged in all three of these types of relationships with students, but in recent years the increased size of colleges and universities and the development of more comprehensive and complex programs have made a functional di-

---

45. Lloyd-Jones, Esther, "Personnel Administration." *The Journal of Higher Education,* Vol. V (March, 1934), p. 142.

vision of responsibilities inevitable. Especially since the Cooke study[46] of business practices in 1910 faculty members have relinquished to business offices practically all business relationships with students. Similarly faculty members have more and more tended to give all their energies to instruction and research rather than to extra-instructional relationships with students. This has been true because in most institutions promotions and increases in salary have come to be determined chiefly by scholarly production.

To assume responsibility, therefore, for extra-instructional relationships with students a new group of officers have within the past few decades been appointed upon practically every campus in the country. These individuals have been, and are, called by all sorts of names, but in recent years they have come generally to be known as student personnel workers. The term is a generic designation for all individuals whose relationships with students are neither routine business relationships nor instructional relationships.

With these three distinct types of institutional-student relationships in mind it is possible to discuss the nature of student personnel work. Obviously personnel work is what personnel workers do, the activities for which they assume responsibility. These activities, as indicated, are distinct from business and instructional activities. An acceptable definition of personnel work must, therefore, state its separateness from business and instructional activities.

Business activities must be ruled out because business relationships with students are, and must be, essentially impersonal. The fact that a college or a university is an educational and only incidentally a business organization should dominate the thinking of every member of the business staff, but business managers and their assistants have their necessary and specialized work to do which cannot include giving attention to the personal development of individual students.

At several points the business and personnel divisions meet. Both organizations are interested in housing, food services, loans, scholarships, and in one or two other activities. The business staff is concerned, however, only with the financial aspects of these undertakings. The personnel staff assumes—or should assume—responsibility for

46. Cooke, Morris Llewellyn, *Academic and Industrial Efficiency*. A Report to the Carnegie Foundation for the Advancement of Teaching. Bulletin No. 5. New York: 1910.

their direction as educational enterprises, keeping of course within the frame-work made necessary by financial considerations. Business departments exist to facilitate the educational work of the institution, but they are not educational units. They serve best by concentrating upon the purposes for which they have been established.

Instructional activities must also be ruled out because faculty people everywhere recognize a distinction between their teaching and their extra-instructional relationships with students. At few institutions have faculty members relinquished all out-of-class responsibilities to personnel officers, but the tendency everywhere is to assign extra-instructional activities to members of the staff who teach part time or do not teach at all. This tendency has been strengthened by the growing conviction that not all professors are temperamentally equipped to deal with students outside the curriculum.

The tendency has further been strengthened by the development of techniques which require special training or unusual aptitude and experience. No matter how much a faculty member may be interested in his students as individuals he is only occasionally prepared to develop, administer, and interpret intelligence tests, personality inventories, and other instruments which have become essential to effective counseling. Moreover, few professors are willing to add to their teaching and research loads such duties as the administration of dormitories, loans and scholarships, placement, discipline, social programs, extra-curricular activities, and other divisions of student life. More often than not it is even difficult to secure the service of professors on policymaking committees for these activities; and, by and large, most faculty members have been willing to see their administration assigned to personnel workers.

If this analysis of the separateness of business, instructional, and personnel activities is correct, what then is the nature of personnel work? The writer proposes the following definition:

Personnel work constitutes all activities undertaken or sponsored by an educational institution, aside from curricular instruction, in which the student's personal development is the primary consideration.

This definition distinguishes personnel from routine business activities by the phrase "in which the student's personal development is the primary consideration." It also distinguishes personnel from instructional activities by the phrase "aside from curricular instruction."

Is this an acceptable definition of personnel work? That remains to be seen. The writer presents it for the critical appraisal of those who may be interested. It can be pointed out, however, that the definition is clearly implied in the discussions of several other, if not most, personnel writers.

In the first place consider the Kóos and Kefauver discussion of guidance. As indicated they use the term *guidance* to designate the counseling function of personnel work which they separate clearly from instruction. Explicitly they write, for example, that "*teaching cannot often be guidance and guidance does not comprehend methods of teaching.*"[47] They also rule out both the supervision of instruction and curriculum problems from the field of guidance. They write that the "*supervision of instruction is concerned with the improvement of teaching and is not guidance.*"[48] In other words instruction and counseling are distinct functions which is much the same as saying that instruction and personnel work are distinct.

Turning to higher education as examination of the itemizations[48] of Jones,[49] Lloyd-Jones,[50] Townsend,[51] Strang,[52] to name but four writers upon personnel problems in colleges and universities, will demonstrate that all of these authors exclude all business and instructional relationships from their list of personnel functions. No one of them, in the opinion of the writer, submits a full compilation; but completeness is not now important. What *is* important is their implicit recognition that personnel work and business and instructional activities are different. The definitions of these writers do not make the clear-cut distinctions proposed in this article, but their lists of personnel activities manifestly do.

It is interesting to compare the functions enumerated by Jones,

47. *Op. cit.*, p. 18. Italics theirs.
48. Because of spatial limitations these cannot be reproduced. The reader is referred directly to the cited statements of the writers.
49. Jones, Lonzo, *A Project in Student Personnel Service Designed to Facilitate Each Student's Achievement at the Level of His Ability.* Pub. by Univ. of Iowa, Vol. V, No. 1, of *Iowa Studies*, November 1, 1928.
50. *Op. cit.*, p. 141.
51. Townsend, M. E., "*Administrative Phases of a Student Personnel Program.*" *Educ. Adm. & Supervision* (December, 1935), pp. 641–56.
52. Strang, Ruth, *Personal Development and Guidance in College and Secondary School.* New York: Harper & Brothers, 1934.

Lloyd-Jones, Townsend, Strang, and still others with those of Hopkins and Clothier. In 1926 Hopkins [53] proposed twenty personnel functions. Six of these had to do with instruction: placement tests, curriculum, selection of instructors, methods of instruction, objective tests, and research concerning teaching. Five years later Clothier, [54] in making his tabulation, dropped five of these six keeping only the selection of instructors as a personnel function. Clotheir's other fourteen items are all clearly personnel activities having no direct relationship to instruction.

Clothier must have checked over the Hopkins table of activities since he referred to his monograph in his article and since the table is its very core. One may assume, then, that he purposely eliminated these five items. And why? Because, it is submitted, he had become aware of the growing opinion that personnel work and instruction are separate. He did not, however, go the whole way, still considering the selection of instructors a personnel activity.

But is it a personnel activity? In a few institutions personnel officers have something to say about the choice and promotion of members of the faculty, but at no institution of which the writer knows have they any real administrative voice in the matter. The selection of faculty members properly belongs in the hands of instructional administrators. Neither by definition nor practice does it belong in the bailiwick of personnel administrators. Personnel people can be influential at this point only by developing attitudes among deans and department heads which are favorable to the choice of instructors who, to quote Clothier, take "a sincere and intelligent interest in the individual student." More will be said on this point in connection with the discussion of the personnel point of view.

VIII. Supplementary Definitions

Before discussing the personnel point of view, however, three other terms should be discussed—*personnel services*, *personnel research*, and *personnel administration*. Two of these may be disposed of promptly. It is

53. *Op. cit.*, p. 7.
54. *Op. cit.*, p. 14–15.

proposed that the term *personnel services* is exactly synonymous with the term *personnel work*. It is proposed that *personnel research* is a type of personnel work, i.e., investigation of problems arising in personnel work. By this definition much of the research being done in personnel bureaus is not personnel research at all. It is really instructional research which personnel people have undertaken because no other agency exists to do it. The sooner instructional administrators see the need of initiating and directing their own research programs the better for higher education. Properly every institution should be continuously and thoroughly studying its curriculums and methods of instruction using the best research techniques available. Such research, however, is not personnel research even though it is erroneously so designated in a number of places.

The third term, *personnel administration*, requires discussion although it may be briefly defined. The word *administration* has different meanings in government, business, and education. In education it means the supervision or direction of an activity or group of activities. Personnel administration may therefore be defined as the supervision or direction of personnel work.

Lloyd-Jones has suggested that "student-personnel administration is one of the three main divisions of educational administration:[55]—the other two being instructional and business administration. The writer has elsewhere[56] made a similar observation. In very few institutions, however, has the importance of personnel administration yet been recognized. Business and instructional divisions have been distinct entities for many decades, but the personnel division in most institutions has not yet achieved a comparable status. Many personnel units have been established on innumerable campuses, but usually they operate independently and without coordination. Personnel work will not attain its potential stature until all agencies which work in the personnel field are correlated and placed under the direction of a major administrative officer.

55. *Op. cit.*, p. 142.
56. *The Personnel Bibliographic Index.* Columbus, Ohio: The Ohio State University, 1932, p. 3. Four instead of three administrative divisions are here listed, the additional one being the administration of research. To this a fifth should perhaps be added, the administration of public services and public relationships. Neither of these two divisions, however, is concerned directly with student affairs.

The present plan of decentralized functioning should be supplemented by centralized policy making and general supervision. Steps in this direction have already been taken at several institutions: Chicago, Duke, Oregon, and Northwestern. At all of these institutions all extra-instructional relationships with students are coordinated under the direction of a major administrative officer. At Chicago he has the title of Dean of Students, at Duke, Vice-president in Charge of Student Welfare, at Oregon, Dean of Personnel Administration, and at Northwestern, Personnel Director. The responsibility of these officers is to see that all functional personnel people work together harmoniously and that extra-instructional relationships with students are developed. It is also their responsibility to coordinate the work of the entire personnel staff of their institutions with the instructional work under the direction of academic deans and heads of departments. Each is the officer to whom the president turns in student personnel matters. Because of the success of this method of organization, it is likely to become more common within the next few years.

Much more than this needs to be said about personnel administration; but since the space is not now available, the discussion may proceed to the definition of a fifth term, i.e., the *personnel point of view*. Many writers use this term, but either they use it as the equivalent of one of the other expressions or their meanings are vague. The writer proposes the following as a desirable definition:

The personnel point of view is a philosophy of education which puts emphasis upon the individual student and his all-round development as a person rather than upon his intellectual training alone and which promotes the establishment in educational institutions of curricular programs, methods of instruction, and extra-instructional media to achieve such emphasis.

This definition has two parts, and each should be examined separately. The first part has to do with *a kind of emphasis*, the second with the media through which the emphasis is expressed. An understanding of the difference between these parts is essential.

The emphasis "upon the individual student and his all-round development as a person rather than upon his intellectual training alone" is not, it should be made clear, the private concern of personnel workers. As a matter of fact personnel people are merely subscribing to the point of view of a long line of philosphers dating at least from Socrates and leading to John Dewey and his adherents. The personnel movement will improve its progress and its status by recognizing that its roots are deeply imbedded in the thinking of some of the world's major social philosophers. The psychology of individual differences from which many personnel activities have directly grown is but a verification by science of an age-old philosophical insight.

Turning to the second part of the definition, it must be similarly emphasized that promoting the establishment of media to achieve the student's all-round development is again not the peculiar responsibility or objective of personnel workers. Many other individuals and groups are striving toward this same end, and personnel people are but co-workers with them. Unfortunately no organization has as yet been established in higher education which undertakes to accomplish objectives similar to those of the Progressive Education Association and other groups in elementary and secondary education. Every year, however, more administrators and faculty members are stressing the need for a more intelligent interest in individual students. The programs at Harvard, Princeton, Swarthmore, Bennington, and several other institutions are monuments to their insight and enterprise. Personnel people, in general, have had little if any part in developing them.

In many colleges and universities, however, personnel workers are the chief proponents of the concept of all-round development. Most faculty members are so completely engrossed in their own subjects that they perceive only a single facet of the student's mind and personality. In such institutions personnel people must carry the torch. By education and persuasion they must seek to stimulate faculties to modernize and humanize their curriculums, their methods of instruction, and their attitudes toward personnel work. At all times, however, they must remember that the philosophy which they call the personnel point of view is a common heritage of several groups of progressive educators who know it by many other names. Personnel workers prejudice and sometimes defeat their purposes when they give the impression, as they too frequently do, that they want to run the entire educational show.

Is this proposed definition of the personnel point of view[57] implied in

57. A number of principles stem from the personnel point of view which the writer hopes to discuss at another time.

the literature? The answer seems to the writer to be in the affirmative. Only one reference needs to be cited in support of this opinion. If the reader will substitute the words *the personnel point of view* for the words *personnel work* quoted from Clothier on page 7 of this article, he will have a definition of the personnel point of view which concurs with that which the writer has submitted above. The labeling of this statement as a definition of personnel work is not consistent with Clotheir's enumeration of personnel functions, but it makes a most acceptable definition of the personnel point of view.

IX. This an Incomplete Discussion

A short review of the personnel field, such as this, must necessarily leave much ground untouched. A great deal more, for example, should be said about personnel administration; and several pages should properly be devoted to a discussion of the relationships of academic deans, department heads, and ordinary faculty members both to personnel administration and the personnel point of view. A complete list of personnel services should also be developed. These and other developments of the proposed definitions must be left to another time.

Two considerations, however, need brief attention to avoid misunderstanding. In the first place the distinctions proposed between business, instructional, and personnel administration do not mean that the student needs to be compartmentalized. A division of labor is both unavoidable and desirable, but at every institution some one individual must seek to know the whole student. Properly that individual should be his educational counselor, who is often a faculty member serving part time as a personnel officer. To him should come data from all sources so that he may counsel the student intelligently. In a later article on personnel coordination the writer hopes to develop this idea. Enough now to indicate its importance.

In the second place, the proposed separateness of instructional and personnel activities does not mean that personnel work should be undertaken only by a special staff of personnel workers completely distinct from the instructional staff. A number of technical services such as the management of health programs and the making of thorough personality analyses of students must be done by experts, but faculty members almost universally participate in practically every variety of personnel work. This arrangement is inevitable and desirable; but when members of the instructional staff are doing personnel work, they are working (or should be working) under the direction of a personnel administrator and not under their department heads or academic deans. Institutional morale as well as economy require that many faculty members act both as instructors and personnel workers, but this necessary dual service should not confuse the difference between personnel work and formal instruction. These interrelationships the writer hopes to discuss at greater length in the article he plans on the coordination of personnel activities.

X. The Need of Agreement

In conclusion the writer should like to observe that the point of view presented in this article seems to him to be but a summarization of the thinking of a number of individuals. Personnel people in rather widely separated areas are recognizing the natural affinity of their work. In 1934 seven personnel organizations[28] came together to organize the American Council of Guidance and Personnel Associations. Kitson reported the organization meeting, in part, as follows:

At the Cleveland meeting (February, 1934), the centripetal force of our idea became so strong that we exclaimed: "Why, we are kinfolk!" And at an enthusiastic luncheon we instructed our several presidents to appoint delegates who should meet and organize a national association through which we might jointly work for the realization of our ideals.[59]

A conviction of kinship among personnel people is undoubtedly developing with some rapidity. It is particularly obvious among personnel workers in colleges and universities. The time is perhaps ripe, there-

58. American College Personnel Association, National Vocational Guidance Association, National Association of Deans of Women, Collegiate Bureaus of Occupations, Personnel Research Federation, Institute of Women's Professional Relations, and Southern Woman's Educational Alliance.

59. Kitson, Harry D., "Our Common Cause." *Occupations*, Vol. 13, No. 8 (May, 1935), p. 709.

fore, for representatives of all college personnel groups to come together for a definitive discussion of the nature of their common task. Nationally and on every campus personnel officers should be working together in a coordinated effort to spread the personnel point of view and to develop programs commensurate with the extra-instructional needs of college students. Such coordination requires an understanding of the unity of their several fields of activity under the basic term *personnel work*. Until a generally acceptable definition is achieved, coordination will very likely not be realized. More than that, faculty members and administrative officers will continue to be perplexed and therefore uncooperative.

The Student Personnel Point of View

Foreword

In January 1925 the Division of Anthropology of the National Research Council sponsored a meeting in Washington, D.C., of representatives of fourteen institutions of higher education to discuss the problems of vocational guidance in college. Out of this conference developed the Intercollegiate Council of Personnel Methods which undertook to investigate ways and means of making available to educational institutions knowledge concerning students as individuals. In 1926 this group requested the American Council on Education to sponsor a study of personnel practices in colleges and universities. As a result of this request the Council established the Committee on Personnel Methods with H. E. Hawkes as chairman.

The initial undertaking of the Committee on Personnel Methods was a survey by L. B. Hopkins to determine what a number of institutions were then doing to assist the students to develop as individuals. The publication of the Hopkins report in *The Educational Record* of October 1926 focused national attention upon the importance of this area and upon the need for further research. During the next several years, the Committee on Personnel Methods, working through a number of subcommittees, inaugurated studies on certain aspects of the total student personnel problem. As a result of these studies, certain tools were prepared including the cumulative record cards, personality rating scales, and comparable achievement tests, which have influenced the improvement of student personnel services.

The American Council on Education in 1936 received the report of the Committee on Review of the Testing Movement[1] which recom-

1. *The Testing Movement*, American Council on Education Studies, Series I, Vol. I, No. 1, (February 1937).

mended the establishment of a Committee on Measurement and Guidance to coordinate activities of the Council in the preparation of measurement materials. As a result of this recommendation, the Council discharged the Committee on Personnel Methods and assigned its measurement functions to the new committee. The Council, however, recognized the need for further investigation of certain fundamental problems related to the clarification of so-called personnel work, the intelligent use of available tools, and the development of additional techniques and processes. Consequently, the Executive Committee authorized the calling of a conference to discuss the possible contribution of the Council in this area.

The following individuals met in Washington, D.C., on April 16 and 17, 1937, and unanimously adopted the following report. The group voted to refer the report to the Committee on Problems and Plans in Education of the American Council on Education.

Thyrsa Amos	D. H. Gardner
F. F. Bradshaw	H. E. Hawkes
D. S. Bridgman	L. B. Hopkins
A. J. Brumbaugh	F. J. Kelly
W. H. Cowley	Edwin A. Lee
A. B. Crawford	Esther Lloyd-Jones
Edward C. Elliott	D. G. Paterson
Burton P. Fowler	C. Gilbert Wrenn

C. S. Marsh
D. J. Shank
G. F. Zook

The Committee on Problems and Plans in Education at its meeting on May 6, 1937, approved the report of the conference and recommended to the Executive Committee of the Council that a Committee on Student Personnel Work be established with instructions to propose a program of action in line with the general statement of the conference. The Executive Committee authorized the organization of the new committee at its last meeting.

George F. Zook
President

June 1937

Philosophy

One of the basic purposes of higher education is the preservation, transmission, and enrichment of the important elements of culture—the product of scholarship, research, creative imagination, and human experience. It is the task of colleges and universities so to vitalize this and other educational purposes as to assist the student in developing to the limits of his potentialities and in making his contribution to the betterment of society.

This philosophy imposes upon educational institutions the obligation to consider the student as a whole—his intellectual capacity and achievement, his emotional make-up, his physical condition, his social relationships, his vocational aptitudes and skills, his moral and religious values, his economic resources, his aesthetic appreciations. It puts emphasis, in brief, upon the development of the student as a person rather than upon his intellectual training alone.

A long and honorable history stands behind this point of view. Until the last three decades of the nineteenth century interest in the whole student dominated the thinking of the great majority of the leaders and faculty members of American colleges. The impact of a number of social forces upon American society following the Civil War, however, directed the interest of most of the strong personalities of our colleges and universities away from the needs of the individual student to an emphasis, through scientific research, upon the extension of the boundaries of knowledge. The pressures upon faculty members to contribute to this growth of knowledge shifted the direction of their thinking to a preoccupation with subject matter and to a neglect of the student as an individual. As a result of this change of emphasis, administrators recognized the need of appointing a new type of educational officer to take over the more intimate responsibilities which faculty members had originally included among their duties. At the same time a number of new educational functions arose as the result of the growing complexity of modern life, the development of scientific techniques, the expansion of the size of student bodies, and the extension of the range of educational objectives.

These officers were appointed first to relieve administrators and faculties of problems of discipline; but their responsibilities grew with considerable rapidity to include a large number of other duties: educational counseling, vocational counseling, the administration of loans and scholarship funds, part-time employment, graduate placement, student health, extra-curricular activities, social programs, and a number of others. The officers undertaking responsibility for these educational functions are known by many names, but during the past two decades they have come, as a group, to be called personnel officers.

A number of terms are in general use in colleges and universities related to the philosophy of education which we have outlined. Illustrative of these terms are "guidance," "counseling," "advisory," and "personnel." Of these, we believe the term "personnel"—prefaced by "student"—to be the least objectionable. Rather than attempt a specific definition of "student personnel" as it is combined with such nouns as "work," "service," "administration," "research," etc., we offer the term, "the student personnel point of view" as indicative of the total philosophy embodied in the foregoing discussion. The functions which implement this point of view—indicated in the next section—may be designated as "student personnel services." Similarly, the performance of these functions may be designated "student personnel work."

This background and discussion of terminology we believe to be important. Personnel work is not new. Personnel officers have been appointed throughout the colleges and universities of the country to undertake a number of educational responsibilities which were once entirely assumed by teaching members of faculty. They have also, because of the expansion of educational functions, developed a number of student personnel services which have but recently been stressed. The philosophy behind their work, however, is as old as education itself.

I. Student Personnel Services

This philosophy implies that in addition to instruction and business management adapted to the needs of the individual student, an effective educational program includes—in one form or another—the following services adapted to the specific aims and objectives of each college and university:

1. Interpreting institutional objectives and opportunities to prospec-

tive students and their parents and to workers in secondary education.

2. Selecting and admitting students, in cooperation with secondary schools.

3. Orienting the student to his educational environment.

4. Providing a diagnostic service to help the student discover his abilities, aptitudes, and objectives.

5. Assisting the student throughout his college residence to determine upon his courses of instruction in light of his past achievements, vocational and personal interests, and diagnostic findings.

6. Enlisting the active cooperation of the family of the student in the interest of his educational accomplishment.

7. Assisting the student to reach his maximum effectiveness through clarification of his purposes, improvement of study methods, speech habits, personal appearance, manners, etc., and through progression in religious, emotional, social development, and other non-academic personal and group relationships.

8. Assisting the student to clarify his occupational aims and his educational plans in relation to them.

9. Determining the physical and mental health status of the student, providing appropriate remedial health measures, supervising the health of students, and controlling environmental health factors.

10. Providing and supervising an adequate housing program for students.

11. Providing and supervising an adequate food service for students.

12. Supervising, evaluating, and developing the extra-curricular activities of students.

13. Supervising, evaluating, and developing the social life and interests of students.

14. Supervising, evaluating, and developing the religious life and interests of students.

15. Assembling and making available information to be used in improvement of instruction and in making the curriculum more flexible.

16. Coordinating the financial aid and part-time employment of students, and assisting the student who needs it to obtain such help.

17. Keeping a cumulative record of information about the student and making it available to the proper persons.

18. Administering student discipline to the end that the individual will be strengthened, and the welfare of the group preserved.

19. Maintaining student group morale by evaluating, understanding, and developing student mores.

20. Assisting the student to find appropriate employment when he leaves the institution.

21. Articulating college and vocational experience.

22. Keeping the student continuously and adequately informed of the educational opportunities and services available to him.

23. Carrying on studies designed to evaluate and improve these functions and services.

Coordination

The effective organization and functioning of student personnel work requires that the educational administrators at all times (1) regard student personnel work as a major concern, involving the cooperative effort of all members of the teaching and administrative staff and the student body; and (2) interpret student personnel work as dealing with the individual student's total characteristics and experiences rather than with separate and distinct aspects of his personality or performance.

It should be noted that effective personnel work may be formally organized or may exist without direction or organization, and that frequently the informal type evidences a personnel point of view in an institution. In either case the personnel point of view is most likely to permeate an entire staff when it is the result of an indigenous development in the institution. Imposition of personnel theories and practices from above or from outside is likely to result in pseudo-personnel work, with probable antagonism developing therefrom. However, it is obvious that coordination of student personnel work is urgently needed. We suggest several varieties of such needed coordination.

I. Coordination within Individual Institutions

The student personnel functions set forth earlier in this report should be coordinated within each educational institution. Existing conditions emphasize the need for such coordination. All personnel workers within an institution syould cooperate with one another in order to avoid duplications of effort and in order to develop student personnel work evenly. The plan of coordination and its administration will, of course, vary with institutions of different types.

II. Coordination between Instruction and Student Personnel Work

Instruction is most effective when the instructor regards his classes both as separate individuals and as members of a group. Such instruction aims to achieve in every student a maximum performance in terms of that student's potentialities and the conditions under which he works. Ideally each instructor should possess all the information necessary for such individualization. Actually such ideal conditions do not exist. Therefore a program of coordination becomes necessary which provides for the instructor appropriate information whenever such information relates to effective instruction.

An instructor may perform functions in the realms both of instruction and student personnel work. Furthermore, instruction itself involves far more than the giving of information on the part of the teacher and its acceptance by the student. Instructors should be encouraged to contribute regularly to student personnel records such anecdotal information concerning students as is significant from the personnel point of view. Instructors should be encouraged to call to the attention of personnel workers any students in their courses who could profit by personnel services.

Certain problems involving research are common to instruction and student personnel work. Any investigation which has for its purpose the improvement of instruction is at the same time a research which improves personnel procedures. Similarly, the results of any studies, the aim of which is to improve personnel procedures, should be disseminated throughout the instructional staff. In both cases wherever possible such projects should be carried on as cooperative ventures.

II. Coordination between the Business Administration and Student Personnel Work

In all financial or business matters having to do with student activities or student problems, either in terms of individuals or groups of individuals, coordination and correlation must exist between business administration and student personnel work. Examples of such matters are:

Student loans
Dormitories
Dining halls
Scholarships
Student organizations
Athletic management
Deferred payments of fees
Student participation in business management of instituion.

IV. Coordination of Personnel Work between Institutions of Secondary and Higher Education

There is a pressing need for further coordination between secondary schools and institutions of higher education. Since a special need exists for coordination between student personnel work in colleges and in secondary schools, copies of the data sent to the admissions department should be available to other college personnel officers. This would be a desirable place to begin coordination. The selection of students, where conditions will permit, should be based upon total personnel records as well as grades in courses. Examples of items in such a record are:

Ability in critical thinking
Ability to cooperate
Physical and mental health
Aesthetic appreciation
Test records such as aptitude tests, reading ability, etc.
Vocational objective
Summarized predictions of college performance.

Coordination should also result in more effective interchange of information, problems, and techniques between the personnel units of colleges and secondary schools. Competent individuals should be available whenever secondary schools desire a presentation, either to students or faculty, of college opportunities and requirements.

Problems of research which require coordination between secondary schools and colleges reside in such areas as:

a. Transfer from high school to college with particular reference to the last year in high school and the first year in college.

b. The basis upon which high schools guide toward college.

c. The basis upon which colleges select entrants.

d. Freshman failures.

e. Variations in the total requirements of different types of colleges; for example, engineering, dentistry, liberal arts, teacher training, etc.

f. Existing types of coordination between secondary schools and colleges; for example, high school visitors, examination systems, coordinating committees, experimental investigations, etc.

V. Coordination among National Personnel Associations

During the past two decades a number of associations of various types of student personnel workers have come into existence. These associations perform valuable services in furthering personnel work and in bringing workers in the field into closer professional and personnel contact. We believe that the point of view for which all personnel people stand and the services which they render would be greatly enhanced were closer coordination developed between these assocations. Hereinafter we propose that the American Council on Education establish or sponsor a committee on student personnel work in colleges and universities. We recommend that this committee, as one of its functions, undertake to bring about closer relationships between these associations.

VI. Coordination of Student Personnel Work with After-College Adjustment

Effective student personnel work should include as its culminating activity adequate provision for induction of students into after-college life.

The satisfactory adjustment of graduates to occupation life constitutes one important basis for evaluation of an institution's educational
effectiveness, since it stimulates a continual re-examination of educational procedures and the effect of those procedures upon the men and
women who make up the student body of the college. Moreover, coordination between college and occupational life rests essentially upon
more complete information covering the various types of work into
which college graduates go.

This conference also wishes to emphasize the necessity for conceiving of after-college adjustment as comprehending the total living of college graduates, including not only their occupational success but their
active concern with the social, recreational, and cultural interests of
the community. Such concern implies their willingness to assume those
individual and social responsibilities which are essential to the common
good.

Future Development

Student personnel work is developing with some rapidity throughout
the country. Annually a large number of institutions undertake for the
first time additional student personnel functions or they further develop
services already established. At the same time new methods of organizing student personnel services are coming into prominence; the literature of the field is expanding voluminously; and problems in need of
careful investigation become more numerous every year.

Because of these and other considerations a need for national leadership in student personnel work is becoming continuously more obvious.
If the expansion and development that the colleges and universities of
the country are experiencing in the student personnel field is to be as
desirable and effective as it should be, some national agency needs to be
available to assist administrators, faculty members, and student personnel officers in their developmental efforts. No such national agency
now exists, and a careful canvassing of the student personnel associations which have grown up brings us to the unanimous conclusion that
no one of them is able to become that national agency.

We, therefore, propose that the American Council on Education establish or sponsor a committee on student personnel work in American colleges and universities. This committee should, in our judgment, undertake the following activities:

I. National Survey of Student Personnel Work

This survey should be conducted throughout the country after the pattern of the one undertaken by L. B. Hopkins for the American Council on Education in 1926. Such a study would require the services of but one individual who would visit five or six institutions in each of half a dozen institutional categories. The undertaking would result in an overview rather than a detailed study, and its publication would satisfy the growing demand for current authoritative information about the student personnel field. It would be built around a check list of the functions we have listed. The Hopkins survey had such great influence that we believe an up-to-date and analogous study published in concise form would be of immediate interest and value to administrators and faculty members throughout the country.

II. Interpretation of the Problems of College Students

A short volume with some such title as "The College Student and His Problems" should be written and published. The purpose of this volume would be to inform administrators, faculty members, and the general public of the complex human problems that are involved in education. Stressing scholarship and intellectual development, educators frequently take for granted or actually overlook the philosophy which we have hereinbefore called the student personnel point of view. The preparation and publication of the volume which we propose would, we believe, do much to bring this philosophy to the attention of all individuals concerned with higher education. It would, moreover, bring this philosophy to their attention in terms of the actual experiences of students rather than through an abstract discussion.

III. Handbooks on Student Personnel Functions

A series of handbooks on particular student personnel functions should be written and published. The survey proposed above would provide a panoramic picture of the entire field. The handbooks that we are suggesting would furnish detailed information about specific personnel functions. Data for these handbooks would come from two general sources: first, from the information gathered by the surveyor on the detailed operation of specific personnel functions in the institutions he visits and, second, from the literature. Each handbook would stress the best practices developed in the handling of each function. The work of writing each handbook should be under the direction of a committee of three. This committee should include an active worker in the special field under discussion and a representative of the appropriate national personnel organization.

IV. Research

Obviously, student personnel services will never develop as they should unless extensive and careful research is undertaken. We, therefore, urge that the facilitation and direction of research be considered an essential responsibility of the committee. In this field we envisage the committee as important in two directions: first, in encouraging other agencies to undertake investigations, and, second, in carrying on several investigations on its own. We list below projects of both types.

Research by Other Agencies

We propose that the Committee on Measurement and Guidance of the American Council on Education be requested to consider the desirability of the following four investigations:

1. *Aptitude testing.* The investigation of aptitudes on a national scale comparable to the work undertaken by the Cooperative Test Service but in the field of differential vocational as well as educational aptitudes.

2. *Social development.* The development of instruments for measuring social adjustment and social maturity.

3. *Diagnostic techniques.* The study of the field of usefulness of existing diagnostic instruments and the development of new instruments.

4. *Scholastic aptitude test scale.* Bringing together on a comparable scale the norms of various widely used scholastic aptitude tests.

We also propose that the National Occupational Conference be requested to consider the desirability of carrying forward the following work:

1. *Occupational information.* Gathering and publishing occupational information for college students with particular emphasis upon periodic census data and trends.

2. *Traits needed in occupations.* Working with the Committee on Measurement and Guidance in the study of human traits significant for various occupations, particularly those which college students enter.

Research by the Committee on Student Personnel Work

A number of research projects need to be undertaken in the immediate future, responsibility for which no existing agencies seem able to assume. We, therefore, propose that the committee secure support for the following four studies:

1. *Student out-of-class life.* College students spend the majority of their time outside the classrooms and laboratories. We have, however, no significant data as to the activities in which they engage. In order to understand the educational importance of their activities we propose that on a score of campuses throughout the country data be collected. Incidentally, this research would be relatively inexpensive since on every campus individuals may be found to do the work without compensation.

2. *Faculty-student out-of-class relationships.* Much is said frequently of the place that faculty members have in student personnel work. We have, however, few facts and we propose that data should be gathered from a number of institutions following much the same technique as proposed in study "I" above.

3. *Financial aid to students.* Large sums of money are available in many institutions for scholarships and loans. In addition the National Youth Administration has been spending many millions during the past three years to help students to stay in college. The problem of who should be helped and how much is growing more important every year.

We propose that this problem in its wide ramifications might well be studied. Perhaps funds for much of this work could be secured from the National Youth Administration.

4. *Follow-up study of college students.* Every year over a hundred thousand students graduate from our colleges. What happens to them and what effect their college work has had upon their vocational and personal adjustments we can only guess. We, therefore, propose that the committee develop a method for making follow-up studies and that this method be made available to interested institutions.

V. Advisory Service to Colleges and Universities

An advisory service to colleges and universities interested in the improvement of student personnel work should be developed. While the proposed survey is being undertaken and while the suggested handbooks are being written, the committee will inevitably have addressed to it a number of inquiries about problems within its field of interest. These inquiries cannot be answered authoritatively until these two ventures are finished, but meanwhile the committee should assume responsibility for directing such correspondents to the individuals best qualified to assist them. When the survey is finished, and the handbooks available, however, we propose that the committee actively promote the best student personnel practices which its work has brought to light.

II

Reaffirmation After World War II

Educators turned their attention to their professional roles in the late forties as hostilities ceased and educational institutions were called upon to help the armed forces veterans return to civilian life. At the same time, the traditional aged high school graduates were seeking college admission in greater numbers than ever before.

From this changed setting, attention was again given to the need to identify the parameters of the student personnel field. One of the first authors to continue the examination of the field was E. H. Hopkins in his article, "The Essentials of a Student Personnel Program." Hopkins, one of the early Vice Presidents for Student Affairs, included the list of services to be provided as well as basic and fundamental assumptions. He acknowledged the importance of the American Council on Education pamphlet published in 1937. His greatest concerns in this new post World War II era were getting more faculty participation in implementing the student personnel point of view, and secondly, obtaining more research-supported facts about students and the programs that serve them.

In 1949 Williamson edited the book *Trends in Student Personnel Work*. He invited Kate Mueller to address problems in counseling women. She argues that since the student personnel point of view calls for development of students as a whole, it should mean both men and women. She examines life patterns, differing social pressures, frustrations of women, and even considers the question of a special curriculum for women. Her insights and conclusions provide a background for the issues that surround sexual equality among staff, students and faculty on campus today.

A speech delivered by W. W. Blaesser at the National Educational Conference in 1948 and published in 1949 as one of the collection of papers, *Higher Education in American Society*, provides another view of the field that links the American Council of Education 1937 statement with the decade of change and concludes with a look to the future. This article is a synthesis of definitions of student personnel work, a review of the essential aspects of a student personnel program, and an indication of how student personnel work in the future might be related to the objectives of higher education as set forth in the President's Commission on Higher Education. This work by Blaesser is an impressive and comprehensive outline of the current status of the profession and an accurate indication of how student personnel work in the future must be related to various processes and functions of higher education. It is apparent that Blaesser brought much from this document to the American Council on Education 1949 report, *The Student Personnel Point of View*, where he was one of the committee members responsible for this document.

The American Council on Education continued its support for student personnel work by authorizing Williamson to convene a committee of twelve to reexamine the purposes of higher education as they affect the student personnel workers. They focused on goals that were obviously related to the upheaval of World War II and the post war social climate. This 1949 A.C.E. document builds on the 1937 A.C.E. document by expanding the statement of professional goals and objectives. The section on student needs and services includes a first time awareness of new types of students—married, veteran, and international. The committee concluded their work by calling for careful attention to the manner of administration of student personnel work— campus interrelationships, and program evaluation. For many newly appointed student affairs staffs, this statement provided the rationale for and a definition of their work on the campus.

The final paper to be selected from that productive year was the American College Personnel Association Presidential Address (1949) delivered by C. Gilbert Wrenn. After giving assurances of personnel work's legitimacy, he proceeds to identify certain faults that stand in the way of an even higher level of performance. He tells us why it is unnecessary to be either belligerent or apologetic about the significance of our work, and improper for us to fail to make a distinctive contribution as specialists in human behavior and human need. He warns about other psychological problems in the life of the personnel worker. Wrenn uses his counseling orientation to suggest ways to handle the factors that cause tensions in our lives. It may be reassuring to know the fatigue and burnout that concerns student personnel professionals today has been a continuing problem—a perplexing one, but not one that has destroyed our effectiveness. Wrenn's message is current.

W. H. Cowley, a higher education historian, had a particular interest in the history of student life. In 1957 he forecast the campus as a likely setting for agitation and destruction if social conditions galvanize the increasing numbers of students to demonstrate. Deans of Students should prepare for this possibility by research on the historical continuum of student life. He also gives considerable attention to the relationships among 7,500 student personnel workers. He sees their communication and mutual support systems in complete disarray and calls for a linking together of all the national associations whose members are engaged in student personnel work in colleges and universities. He accurately forecast the movement that later resulted in the formation of The Council of Student Personnel Association (COSPA), an organization that was to help unify the fast growing profession from the early 60s through the early 70s.

The Essentials of a
Student Personnel Program

E. H. Hopkins

. . . let me state very briefly the outline of this paper. . . . *First*, I shall merely list those essential and specialized student personnel services, which in one form or another, must be provided as an integral and inseparable part of any program of higher education. *Second*, I shall list a group of basic and fundamental principles and assumptions, which are just as essential as the student personnel services themselves. *Third*, I shall make a plea for "optimum" instead of "minimum" essentials in student personnel work, and education generally. *Fourth*, there is a degree of urgency about all of this which we as educators, and citizens, have not fully appreciated, or if we have, we have done little about it. And last, I wish to single out for special consideration and discussion two of the eleven essential principles which I shall propose.

Essential Student-Personnel Services

For the sake of brevity, I shall merely list eleven specialized student personnel services, which I consider to be essential to a sound program of higher education. Each of these could be discussed at length, but let us merely assume that each of these services should be organized, coordinated, and integrated into the total educational program, in a sound and effective manner. With this assumption, I shall eliminate further discussion with respect to the "hows" and "whys" of these eleven essential services. They are as follows:

1. A program of *pre-college counseling, selection, and applicant-centered admissions.*

2. An organized program for diagnosis and counseling of students. This includes both *intensive clinical* counseling and the normal day-to-day educational and personal counseling provided by the faculty and other less professionally trained counselors.

3. An effective *orientation* program, spread throughout the entire first year.

4. *Remedial assistance in various areas* for those students who need it.

5. Definite provision for the supervision, coordination, and integration of the "*co-curricular*" program on the campus.

6. A *student health service*, providing professional services in areas of both physical and mental health.

7. An adequate program of *supervision of living arrangements*, including the food service program. This program must be provided in such a manner as to contribute to the maximum extent possible to the social-educational objectives of the institution, as they relate to the individual student.

8. A well-organized program for administering *financial aids, student employments, post-graduate placements, and job follow-ups.*

9. Special facilities for developing and evaluating the *religious life and interests* of students on the campus.

10. There must be devised and maintained an adequate system of permanent *cumulative personnel records*, which include pertinent information relative to *all* aspects of student life and student accomplishment.

11. At the present, and for the next few years, a special service providing for the coordination of Veteran's affairs is an essential part of the total program.

Basic Principles and Assumptions

There are certain basic principles and assumptions which are just as essential as are the student personnel services. . . .

1. First, of course, is the student personnel point of view. . . . It

must be considered as the fundamental and basic principle underlying the total program. It is well defined and described in the American Council on Education pamphlet, entitled *The Student Personnel Point of View*, published in 1937. In essentially the same form and in 1938, it was adopted as the first chapter of the charter of this association. It is just as up-to-date in 1948 as when it was adopted in 1938.

2. The second principle. . . . is the necessity for thorough-going and effective coordination not only between and among the services and principles themselves, but between the services and the instructional program. This coordination must prevail both horizontally and vertically, not only within the institution, but with the pre-college program and with post-college adjustments. A program of student personnel services, of and by itself, just does not exist.

3. Education and the processes of education are strictly individual processes. The individual student must be considered as a total unique personality. Consequently, education must be flexible to the needs of individual students. This principle of considering the individual student as an individual is absolutely essential to a sound program of education which is based upon the student personnel point of view. Furthermore, there is nothing in this principle which is in conflict with the social objectives of education; there is no dichotomy between education for the needs of the individual and education for the improvement of society.

4. Educational programs, policies, and procedures cannot be established at least in a healthy manner by administrative edict or by fiat. These are matters demanding the combined wits and wisdoms of the entire faculty—with the additional help of the students. In addition, such a democratic policy is psychologically necessary for the success of the program.

5. Another essential principle, at least as it applies in coeducational institutions, has reference to what I consider to be a psychological fallacy apparent in some institutions where separate and parallel organizational structures prevail, one for women students and one for men students. I, of course, have reference to the traditional "Dean of Men" and "Dean of Women" organizations. Therefore, I consider it a sound principle to assume that the problems of men and women students on the campus are of the same order, and that the principles and methods for solving them are the same.

6. The college campus, both in action and in spirit, must be made an efficient *laboratory for training in democratic living.*

7. While I have no intention, here and now, of listing all of the principles or assumptions basic to education generally, there is another educational or psychological principle which I regard as being . . . closely akin to the objectives of student personnel services . . . I have reference to the concept of "deferring the selection of a major." The actual process of "selecting a major" is an individual student process, and a mental process. Therefore, there can be *no* institutional edict which says categorically to the student that you may not select a major field of study until "such and such a time." On the other hand, there should be a policy which prevents students from being forced into such decisions too early in their college careers. Along with this principle goes a strong endorsement of the principles and objectives of general education, *but not to the exclusion of training for jobs.*

8. As a principle, student discipline, in the broad as well as the narrow sense, must be judiciously administered and in such a manner that the individual student will be strengthened and the welfare of the group preserved.

9. As mentioned before, a student personnel program does not exist, per se, in spite of the tendency of most members of the faculty to think so, and to act accordingly. Consequently, when we refer to the essentials of "the student personnel program," we must necessarily refer to "higher education generally." We simply cannot talk about student personnel work, in educational institutions, without talking about *education* itself. Student personnel services *are* education. We must assume that both the objective and the methods of student personnel work, and of education generally, are *absolutely* inseparable, if not identical. The plain truth *is* that student personnel work *still* is considered by far too many faculty members, deans, and presidents simply as a fifth wheel. And they are not referring to the "steering wheel." Consequently, it is imperative that you bring the *entire* faculty, administration, student body, and alumni into active and constructive participation in the practical implementation of the program.

10. In discussing the principle of "faculty participation" and other sound principles of organization, I should like to take issue with one of the currently accepted university organizational patterns which organizes the President's office into four divisions: Namely, the academic,

the student personnel, the business management, and public relations. This *is* the current trend in the larger institutions. I am aware that on many campuses it has been a *struggle* for status, particularly for the Dean of Students, or Director of Student Affairs. I am indeed happy that on many of these same campuses, the Dean of Students now has a parallel position with the Dean of Faculty. That is appropriate. However, I do not concur with an institutional organization which permits the student personnel program on the one hand, and the academic program on the other, to be so separated that they are brought together *only* by the President.

11. There must be a principle, a policy, in fact a plan for continuous appraisal and evaluation of the program and a *willingness* to adjust and readjust it to fit changing conditions. Closely related to this principle, in fact a part of it, is the compelling need for curricular and student personnel research at all levels of the higher educational ladder, but most important at the post-graduate level, i.e., a follow-up of our graduates, and for that matter of all others who leave our schools before graduation, in order to find out what are the results of our particular brand of education. Just how effectively are we doing what we propose to be doing? This point, also, I shall discuss later.

Too Much Emphasis on "Minimum Essentials"

In the first place, I am reminded of the Office of Education publication, published, I believe, in the middle 'thirties, entitled *Minimum Essentials of a Guidance Program*; for our purposes, it must just as well have read, "Minimum Essentials of a Student Personnel Program." I fear that too many of us, and our deans, our presidents, and our governing boards, think too frequently in terms of *minimum* essentials, when thinking of the student personnel program in our respective institutions. Why should we put ourselves so clearly on the defensive? Why should we show such lack of confidence, such half-heartedness, such weakness of moral courage, when we try to sell the student personnel point of view, and the kind of program which will put that point of view to work? That point of view, with which we are all familiar and to which we all subscribe, is of little consequence until and unless we put it to work in rather concrete and practical situations. Indirectly, we have been apologizing for what we have to offer, by asking merely for *minimum* essentials. Perhaps we have not called them that, and in some cases probably we have not even been aware ourselves that we were seeking merely minimum essentials.

If we really *want* to make education effective . . . let us start defining the *optimum essentials* of education, and gear these essentials and their practical implementation to the *immediate* problems facing education today. Let us direct our thinking, and therefore our *actions*, toward the *maximum potentials* from *optimum conditions*, rather than toward the *limited potentials* from *minimum conditions*. Without this kind of forward thinking, without this courage to face reality—and I mean facing reality in 1948, not in the distant future—we might just as well toss whatever strength we have into the military machine and wait for the consequences.

Urgency for More Effective Higher Education

In asking for optimum conditions we must stress the *urgency* of our purpose, and we must also get across the idea that we have no "vested interests," no selfish motives, no axes to grind, but that these conditions are essential, and essential now, if we are to do the kind of job we *must do—for our own survival.*

The situation is both critical and urgent and further complicated by emotions of fear, distrust, prejudice, selfishness, indifference, and general "uneasiness."

This "uneasiness" and its consequent fearful speculation are very real, and undoubtedly represent a significant "cross-roads" in civilization as we know it. The first question is "Can we survive?" and the second, "How can we adapt ourselves to the new age if we do survive?" In either case, the "cross-roads" unquestionably is here. But let us concentrate on the first question; there is no time in this discussion to concentrate on the second. What consequences are likely, if we become a world frightened by our own disorganized efforts to cope with it? If fear is an individual's greatest enemy, as the psychologists say it is, it is a far greater enemy of a nation—or for a world—because in an individual.

therapy is more easily and more effectively administered. We must meet this world-wide fear with *understanding* and with *education*. How else can we bring about changes in the attitudes and motivations of individuals, except through education? But do we have the "stuff" in ourselves and in our ranks to provide the leadership needed in these critical times? I am confident that we do have, but it is absolutely essential, and essential now, that organized education in this country come decisively to grips with the worldwide crisis of mankind. We cannot afford to let this crisis just "take its course."

The second urgent and compelling reason for a fresh view and a revitalized program of higher education based upon the student personnel point of view is the fact that too often our graduates simply do not measure up to our expectations, to their own capacities, or to the demands of the society of which they become a part. While there is continuously mounting evidence which clearly indicates this weakness in higher education today, for the sake of brevity I shall use but a few references. Perhaps the overall problem in this connection is nowhere better summarized than in the Editor's Foreward to Robert Pace's report of the Minnesota study, completed just prior to the war, entitled *They Went to College*. This foreward, as you would expect, is based upon the findings of the study, in which Pace reported on the differences between college graduates and non-graduates, at the University of Minnesota. I quote:

> We need desperately to know why there appears to be little or no difference between graduates and nongraduates, between high-ranking students and low-ranking students, after they have been a decade away from the campus. Why most of them appear to want security and contentment instead of taking a vigorous delight in 'looking upon the bright face of danger' and welcoming blood-stirring change. Why, if we have taught them—far above their fellows—to think critically, they are in after-college years so obviously uncritical and inconsistent in their thinking. Why, if we have taught them to read good books, most of them read only 'slick' magazines of huge circulation, newspapers, a few books of a standard below that of the freshman English class. Why, in a democracy, the most highly educated people we have fail so miserably to engage in community and political activities.

Much more could be said with respect to the *need* for an effective student personnel program, one which is thoroughly meshed into the total educational program and which would be capable of producing products of which we could be proud. Just take a look at our attrition rate, throughout the country, where from fifty to sixty-five per cent drop out before embarking upon the third year of college. Just take a look, without even a pretense at scientific evaluation, at the appropriateness and effectiveness of the training which from year to year is being given those who do drop out along the way. Just find out, in your own institutions, what percentage of *your* students do not know what occupational objectives they wish to follow, or for what occupational pattern they are best fitted. Just find out, *in your own institutions*, the extent to which individual students *are* following intelligent and *planned* college careers.

While this picture is a rather discouraging one, representing a combination of a critical, serious, and urgent national and international situation, and what appears to be an inefficient and ineffective educational system, I do feel that there *are* ways out.

Although I do not recall the specific reference, I recall reading not long ago in another article by President Hutchins in which he made some such statement as this:

As a means to a peaceful world, education is either everything, or else it is nothing; if it really is everything, then it should be encouraged, implemented, financed, and made to work; if on the other hand, it is nothing, there should be no more time nor money wasted on it.

I think we agree on the fundamental importance of education; I think we agree that it *is* everything, so far as progress is concerned. We agree on the wisdom of the student personnel point of view in education, but apparently we have had little agreement on what constitutes the most fruitful means of putting this point of view and education to work.

Two Positive Approaches

In the light of this setting: first a war-torn, tattered, and unstable world; second, a rather unenviable record of civic and social participation and contribution on the part of the average college graduate, as compared with non-college graduates; and, third, a heterogeneous and conglomerate mass of student personnel and educational practices being used and misused throughout our respective institutions; I should like to focus more attention on two of the eleven essential principles which I mentioned at the beginning of this paper: *first, the principle of getting more active faculty participation in the implementation of the student personnel point of view, and secondly, the need for many more facts, i.e., curricular and student personnel research.*

Regarding the first: if we are going to have an effective educational program, based truly upon the student personnel point of view, that point of view must be known, believed, accepted, and *practiced* by the teaching faculty, by the administration, and by those responsible for the specialized services within the institution. This is essential—but "How?" This is where you come in—in fact, it is *your* first essential. We must first create an organization, a faculty, in fact, an institution, which by its composite and coordinated efforts, by its sound educational policies which will have been put into action, will do for the masses what a few counselors and a few instructors have been trying desperately to do for too few students. Certainly, I do not mean that you will eliminate the need for individual counseling by specially trained and qualified workers . . . but we will get far greater results with the masses of our students, if we provide on a wholesale and preventive basis, what we have been attempting to provide on a retail and therapeutic basis. It is comparable with the effects of a public health program. You need relatively fewer physicians in a community having an intelligent and carefully administered public health program than in communities where no such program exists.

This would be merely empty "mouthing" if I did not believe that we *can* go a long way, in a relatively short time, toward the development of this kind of a program. You are the people who must carry the torch; you must become crusaders, and maintain that zeal and enthusiasm, along with a necessary amount of patience and diplomacy, until the process begins to "take." More than ever before, you must devise better means of informing your faculties, and doing it repeatedly, of the significance of the student personnel point of view. In weekly or periodic staff bulletins, report and review individual cases, report and review the kind of facts which Pace reported in the study of the 951 graduates and non-graduates of the University of Minnesota. If possible, find out these facts from your own institution and your own students. Also, report continuously and repeatedly what other institutions are doing, significant, urgent, and compelling statistics on such matters as student failures, student drop-outs, the criteria for success and the reason for failure on post-graduation jobs, and the failure of college graduates to assume more than a minimum of civic responsibility.

Why not prevail upon your President, your Dean of Faculty, or your Budget Committee for enough money—and it would take a surprisingly small amount—to purchase sufficient copies of the *Report of the President's Commission on Higher Education* so that each department in your college would have copies of the complete report, and insist that it be rotated among the members of the respective departments until all had read it. The reading of that report should be an absolute requirement of every person who justifies his name on a college faculty payroll. Also, for a very small budgetary consideration (75¢ per year per person), your institution can subscribe to *Higher Education*, the semi-monthly publication of the Higher Education Division of the U.S. Office of Education; I recommend it as a good investment by the institution for every single member of your faculty.

How many of you take time, or make time, to visit *regularly* with members of your instructional staff to discuss with them common policies and procedures, institutional objectives and your *joint* responsibilities for achieving them, to encourage or solicit constructive criticism from them, to demonstrate through a discussion and consideration of *their* teaching and research interests that you understand and appreciate *their* important role in the overall educational program of the institution?

This year on our campus we inaugurated a series of monthly faculty meetings, for *all* members of our faculty; such meetings are devoted exclusively to lectures, discussions, and panels covering matters of current educational and faculty personnel policies. Although our faculty probably is as busy and overworked as the average faculty, I am happy to say that these meetings have been unusually well-attended and unusually successful. As a result we have set aside $10,000 for next year, to bring to the campus outstanding authorities, consultants, and visiting lecturers on matters of current educational interest to the faculty.

Another example of the degree of genuine interest in, and willingness to participate in and contribute to, a dynamic program of educational improvement on our own college campus, was demonstrated a few weeks ago when I called for volunteer memberships on a large number of subcommittees of the Educational Policies Committee. It was understood that these subcommittees were to delve *deeply* into such matters as "improvement of instruction and the relating of instruction to contemporary issues," "integrated courses," "instruction in community, national, and international affairs," "student counseling," "Graduation requirements," "a deferred-major plan," "the integration of student activities into the educative processes," "terminal education," "how to teach worker education," and a number of others. With faculty members already "committied to death," you would be astonished to know that we had approximately one hundred and fifty faculty volunteers who indicated both an interest in, and a willingness to serve on, such committees. Those committees are going to stir up a lot of grass-roots thinking on the Washington State College campus within the next few months, and the next year. Our faculty has just completed working out its own plan for faculty evaluation. This means appraisal of faculty performance and effectiveness in areas of instruction, research and publications, and in over-all benefit to the institution and to the community. They have now asked that the faculty be evaluated by the students and by the alumni. They *are* deeply interested in self-improvement and in the improvement of instruction and education generally. Our faculty voted, as a result of their own deliberations, not merely to adopt a deferred-major plan, but to place the administrative responsibility for the entire lower division in the hands of the Dean of Students and his student personnel staff. This plan has been in operation for two years. They are sold on it, and are improving it.

In connection with institutional committees, may I suggest also that you, as student personnel workers, have an important and urgent role to play in the determination and implementation of educational policies within your respective institutions. Therefore, you should see to it somehow that you and other selected members of your student personnel staff are placed on such committees as the curriculum committee, educational policies committee, admission policies committee, and other important committees charged with policy determination functions. Also, on your important policy committees, place some of the best students on your campus. If you have not already tried this, I think you may be both amazed and pleased with the nature of the contribution which they can and will make.

The second postulate on which I wish to focus more attention has to do with the dire need for *curricular and student personnel research* to guide us in our policy determinations. How on earth can we expect to develop new curricula, new programs of study, proper combinations of general and specialized courses, integrated courses which we know are effective, adequate vocational and other counseling services, student activity programs which are supposed to train for democratic living, sound admission policies, sound re-instatement policies, sound and defensible graduation requirements, when we do not even know what the effects and the results of our present curricula, instructions, and services are?

We set up admission policies without knowing what really makes for success in college. For example, we are still clinging to high-school graduation and certain patterns of high-school subjects, when we have known for years that there is no scientific basis for believing that high-school subject-matter patterns are related to academic success in college.

In addition, we should know far more about the students who come to our campuses for educational training. Before we admit them, we should know something of their aptitudes, interests, personality characteristics, as well as their scholastic achievements. We have no right to admit them, and then later to tell them that we are sorry, but we just do not have what they need. Usually we do not even tell them that; they struggle along for a year or two, and then discover for themselves that not only are they swimming upstream, but up the wrong stream. We need to know what the individual need of our prospective students are, and in addition we need to know the overall pattern of individual, social, and employment needs of the regions which we serve, if we are to fulfill our missions efficiently and to the best of our abilities.

In my opinion, the effectiveness of any educational institution, and therefore the effectiveness of its governing board, of its President, and of those others responsible for educational policies and practices within the institution, should be measured by the quality of the product which the institution produces. This, of course, assumes that the qualities and qualifications of the product would have to be measured, and measured consistently and continuously. It means, in all institutions, that such studies as the one reported by Pace at Minnesota should be made, and the data should be kept current. "But," you say, "this would cost money." I can only say that it would cost for less than what is now being spent providing teaching faculties, services, housing, and other provisions for the students who are "swimming up the wrong streams," not to mention the loss of time, money, prestige, and "face" of each student in that category. Consequently, if we really are interested in developing an educational program based upon the student personnel point of view, let us find out a little more about the individual needs of those students who come to us for training, the social and employment needs of the regions which we serve, and the effects and results of the training which we are now providing for our students. *This research is essential*, and you are the people who are best qualified and who are in the most strategic positions to carry it on. You are the persons to see to it that the findings of such research become the common property of your administration and your faculty.

Summary

1. The *essentials of a student personnel program* consist of:
   a. The student personnel point of view as applied to all educational processes;
   b. A group of at least eleven specialized student personnel services, requiring specially trained counselors and technicians;
   c. Certain basic and fundamental principles and assumptions which apply to all phases of the program. Eleven such principles and assumptions have been specifically mentioned.
2. We must strive harder than we have ever striven before for "optimum" conditions and the wherewithal to carry out an effective educational program.
3. We must devise countless practical and spirited means of transforming the student personnel point of view into institutional and *faulty action* patterns—not only as a long range objective, but as an immediate one.
4. Through scientific research we must *get at the facts* which are basic

to an intelligent and effective program. *We must know wherein we are ineffective or weak.*

5. There is a degree of urgency which we can ill afford to ignore. In short, all that I have been trying to say is that it is high time that we come down from the ivory towers, that we face the urgency before us, that we follow the courage of our convictions, and develop an educational program which will bring about the full realization and meaning of *democracy in action.* This means an educational program which will turn out emotionally mature men and women *capable, willing,* and *desirous* of acting intelligently in a world where men depend upon men, and in a civilization which depends upon understandings among men. In the words of the President's Commission on Higher Education, "the responsibility for the development of these personal qualities (in our students) can no longer be left, as heretofore, to some courses, or a few departments, or some scattered extra-curricular organizations; *it must become a part of every phase of college life.*"

Problems in Counseling Women

Kate Hevner Mueller

The college years always represent a period of accelerated progress and a telescoping of previous rates of growth. The half-decade of adolescence has its own characteristic misdirections, frustrations, and disillusionments, to say nothing of irresponsibilities and impertinences. Youth is in the process of establishing independence of family. He is working out his relationships with the opposite sex. He is deciding on and preparing for his career. And with more or less conscious effort he is fusing his varied assortment of values into a usable system and his conglomeration of personality traits into a smoothly functioning whole.

These findings are equally characteristic of both sexes, but there is a differential impact of the college campus on men and women. Counselors who are responsible for putting their students in rapport with their environment, both present and future, need to be aware of what is happening in the world so that they can pick up their cues the more expertly.

Sex Differences

In considering the special problems encountered in counseling women, our first question is, How do women differ from men? Although there is no lack of differences if we select at random any one man and any one woman, it is more difficult to divine strong and important differences that are significant for the sexes as a whole (2, chapters 14 and 15). Physical differences in size and shape are obvious, but the more important differences of endurance and vitality are questionable. It is difficult to find reliable differences in amount and variability in intelligence; in achievement, however, there are very consistent differences, with girls excelling in verbal ability, in memory, and in certain curriculum areas corresponding to their interests.

Various tests bring out certain differences or similarities in personality which are probably more related to the nature and technique of the testing procedure than to the two sexes. Men are said to give highest values to things economic, political, and theoretical; women to the aesthetic, social, and religious. The feminine are more interested in domestic affairs, aesthetic objects, sedentary and indoor occupations, and ministrative occupations, particularly with the young, helpless, and distressed. The masculine have more self-assertion, aggressiveness, hardihood, fearlessness, and roughness of manners, language, and sentiments. The feminine are more compassionate and sympathetic, timid, fastidious, aesthetically sensitive, probably more emotional, and the severer moralists.

The more important investigators (19) emphasize the role of cultural factors in establishing these differences, and show that the masculinity-femininity index is related to the amount of education, to occupation, and to the domestic milieu (e.g. deprivation of one parent and number and sex of siblings). In summary, it is difficult to discern any fundamental differences in the abilities of men and women (even though masculinity and femininity can be more accurately defined than formerly) because the issue is always confused by differences in opportunity. *Women are closest to the pattern for men in abilities, farther apart in interests, and farthest apart in opportunity.*

Men and Women in Society

Life Patterns

Since it is the social expectancy which is so very different for men and for women, it will be necessary to analyze at some length the roles of men and of women in society, and to describe and differentiate their life patterns.

The role expected of man is much more clear-cut and well defined than the role—or better, the various roles—expected of woman. Woman must be prepared to alternate between at least two roles, her business or professional or citizenship career, and her life as a home-maker. Her life pattern will include several well-defined periods, when the time and emphasis will shift from inside to outside the home. A typical adult life pattern for the upper middle class woman might include first a business or professional period; then a family period of perhaps ten or fifteen or even twenty years, during which she may or may not be able to keep up her professional contacts or build the bridges into the world of civic and economic responsibility; and finally a period relatively free from family duties and from financial strain during which some of her best creative or organizational activities may occur.

These life patterns of modern women of the upper middle class have changed quite definitely from those of even fifty years ago. The family period—child bearing and rearing—has been shortened very perceptibly with our lowered birth rate and the cutting off of the third and fourth children (14). Women live longer and enjoy better health, and their housekeeping routines—cleaning, cooking, canning, sewing—have been shortened and lightened. These changes become effective especially in the third period, making it possible and even necessary for a woman to find some worthwhile activity outside the home during the years of her later maturity.

Technological advances and urbanization in the past century have brought about larger changes in the life patterns of women than in those for men; therefore women more than men feel the conflict between these advancing forces and the slower moving mores and ideologies.

Advances in the field of clothing, grooming, and personal services have greatly enhanced woman's attractiveness. Such heroines of fiction and fact as Amber, Scarlett O'Hara, Anna Karenina, and Lillian Russell created problems for themselves because they were beautiful. Beauty was an unusual trait in their day, making them stand out from the masses of lesser, unhistorical women who had no beauty and therefore no problems of interest to the tellers of tales. In 1847 the average woman of forty was dowdy and provincial in her dress. She had no permanent wave and no silk stockings, and she had a large family whose constant needs kept her close at home. Today the woman of forty is slim, fashionably dressed, and well groomed, as attractive as the heroines of fiction, and she therefore encounters some of their problems. As she moves about in her car, she meets a large circle of men who also show the effects of technological improvements. Unfortunately, she also meets the same old mores—the Christian ethic, the Victorian code—all very little changed from the time of her grandmother. Obviously she needs help.

Differing Social Pressures

Neither men nor women can be conceived of merely as human beings free and self-determined according to their inner needs and stresses. Man is a social being as well as a human being, and his personality is a social as well as a psychological construct, growing out of the many roles he plays and the status he enjoys. We could not, of course, claim that this social milieu is more important for women than for men, or more effective, or even more oppressive, or more unfavorable. We could be persuaded to believe, however, that it does give to men a greater amount of freedom in several respects.

1. *Sex behavior and social standards.* A woman is not quite as free an agent, not equally in control of the situation, in regard to choosing a mate. She is forced into the more passive role, which gives her a feeling of greater helplessness, a feeling on which she may or may not be able to capitalize. If a woman is unsuccessful in the art of attracting the attention of men, she has no opportunity to use many of the other skills and knowledge with which she may be richly endowed (7, p. 560). Men in the more active role can always do something about such a situation and avoid the ensuing frustration. Women, forced into more devious methods of approach, suffer more readily from maladjustments.

Most of us are well aware that "the present state of our love and sex mores is chaotic, inconsistent and transitory" (7, p. 563). "The most accurate picture of current attitudes would be in terms of ambivalence and conflict" (17). One writer reports that there is nothing really strong enough and firm enough to warrant the term *conflict.* There is, especially on the college campus, just an ooze, with everybody worming around in it. Most of us have likewise noted the decline in the efficacy of religious sanctions and the effect of the increasing availability of contraceptives. There is also to be observed in these troubled and complex times an increasing need for personal intimacy, for escape in terms of "whatever happens at least we have each other"—even though this solution represents merely an exchange of one set of compulsions for another, and often prove, no matter how satisfying and consoling, no real substitute for these other needs (17).

As other arguments for sex behavior become less cogent, sex and morals educators are forced to rely increasingly on the idea that exclusiveness beautifies and ennobles intimacy. The very intensification of these uplifted expectations of monogamous bliss call for substitute satisfactions (6, p. 722). Our culture continues to emphasize "youth and beauty" as the only love stimulants, although we might do better to develop a higher valuation of woman's personality, intellect, and health.

What can women be sure of in our culture? Acquisitiveness, competitiveness, emphasis on feminine sexual attractiveness, socio-political irresponsibility, and the cult of success (9, p. 321). On these values she must build her own, her husband's, and her daughter's social position, buttressing them with whatever attitudes, prejudices, and sentiments she can lay her hands on.

In summary, social pressures and technological advances are creating new problems for women; social expectations are misleading her; and the techniques for building new values and teaching them to her are inadequate.

2. *Economic limitations.* Women are, to say the least, less free than men in regard to their professional or business or civic careers. The economic limitations for women, following Folsom's analysis, are these: (a) she receives lower pay for the same work; (b) positions requiring greater skill and authority are closed to her in favor of men; (c) her geographic location and socio-economic status are dependent on her husband; and (d) housekeeping (her fundamental occupation) offers no regular pay and gives no prestige.

The fact that women are paid less for the same work than men, especially in the professions and white collar jobs, is too obvious to argue. Except for a few areas where equality prevails, professional women earn about a thousand dollars less annually than men in a parallel position. Some women feel that this gives them an advantage in the hiring market, without which they could not compete even as well as they do.

There is also some justification for the differential—not, as many would like to think, because woman has less financial responsibility and does not need the money (15, p. 41), but because she is a less permanent worker. She may leave her work to have a child, or her husband may move his household to another part of the country.

The more important economic limitation is the prejudice which the woman professional or business or civic worker finds barring her advancement to better paid positions with more authority and responsibility. Sometimes the limiting policy is stated quite openly and frankly. More often it is concealed under the guise of sentiment and chivalry.

How deeply this prejudice is imbedded in our thinking appears in Allport's explanation for the superiority of women in interpreting attitudes. He says a woman learns the skill because ". . . her success depends upon the attitudes of people toward her. It is important for her to know, for example, whether her male associates in business have an antagonistic, jocular, patronizing, or fairminded point of view regarding her presence in their profession" (1, p. 517). What man labors under this added handicap in his business or professional dealings?

The whole ideology of the "success story," and the emphasis given to the more glamorous careers by the smart women's magazines has a vicious effect on the morale of young women workers. "In our present culture she must have a source of prestige in the form of a career if she is to be well thought of. She must work, and the more her work is a career preceded by specialized education and yielding great monetary rewards, the greater will be her prestige" (5, p. 118).

This confusion in motivations, this unrealistic attitude is the more damaging because the career ideology has already declined with men. "No longer are boys brought up on the Alger and Henty books, which suggest that any boy can become President and that only the right attitude is necessary to insure a steady rise from office boy to general manager" (7, p. 617). Women must learn that vocational life is unpredictable and subject to many forces outside our personal control. Sociologists have given us more careful analyses of these factors in our culture, and neither women nor their counselors can afford to ignore them.

Another discouraging factor in the status of the professional woman is the defection among her own kind, the lack of solidarity within her own ranks. Every contented housewife, every pretty little secretary or schoolteacher who works a few years before marriage, even if they can be aroused to an awareness of the situation, are on the man's side of the argument. Women, especially young college women, need a longer perspective as well as a more objective analysis of their status in society and their personal and emotional needs. It has been suggested that the emancipation of women is really a part of the long emergence from feudal society, in which men were driven from the home at an earlier stage by the growth of capitalism but in which women have lagged behind (3, p. 15).

Women on the Campus

How can this complex societal background which we have sketched be related to the problems of women on the campus?

First, let us remember that on the college campus woman's environment is most nearly the equal of man's. She takes the same courses, and in the intellectual realm her successes are welcomed and encouraged by her teachers. She is a vital part of the social life, and conditions favorable to her participation in extracurricular activities are usually arranged for her. Her college situation is therefore peculiarly misleading to her, which means that her counselors must take special pains to devise and apply the necessary correction or prediction formulas so that her later disillusionment will be, nor a bitter one, but as good humored as it can possibly be made.

Both her formal academic training and her informal training through day-to-day campus life introduce the college woman to a pattern of living which will show a cruel discrepancy with actual life experience. The concentration of the upper middle class and especially the age structure on the campus are both abnormal. There is a parasitic existence in a sort of socio-political vacuum (9, p. 326). All the adolescent enthusiasms and irresponsibilities are reinforced in daily contact and are at the same time unrestrained by the social controls that result from closer contact with older ages, family life, business, and civic obligations. Added to this is the present confusion in the minds of both men and women because of the tempo and the radical nature of current economic, psychological, political, and social changes.

Vocational Problems

The *central* problem for the young college woman of today is the diffi-culty of choosing and preparing for the ambiguous life pattern described above, especially of fitting the role of homemaker into all the other roles she wants to play in her life. She is uncertain as to whether she will even have the opportunity to play the role of homemaker; whether her husband's economic status will be high or low; whether the family period in her life pattern will be a long one, keeping her closely at home, or a short one with plenty of leisure in which to experiment. Fortunately for her present peace of mind the later and perhaps more devastating conflicts do not immediately unfold themselves before her. She cannot yet imagine that the heavy costs in time, energy, and money of freeing her personality from the soporific of homemaking may be more than she can ever afford to pay, or that she may have to fight for the privilege of using her talents to build a better social and eco-nomic world.

The old problem of *career or marriage* has become, at least in the minds of the girls, the new problem of *career and marriage*. It is no longer an either-or dilemma; it is merely a question of assigning the proper emphasis to achieve the nicest balance between the two inter-ests. The marriage rates for college graduates no longer lag so much be-hind the rates for other women of comparable age and status, and col-lege girls now frankly admit, 99 percent of them, that they would prefer to marry if they can. At the same time they crave the independence that goes with earning power, and they dread the thought of inactivity after the exhilaration of campus life.

This does not make vocational and educational counseling easy. Freshman women and other women students will exhibit a strong re-sistance to preparation for any role except the professional or business career. This is partly because the role of earner is the only one a woman can be sure of, the only one she feels is within her control, and partly because her mother has convinced her that homemaking skills and knowledge can be "just picked up somehow." She will probably resist also the exclusively women's vocations in which she has the best chances for advancement and material success, because they have no prestige value, or because she knows, without Mr. Popenoe's warning, about the certain "occupational segregation" (18) that will lower her chances of finding her future husband through her business contacts.

The process of working through with a freshman girl the problems involved in choosing a vocation and preparing for any one of the various life patterns which she may try to arrange for herself involves continuous and specialized effort: not only her academic program but also her extracurricular activities and her group living can be organized to make invaluable contributions to this phase of her development.

Personal Problems

Fortunately the freshman will talk quite frankly and has a good deal of insight into her problem of career and life pattern. She is equally harassed—but no so able either to formulate her problem or to ask for help—in her daily routine of keeping herself socially afloat in the campus marriage market. The counselor who works with women will soon learn to shift the fulcrum and achieve a better balance between personal and vocational needs. For this reason, with women it is more difficult to divide the functions of educational and personal counseling between two sets of counselors in two different departments. The best means of entry into the uncertain area of personal problems is often through the well-traveled paths of vocational problems.

Personal counseling becomes largely sex and social behavior counseling, because "for most persons, the dominant motive of college attendance is the desire to rise to a higher social class. Behind this we see the ideology of American life, the projection of parents' ambitions upon children" (20, p. 727). The college freshman never heard of Mr. Popenoe's mating gradient, "the widespread (and praiseworthy) tendency of women to marry above their own level and of men to want to marry below," but she has, nevertheless, exactly the same idea in mind. "In the absence of help from the curriculum, she has had to get her education on marriage from the other great educational agencies of the present day" (18, p. 739): the movies, the women's magazines, the radio, the advertisements. She has strange ideas and strong feelings, very little organization, and some surprising resistances.

In this area the counselor, in order to be successful, needs to understand the social milieu of the campus, the hierarchy of the various

groups and organizations, and the social complex of "rating and dating." He should know the functions and techniques of courtship as described by the sociologists (20), as well as from the more naive points of
view of the students and their parents. How much of college dating is a
"sort of dalliance relationship, largely dominated by the quest of a
thrill, and regarded as an amusement and a release of organic tensions"?
Under what conditions and for how long will a date bureau flourish and
who will reap the advantages and suffer the disadvantages? When shall
he use Moreno's technique (16) for analyzing a group of persons in
terms of attractions and repulsions among individuals?

Women students will spend a substantial portion of their time discussing among themselves these personal and romantic problems. The
counselor who can introduce perspective and objectivity into these discussions needs a strategic position from which to work as well as special
knowledge and perfected techniques. College freshmen can learn much
from the discussion of such questions as these: How many persons of the
opposite sex hve you known well enough to pass judgment on whether
they would be a fit marriage partner? How does the progress of your
campus love affair differ from the typical charts? How many ways can
you use to enhance your attractiveness for a man other than the use of
your body? They will be glad to know about the research studies which
show that college men and women have an average of approximately
2.2 campus love affairs, of which about 70 percent are broken off (10,
11). They will give openminded attention to the advice: "Young
women should take into account the age differential in marriage and
cultivate the acquaintance of men a few years older than themselves"
(18).

A Special Curriculum for Women?

There are many who feel that a special curriculum or a core curriculum for women, or the establishment of a women's college within each
university, is the next important step in the solving of women's problems. But these earnest well-wishers fail to pay enough attention to two
major factors: (1) the wide range in abilities, interests, and cultural
backgrounds of women students, which makes any one curriculum or
even a core curriculum as ridiculous as one curriculum would be for

men; and (2) the tremendous and admirable energy and dynamic force in the modern woman, which, in combination with technological advances, gives her the leisure and the verve to play two roles—which, in fact, probably makes it necessary for her to play two, or any additional number of roles it pleases her to undertake (13).

The determining factors in a curriculum for women are: (1) The educational requirements of the field of study itself, which are given most weight in the academic world and without which the field cannot be mastered. (2) The requirements of society, for higher education is inevitably concerned with the critical problems of the day and all hands, including women's, are needed for the job of solving them. The special skills and interests and point of view of women are essential and should be used to best advantage equally with men's. (3) The special needs which grow out of the life patterns of women, whether their home life and family relationships are absorbing and continuous or of incidental interest, or intensive but concentrated in a certain period of years.

The range of women's interests is as large as men's, although there is no overlapping throughout the whole of these ranges. Therefore, women's needs are best met through a broad framework, not merely the elective system, but a whole range of college and university programs, liberal, general, pre-professional, and applied arts and sciences. The emphasis in any one institution should be keyed to the demands of its student body and the proportions of various kinds of students of all ages, sexes, and classes which are to be found in it. Women should then have the best possible advice in choosing their courses, but so also should men. Some women should be advised to take courses in homemaking, and some men should be urged to take courses in family relationships. Volunteer community service should be an extracurricular activity for both men and women.

The inclusion of nutrition, applied economics, and child care as a core curriculum for women has been advocated for practical reasons: the inadequate preparation for meeting life's daily problems without these emphases; on a scientific basis, namely, women's different biological structure and function; and more recently on a psychoanalytic claim that woman finds satisfaction only in filling her role as wife and mother and that conflict follows any attempt to change it into a career or intellectual life. These arguments distort the problem by making it seem the woman's only; they ignore the possibility that the husbands (that is society, "the man's world") may be equally at fault. Besides, there is no evidence that any certain courses or curriculums would be effective in correcting this or any other of our educational faults.

Extracurricular Activities

Sex differences in interests and values are apparent in the extracurricular activities which women plan for themselves and in their attitudes toward these activities. They are more self-conscious about them and plan them with much more thoughtfulness and in a more democratic spirit. Fewer women see these activities as a means to climbing the campus success ladder which leads to future employment advantages. More of them seek the opportunity for both personal development and campus service. This situation does not obtain because of any innate highmindedness of women; again it is the obvious result of circumstances and social pressures.

Both historically and currently the "double standard" has made it necessary to regulate campus life for women more than for men. Because of society's insistence on getting the girls into their residences early at night and on regulating the hours when their halls and their parties should be open to men, supervision becomes a vital part of women's campus life. Supervisors, whether they are called chaperones or housemothers or wardens or deans or counselors or personnel workers, have always been aware that these social regulations (in contrast to the business or academic regulations) can be effective only with full student participation in making and supporting them. Therefore, the fundamental assignment of any counselor who works with women is the building of morale high enough to contain this particular problem.

High morale and effective student governments are especially characteristic of the women's colleges. Long traditions of responsibility and success and high selection of student bodies have furnished the undergirding; and there is a continuous process of buttressing, including careful curriculum adjustments, more attention to the teaching process, a more elaborate religious program, and the use of counselors experienced in women's problems. The honor system in examinations and even in social regulations is a commonplace in women's colleges, and is practically 100 percent successful, a phenomenon which men find it difficult to believe, because it is almost if not quite impossible to achieve on the coeducational campus.

Other Personnel Functions

In similar fashion it is obvious that any single function of campus personnel services—housing and group living, discipline, finances, government, leadership, and social programs—is different in certain aspects for men and women. Woman has much more to lose than man under disciplinary action, because social position and prestige are so much more important in her life. The bad manners or behavior deviations of a man will be dwarfed and overshadowed by his business successes, but a woman's little inadequacies are sometimes the only things by which she can be remembered.

Woman's social prestige often suffers when she engages in certain types of part-time campus employment. She cannot so easily rationalize her work as employment experience. She is also a poorer risk for loans because of her lower salaries, shorter working period, and restricted opportunity for work. Because she must at all costs maintain her respectability, her standard of living must be higher, which means higher living costs.

Conformity and acceptability in dress and grooming have become almost a fetish on the college campus and are more difficult to achieve for women than for men. No single item in the maintaining of appearance is as easy for women as for men. Choosing, designing, fitting, cleaning, and repairing of clothing and caring for and camouflaging the skin, figure, and hair make tremendous inroads on the time and energy of women students.

Home ties are stronger for women students, and parental attitudes and prejudices are harder to shake off (17). Parents are at the same time more in evidence, and more deeply embarrassing when off-standard in manners or behavior.

More women than men read the current popular magazines with their misleading ideologies and their dishonest advertisements. More women than men attend the movies and listen to the radio to absorb their romantic infantilism. Women will, therefore, offer more resistance to the objective and realistic point of view so necessary to the solution of the current problems of the social order.

The leadership which women must develop is different from the leadership qualities appropriate for men. To be sure, they must learn the techniques of the men in order to be able to deal with them, but in so far as a woman's own leadership may be exercised among other women, it must be based on different personal qualities and different interests to meet the different social forces. A woman's leadership, or perhaps we should call it a certain kind of "followship," for dealing with men must also be of a special kind. She can never assume that men will have acquired her point of view, and she must learn to teach it to them with patience and good humor while she indulges them by pretending to learn their patterns of ideas and behavior, which she already knows. "We will ask these men to meet with us," offered one college adviser in a moment of crisis, "and ask them what they think about the situation, which will probably be the best way for us to tell them what we think."

The naiveté of women in dealing with the techniques of "leadership" exercised by men is, of course, very patent both on the campus and in the economic and political arenas. Here especially it would be important for the college woman to acquaint herself with the history of women's groups and their accomplishments so that the gains already made can be evaluated and the losses appreciated.

Another function in which the personnel division sometimes plays a part is the interpreting of the college to its constituency. More than this, the institution sometimes feels an obligation to introduce a better perspective, or to disseminate information necessary and important for a progressive social or economic program. Without knowledge of and insight into women's problems, which under present conditions men have no adequate means of acquiring, mistakes will be made and opportunities for leadership in women's work will be missed when women are not given a voice in administrative councils. Few men understand the nature and hierarchy of women's clubs and professional organizations or can differentiate among those which are progressive and realistic and those which are anachronistic and reactionary. In this respect the leadership shown by some of the women's colleges is in sharp contrast to the failures of the coeducational schools in serving, not the interests, but the best interests of women.

Conclusion

According to the popular press the frustrations of women seem to be, if not increasing, at least claiming more attention in recent decades. At least we have no books entitled *Modern Man, The Lost Sex* (12), *Men After Forty* (4), or *Men After College* (8). Up to this time the correctives are being applied in terms of a more elaborate understanding of woman's emotional and physiological nature in addition to manipulations of her education. It might seem more feasible to attempt manipulation of the social forces in her situation, since they are now in a fair way to being understood. If women have more frustrations then men, it might be logical to explain them in terms of the factors in which women are most different from men, namely, in their social expectancies and their life patterns.

Because of these still greatly different life patterns, women students must be helped toward greater insight into the psychological and social forces which lie behind them. An important factor in building these insights is the knowledge of the history of women and the perspective gained by differentiating her nature and her problems from those of men and projecting them against the background of society as a whole. Are men interested in this field, the history and status of women? Will men develop it and introduce its study into the curriculums of both men and women? Is not the denial of its importance by men one of the techniques by which they cheat women of the opportunity to solve their problems and eliminate their frustrations? Does not the failure to include women as active and competent (that is, equal) participants in planning and administering the curriculum and personnel work insulate the men from their most useful source of information in this area?

The student personnel point of view in education declares that it is the task of the colleges to assist the student in developing to the limits of his potentialities and in making his contribution to the betterment of society. It puts emphasis, in brief, upon the development of the student as a person rather than on his intellectual training alone. It seeks to train the student *as a whole*. Or is it merely the man as a whole? Or is it perhaps the student, man or woman, as a psychological but not a social whole?

References

1. Allport, G. *Personality: A Psychological Interpretation*. New York: Holt, 1937.
2. Anastasi, Anne. *Differential Psychology*. New York: Macmillan, 1937.
3. Bruton, Margaret P. "Present-Day Thinking on the Woman Question," *Annals of the American Academy of Political and Social Science*, 251:10–16 (May 1947).
4. Elliot, Grace. *Women After Forty*. New York: Holt, 1940.
5. Farnham, M. F. "Battles Won and Lost," *Annals of the American Academy of Political and Social Science*, 251:113–19 (May 1947).
6. Folsom, Joseph K. "Changing Values in Sex and Family Relations," *American Sociological Review*, 2:717–26 (October 1937).
7. Folsom, Joseph K. *The Family and Democratic Society*. New York: John Wiley and Sons, 1943.
8. Foster, R. G., and P. P. Wilson. *Women After College*. New York: Columbia University Press, 1942.
9. Hartshorne, Edward Y. "Undergraduate Society and the College Culture," *American Sociological Review*, 8:321–32 (June 1943).
10. Kirkpatrick, Clifford, and Theodore Caplow. "Courtship in a Group of Minnesota Students," *American Journal of Sociology*, 51:114–25 (September 1945).
11. Kirkpatrick, Clifford, and Theodore Caplow. "Emotional Trends in the Courtship Experience of College Students," *American Sociological Review*, 10:619–26 (October 1945).
12. Lundberg, F., and M. F. Farnham. *Modern Woman: The Lost Sex*. New York: Harper, 1947.
13. McBride, K. E. "What Is Women's Education?" *Annals of the American Academy of Political and Social Science*, 251:143–52 (May 1947).
14. Metropolitan Life Insurance Company. *Statistical Bulletin*, Vol. 25, No. 8, August 1944, and Vol. 27, No. 7, July 1946.
15. Miller, Frieda S. "Women in the Labor Force," *Annals of the American Academy of Political and Social Science*, 251:35–43 (May 1947).
16. Moreno, J. L. *Who Shall Survive?* New York: Nervous and Mental Disease Publishing Co., 1934.
17. Newcomb, T. "Recent Changes in Attitudes toward Sex and Marriage," *American Sociological Review*, 2:659–67 (October 1937).
18. Popenoe, Paul. "Mate Selection," *American Sociological Review*, 2:735–43 (October 1937).
19. Terman, L. M., and Catherine C. Miles. *Sex and Personality*. New York: McGraw-Hill, 1936.
20. Waller, Willard. "The Rating and Dating Complex," *American Sociological Review*, 2:727–34 (October 1937).

The Student Personnel Point of View

E. G. Williamson, Chairman
Willard W. Blaesser
Helen D. Bragdon
William S. Carlson
W. H. Cowley
D. D. Feder

Helen G. Fisk
Forrest H. Kirkpatrick
Esther Lloyd-Jones
T. R. McConnell
Thornton W. Merriam
Donald J. Shank

I. Philosophy and Objectives

The central purpose of higher education is the preservation, transmittal, and enrichment of culture by means of instruction, scholarly work, and scientific research. During the past few decades experience has pointed up the desirability of broadening this purpose to embrace additional emphasis and objectives. Among these new goals, three stand out:

1. Education for a fuller realization of democracy in every phase of living;
2. Education directly and explicitly for international understanding and cooperation;
3. Education for the application of creative imagination and trained intelligence to the solution of social problems and to the administration of publications.[1]

Although these added goals aim essentially at societal growth, they affect positively the education and development of each individual student. The development of students as whole persons interacting in social situations is the central concern of student personnel work and of

1. Adapted from *Higher Education for American Democracy: The Report of the President's Commission on Higher Education, Establishing the Goals* (Washington: Government Printing Office, 19475 New York: Harper & Bros., 1948).

other agencies of education. This emphasis in contemporary education is the essential part of the student personnel point of view.

The student personnel point of view encompasses the student as a whole. The concept of education is broadened to include attention to the student's well rounded development—physically, socially, emotionally and spiritually, as well as intellectually. The student is thought of as a responsible participant in his own development and not as a passive recipient of an imprinted economic, political, or religious doctrine, or vocational skill. As a responsible participant in the societal processes of our American democracy, his full and balanced maturity is viewed as a major end goal of education as well, a necessary means to the fullest development of his fellow-citizens. From the personnel point of view any lesser goal falls short of the desired objective of democratic educational processes, and is a real drain and strain upon the self-realization of other developing individuals in our society.

The realization of this objective—the full maturing of each student—cannot be attained without interest in and integrated efforts toward the development of each and every facet of his personality and potentialities. His deepening understanding of his world is not sacrificed to his emotional maturing. His physical well-being does not become a limited end in itself. His maturing sense of values, social and spiritual, is not sacrificed to his understanding of the world of man and nature. His need for developing a sound philosophy of life to serve as the norm for his actions now and in adult life is not neglected in the college's emphasis on his need for intellectual and professional competence. Rather are all known aspects of the personality of each student viewed by the educator and personnel worker as an integrated whole— as a human personality living, working, and growing in a democratic society of other human personalities.

A long and honorable history stands behind this point of view. From the Middle Ages until the beginning of the nineteenth century, European higher education and its American offshoots gave as much attention to the social, moral, and religious development of students as to their intellectual growth. But the rise of the modern research centered German university early in the nineteenth century led to the abandonment of this personal concern for students and centered on an intellectualistic concern. Influenced by German models, American educators steered American higher education toward intellectualism.

Prosecution of scientific research and the stimulation of the intellectual development of students became the dominant emphases in American higher education. The earlier concern of Colonial educators for
the spiritual, social, and personal development of students was shunted
aside for more than a half century in most universities and in some colleges. At the turn of the present century certain great social forces matured and converged to shift attention back to the student's broad development in all aspects of his personality.

The student personnel movement developed during the early twentieth century in part as a protest against German-born intellectualism
and also as the result of the findings of the psychology of individual differences during the second decade of the present century. Its evolution
was stimulated by the huge growth of American colleges and universities following the First World War. With hordes invading institutions
of higher education, colleges sought means to maintain some personal
and individual relationship with students.

Present-Day Objectives

The student personnel movement constitutes one of the most important efforts of American educators to treat the college and university
students as individuals, rather than as entries in an impersonal roster.
The movement, at the same time, expresses awareness of the significance of student group life in its manifold expressions from student residence to student mores, from problems of admission to problems of job
placement. It has developed as the division of college and university
administration concerned with students individually and students as
groups. In a real sense this part of modern higher education is an individualized application of the research and clinical findings of modern
psychology, sociology, cultural anthropology, and education to the task
of aiding students to develop fully in the college environment.

The specific aspects of the student personnel program stemming from
the above point of view will be discussed in a later section. In addition,
however, certain fundamental issues in education are affected by the
application of the personnel point of view.

The optimum development of the individual necessitates the recognition by teachers and administrators, as well as by professional personnel

workers, of individual differences in backgrounds, abilities, interests, and goals. In the light of such individual variations each institution should define its educational purposes and then select its students in terms of these purposes. This concept of development demands flexibility in methods of teaching and in the shaping of content to fit the individual differences found in students. It also requires integration of various aspects of the curriculum.

The individual's full and balanced development involves the acquisition of the pattern of knowledge, skills, and attitudes consistent with his abilities, aptitudes, and interests. The range of acquisition is a broad one. Through his college experiences he should acquire an appreciation of cultural values, the ability to adapt to changing social conditions, motivation to seek and to create desirable social changes, emotional control to direct his activities, moral and ethical values for himself and for his community, standards and habits of personal physical well-being, and the ability to choose a vocation which makes maximum use of his talents and enables him to make appropriate contributions to his society.

But such broad-gauge development of the individual should in no sense be considered as a sufficient and complete goal in itself. It is axiomatic today that no man lives in a social vacuum. Rather individual development is conditioned by the kind of society in which a person lives, and by the quality of interpersonal and group relationships which operate around him. He is constantly affecting society; and society is constantly shaping him. These relationships constitute the cultural patterns with which higher education must be concerned in its efforts to stimulate and guide the development of each of its students.

The cultural patterns of America have been, and will continue to be, deeply affected by the emergence of the United States as a world power. With the nation's new status in world affairs, the preservation of basic freedoms and responsibilities at home becomes increasingly important. Our way of life depends upon a renewed faith in, and extensive use of, democratic methods, upon the development of more citizens able to assume responsbilities in matters of social concern, and upon the active participation of millions of men and women in the enterprise of social improvement.

Such a social philosophy as that outlined above thrust upon the college an urgent responsibility for providing experiences which develop in its students a firm and enlightened belief in democracy, a matured understanding of its problems and methods, and a deep sense of responsibility for individual and collective action to achieve its goals. Both classroom and out-of-class activities of the college should be related to these ends, and students' organizations should be incorporated in the institution's total educational program. In both the curricular and the cocurricular program of the college the dynamic forces of society should be skillfully organized for the use of their learning values in furthering the development of students.

As educators, our attention should be focused upon the social forces of the institution itself, which also provide learning experiences for the student. For example, the relationships among the various groups on the campus affect such social development. If faculty and students and faculty and administration work closely together in achieving common objectives, curricular and cocurricular, the learning of socially desirable processes is thereby enhanced.

The college or university which accepts these broad responsibilities for aiding in the optimum development of the individual in his relations to society will need to evaluate carefully and periodically its curricular offerings, its method of instruction, and all other resources for assisting the individual to reach his personal goals. Among its important resources, it also will need to provide and strengthen the type of services, as outlined in the next section, encompassed within the field of student personnel work.

II. Student Needs and Personnel Services

During their college years, students have opportunities for intensive classroom learning supplemented by many of the major elements of community living. Students live, work, make friends, have fun, make financial ends meet—all within the community of scholars. Since colleges seek to assist students to achieve optimum development of powers and usefulness, a comprehensive and explicit plan and program embracing many personnel services are necessary for this undertaking. The essential parts of such a plan and program are outlined in the following sections.

The student personnel point of view holds that the major responsibility for a student's growth in personal and social wisdom rests with the student himself. Necessarily, however, his development is conditioned by many factors. It is influenced by the background, the abilities, attitudes, and expectancies that he brings with him to college, by his college classroom experiences, and by his reactions to these experiences. A student's growth in personal and social wisdom will also be conditioned by the extent to which the following conditions are attained:

The student achieves orientation to his college environment. Individuals are freer to learn, are under less strain, suffer less confusion, and have more consistent and favorable self-concepts if they feel at home and oriented in relation to their environment. The personnel worker attempts to help students feel at home in their college environment through:

1. Interpreting institutional objectives and opportunities to prospective students, to their parents, and to high school faculties;
2. Selecting students who seem, after study, to be able to achieve in relation to the college offerings and requirements;
3. Orienting students to the many phases of their college lives through a carefully designed program that involves such methods and experiences as personnel records, tests, group instruction, counseling, and group life.

The student succeeds in his studies. The college or university has a primary responsibility in selecting for admission students who have the basic qualities of intelligence and aptitudes necessary for success in a given institution. However, many otherwise able students fail, or do not achieve up to maximum capacity, because they lack proficiency or personal motivation for the tasks set by the college, because of deficiency in reading or study skills, because they do not budget their time properly, have emotional conflicts resulting from family or other pressures, have generally immature attitudes, are not wisely counselled in relation to curricular choices, or because of a number of other factors. In order that each student may develop effective work habits and thereby achieve at his optimum potential, the college or university should provide services through which the student may acquire the skills and techniques for efficient utilization of his ability. In addition to the contribution of counseling in removing blockages from his path toward good achievement, the student may also need remedial reading and speech services, training in effective study habits, remediation of physical conditions, counseling concerning his personal motivations, and similar related services.

He finds satisfactory living facilities. Comfortable and congenial living arrangements contribute to the peace of mind and efficiency of the student. If effectively organized and supervised, the facilities that provide for food and shelter can also contribute to his social development and to his adjustments to group opportunities and restraints.

The student achieves a sense of belonging to the college. To a large extent the social adjustment of an individual consists of finding a role in relation to others which will make him feel valued, will contribute to his feeling of self-worth, and will contribute to a feeling of kinship with an increasing number of persons. The student personnel program will help him achieve these goals through:

1. Stimulating the development of many small groups;
2. Fostering the development of a program of student-initiated activities;
3. Encouraging the development of a diversified social program;
4. Developing opportunities for participation in college-community cooperative activities;
5. Fostering teacher-student intellectual and social relationships outside of the classroom.

The student learns balanced use of his physical capacities. It is not enough to conceive of a health service as an agency only for the treatment of illness in order to keep the student operating in the classroom at regular maximum efficiency. To be broadly effective, the health program should also aggressively promote a program of health education designed to equip each student with self-understanding and self-acceptance at his optimum personal level of physical competence. The adjustment of the individual to his physical potentialities as well as to his irremediable limitations is a basic element in his full development of personality.

The student progressively understands himself. This is the process of self-discovery and rediscovery which, progressively over a period of time, must unfold for the student in terms of his individual readiness for it. Through a rich program of experiences and skilful counseling, the student may acquire an understanding of himself, his abilities, interests, motivations, and limitations. With such understanding the student becomes ready to make long-range life plans; he acquires the understandings and skills necessary to cope with life problems; he learns to face and solve his own personal problems; he grows personally and, in the process, make constructive social contribution. To aid in this development, the college or university provides:

1. Adequate services for testing and appraisal;
2. Skilled counselors trained in the art of stimulating self-understanding without directing decisions;
3. Useful records available for study so that the student may inform himself of his present status and be apprised of whatever growth and development he has thus far achieved;
4. Other services which will help the student acquire such specialized knowledge as the individual should have concerning himself in order to make reasoned and reasonable choices and decisions.

The student understands and uses his emotions. As mainsprings of action, emotions either may lead to disorganized and random behavior or to concerted, directed, worth-while accomplishment. Directed emotions may enrich and strengthen action which is otherwise sterile and terminal. A human being is a creature of emotions as well as intellect. Effective personal counseling will help the student to understand and use his emotional powers for maximum, directed action. Without such understanding and self-direction the student may soon find himself not only ineffective, but also socially inept and unacceptable. The counseling service, psychiatric services, and organized group activities are among the parts of the student personnel services which may assist the student in this area of achievement.

The student develops lively and significant interests. Many aspects of personality directly related to attractiveness, alertness, and forcefulness are conditioned by the number and depth of interests an individual is able to cultivate. The effective college will recognize this by:

1. Helping the student to discover his basic interests; and,
2. Fostering a program of recreational and discussional activities that is diversified.

The student achieves understanding and control of his financial resources. Learning how to live within his income, how to increase that income, how to find financial aids that are available are part of an understanding of the student's economic life. Such an understanding of money-values must be achieved in balanced relationships to physical energy, curricular, and social demands.

Counseling students on financial matters and administering financial aids in such a way as to help the most worthy and most needy are important parts of the student personnel program.

The student progresses toward appropriate vocational goals. Some students enroll in college with a definite plan of preparation for a career. Others will modify their plans as they acquire new interests or gain clearer understanding of their own capacities and of requirements for certain occupations in relation to the needs of society. But many men and women who come to college do so without any plans or understanding of themselves in relation to the world of work. The college has a responsibility to see that these students have access to accurate, usable information about opportunities, requirements, and training for various occupations appropriate to their possible levels of vocational preparation. Vocational counseling given on a basis on insight, information, and vision can help students to relate their future work to their life goals. When conducted with social imagination, such counseling can help to develop these leaders who will pioneer in new professions and in the extension of needed services for the country's welfare.

The student develops individuality and responsibility. Progressive emancipation from the restrictions of childhood is a major challenge to every adolescent. Reveling in his new found freedoms, for which he may not yet be prepared by adequate self-discipline, the college student may find himself in conflict with accepted social patterns and standards. Other students, whose domination by their families may extend to the college campus, may voice their rebellion in actions offensive to their fellow-students or embarrassing to the college family to which they now belong. In such situations, preventive therapy may be accomplished by enlisting parental cooperation in counseling in such personal problems when they are discovered and diagnosed. When the need for social discipline does arise, the college should approach the problem as a special phase of counseling in the development of self-responsibility for behavior rather than in a spirit of punishment of misbehavior.

The student discovers ethical and spiritual meaning in life. For many students the introduction to scientific understandings and meanings in the classroom may necessitate a drastic reorientation of religious ideology at a new level of objectivity. The time-honored teachings of organized religion may lose their effectiveness both as explanatory and guiding principles. The resultant disturbance may have deep and far-reaching ramifications into personal as well as family, and even broader, social conflicts. In his new search for values which are worthy of personal allegiance in a time of social conflict, the student needs mature guidance. The religious counselor and the religious-activities program with a broad social reference may assist the student in developing an understanding of proper concepts of behavior, ethical standards, and spiritual values consistent with his broadened horizons resulting from newly acquired scientific and technical knowledge.

The student learns to live with others. The maintenance of individual integrity within a framework of cooperative living and working with others in a spirit of mutual service is the highest expression of democracy. By intelligent followership as well as by permissive leadership the student prepares himself for his social obligations beyond the college. By means of special-interest groups, student government, dormitory and house councils, and other guided group activities, the student personnel program can provide opportunities for developing in the student his capacities for both leadership and followership. The counseling service will also use such activities as may be appropriate for individual therapy and development as the needs may be revealed through suitable diagnostic procedures.

The student progresses toward satisfying and socially acceptable sexual adjustments. During the years when young people are in college, they are normally deeply, although perhaps covertly, concerned with finding congenial marriage partners. This concern may produce anxieties which eventuate in behavior that may be either acceptable or unacceptable to society, and satisfying or unsatisfying to the individuals. Since marriage adjustment is basic to family stability, and since the family is our most important social institution, colleges should help students to effect satisfying, socially acceptable, and ethically sound sexual adjustments by (1) encouraging the development of a rich and diversified social and recreational program, (2) providing counseling on relationship and marriage problems.

The student prepares for satisfying, constructive postcollege activity. For most students the activities of postcollege years will be a combination of the practice of a profession, progression in an occupation, marriage and family life, and service as a community and world citizen.

Personnel services of the college appropriate to these attainments may include job placement, information about jobs, internships, graduate training programs, or opportunities for volunteer service. Some colleges include also some periodic follow-up contacts to determine the success of their graduates.

Elements of a Student Personnel Program.

The achievement of the foregoing objectives requires the cooperative and integrated functioning of classroom and extraclass activities with the growth and development of the student as the focal point of all that is implied in the educational process. To be sure, not every student will need or make use of all the student personnel services just as, by the same token, not every student studies courses in every academic department. But the college should make optimum provision for the development of the individual and his place in society through its provisions for:

1. The process of admissions, not as a credit-counting service, but rather as a first step in the counseling procedure designed to interpret the institution to the student, his family, and his high school teachers in terms of its requirements for success, its services, and its ability to satisfy his educational and personal needs.
2. The keeping of personnel records and their use in the improved understanding of, and service to, the individual student as he has contact not only with the classroom, but also in all phases of his college or university life.
3. The service to the student of trained, sympathetic counselors to assist him in thinking through his education, vocational, and personal adjustment problems. Such a service should be so designed as to be in effect a cohesive agency drawing together all the institution's resources in the process of facilitating the student's efforts to achieve the objectives of higher education. This service will have access, either through direct association or as a supplementary service, to psychological testing and other special diagnostic services as may be necessary to achieve better and more objective appraisal and understanding of the individual.

Resources for adequate vocational information as may be needed by the student in the process of his orientation should be closely correlated with the counseling program. Special attention should be given to the educational importance of supplementing the efforts of counseling specialists by the use of carefully selected, specially trained faculty members serving as advisers and counselors.

4. Physical and mental health services whose orientation is not only the treatment of illness, but also, and even primarily, an educational program of preventive medicine and personal-hygiene counseling.

5. Remedial services in the areas of speech, reading, and study habits, recognizing that the presence of defects in these areas may seriously impede the functioning of many able students and also restrict the contributions which may be made by otherwise adequate personalities.

6. Supervision and integration of housing and food services to the end that they shall not only provide for the physical comforts of students, but also shall contribute positively to education in group living and social graces.

7. A program of activities designed to induct the student into his new life and environment as a member of the college or university family.

8. The encouragement and supervision of significant group activities arising from the natural interest of students.

9. A program of recreational activities designed to promote lifetime interests and skills appropriate to the individual student.

10. The treatment of discipline as an educational function designed to modify personal behavior patterns and to substitute socially acceptable attitudes for those which have precipitated unacceptable behavior.

11. Financial aid to worthy students, not as a dole, but as an educational experience in personal budgeting and responsibility.

12. Opportunities for self-help through part-time and summer employment, geared as nearly as possible to the defined vocational objectives of the student.

13. Assistance to the student in finding appropriate employment

after leaving college and subsequently assisting alumni in further professional development.

14. The proper induction, orientation, and counseling of students from abroad.

15. The enrichment of college and postcollege life through a well-integrated program of religious activities, including interfaith programs and individual religious counseling.

16. Counseling for married students and for those contemplating marriage to prepare them for broadening family and social responsibilities.

17. A continuing program of evaluation of student personnel services and of the educational program to insure the achievement by students of the objectives for which this program is designed.

III. The Administration of Student Personnel Work

The administrative pattern of student personnel work in any one college or university will necessarily be adapted to the local resources and personnel. Although no definitive and evaluative studies of different types of administrative organization are available, yet in the last decade of student personnel work, the following generalizations have evolved.

Interrelation of Campus Resources

Everyone on a campus, from the students to the president, participates in some phase of the student personnel program. But certain personnel functions are usually the direct responsibility of designated staff members. Interested teachers devote time to counseling and the guidance of student organizations. Dormitory directors organize recreational and hobby activities. Such specialists as counselors, medical officers, psychiatrists, and psychometrists assist students in various ways. Many other examples of the range and types of personnel workers will be identified by the interested observer.

The nature of student personnel work is such that certain aspects of most activities may involve the interrelationship of a number of individuals in varying ways. For example, the operation of an effective orientation program for new students draws on many different persons. The teacher-counselor, the admissions officer, the doctor, other students, the administrative heads of the institution, the housing officer, recreational leaders, and others must contribute to an effective orientation program. Such interrelation of resources makes coordination necessary.

Administrative Structure

Experience indicates that specialized functions performed by trained personnel staff members should be organized with the customary definiteness found in instructional departments and colleges. For example, functions related to counseling need to be organized in a department, bureau, or center manned by the staff performing such functions. In similar manner, the functions of admissions, supervision of extracurricular activities, and many others of those discussed in the previous section need to be assigned to designated persons and departments.

This is not to say, however, that each personnel function needs to be organized in a separate bureau or assigned to a different individual or that each bureau or individual has a monopolistic control over its special functions. In smaller institutions, where the volume of work and the number of available staff members are limited, the form of organization can be simpler. But the principle of definiteness of assigned responsibility for each personnel function should be clearly established, even though only one member of a staff may be available to perform the function. In larger institutions, the volume of work permits, and sometimes compels, more formal organization and greater degrees of specialization.

As volume of services and size of staff increase, the necessity for centralization of administrative responsibility of an over-all nature becomes more readily apparent. The experience of the past decade indicates the desirability of assigning the responsibility for personnel work to an administrator. This generalization follows the pattern clearly established historically of designating instructional responsibility in the dean of a faculty or in the president in a small institution. When volume of work and other factors warrant it, a personnel administrator should be free from responsibility for any one personnel function or service in order that he may be able to deal effectively with over-all program development and coordination on a college-wide basis. As in the case of the instructional program of a college, the major personnel administrator, working with and through a staff council of personnel workers, should be held responsible for such administrative functions as budget-making and distribution; recruitment of staff; appointment and induction of staff members; stimulation of professional growth of personnel staff members; planning the continuous development of cooperation and coordination among the personnel specialists and between personnel work and the instructional program of the institution; and evaluation of the effectiveness of the total program.

The advocacy of a single administrative head for personnel work does not imply the assignment to such a person of complete and arbitrary authority. Instructional administrators have developed modifications of this centralization of authority in the form of program and policy committees composed of deans and faculty members and students. Indeed, the president of a college leans heavily upon his council of deans for aid in administration. In turn, each dean shares his administrative responsibilities with an executive committee of his faculty. In similar manner personnel administrators must enlist the help of specialists and of members of the instructional staff in determining policies and in planning personnel programs. Policy committees and coordinating councils should assist in administration and in continuous development of more effective services to education.

Decentralization of functions, as opposed to centralization in one person or one department, actually may increase the direct effectiveness of these services to students, provided that coordination produces the exchange of information and leads to the avoidance of conflict of services. Each institution must develop its own coordinating mechanisms for bringing together these decentralized services into a balanced, institution-wide program. Coordinating councils, informal meetings, exchange of memorandums, the maintenance of friendly working relationships—these and many other administrative devices need to be developed and maintained at a high level of effectiveness.

Process in Program Administration

Preoccupation with problems of administrative structure should not lead to neglect of process. Personnel literature to date is full of discussions of structure, of line and staff relationships, the points at which various responsibilities should rest, assignments of responsibility to various points of the structure, the ways in which parts should fit together, how they may be expected to work in relation to each other, and related topics.

Equal attention should be given to process. In a simple line and staff structure, for example, communication involves sharing information through organizational lines—down from the top in a relay pattern and sometimes up from the bottom along the established lines. Personnel administrators recognize that even two-way communication, however efficiently carried out, is not adequate for personnel work, and further experience is needed with respect to alternative forms of communication and administrative relationships. For example, personnel workers of all types need to meet regularly for discussions of common problems and for planning of interrelated programs of services. Experience indicates that not only information, but also feelings, always important in cooperative undertakings and other types of human relations, can best be transmitted in such face-to-face situations, and in well-planned and executed staff discussions of common problems and cooperative enterprises. Similarly, group planning of programs and discussions of issues and problems may produce better results than are obtained through the efforts of any single staff member. Furthermore, although each group will almost always create a leader role and ask someone to take this role, full participation of all members is best achieved when the role is passed from person to person within the group in terms of the differing competencies and experiences of the members in relation to the varying needs of the total program.

Participation in Institutional Administration

Personnel workers at all levels of specialization and administrative responsibility should be given appropriate opportunity and responsibility for participating in planning and policy-making for all phases of the institution's instructional and public-relations programs.

Students' Participation in Administration

Students can make significant contributions to the development and maintenance of effective personnel programs through contributing evaluations of the quality of the services, new ideas for changes in the services, and fresh impetus to staff members who may become immersed in techniques and the technicalities of the professional side of personnel work.

In addition to the use of advisory student councils and committees for reviewing programs and policies, personnel administrators and specialists should avail themselves frequently of opportunities for informal consultation with many individual students.

A Balanced Staff

Personnel specialists as well as personnel administrators should be chosen for their personal and professional competence to discharge their responsibilities. Personnel specialists and administrators, both men and women, should be available in all of the personnel departments. That is, competent men counselors should be available for those students who prefer to consult a man. In like manner, competent women counselors should be available for those men and women who prefer to consult a woman about scholastic or personal adjustments. Both men and women administrators should be members of top policy-making councils.

Special attention needs to be given to the maintenance of balance in another respect, namely, narrow specialization in one type of technique, adjustment problem, or school of thought. Each personnel staff should be maintained in a balanced manner with respect to desirably varied professional points of view and professional backgrounds of specialists.

Criteria for Evaluating Program

The principal responsibility of all personnel workers lies in the area of progressive program development. Essentially this means that each worker must devote a large part of his time to the formulation of new plans and to the continuous evaluation and improvement of current programs. The test of effectiveness of any personnel service lies in the differences it makes in the development of individual students, and every worker must develop his own workaday yardsticks for evaluation. The following suggest themselves as possible criteria for a continuing day-by-day appraisal of the program. No single criterion, alone and independent of others, would probably have much validity, but, taken together, they may provide an effective working relationship among staff members with respect to their program responsibilities.

These criteria are:

1. Students' expression of satisfaction and dissatisfaction with services received. These expressions may be informally collected or may be gathered systematically. Obviously such expressions need to be critically evaluated in terms of the total situation.

2. Expression of satisfaction and dissatisfaction with the program by members of the teaching staff. Again, such expressions need to be evaluated.

3. The extent of students' uses of the personnel services. Again, this criterion must be applied with full cognizance of the limitations of financial resources and other institutional factors balanced against the needs of the personnel departments.

4. The continuance of improvement in the professional training and professional status of members of the personnel staff through additional formal training, experiences, committee assignments, and other local, regional, and national recognition.

5. The quality of the interpersonal relationships and cooperation between personnel workers and members of the instructional and noninstructional staffs, and among personnel specialists themselves.

Institutional Mores and Policies

The effectiveness of a student personnel program is determined not solely by either its technical quality or its administrative and financial structure, but even more by its institutional setting. In an institution where conditions are favorable to the maintenance of friendly, informal working relationships between teachers and students, and where the institutional leaders explicitly support such relationships, effective counseling may be developed far more readily and effectively than would be the case in institutions burdened with an anti-faculty attitude established among student leaders.

Personnel workers of all types, particularly those involved in group-work functions, need to give continuous attention to the development of positive relationships in their work with student leaders. But, essentially, the institutional leader, the president, must set the standard of such mores. He can accomplish this by making clear his own basic attitudes toward students, teachers, and personnel workers, and the interrelated contributions of each group to the total institutional program of assistance to each student in his efforts to achieve full and broad development.

The Future of Student Personnel Work in Higher Education

W. W. Blaesser

Our title, "The Future of Student Personnel Work in Higher Education," may sound rather ambitious for a symposium entitled "Counseling, Guidance and Placement." Possibly the theme of this conference, "Improving the Effectiveness of Higher Education," prompted it. We prefer to use the term "student personnel work" because it encompasses more accurately those educational services which need greater emphasis today. We shall discuss the meaning of student personnel work shortly, but let us first briefly outline the full paper. First, we wish to discuss the student personnel point of view, the meaning of student personnel work, and the need for a much broader application of this point of view and meaning to educational practices today. Secondly, we shall review what we consider to be the essential aspects of a student personnel program, as well as the major assumptions underlying the total program. We shall treat very briefly the history of student personnel work, its status today, and lastly we shall comment upon those aspects of the program which we consider most in need of emphasis in the future.

The philosophy underlying student personnel work was clearly stated by the American Council on Education in 1937 as follows:

One of the basic purposes of higher education is the preservation, transmission, and enrichment of the important elements of culture—the product of scholarship, research, creative imagination, and human experience. It is the task of colleges and universities so to vitalize this and other educational purposes as to assist the student in developing to the limits of his potentialities and in making his contribution to the betterment of society.

Author's Note: E. H. Hopkins, State College of Washington, was co-author of this paper.

141

This philosophy imposes upon education institutions the obligation to con-sider the student as a whole—his intellectual capacity and achievement, his emotional makeup, his physical condition, his social relationships, his voca-tional aptitudes and skills, his aesthetic appreciations, his moral and religious values, his economic resources. It puts emphasis, in brief, upon the develop-ment of the student as a person rather than upon his intellectual training alone.[1]

This philosophy has had a profound influence upon recent trends in higher education. We choose to use it as a point of departure, a point of view in defining more specifically what we have in mind when we refer to student personnel work.

Obviously, any institution of higher education must offer a sound and adequate program for the intellectual development of its students or its very existence is not justified. But that is not enough. We suggest a broad definition. In our opinion, student personnel work consists of all those processes and functions undertaken by an educational institution which place emphasis on:

1. the individual student and his intellectual, social, emotional and physical development;
2. the building of curricula, methods of instruction and extra-class-room programs to achieve the preceding objective;
3. democratic procedures in working with students in order to help bring about their greatest possible self-realization;
4. the *performance* of student personnel functions rather than on specifically designated individuals to perform them.

If we analyze this definition, we find that it has several implications.

It has reference to the *application* of the student personnel point of view, the *application* of a democratic method, and the *application* of a consistent purpose in education. It puts emphasis upon work actually done by the various members of the staff, and not merely upon a point of view which may be accepted enthusiastically because it sounds good, but which may not reach a stage of practical use by the members of the faculty and staff who have immediate contacts with the students.

It should help to eliminate the controversy between "student person-

1. *The Student Personnel Point of View*, American Council on Education, Series 1, Vol. 1, No. 3, 1937.

nel work" on the one hand, and "instruction" on the other. It assumes that student personnel work can and should be done by *all* members of the academic, instructional, and administrative staffs, differing only in extent and in the respective roles of the staff members involved. It implies the concept of "every teacher a personnel worker." It does not imply that *all* teaching (good, bad, or indifferent) is personnel work. The researcher, and even the good teacher, normally would be spending far less of his time in actually performing student personnel work than would the clinical counselor, the dean of students, or the faculty counselor. Thus, student personnel work is carried on *throughout* the institution, differing from staff member to staff member, but only in terms of role, degree, and types of specialization.

The definition does not assume that a hard and fast line can be drawn between student personnel work on the one hand and instruction on the other. It does assume, however, that each of these functions can be defined and that each may exist alone or that each may overlap in any single instance. In other words, some teaching and particularly good teaching, might well be student personnel work. Certain types of student personnel work would also be teaching. This concept may be illustrated by showing at one end of a graphic continuum the strictly teaching functions, and at the other end, the strictly student personnel functions, but in the middle a "gray" area of service which could and should be referred to as both teaching *and* student personnel work. An example of this dual purpose function would be an instructor teaching a course in "Vocational Guidance," or a course in "Mental Hygiene." These are the obvious examples of the dual functions, where a distinctive line between student personnel work and teaching cannot be drawn—but by definition they clearly overlap. This overlapping is good, it is healthy, it is an objective for which to strive.

We are not proposing anything new. We are merely emphasizing a broader concept of student personnel work than is currently prevalent. We think that this broader view is urgently needed if student personnel work is going to contribute its maximum to higher education. There are some critics who believe that student personnel work is solely a field of specialization engaged in by those who are *professionally* trained—that the regular faculty member or the "untrained" administrator must not venture into the sacred bounds of the student personnel specialist. There is nothing in our proposed definition which excludes the profes-

sionally trained clinical counselor, the professionally trained full-time
student personnel administrator, or any other professionally trained and
competent personnel technician. All are sorely needed, and with
higher standards of professional competence than we now have generally. The wide variety of student problems and the various ways by
which the student can get individual help from his teachers, his counselors, his deans, and others who are in strategic positions to help him,
necessitate a recognition of these various roles within the field of student personnel work. All these roles are equally necessary and are
equally important. When they are all truly coordinated into a single-
purpose program, then we believe we will be *well on our way* to an effective program of student personnel services, and therefore a *more effective program of higher education.*

Six major assumptions underlie the foregoing concept of student personnel work:

1. That individuals will inevitably have problems in adjusting to a
   complex society.
2. That personality must be considered as a whole.
3. That there must be emphasis on prevention.
4. That personality and environment are interrelated.
5. That the individual has the capacity to take the major responsibility for his learning and for the solution of his problems.
6. That a common purpose must be defined and must operate in an
   interdependent democratic society.

The first fundamental assumption is that individuals inevitably will
have problems in adjusting to a complex society. Many problems confront the college student making the necessary social, physical, and
emotional adjustments. Some students, without being "problem cases"
in themselves, need assistance in meeting the stress and strain of these
adjustments. Problems differ from individual to individual and each student must be recognized as having unique problems and characteristics.
It is in this area that the *specialized* personnel services make their major
contribution. It follows that personal problems should be turned into
constructive learning experiences.

Second, in considering the wholeness of personality as a basic factor
in sound personnel work, we must assume that the intellectual person,
without his emotional, physical, and social reactions, is a logical abstraction rather than a reality. The natural but regrettable tendency is

to consider each individual in terms of parts. With the integrated personality as a goal, we must of necessity eliminate any distinction between the primary objectives that have been separately designated in the past to personnel workers on the one hand and faculty members on the other. The student must be helped to understand that the educative process is a vital part of "real life," of living now.

In considering the third assumption, the necessity for the emphasis on prevention, it is assumed that the development of the whole student can best be achieved by preventing the more serious problems. More failures can be avoided by appropriate admissions and distribution policies than by adjustive measures employed after the student has become educationally and personally demoralized. These adjustive measures are of course important because their services are essential as a means of further prevention. Unless institutions of higher learning are prepared to exercise adequate adjustive measures to alleviate problems that have their roots in earlier development, such institutions are to a large extent responsible for the continuance and even the further aggravation of social and emotional maladjustments.

The fourth assumption calls attention to the interaction of the personality and the environment. A student's highly individual responses to his college experiences, and their cumulative effect, will have influence throughout his lifetime. The individual functions always in a social medium; consequently, the educational program must take into account the social pressures, mores, and accepted cultural patterns of the college community. Furthermore, the college environment cannot be assumed to be identical for all individuals.

Because of our conviction that the integrity of each person must be respected, our next assumption, that the individual has the capacity to take the major responsibility for his learning and for the solution of his problems, is of outstanding importance. People have a right to assume responsibility for their own action and development. We believe strongly that each individual has the inner drives and the capacity for self-development—that all learning basically is self-education. It is imperative that students have the opportunity to direct their lives in constructive ways. Good personnel work strengthens the decision-making abilities of students and aids in this self-growth process. Students can develop to their fullest and function effectively only in a democratic environment in which they have roles to play. In such an environment they should be encouraged to participate with the faculty and administration in making policies and setting up educational programs.

The sixth assumption is a rhetorical one. The need for common educational purposes for both personnel workers and instructional staff is being emphasized throughout this paper. Such an institutional atmosphere is imperative.

We need now to indicate the services and functions which are essential to a sound program of student personnel work. The American Council on Education published a list of twenty-three student personnel functions in 1937, and since that time a number of revisions and regroupings have been made.[2] We have regrouped them as follows:

1. Interpretation of institutional objectives to prospective students and to workers in secondary education.
2. Selection and admission of students.
3. Orientation of the new student to his college environment.
4. Provision of diagnostic and counseling services.
5. Remedial assistance in speech, reading, and other subjects as needed.
6. Supervision, coordination, and integration of the "co-curricular" program on the campus.
7. Provision of physical and mental health services.
8. Supervision of living arrangements, including the food service program.
9. Administration of financial aids, student employments, postgraduate placements, and job follow-ups.
10. Development and evaluation of the religious life and interests of students.
11. Development and use of permanent cumulative personnel records.
12. Application of a knowledge of student needs to the curriculum and to the instructional functions of the institution.
13. Use of both preventive and counseling procedures in carrying out discipline work.
14. Systematic evaluation of student personnel services.

2. Wrenn and Kamm, "A Procedure for Evaluating a Student Personnel Program," in *School and Society*, Vol. 67, April 3, 1948; E. H. Hopkins, "The essentials of a Student Personnel Program," in *College and University*, July, 1948.

15. On-the-job training, development, and stimulation of all persons performing student personnel functions.

While this paper is concerned mainly with needed emphases in student personnel work, we should like now to comment very briefly about
its heritage. The minutes of the early faculty meetings at the University
of Wisconsin are excellent source material, but we will have to limit
ourselves to a few generalizations.

We know that Professor Sterling was not the least bit concerned
about the *definitions* of student personnel work when he welcomed the
first University of Wisconsin students about one hundred years ago.
Nevertheless, in the tradition of American collegiate education at that
time, he thought of education as involving a concern for *all* aspects of
the student's life. James F. A. Pyre's book, *Wisconsin*, informs us that on
the afternoon of Chancellor Lathrop's inauguration in 1849, the Board
of Regents reported to the legislature the urgent need for dormitories if
the University was to begin "its proper work."[3] The only new buildings
constructed between 1849 and 1855 were dormitories, and one of
these, South Hall, contained quarters also for members of the faculty
and their families. This made it easy for the faculty to watch over the
students, checking on student conduct, study habits, sleeping habits,
etc. In fact, the minutes of the University of Wisconsin faculty meetings of those early years abound with references to faculty concern for
the manners, morals, and character of the student as well as his intellectual growth. Misdemeanors were solemnly reported in the minutest
detail at these faculty meetings; there was serious consideration of the
action that should be taken for the welfare of both the student and the
institution.

Wisconsin was not unique in this regard. Cowley's research into the
history of higher education has revealed that these "Alma Maternal
ministrations to students had characterized the universities of the Middle Ages and had been the most notable element in American higher
education up to the time of the Civil War."[4]

Personnel activities in American institutions of higher learning, according to Cowley, fell into disrepute because of secularization, special-

3. James F. A. Pyre, *Wisconsin* (New York, 1920).
4. W. H. Cowley, "The Past and Future of Student Personnel Work," *Proceedings, University of Minnesota Personnel Institute*, November, 1947.

ization, and especially as a result of the influence of the intellectualistic impersonalism imported by American scholars trained in Germany. He places the heyday of the intellectualists between 1870 and 1920 and relates that during this period personnel work was considered to be a necessary evil. Reactions, however, came from (1) the humanitarians who tried to promote mental hygiene, vocational counseling, and other individual services for college students, (2) from far-seeing administrators like President Gilman of Johns Hopkins who created the country's first system of faculty advisers, or like President Harper of Chicago who emphasized *residential housing*, (3) from the applied psychologists who began to identify individual differences in intellectual capacities and personal characteristics, and (4) from the students themselves who began to build an extensive extracurriculum.[5]

The personnel movement made considerable headway after World War I as psychologists, interested in the measurement of intelligence, turned their attention from the Army to colleges and universities and to industry. Also, during this period, the professional aspects of student personnel work were stressed heavily by the applied psychologists, interested administrators, and the professional organizations in the field. Research efforts brought forth improved tests, inventories and other devices to measure interest, aptitude, and personality characteristics. Findings were applied to the development of a systematic approach to educational, vocational, and personal counseling, in which diagnostic procedures played an important part.

There were also numerous attempts during the thirties to identify relationships among the many student personnel services and functions. This effort was devoted largely to keeping each function from obstructing the other. This made possible the development of neat organization charts with box-tight compartments—but with relatively unsatisfactory results.[6]

Services and functions did expand rapidly during this period. This led to considerable talk about centralization, although a somewhat counter trend toward coordination of decentralized services was in evidence.

5. W. H. Cowley, "The History and Philosophy of Student Personnel Work," in *Proceedings, American College Personnel Association*, February, 1940.

6. Esther Lloyd-Jones, "Personnel Work Today," in the *Journal of Higher Education*, 13:81–86 (February, 1942).

In the years immediately preceding Pearl Harbor, there was a definite attempt on the part of student personnel work to discover its role in relation to the objectives of higher education. Several new colleges began to develop a more unified plan of education by appointing faculty members who were good teachers and good scholars and who in addition had ability, interest, and successful experience in working with students.

Student personnel work became almost entirely military personnel work after Pearl Harbor. Most of the specialized personnel workers donned uniforms and helped to develop the vast testing, interviewing, and classification programs of the Army and Navy. Others did urgent research on tools, techniques, and training devices. Some went into industrial and government personnel work. A few remained on college campuses to help administer wartime training programs and to keep alive a minimal personnel program for the greatly reduced numbers of civilian students.

A challenging book by Carl Rogers reached the colleges early in the war, in time to start a ground swell of controversy about the counseling procedures which he advocated.[7] His book attacked the diagnostic tools and techniques of the clinical counselor and argued for a counseling approach which relied upon the counselee's capacity for self-growth rather than upon the counselor's diagnostic skill. Although the full implications of Rogers' approach for student personnel work are only now being recognized, special note is made in this section to record its origin during the war years.

The Veterans Administration Guidance Centers appeared on many campuses at the end of the war. These centers have affected the development of student personnel programs on numerous campuses, but their full significance cannot yet be determined.

Today, we have a situation representing the composite influences of all these forces. Especially pertinent were the developments during and since the war.

The complexity of the present situation at best is baffling to all of us. We are faced with a changing, groping, unstable world. We have a heterogeneous mass of educational practices being used and misused throughout our respective institutions. The rapid postwar expansion of

---

7. Carl R. Rogers, *Counseling and Psychotherapy* (New York, 1942).

all our educational services, the vast increases in student enrollments caused principally by the influx of veterans, the personnel problems arising from these increased enrollments—in teaching, housing, feeding, and counseling—have all tended to complicate further the picture of "student personnel work today." In addition to these, we have a shortage of qualified student personnel workers, teachers, and administrators. As a consequence, the standards for all this work have necessarily fallen, and at a time when quality is needed more than ever. Student personnel services, as well as other educational functions, have been greatly multiplied on most of our campuses, and frequently without adequate regard to sound administrative and coordinating structure. Inadequate faculties, heavy teaching loads, research demands, and other institutional responsibilities are preventing even the good teachers from doing the kind of job they would like to do and are capable of doing.

Out of all this, however, some promising trends can be identified. There is an increasing tendency to assign to one person the coordinating and administrative responsibility for the student personnel program. There is an increasing emphasis on the need for the improvement of standards and "quality" of work performed. More attention is being given to personal-adjustment counseling. Finally, but very important, is the prevalence of institutions' evaluations of their own programs. Many college faculties, in the past three years, have taken an inward look at their institutions, their curricula, their objectives, and the relation of all these to the crucial problems ahead. This is significant. Improvements should follow.

This leads us to the important question, "What about the future of student personnel work?" The formula for the future is no different now from what it might have been at any point in our historical past. It calls for an analysis of our problem, including a study of the past and an unbiased appraisal of the present, a critical determination of accepted, pertinent, and constructive educational objectives, followed by a concrete and realistic plan of action. This formula is relatively simple and is applicable to virtually all problems. It involves also the responsibility for following through with constructive programs of action. However, the current societal situation *is* different from any other even remotely comparable situation in history, and therefore may call for a program of action heretofore considered inappropriate or unnecessary. "Urgency" is now the driving force behind any analysis and program of action. The tremendous complexity and the "interwoveness" of our social, economic, political, military, and security problems have never before been so strategically related, and the responsibility of higher education in these areas is a matter of real concern.

While our instruments for dealing with these problems need far greater refinement than yet has been achieved, we do have more scientific "know how" in dealing with social problems than we have had previously. We not only have more refined research and statistical techniques, but recent fruits of scientific research have given us a broadened understanding of the learning processes and an appreciation of the significance of individual and trait differences. Also, we have revised our concepts of mental discipline theories. We have developed new emphasis on motivation and purpose in learning. We have reached a better understanding of the importance of "learning by doing" (hence the college campus as a laboratory in democratic living), and we have a new emphasis upon "teaching for generalized meanings and abilities" rather than knowledge for knowledge's sake. These are examples of only some of the current findings which have a significance to the over-all problem of determining the most appropriate programs of student personnel services and, in fact, the most approrpiate programs of higher education generally.

A consideration of the future of student personnel work leads directly into the last process included in the simple formula already indicated. We need a vigorous "action" program, based upon the findings of scientific research and upon a concerted effort to apply the revised definition or concept of student personnel work at the various levels and in the various roles of educational work.

One of the best attempts to do just this is represented by the prodecure followed, the appraisals made, and the "proposals for action" set forth by The President's Commission on Higher Education. This report is a truly significant document. One part of the report contains a critically determined list of constructive and attainable objectives of higher education for the future. The commission's method of stating objectives, i.e., in terms of individual student outcomes desired, is itself a result of research in the problems and nature of learning and of human behavior. These outcomes demand further attention, since we are concerned with "mapping out" a program for future action. They illustrate clearly the implications of our broader definition of student personnel work. They are paraphrased from Volume I of the commission's report as follows:

1. Development for the regulation of one's personal and civic life of a code of behavior based on ethical principles consistent with democratic ideals.
2. Participation actively as an informed and responsible citizen in solving the social, economic, and political problems of one's community, state, and nation.
3. Recognition of the interdependence of the different people of the world and one's personal responsibility for fostering international understanding and peace.
4. Understanding the common phenomena in one's physical environment, application of habits of scientific thought to both personal and civic problems, and appreciation of the implications of scientific discoveries for human welfare.
5. Understanding the ideas of others and the ability to express one's own ideas effectively.
6. Attainment of a satisfactory emotional and social adjustment.
7. Ability and willingness to maintain and improve one's own health and to cooperate actively and intelligently in solving community health problems.
8. Understanding and enjoyment of literature, art, music, and other cultural activities as expressions of personal and social experience, and participation to some extent in some form of creative activity.
9. Acquisition of the knowledge and attitudes basic to satisfying family life.
10. Choice of a socially useful and personally satisfying vocation that will permit one to use to the full his particular interests and abilities.
11. Acquisition and use of the skills and habits involved in critical and constructive thinking.

With these realistic objectives in mind, let us indicate how student personnel work in the future might be related to these various processes and functions in higher education.

1. *Student Personnel Work and Instruction.* More consideration should

be given to the instructor as a personnel worker. In our brief treatment of the history of student personnel work, we indicated that in the early American college the instructors usually maintained an informal and personal relationship with their students. This relationship was not usually restricted to instructional or subject-matter problems but extended to all sorts of extracurricular and personal problems as well. We might decry the paternalistic emphasis of these early professors but not their basic interest in the total education of their students.

We have already indicated that during the period between the two world wars the pendulum swung too far in the opposite direction. Student personnel work and instruction became further and further apart. An impression was developing that teachers were to teach and personnel workers were to do the counseling; that teachers had neither the time, the inclination, nor the training to perform this function. We urge that the pendulum should swing back to some extent, at least to the point where teachers will continue to play an important role in the over-all program of student personnel work on the campus. We have already indicated that this point of view is not a new one. As a matter of fact, Williamson in 1938 presented the following list of student personnel functions which may be performed by the teacher:

(1) Creating and maintaining in the classroom an atmosphere psychologically conducive to the development of optimum motivation, healthy emotional balance and socialized attitudes.

(2) Maintaining friendly and personalized relationships with each student.

(3) Cultivating in each student an intense desire to learn what can be learned and to achieve satisfaction as well as success in life adjustments.

(4) Maintaining constantly a student point-of-view as opposed to the textbook emphasis.

(5) Modifying teaching techniques and subject-matter in terms of the needs and readiness to learn of each pupil; i.e., individualizing instruction and making it appropriate to the capacities and needs of each student.

(6) Observing and recording significant and relevant data about those intangible but important factors we call motivation, attitudes, and social skills.[8]

8. E. G. Williamson, "The Teacher as a Personnel Worker," in *Proceedings of the 1938 Annual Meeting*, Association of Texas Colleges, *Bulletin*, July 15, 1938.

The emphasis needed, now and in the immediate future, is one which assumes that all members of the instructional staff should consider as one of their most important responsibilities the job of relating instruction and counseling directly to such educational objectives as were proposed by the President's Commission.

One more needed emphasis in this general area is a new role for the graduate schools throughout the country, since they produce practically all of our college and university teachers. Approximately two thirds of all persons with Ph.D. degrees are engaged in, and probably will continue to engage in, college or university teaching or other phases of educational work. Would it not then appear appropriate to include, as an integral part of the graduate training program, some definite preparation for the important job of teaching? Beyond this, there should be effective programs for the improvement of instruction at all levels on every campus.

2. *Student Personnel Work and Academic Administration.* By the same analogy a certain portion of almost every administrator's work could and should be referred to as "student personnel work." This is true whether he is the business manager, the registrar, the manager of dormitories, or the president of the college or university. It is just as important for these officers to perform their jobs in harmony with the student personnel point of view, by democratic methods, and with the basic purposes of the institution in mind, as it is for the instructor or for the dean of students.

In relation to academic administration, a dean of a college—liberal arts of professional—should be encouraged to perform many of the duties of a student personnel worker. He should devote much of his energy to the implementation of the student personnel point of view and toward the use of democratic methods both in relation to his staff and in the relation of his staff to their students. Finally, he should consider the paramount purpose of his academic program that of developing to the fullest extent the individual capacities, interests, and abilities of the students enrolled in his college. Such a person, in such a position, could contribute as much to the over-all program of student personnel work on his campus as any other person on the staff, including the dean of students. On the other hand, such a dean might actually be engaged in a type of academic administration and research which could not, by any stretch of the imagination, be included within the scope of the definition of student personnel work referred to earlier.

The same could and should be said for other administrators on the campus, particularly those engaged in the business and financial aspects of educational administration. Unless current and sound educational objectives are constantly in the minds of the persons administering these programs, the tail is very likely to wag the dog. Here, then, lies the second and urgently needed emphasis in higher education today.

3. *Student Personnel Work and Public Relations.* If higher education is to do the job which all of us feel that it must do, it is precariously in need of far greater understanding and financial support than it now has. It is our contention that if a college or university first defined its objectives in some such terms as those just outlined, if its faculty dedicated itself to the task implied by those objectives and definitions, and if the public-relations program conveyed this message adequately and forcibly, adequate support would be forthcoming. If it is to get this support it must do a better job of public relations, which like teaching and counseling involves an educational point of view. Our publics want to know, and are entitled to know, what we are doing in an *educational sense*, not just to know that "we need money."

In this connection, it is significant to quote from the September 16, 1948, issue of the *Educator's Washington Dispatch* in which the following question was asked:

What would an industrialist do if he were faced, like many a school executive is today, with lack of trained personnel, antiquated plant, outworn equipment, and lack of funds?

This *Dispatch* query went to a top United States manufacturer, who was quick to answer:

He'd put on the biggest selling campaign you ever saw. And he'd have a moral right to, because he has the best product in the world to sell. If the manufacturer were in the unhappy position of that schoolman, he'd tell every parent, every citizen, every taxpayer about his problem. If he did that he'd get the resources he needed. No community will starve its schools. But it has to know what the school system faces. And it has to be assured that the money raised will be spent soundly. Give business men these facts, and they will go to the limit supporting the schools.

This then is the third needed emphasis today, namely, the consideration of broad educational objectives and the essentials of student personnel work in the public-relations programs of our respective institutions. It should pay great dividends.

4. *Student Personnel Work and the Students.* If the broader definition of student personnel work and the President's Commission's objectives of higher education should bring about corresponding institutional patterns on the college campus, there would spring up dozens of "democratic laboratories" in nearly every phase of student activity and student life, including the instructional classrooms. Rogers and other client-centered counselors have brought forth some very significant clinical and research data regarding a person's capacity for growth and self-realization under proper psychological conditions. They report that many of the same principles seem to apply to groups—in group therapy, in staff relationships, in classroom teaching. The broad implications of their approach merit serious consideration and experimentation in many phases of the student personnel program. It must be kept constantly in mind that it is the student for whom our institutions exist. If the results of all our efforts are not reflected in the development of desirable educational outcomes in our students, we might just as well "turn in our suits."

5. *Student Personnel Work and Institutional Research.* Another emphasis which is sorely needed to guide the kind of program we have outlined is a vigorous, critical, but constructive plan for student personnel and institutional research. This program should be designed to find out what the real needs of our students are, what the needs of society are, and how effectively or ineffectively we are now meeting these needs. We need this kind of information not only to guide policy determinations, but to convince ourselves, our faculties, our administrations, our governing boards, and our publics what is really important.

We can't develop adequately new curricula, new programs of study, proper combinations of general and specialized courses, truly integrated courses, vocational and other counseling services, student activity programs which will train for democratic living, sound admission policies, sound reinstatement policies, and sound and defensible graduation requirements until we know about the effects and the results of our present curricula, instruction, and services.

6. *Top-Level Coordination Needed.* We believe that each institution must provide the organizational mechanics, and the necessary leadership at the appropriate levels, if it is to expect noteworthy results. In our opinion, this calls not only for a faculty and institutional organization which provides for a definite coordination through appropriate consultation among staff members, but also for a carefully planned line and staff organization designed to accomplish these objectives. In addition to carefully planned faculty and staff organization, with optimum use of student-faculty advisory committees on all aspects of educational policy, there is a need, especially in the larger colleges and universities, for a "top-level" educational *staff* officer, whose chief responsibilities would be to provide this coordination and this educational leadership, the kind of leadership that the president would provide—if he were twins, or in some cases, triplets. Since few presidents have the time actually to pull together all these important educational functions, at least in a day-to-day and practical manner, we suggest a top-level *staff* administrator, especially for the larger institutions. The importance of these duties should be properly emphasized by the title of educational or academic vice-president, an administrator who could devote his full energies to this broad-gauge program.

Let us summarize briefly: First, we attempted to clarify the meaning and philosophy of student personnel work, with an increased emphasis upon its broader applications and implications throughout educational institutions. Secondly, we stressed that such a program, if sound, must be predicted upon certain basic and fundamental assumptions. These were identified. Thirdly, and to further clarify the scope of a sound program of student personnel work, the essential elements comprising such a program were enumerated. Fourthly, to interpret more intelligently the role of student personnel work in education today, and in the future, a minimal historical sketch was included, as well as a brief overview of its present status. Lastly, six aspects of the student personnel program were chosen for more detailed consideration, in an attempt to emphasize those functional aspects of student personnel work most urgently in need of emphasis now, in order that higher education will be able to provide the type of leadership which is so imperative today.

"The Fault, Dear Brutus—"
C. Gilbert Wrenn

A logical interpretation of this quotation would lead to the conclusion that I believe that personnel workers are in the position of "underlings." There are times, of course, when each of us is quite sure that he is an underling, subordinate to far too many people, but it is not my belief that the profession is now in a position subordinate to that of other educational specialties. I think we have grown out of our swaddling clothes, that personnel work is a distinct personality in the family of professions. Personnel work never was an unwanted child for it was born of a need, a need well recognized by both students and administrators. It is true that some of our relatives, our academic aunts, uncles, cousins and the like, have raised their eyebrows at us, but we are now a member of the family, whether always approved or not, and we are here to stay. I am, however, suggesting that certain faults in the performance of personnel work lie within us as individuals and that we might examine these and learn a bit thereby.

Compensations for Lack of Assurance

Our very lack of assurance . . . is one of our greatest faults. We are too young to be a science and not old enough to be a tradition. We are on the way toward accumulating a science of practice, and certainly psychology upon which we depend can be considered a young science, but upon the whole we cannot stand out in an academic gathering with the assurance of the natural scientist, nor yet with the complacency of our older academic relatives, such as literature, history or the languages. In many a social gathering I have seen this lack of self-assurance

158

upon the part of the college personnel worker. It is often evident in one of the two familiar patterns in which defense behavior is expressed. When we are defensive against questions that we cannot answer, accusations about which we think there may be some truth, or in the presence of such ignorance of our work as to give us doubt that it is as important as we thought it was, we are apt to respond with either belligerent behavior, on the one hand, or apologetic behavior on the other. Both, as all psychologists know, are expressions of the same sense of inadequacy.

A belligerent pattern is frequently expressed in overselling of personnel work. This is done by claiming more for student personnel work than it can legitimately perform or by claiming outcomes for personnel services for which no proof can be offered. This pattern of behavior is common for the younger members of the profession who have not yet learned the limitations of the work in which they are engaged. Nor have they learned that such over-salesmanship is resented by professional colleagues with whom personnel people must work cooperatively. "It is better to remain silent and appear a fool, than to speak and remove all doubt." One does not have to be too boastful about one's self or one's vocation to assure the other person that either the person or the vocation is significant. This same belligerency is sometimes revealed in an over-sensitiveness to criticism of one's vocation or of one's own part in personnel work. It is again well known that the over-sensitive person is merely revealing his basic insecurity. One of our problems in this area is that we are not well enough assured of the really valid and stable contributions of our vocation so that we can readily take criticism of the many aspects of our work that justify criticism.

The opposing attitude, that of apologetic response to criticisms or discussions of our professional field, is perhaps even more reprehensible than the belligerent attitude, for, in so being apologetic, we are betraying both ourselves and our profession. We have nothing to apologize for in spite of the fact that we are doing many things poorly. We should make known that we are engaging in a work so complex that we shall never perform as well as we should like to do. We must admit failures and weaknesses and at the same time be proud of certain achievements and basic concepts that will stand up under the most rigorous examination. I well remember Dean Harold Benjamin some years ago speaking of the fact that until teachers held their heads up and stuck their chins out and said "I am a teacher and proud of it" that the teaching profession would never get the respect from the public that it deserves. With this I heartily concur. We must start that, it seems, by attaching importance not to the quality of what we are doing, but to the *significance* of the job to be done. Furthermore, as I have said, there is much more to be proud of than we have sometimes admitted.

One can honestly say to young people that society . . . has done too good a job of making them aware of their liabilities and weaknesses. Perhaps we, as a young profession, are in the same category. There is no reason for us in personal conversations with colleagues or in professional meetings to be other than realistic about the work that we are doing. This realism consists, in part, of admitting our weaknesses, but, also, in stating our strengths. We have many more strengths, as a matter of fact, than some of the academic disciplines that have prestige because of long life. Age does not necessarily bring wisdom. . . . I propose that we accept ourselves as a young profession with much to learn, but at the same time that we consider it unnecessary to be either belligerent or apologetic about the significance of our work. Let it speak for itself—with some assistance from us! And, most of all, let us accept gracefully criticisms of our personal part in the performance of personnel work without puffing up our dignity . . . or exhibiting more obvious signs that our feelings have been hurt.

A second psychological problem of personnel workers is the strain upon the individual of constant contact with human beings. No one but teachers and individuals in similar human relations occupations appreciate the drain made upon nervous energy by the daily routine. For many people, those in the academic field have a soft life. We know differently. The only trouble is that we know it in such terms that it frequently cannot be understood by anyone outside of our own field. I am . . . drawing attention to the effect of this constant contact with people and their troubles, decisions that must be made in terms of human reaction rather than objective fact, the necessity for constantly shifting in terms of the various personalities whom we meet from time to time throughout the day, the necessity for attempting to see beneath the surface and to infer attitudes and conflicts from exterior behavior and verbalization. These, and other conditions of our work, cause us to suffer a kind of nervous fatigue unlike that experienced in most other fields.

This fatigue leads to a peculiar danger of personnel workers, the adoption of a kind of surface defense to protect us from the results of fatigue. This mask frequently results in a blunting of our sensitivity to intimate human reactions. Administrators are more often accused of this than are counselors or teachers. The solution rests within ourselves and our own program of personal mental hygiene. It rests with our own program of conserving our energies so that the more important things can be handled adequately. The most important thing is the reaction and the growth of each individual human being with whom we deal.

One of the solutions in this connection is for us to become less concerned with paper work and less concerned with personal prestige than we are with the significance of the behavior of the persons with whom we deal as professional workers. It is not easy to ignore a crowded desk and a crowded schedule, to appear at ease and wholly absorbed in the self-revelations of a given individual, whether a student or colleague. It is not easy, but it is *essential* if we are to fulfill our highest obligation as personnel workers.

If we are crowded at our office by people who wish to see us and if we, at the same time, must get out certain correspondence or perform other essential tasks, then perhaps we should perform these other tasks away from the office, so that our office time will not be jammed with affairs not connected with personal relationships. If we are truly to act as counselors, whatever our personnel title, then we must give every indication that our primary concern is with the individual who is consulting with us. And in order to do a good job of dealing with that person's needs, we must give our undivided attention to observation of what might be called the clinical signs of behavior. To allow ourselves to be licked by the human fatigue factor, to become insensitive to the nuances of human behavior, is to lose our distinctiveness as specialists in human behavior and human need.

Self-Glorification

There is a third danger. . . . This is the temptation to become smug and superior in our attitudes toward others. Because the other person comes to us for help and because we try honestly to help him, we are apt to feel pretty good about ourselves, a little like Jehovah and his children. The client *is* grateful and we have seen him, but we should not take particular satisfaction from that reaction. Being bluntly realistic, it is our chosen task to help people and there is no particular merit in our doing so. All of us like love and admiration from others, although sometimes we ask for it a little too obviously. When the student or the client gives us gratitude and affection, deserved or not, we are apt to glorify ourselves a bit, although we would not admit it to anyone but ourselves!

One way to keep one's self from this particular psychological temptation is to constantly remind one's self of the social obligations and social aims of personnel work. Our job is to help individuals become more effective and integrated members of their current society. The fact that they are grateful for our helping them in this regard is of little moment. The real point is that it is our job. If we are completely honest we will admit that what we do for others is seldom done as well as we should like or well enough for us to feel complacent about it. Another thing to consider is that much of the value to the student comes from his own reactions to himself rather than from anything that we have done. I am increasingly convinced that we have placed too much stress on techniques and not enough upon the interaction of the two personalities in the counseling situation. The interaction of these two people may bring a considerable degree of the benefit to the counselee without regard to what either one may have consciously done or of the particular techniques employed by the counselor. The student *may* have benefitted in this way—we do not know that he did. In fact, so little is known of *how* counseling benefits others, that all of us who counsel would do well to take little credit for ourselves.

Discouragement

Now to look at a fourth psychological problem. . . . This is the opposing danger of self-disparagement over the enormous complexity of the human problems faced by any personnel worker. Here I am speaking not only of counselors . . . but of personnel workers who counsel with colleagues or who are responsible for colleagues in their own institution. Because we have the title "personnel" attached to us, it is assumed that we are interested in people and their welfare, and, for this reason, many problems come our way which are not necessarily those of a student-counselor type. If our interest in people is a thoughtful interest, we are frequently discouraged at the enormity of the need, on the one hand, and the smallness of our possible contribution, on the other. Of course, we frequently expect too much of ourselves. We frequently forget that growth in any essential characteristic takes time and that no one or two interviews are going to change a person's life unless we can assume that certain dramatic cases that have been publicized in literature are common occurrences. We frequently become emotionally involved in the client's problems and identify ourselves closely with him. In this we lose one of the great advantages of a professional counselor, his ability to remain objective and neutral in spite of the client's perturbation.

We must constantly tell ourselves that the goals of counseling are limited and that we cannot remake a person's life. We merely assist him in one connection. We furthermore must know that what we are trying to achieve is a process of re-education of the individual, that is, helping him to re-educate himself. This is not done quickly. It takes time to translate a change of attitude into a change of behavior. If we are realistic about ourselves and our job we will not assume that we are going to make great changes in a person's life, and we will, therefore, not be discouraged over a lack of achievement. The counselor is but a tool or a catalyst in the life pattern of the individual with whom he is dealing at the moment. Many other factors are present; he is but one. He can neither take credit nor blame for all that happens.

Perhaps one of our peculiar liabilities arises out of this limitation. This is the liability of never actually feeling mastery over situations. The intricacies of human nature are so great, the bulk of what we do *not* know is so large, the rapid growth of new knowledge so perplexing, that we never seem to feel that we are doing a complete and thorough job in any of our human relations responsibilities. One of the perplexing things for those of us who have been in the field for some time is that the thing which we once thought right is now considered wrong, or is, perhaps, *proved* wrong. This, of course, is not unique to our field of endeavor. It is true in medicine and many other areas, but it seems to hit us with peculiar force. I think this matter of never feeling complete mastery over a situation or never feeling that we are right without equivocation is one of the penalties of dealing with intricate human behavior. We must simply live with this particular liability. We will probably never dispense with it.

Strain of Indecision

Another of our peculiar problems is that of being so frequently undecided as to the best course of action. Psychological counseling and any of the professional personnel functions that deal with human decisions are particularly subject to this strain of indecision and for a specific reason. Our problem is always that of "how far shall we go in transmitting to the other party our convictions with regard to his best course of action?—how far shall we attempt to load the dice in terms of a particular alternative by the way in which we discuss the alternatives or by our very tone of voice?—how far shall we simply keep quiet and allow the individual to work through completely on his own?" These are the questions that trouble us and bring about, it seems to me, an unusual amount of strain upon the part of those who are conscientiously trying to work with individuals in terms of facilitating the process of growth within the individual himself. We may know what is best for the student or best for our colleague, but our knowing it will never solve the problem for him. The real situation is solved only when the individual concerned finds for himself a resolution of conflict, a best way out, a changed attitude.

The Temptation of Authority

In speaking tonight of the personnel worker, I am stressing the point that he or she is, without question, the most important element in the personnel program. Henry Murray has spoken of "psychology's forgotten instrument—the psychologist." Rapaport[1] lists four factors essential to

1. Rapaport, David. "The Status of Diagnostic Testing." *Journal of Consulting Psychology.* XII (1948), 4–7.

the understanding of diagnostic information: the basic personality theory that is held, test rationale, familiarity with previous research, and the self-knowledge of the counselor. He writes that "the richest source book of psychological understanding is carried by the individual within himself," that through a process of self-examination and heightened self-awareness as an instrument in the psychological process, we can develop a greater sensitivity to the meaning of information about human behavior. All of this is just as true about the personnel administrator. About one-half of the membership of ACPA is classified as personnel administrators, and certainly they have no more important function than the consideration of the personnel worker, his qualifications, his welfare and his progress. If the personnel administrator gets too much engrossed in programs and forms, in public relations and budgets, he misses his chance to make his greatest contribution to the personnel work of his institution—the development, encouragement and support of the personnel workers subordinate to him.

Administrators, as such, have rather distinctive psychological problems. In the first place, many administrators such as Deans of Men, Deans of Women, or Deans of Students, actually have authority over the lives of students, and the temptation is to use that authority in ways that will facilitate a given situation but which may not necessarily be best for the student concerned.

Part of this arises from the administrator's tendency to look at the outcomes of programs rather than at the outcomes in the lives of individual students. Part of it may come from the fact that he is frustrated at times in dealing with his colleagues or with his superiors in the academic organization, and this frustration leads to arbitrariness with students or with subordinates, the only people with whom he can be arbitrary. Our most dangerous time in dealing with individuals who are in any sense subordinate to us is just following some frustrating experience upon our own part. The phenomenon of projection is too well known to demand emphasis here, but it is not too readily recognized by the person exhibiting the mechanism.

The administrator may be engrossed in a complex program, but he cannot forget that impersonal manipulation of staff personnel, no matter how immediately helpful to program development, will only result in lowered morale for these and *every other* staff member who hears about it. The tolerance of leader domination of group activity seems to increase with the size of the group . . . but even here the efficiency of result may decrease in spite of tolerance. The power factor, the authority complex, the advancement of program at whatever cost to staff security, is the worst and riskiest kind of personnel administration.

There is excellent argument for an emphasis upon a clear-cut line-and-staff organization of the student personnel functions and staff of an institution. The administrator in higher education must remember . . . that he is dealing with individuals on a staff who are . . . his colleagues. In policy making and in the initiation of new ideas, they must work *with* him and not *for* him. I have written elsewhere ". . . the student personnel program should operate under policies established by an agency representing the administration, faculty and students," and "Student personnel procedures do not function well under an administrative *fiat* arrangement."[2]

Misinterpreting the Administrator's Relationship to his Staff

Another problem of administrators is their frequent failure to recognize that in dealing with the staff they are *not* dealing with students but are, at the same time, responsible for people who have common human need for counsel and encouragement. The prestige factor is an important one in a decision to assume administrative responsibilities as is the realization that certain things could be done with the program if the individual had more control. When this move is made, however, the thing which is frequently not realized is that one must change within himself when he changes from teaching or counseling to administration. Now he is engaging in a process of *adult* education and counseling. He is responsible for staff intellectual and emotional growth, their independence, their morale. Williamson[3] states that "developing counselors" is one of the three major objectives of a program of supervision of counseling services. He writes, "The counselor, himself, is as often as much in need of counseling as the client is, and any administrator that

2. Wrenn, C. Gilbert. "The Administration of Counseling and Other Student Personnel Services." *The Harvard Educational Review*, May, 1949.

3. Williamson, E. G. "Supervision of Counseling Services." *Journal of Consulting Psychology*, VIII (1948), 297–311.

forgets that is not a good administrator." ". . . in administration we almost refuse to do for the doctor what the doctor does for his patients."

Perhaps it is hard to be both an administrator and a counselor. Dean Clifford Houston, in writing to me of the work of his Committee on Professional Standards, makes the following observation: "One does not draw conclusions from so few cases, but it is becoming very obvious that the personal and professional qualifications of a good counselor are not *always* identical with those of a good Dean of Students. Leadership and persuasiveness are very important characteristics for the latter. On the other hand, the careful research type of psychologist might find it difficult to become a real influence with the interfraternity council."

If the personnel administrator states that he is concerned with the morale of the *students* in his institution, he must first be concerned with the morale of the *staff members* who deal with those students. His primary responsibility is to his staff and through them to his students. This is not an easy thing to accept, particularly if one likes to deal with students. One is apt to relegate staff to a position of subordinate responsibility, but this the administrator cannot and must not do. He must depend upon these staff people for their interpretation of student needs. Yes, the administrator has difficult enough problems in terms of developing his program and keeping his various bosses satisfied, but that is nothing to the problem he has in dealing adequately with his staff.

I have said nothing here of the difficulty faced by the personnel administrator by virtue of student reaction to his title, whatever it may be. This is serious enough in the case of the "Dean," for this word carries with it a connotation of authority and officialdom that the personnel administrator would like very much to avoid.

This might sound as though I were overly aware of psychological problems in the life of the personnel worker. Perhaps what I have been doing is reflecting the problems in my own life at various stages in my development, and I may have had more difficulties than the average person. There seems to be some basis, however, for believing that these problems and temptations of the personnel worker are common to many. What, then, can be done about them? Is there anything that could be suggested that would help point the way for a personnel worker to become more effective in dealing with these intimate psychological factors in his life?

One might use a basic approach and examine the factors that *cause* tensions in our lives. This has been ably done by Lewin in several of his brilliant essays collected under the title *Resolving Social Conflicts*.[4]

If it is not presumptuous, let me suggest some simple rules of mental hygiene that may be appropriate to each of us as personnel workers. These suggestions are for me even more than for you.

The first thing to suggest is that we attempt to have fun from our associations with people. I feel that sometimes we take people, and their relationships to us, too seriously. We become involved in what they think of us, or become involved in their troubles, and much of the actual joy of human companionship is lost. Perhaps we could adopt a principle that we might *learn* more from others and *instruct* them less frequently. This would put us in a different relationship to many people, particularly our clients and our associates. None of us should have entered the field of personnel work unless we had enjoyed constant personal contact with people. This enjoyment may have been evident in the beginning, but now some of us have become so engrossed with programs, public relations, publications, and promotions that the joy we once had from simple human contacts has been greatly diminished. When this has happened, we become less effective in all of our personal relationships. People enjoy less being around us, since we enjoy less being around them. Any uniqueness we may have had as far as understanding and sensitive personality is concerned, has been merged in the common pattern of personal ambition and drive.

A second point is that we should recognize our fatigue points and deliberately avoid any extensive contact with people once that point has been reached. We certainly are not effective after we have reached this fatigue point. It is at this time that our voices become sharp, our attention wanders, our patience with the slow progress of others falters, and our effectiveness drops to the vanishing point. This fatigue point will be different with each individual. Furthermore, we must learn to recognize the symptoms of that approaching state of tension. Perhaps only a brief respite is necessary to reduce the fatigue and tension. For some this respite is in a candy bar. Others read something light, and still others will look out the window. Someone else may stretch for a

---

4. Lewin, Kurt. *Resolving Social Conflicts*. Harper and Brothers, 1948. (See especially pp. 89–90.)

few seconds or take a deep breath. All of these have a combined effect of releasing our physical tensions and at the same time bringing new associations into our intellectual existence.

A third suggestion is that we stop setting up impossible goals for ourselves in terms of the amount to be accomplished each day. If we plan on *less* than we actually expect to do each day, the unexpected things that always arise will fill in the chinks of our time without strain. We almost *always*, on the contrary, plan on more than we can do and then feel frustrated and unhappy because the impossible has not been accomplished.

A fourth possibility is a habit of blocking out a small amount of professional reading each day and thereby reducing the feeling of frustration that we develop because we are not making professional progress. Most of us know that we have several hours reading ahead of us each day and seldom get more than a fraction of it done. Our journals pile up. The books that we have to review become older month by month.

The fifth point that I should like to suggest is that we deliberately practice small courtesies in our relations with other people. In the first place, it is easier on others and will pay large dividends in social effectiveness. In the second place, by practicing these small social courtesies, we are actually demonstrating that we believe in the integrity of each human personality with whom we deal. This point is not easy to express, but I am trying to say that if we practice courtesy and consideration for the welfare and dignity of the other person in small affairs, then it will be easier for us to measure up to our ideals in major human relationships.

Finally, I would like to suggest that we should remember that ultimate values persist regardless of what happens to our personal lives. Things that we believe in, that have permanent significance, do not change no matter how much the world about us seems to deteriorate. We may be personally in a minor position and we may suffer in comparison with others. We may have little in the way of goods or money. Prices may go up, and our state legislators may rob the schools to pay bonuses to veterans and pensions to the elderly. The United Nations may lose its prestige and we may have grave fears about our policy with regard to the atomic bomb. But in the face of all these, certain basic values do not change. Human rights and dignities, the integrity of each human personality, the warmth of love and friendship, the beauty of the earth, the eternal significance of the spiritual,—these things endure. The physical and the political world about us may cause suffering of body and mind, but the things of the human spirit do not die and it is with these eternals of human life that we must be concerned if we are to live up to our high calling as specialists in human relationships and as trustees of human values.

Student Personnel Services in Retrospect and Prospect [1]

W. H. Cowley

During the past century, American college students have been extraordinarily well behaved in comparison with former times. Until the Civil War, riots and rebellions broke out in most colleges every few years. Some of them led to bloodshed, some even to killing. The pattern went back to the town-and-gown riots of the Middle Ages, the most famous being the Oxford outbreak which began on St. Scholastica's Day, 1355. More than 50 students and townsmen died in that encounter. It lasted almost a week, and because of it the City of Oxford annually paid fines and obeisance to the University of Oxford for the next 470 years. To this day, Cambridge University continues to be prepared for the consequences of such outbreaks, the only duty of its High Steward being "to attend the hanging of any undergraduate."

Nothing in the history of American student life compares with European antecedents, but, during the early years of the 19th century, Princeton students blew up Nassau Hall three times with dynamite, Yale students stabbed to death at least one New Haven fireman in their annual spring "hose riots," and a student blinded the left eye of the famous historian, William H. Prescott, by hitting it with a piece of stale bread in one of Harvard's numerous food riots. Describing these uprisings as they occurred at Harvard, its tercentennial historian, Samuel Eliot Morison, has written that

. . . the half century from 1807 to 1857 is studded with explosions in lecturehalls, bonfires in the Yard, smashing tutors' windows, breaking up chapel exer-

1. Adapted from an address before the National Association of Student Personnel Administrators, Stanford, Calif, June 21, 1956.

cises, and rebellions. There was even a traditional Rebellion Tree opposite the south entry of Hollis, where they started. . . . Josiah Quincy, who lived in Wadsworth House when he was President, complained after his resignation that he could not sleep in Boston—it was so quiet compared with the Yard! [2]

In the high-spirited South even fewer restraints prevailed, as witness the following summary statement of conditions there:

In North Carolina they [students] rode horses through the dormitory and "shot up" the place generally. At a great drinking bout, attended by students and faculty, that signalized the celebration of Washington's birthday in 1804, a young instructor, according to a student's letter, achieved a feat of getting drunk twice. Shooting, blocking stagecoaches, and singing ribald songs in front of churches are reported from the University of Virginia. Students here went even further and on occasion assaulted and whipped members of the faculty. In the course of the riot of 1842 Professor Davis was shot and killed by an exuberant undergraduate. A similar outrage was the murder of President Jeremiah Chamberlin of Oakland College in Mississippi. During the political excitement attendant upon the discussion of the Compromise of 1850 a drunken student, enraged over a fancied injury, stabbed him to death. [3]

Compared with the lawlessness of pre-Civil War college students, today's panty raids seem so mild that the historian of college life is tempted to dismiss them as inconsequential. Deans of students, however, cannot be so complacent and must deal with them wisely if they occur and prevent them if they can. In both enterprises the historical continuum provides the richest available case records as well as foreshadowings of potential dangers and of possible ameliorations.

Panty raids may even constitute a blessing in disguise for deans of students, because, if they will view them as events on the historical continuum of student riots and rebellions, they can learn what—about a hundred years ago—stopped the gory atrocities of earlier periods, what remedial techniques of the past have relevance today, and what to expect in the future.

2. S. E. Morison, "The History and Tradition of Harvard College," *Harvard Crimson*, 1934, pp. 20–21.

3. G. P. Schmidt, "The Old Time College President," (New York: Columbia University Press, 1930), p. 86.

At least six factors seem to have been involved in reducing the number and intensity of student outbreaks. Administrators initiated three of them, and three emerged from the changing times. The three administrative devices were: changing the college calendar so that vacations would come at time of the year during which students had been prone to hell raising (including the Christmas season which did not become a vacation period until about 1850), abandoning dormitories (a solution which led fraternities to change from literary societies meetings once a week to housing units and social clubs), and helping students to organize for self-government.

Meanwhile, three powerful social developments in American life at large forced the colleges to change spectacularly: coeducation, organized athletics, and the establishment of curriculums for the training of kinds of students that universities never before had served—engineers, dentists, farmers, intending scientists, and a growing variety of others, including those planning to become businessmen. Among these three societal influences upon the colleges, the third seems to be the most important because those preparing for careers as individualistic workers in medicine, law, and in the professions generally do not have to explain to potential employers their student behavior as do those going to work for large organizations. Upon investigation, deans of students will probably find that those planning to work for large industrial and governmental units constitute their best resources for maintaining law and order.

In any event, panty raids present deans of students with the challenge of research. Should another serious depression strike, the deans might not be dealing with coed panties but, instead, with the banners of political agitators from both the left and the right. We had a taste of such agitation during the 30's, and another long depression would probably make those years seem placid. Because, today, college campuses bring together such a large proportion of the youth of the nation, groups of agitators would descend upon them; and students, believing their prospects to be blighted, would flock to their banners and do their destructive bidding.

This is a possibility for which deans of students ought to be preparing. How? The only answer is research, research on the historical continuum of student life—that is, investigating the present in the light of the past with a view to preparing for the constantly arriving future.

The same formula can be used in meeting the issues raised by the U.S. Supreme Court decisions concerning racial segregation, in studying fraternity and sorority trends, in administering admissions and financial aid programs, and, indeed, in every sector of student life. The history of each sector has shaped its present characteristics, and both the past and the present can be assessed to glimpse and to prepare for the future.

Another question could well be what can be done to promote a better spirit of co-operation among the various kinds of workers who perform student personnel services in colleges and universities. Specifically, what can be done to lessen the antagonism between deans of students as a group and deans of women as a group, to make registrars and directors of health services better co-ordinated members of the student personnel team, to bring the psychological testers more effectively into camp, to educate the growing number of clinical counselors to the points of view of deans of students, and vice versa?

Three kinds of people engage in student personnel services professionally: the humanitarians, the administrators, and the scientists, more especially psychologists. The humanitarians came upon the American scene first and continue to be recruited in fairly large numbers. Next came the first wave of administrators, but a second wave has been more important. Then came the psychologists—first the tests-and-measurement psychologists and next their clinical brothers. These three kinds of personnel people seem to have little in common; hence; the so-called student personnel movement is not a movement at all, but, instead, a collection of independent wheels turning at different rates and often in different directions.

Consider first the humanitarians. Most deans of women, many deans of men, but only a few deans of students belong to their numbers. They are the people who have come into the field primarily because they want to help others. As students or as faculty members, they were appalled by the impersonalism of research-minded professors and the resulting failure of colleges and universities to give students the individual, extra-instructional help so many of them need. They have become personnel workers because essentially they want to do good in the world especially among college students.

The humanitarians have made and continue to make precious contributions to student personnel work; but they incline as a group, recalling William James' classification, to be tender-minded rather than tough-minded. Frequently, therefore, they tend to be sentimentalists in the Deweyan definition of sentimentalism: they often advocate building Utopias without knowing much about architecture and construction engineering. Student personnel services, like all enterprises, need humanitarians—but not too many of them.

The first wave of student personnel administrators came largely from the rank of the humanitarians, and some of them became distorted sentimentalists—that is, individuals who still believe in Utopia and will use any means to bring it into being—and, thus, dangerous people. However, the second wave of administrators includes few simon-pure humanitarians. By and large, those who have come into the field during the past 25 years to administer the huge co-ordinated programs that have developed have been appointed primarily because of their administrative ability rather than because of any compelling interest in students. They are primarily executives in charge of large and important operations.

They come from a wide range of backgrounds: people from almost every subject-matter department, some from industry, and some from other administrative units of colleges and universities. They are the top dogs of the enterprise. They deal with presidents and academic deans; they wangle budgets; they direct the work of staffs that steadily increase in size; but generally they are too busy to talk with students other than presidents of student organizations or those in serious trouble with the administration.

Other limitations seem to include, first, inadequate knowledge of the backgrounds and trends of American higher education in the broad; second, relative ignorance of the preoccupations and points of view of the specialists who work under their direction; and third, an inclination to solve problems by rule of thumb rather than by the slower but more effective method of careful study.

Even though psychologists often take credit for initiating the student personnel movement, they arrived on the scene late. They did not appear until just after World War I; but with their tests, their correlations, and their counseling techniques they rapidly took the center of the stage. Tough-minded in sharp contrast to their tender-minded humanitarians and zealously evangelical for their cause in comparison with the relatively placid administrators, they have jostled both of their groups of associates into frequent antagonism. Yet, they have brought much of incalculable value into student personnel work; and, because of the solid facts they have gathered, they have probably had more to do than any other group with giving the program status with administrators, faculty members, students, and the general public. Every time anyone uses a student's I.Q. or intelligence percentile rating, he salutes the work of the psychologists. Every time an institution modifies its admissions program in the light of studies of the criteria involved, it acknowledges its debt to psychologically initiated concepts. Every time a college or university improves its counseling program, it endorses conclusions reached by psychological investigators.

Beyond doubt, psychologists needed to be engrossed until recently in measuring the capacities of individuals and in amplifying counseling conceptions and procedures. These scientific sectors of the personnel field had to be plowed and cultivated first and must be kept productive. The time appears to have come, however, when more attention should be given to issues involving group psychology—in brief, to the social psychology and sociology of student life.

At least 7,500 persons devote all of their working time to student personnel activities, an average of four in each of the 1,900 colleges and universities of the country. Probably this is too conservative an estimate, and in any case it must be supplemented by the large number who do part-time counseling. These workers come from a wide variety of backgrounds and have many kinds of training and a miscellany of points of view with no recognizable common core of knowledge of, interest in, or commitment to student personnel work. Only a minority are organized into a number of non-co-operating and, what is worse, non-communicating national associations.

Perhaps, at this stage of the student personnel movement such topsy-turviness is inevitable. One day, however, some will conclude that something should be done to pull the sprawl together. Toward that end I have some suggestions.

I begin with two negative proposals. First, it would be folly to try to organize a national association seeking the membership of all personnel people in secondary schools, colleges, and universities. An attempt to do this has been made, and it failed. The interests and loyalties of those in higher education differ so markedly from those in secondary education that all such efforts must inevitably fizzle. Second, it would be similarly profitless to propose to existing organizations—such as the National Association of Deans of Women and the American Association of Collegiate Registrars and Admissions Officers—that they should go out of business. They would be understandably deaf to the suggestion. They have important functions to perform and will continue to perform them. Yet, somehow, all student personnel people should be helped to understand their common interests and their common destiny. The question is how.

My proposal is that this association, in co-operation with any or all of the other 15 in existence which care to join, undertake the establishment of an agency to serve all higher educational personnel workers. For a modest fee the agency could put upon the desk of every subscriber every week a communication something like the Kiplinger Letter. Its essential function would be to keep student personnel people in touch with the major activities and thought of their field. Some of the letters would include only succinct news items; some would report one or two conspicuously important events; some would give brief abstracts of leading articles and addresses; some would be entirely devoted to epitomes of outstanding books; and some would review all important research completed.

How would an agency be organized? Who would edit the weekly letter? What group would make the agency's policies? How much would its services cost? These, clearly, are basic questions; but they and others like them have workable answers which would soon emerge should the desire for these services be widespread enough and strong enough.

The agency would not be a panacea, of course, but it would constitute a significant beginning toward meeting the three needs—helping all groups of personnel workers in higher education better to understand one another, supplying them with information about the historical and current frontiers of their own terrains and of the enterprise in general, and promoting needed research in presently neglected areas.

III

Conflicts and New Theories

College and university campuses, characterized by a period of growth, pride, and relative tranquility during the previous decade, are to be significantly and permanently affected by the dramatic events of the 1960's. This decade, referred to as the "age of student activism," the "downfall of *in loco parentis* and the rise of legalism," and the "years of civil disobedience," produced a body of literature that echoed both traditional perspectives and respected elder statespersons of the profession and heralded the beginnings of a new philosophical and theoretical orientation to the functions to be performed by student affairs practitioners.

Four major themes can be identified in this section of literature: 1) the pressure being applied within higher education to implement various practices and techniques of the business and corporate world to insure cost effective management; 2) the necessity to reexamine the need for and the roles of individual student personnel workers; 3) the descriptions, explanations and reactions to the erupting patterns of student behavior; and 4) the beginnings of a movement later to be called student development.

Shaffer (1961) recognizes that traditional organizational lines have divided the academic community into separate and distinct segments of influence and specialization. He argues for effective education, which will not be realized without an integration of the goals and efforts of faculty, student personnel workers and students. Cooperative relationships must be formed by student affairs personnel if the significant problems identified by Shaffer as confronting higher education are to be resolved.

Crookston and Blaesser (1962) provide an early example of attempts

179

to implement another perspective on the collegiate environment by suggesting the application of Lewin's force-field analysis to issues within student affairs. Viewing the campus environment as shifting between states of equilibrium and disequilibrium depending on constraining and restraining factors, the authors perceive change as the only constant. The new function for the practitioner, therefore, is to plan systematically for change rather than to react to its effects. Crookston and Blaesser are, in a sense, leading the way to the future conceptualization of the professional role as that of change agent.

The renewal of the image of student personnel work in higher education is the focus of Hardee's ACPA presidential address in 1963. From an assumption that the efforts of student personnel workers are integrated with the aims and labors of faculty and the belief that the student personnel program is comprehensive, she recommends that ACPA members contribute to the efforts of the Committee of Academic Affairs of the American Council on Education and the Interassociation Coordinating Committee (IACC), later to become COSPA. For Hardee ACPA must be heard at the national, regional and state levels influencing legislation affecting students, student personnel workers, and their campuses.

An elder statesperson, W. H. Cowley (1964), admonishes current members of the profession for their lack of progress made toward solving issues that he himself confronted in 1938 as a neophyte professional. His contribution of the centric triad as a measure of maturity and status of any field of human activity tells us that our profession has not yet attainted adulthood. Cowley believes that the purpose and functions of student personnel work reside within the complementary sphere of academe; that is, extrainstructional services. Teaching and research are the domain of the faculty and together represent the core function of higher education.

The traditional void between faculty and student affairs professionals begins to be bridged with Trueblood's vision (1965) that the student personnel practitioner will be an educator rather than a procedural technician. The educator's focus of concern will be not only the college student, but also the campus environment.

Using the theoretical framework of Erikson, Kirk (1965) reminds the ACPA convention members that for a profession "to have an identity

. . . we must be recognized and perceived by others" (p. 198). This is the path she suggests as a means of overcoming the identity crisis that gripped ACPA and its members in the latter part of the 1960's. She pleads for a reexamination of values, the creation of innovative methods and the importance of introspection suggesting that members seek that which is internally consistent as the core of beliefs that will survive in future years.

The effects of the womens' movement and student activism as well as an emphasis on accountability help to form the environmental context in which Berdie poses questions about student personnel's identity and purpose. His perception is that student personnel is a part of rather than "different but not apart from other persons and functions in higher education" (p. 240). The methods and purposes of higher education are considered to parallel the methods and purposes of student personnel work. If the role as educator is to become a viable one for the student affairs practitioner, Berdie argues that the skills and competencies of the practitioner must be merged with the functioning of academic administrators.

In contrast to past labels of student personnel officer or worker, Mueller (1966) recommends that we serve as student personnel administrators whose task it is to deal with students in a tertiary relationship rather than a primary or face-to-face basis. She underscores the disadvantages inherent in the increasingly large and complex bureaucratic organizations found on many campuses that result in students being forced to confront the institution.

Humanism as an early and recurring orientation to life and education, receives additional support by Williamson (1967) when he suggests a series of significant questions and paradoxes for the profession. Our mission as deans, he reminds us, is to become "thinkers and researchers"; to help students achieve their potentiality as humane beings.

Another ACPA presidential address mirrors the identity crisis in which the profession found itself in the late 1960's. Greenleaf (1968) questions the future of student personnel administration asking how others in academe see us and concludes that the functions defined earlier by Leonard will persist although the methods or ways in which professionals perform them may undergo alteration.

The disappearance of the Protestant work-ethic is predicted by the year 2000 by Tripp (1968). The next thirty-two years will witness a greater understanding of "Life as a continuous process of change" and an increased respect for "humanness" (p. 280). The student personnel worker of the future will be redefined as a "scholar in student development" applying change agent strategies to achieve a phenomenological mission.

One of the earliest authors to suggest that the student personnel point of view is no longer viable, Penney (1968) identifies issues which will continue to prevent student affairs practitioners from gaining professional recognition on campuses. The increasing specialization of functional areas, the paucity of quality literature and a preoccupation with housekeeping responsibilities are contributing to the field's current identity crisis and low self-esteem.

Student Personnel Problems Requiring a Campus-Wide Approach

Robert H. Shaffer

The traditional organizational structure of colleges and universities has led to an artificial separation of duties for administrative purposes. This structure has led to a classification of many problems into academic, student personnel or business. In turn, this classification has militated against the marshalling of resources, wherever they might be in the campus community, to meet many pressing problems which cut across the artificial lines.

Effective education on the campus depends upon the degree to which the total environment or community provides a consistent, forceful stimulus in the direction of intellectual growth. Various duties within the educational enterprise may be assigned to specific offices. Assignment of responsibility to such offices does not make them solely responsible, however, nor does it free them of responsibility in other areas which might be delegated to other divisions of the college or university.

A significant challenge to educational administrators particularly in the years ahead is to exercise initiative and ingenuity in utilizing the total resources of their institution for the achievement of its objectives. This will require aggressive efforts to overcome the traditional tendency to divide the campus community into discrete line agencies each independent, in its opinion, of responsibility and authority for meeting problems classified as falling under another office.

Student personnel work has particularly suffered from this tendency. Some practitioners have carved little empires for themselves, possibly from feelings of insecurity. In other situations the "academic" or "business" personnel have been so relieved at divesting themselves from various student problems that they have heaved a sigh of relief at the creation of student personnel offices and have promptly disclaimed responsibility for such in the future.

There are a number of significant problems facing higher education which have some personnel implications but which require a unified, cooperative approach by all segments of the campus community. Among them would be at least the following:

1. *Securing a coherence among the many cultures and forces operative on the campus.* Such a coherence must arise from the integration of the goals and efforts of students and faculty alike. All elements of the college community contribute to student growth. Whether this growth is in the desired direction is a question of great concern to all educators. What the student learns in his out-of-class life, for example, determines to a great extent the attitudes, the aspirations, and the motivation he brings to the classroom and the level of achievement he attains there.

For this reason, not only student personnel workers are interested in this environmental influence. All staff members of the college are. It is not enough for the instructor to say, "You keep the residence halls quiet so my students can study and I'll educate them!" Frustrated and exasperated hall personnel can only reply, "If you would work them harder, they wouldn't feel they could play around all night and still make acceptable grades!"

The relation of student conduct to general scholastic achievement is almost exactly the same as the relation of good English usage and achievement in the English class. Some professors say to their colleagues in English, "For heaven's sake! Can't you do a better job of teaching these jokers to write?" The frustrated and exasperated English instructor can only reply, "If you would demand a higher quality of English in your written work, we could and would be able to do a better job."

The "yellow slip" plan used in a number of colleges is a good example of integrating efforts from a number of sources to motivate the student. At Indiana University the English Department provides gummed slips which the instructor in any class may paste to any piece of written work and check one of three comments:

The English in This Paper
Is Not Acceptable

___ It appears to be the result of carelessness. In the future I will expect you to write with more care.

___ The English in this paper is so poor that I have lowered your grade. It would pay you to write with more care.

___ You should take this paper to the Writing Clinic for assistance with your problems in writing. Report to the English Office for an appointment at the Clinic. Do this within the next week; then return this paper to me.

The Writing Clinic is available to any student having trouble with English. Information about it may be obtained at the English Office.

Closer agreement on the goals and objectives by all segments of a college and the aggressive realignment of all forces within the campus community is essential to a vital and effective academic effort. While the student personnel worker is interested in this effort, he must to be successful direct his interest and work towards organizing, uniting and cooperating with all other elements in the university.

2. *Facilitating the conscious and effective interpretation of the concepts of a college, a college education and a college educated person.*

The best interest of any enterprise demands that all associated with it clearly understand its objectives both over-all and of its component parts. Students particularly need to understand what the college feels to be a good education, what it feels to be marks of its greatness and success, and what it expects of its graduates.

Just as a definite relationship exists between communication and employee productivity in a business enterprise, so in the educational enterprise, is there a definite relationship between the effectiveness of the communication of the spirit and meaning of the college and the productivity of its students.

Many students have goals other than those felt by the college to be of primary importance. Such students are satisfied with the relative satisfaction of these goals and usually feel little disturbance if they do not live up to the expectancies of the college. This is particularly true when the expectancies of the college are vaguely stated and communicated. Because they feel satisfied when their own goals are met to a minimum degree, they sincerely do not understand or are not greatly disturbed by anguished cries of faculty members and educational critics that our colleges are not doing an adequate job.

It is important that every institution examine carefully what it is doing to interpret more effectively to its students its nature, goals and expectancies. Included in such an examination should be analysis of literature sent to prospective students, orientation procedures, the approach and content of the opening days of classes, the public relations and alumni programs, the campus extra-curricular program and, particularly, the dominant forces in the student culture.

The importance of this latter aspect of the campus, the student culture, has been emphasized by the reports on the studies at Vassar.

"The student body as an entity may be thought to possess characteristic qualities of personality, ways of interacting socially, types of values and beliefs, and the like, which are passed on from one "generation" of students to another and which like any culture provide a basic context in which individual learning takes place. We contend, in fact, that this culture is the prime educational force at work in the College, for, as we shall see, assimilation into the student society is the foremost concern of most students. Suffice it to say now that in our opinion the scholastic and academic aims and processes of the College are in large measure transmitted to incoming students or mediated for them by the predominant students culture."[1]

Thus, any consideration of securing a more coherent campus environment and interpreting the meaning and significance of this environment to students must take into account the values, the status figures, and forces prevalent in the campus culture.

3. *Assisting each student in understanding the revelance of higher education to his life and problems.*

The writings of the last few years on the relationship, or probably more accurately, the lack of relationship between the formation of certain values and a college education document the need for attention to this function. If colleges are to have serious, motivated and thinking students on their campuses, they must help their students see their college experience as more than a passage of time, the accumulation of credit hours, or merely training to earn a better living.

Nevitt Sanford, also reporting on the Vassar research, concluded that students "perceive the curriculum as more or less irrelevant and look to each other for the instruction that really matters."[2] His observa-

1. Freedman, Mervin B., "The Passage Through College," *The Journal of Social Issues*, 12:4, 1956, p. 14.
2. Stanford, Nevitt, "Changing Sex Roles, Socialization, and Education," *Human De-*

tion had particular reference to sex roles in society but are applicable equally to other societal issues. Whether or not his observations and those of such writers as Jacob, Eddy, and others are completely accurate, the function of helping the student find real meaning in his college experience is an important and necessary one. The personnel program should provide agencies or stimulate forces which will organize resources in the college community to perform this function.

4. *Re-orienting the orientation program.*

Traditionally, orientation programs have tended to emphasize physical and social orientation to the possible exclusion of orientation to the academic and cultural environment. Student personnel workers have given the new freshman tests, told him about the health service, introduced him to the campus, mixed him with students of the opposite sex, taught him the school song and yells, introduced him to the campus leaders and athletes, organized him into groups, and then, at the end of so-called orientation week, dumped him into class with a sigh of relief.

Critical analysis of the content of many of our orientation weeks really reveals them to be dis-orientation weeks when judged by the extent to which the student was introduced to the fact that college is a challenging, disturbing, perhaps even a shocking experience, and one which will demand more from him in the way of self-discipline and motivation than he has been called upon to exercise previously.

It is necessary that student personnel workers review their approach to orientation to make certain the major emphasis is made unmistakably clear amid all the procedural and social exercises. Orientation is a function of the whole institution, not just that of the personnel worker.

5. *Emphasizing that the student must assume responsibility for his education, exercise self-discipline in his behavior and provide self-direction in his personal and intellectual growth.*

Symptoms of the failure of higher education in this regard range all the way from panty raids to cheating on one continuum, usually the dean's, and from choosing easy courses to doing just enough to get by on another continuum, usually the faculty's.

Sound personnel practice is based upon the principle that every contact with a student should lead to his increased independence and abil-

---

velopment Bulletin on the Ninth Annual Symposium, Committee on Human Development, University of Chicago, 1958, p. 66.

ity to handle his problems on his own in the future. Yet many colleges and universities in their relations with students, parents and the public attempt to assume a degree of responsibility which robs society of an important lesson it must learn if higher education is to be truly higher education. That lessons is the fact that a college student must grow up and assume certain responsibilities for himself.

The concept of *in loco parentis* should not lead colleges to assume more authority than the parents themselves would exercise if the students were at home during the comparable four years. Colleges properly have all sorts of personnel workers and aids to help the student achieve this independence and self-discipline but it is important for the whole collegiate community to make certain of the direction of such work. Certainly, student personnel agencies should strive to avoid being what one professor describes them; namely, a "haven for the incompetent."

Faculty members need to review their thinking in this area with care. Many will endorse without reservation the ideas expressed above. Yet in another context they will demand that personnel workers eliminate such time-wasting activities as queen contests, fraternities, automobiles, social affairs, and campus marriages.

Involved in the question is the achievement of a balance between the authority exercised by the institution in all its areas and the freedom granted to students. Vice President Haskew of the University of Texas has described the situation well when he characterized present practice in higher education as one of:

"such alternation between the practice of authority and the practice of freedom that the student is left with nothing more than rudderless motive power . . . . Some schools deal with this issue on the basis of self-defense, I fear, championing enough freedom to keep students reasonably happy and practicing enough authority to keep teachers from resigning . . .

"On three points the protagonists of freedom, the protagonists of authority, and perhaps all the rest of us are agreed. One is that we are not satisfied with the results to date of society's efforts to resolve this issue. The second is that the synthesis to be worked out must include elements of both freedom and authority. The third is that a synthesis for schools is integral with a synthesis for the family and for the community."[3]

3. Haskew, Laurence D., "The Fields Are White Unto Harvest," *Teachers College Record*, 57:6, March, 1956, p. 349.

6. *Developing the optimum use of housing facilities for educational purposes.*

American higher education has passed from the dormitory era, when halls were thought of as a place for the students to sleep and eat while they were being educated in the classroom, to the residence hall era when programming in the halls was emphasized for social and cultural ends. The next phase will surely be the integration of the living-unit program into closer relationship with the academic and intellectual life of the institution. Artificial distinctions between business, personnel and academic interests must be eliminated in favor of a careful analysis of the most effective organization and operation of the halls and other types of housing from the point of view of the entire institution and its institutional objectives.

Residence hall libraries, seminar and classrooms, writing clinics, budgeted aid for educational and cultural programs and faculty relations, and many other innovations must all be considered. These developments are not new on the educational scene. What is new in present-day thinking is the point that provision of funds and expenditure of energy must be directed with the thought of utilizing them where they will accomplish the most from the point of view of education, not from artificial distinctions or past custom. Attention particularly must be directed to experiences of other institutions to see what adaptations might be made or what programs might be adopted even if similar funds or facilities are not immediately available. Too many educational administrators have dismissed promising developments without consideration because their particular institutions did not have the special funds or grants others might have.

7. *Striving for the development in each student of a strong feeling of identification with his college.*

This feeling is not necessarily related to agreement with the stated objectives of the college or even with its efforts to have the highest possible academic standards. Rather, it is a feeling of belonging to and possessing a part of the institution.

American higher education seems to be doing this very well as a whole. In *What College Students Think*,[4] Goldsen and her colleagues re-

4. Goldsen, Rose *et al*, *What College Students Think*, Princeton, N.J., D. Van Nostrand Co., 1960.

port the strongly personal feeling most students in all the eleven universities studied had towards their individual institutions. They did not see them as impersonal entities with just an educational function. Instead most students at each institution saw it as having its own personality over and above the individual students in it.

Such a feeling of identification provides a base for efforts to integrate students and their cultures into the efforts of the total institution. It does not preclude strong criticism of phases of the college, nor should it, but it does furnish a positive basis evaluating differences among and between student groups, eliminating misunderstandings and integrating effort towards common objectives.

Failure to develop further and to use this asset in the years immediately ahead will constitute sheer administrative and professional incompetence.

8. *Assisting institutions in the development of effective positive public relations programs defined in the best and broadest sense of the term.*

Every institution created by a society has the obligation to interpret its work and functions to that society. It is almost a tragedy for higher education that intellectuals as a group have built up such a feeling of disdain if not antagonism toward the concept of public relations for higher education. An important contribution of student personnel work is to work with administrative officers and students in developing a program to explain and interpret the rational way of life, its importance to free society, its essential elements, and the support society must give its institutions if they are to progress in effectiveness and significance.

If the colleges and universities of the country do an effective job with the students currently enrolled, both in giving them something of real value and in helping them understand what it is they have, there should be no real difficulty in explaining the needs and problems of higher education to the various publics involved.

Related to all of the preceding points but particularly the latter, is the importance of the image the students of any institution have of themselves and their institution. In all colleges and universities there are greater resources for a higher quality education than most educators and students recognize. In their student bodies there are probably greater talents, abilities and personalities than commonly recognized. Basic to a release of their latent educational potentialities is the destruction of the image of college students as irresponsible youngsters and the widely held idea that a quality education can be secured in only a small number of colleges and universities across the country.

A systematic approach to this problem area will up-grade higher education very greatly but will require the cooperative efforts of all segments of the educational world. Student personnel workers are in a strategic position to assist in the advancement of such a program because of their relationship with students, parents, high schools and student activities. This is not to imply that a superficial image-building campaign is in order. An effective program can be developed on the highest professional and ethical planes.

In summary, there are a number of pressing problems facing higher education in which the student personnel aspect seems to be particularly important. However, these problems will not be solved by student personnel workers alone because they involve all aspects of campus life. Student personnel administrators specifically and higher education administrators in general must take the lead in overcoming narrow organizational lines to mobilize all resources available in the educational community to meet these problems.

An Approach to Planned Change in a College Setting

Burns B. Crookston and Willard W. Blaesser

Death, taxes, and change are among the inevitable elements of life to-day. In contrast with the first two, change has the potential of improvement, depending upon our value system, as it relates to a particular situation. Change, whether "good" or "bad," has been given increased and more systematic attention during recent years, particularly in the organizational settings of business and industry. There is pressure upon managers as part of their major organizational responsibility to diagnose changes in process, to predict the nature and extent of change in the years ahead, to identify changes which seem more urgent, and deliberately to plan and help execute certain changes. Training departments are asked to develop in-service training programs which will help lower, middle, and top management to work more effectively toward improvements in the total organization. Managers are frequently sent to training laboratories, institutes and courses which include emphasis on skills of analyzing and carrying out change potentialities in organizational settings.

Colleges and universities appear to be giving less attention to systematic approaches to change within their institutional settings. Many have utilized management surveys to outline recommendations for changes in structure and function. Usually these are accomplished by outside consulting firms which are not available for continuing service and training functions. Faculty committees often study various phases of the college program, usually curricula, and develop plans for improvement. However, the concept of deliberate and continued planning for change as the responsibility of administration, teaching faculty, and student personnel staff does not seem to be recognized as a responsibility of higher education today.

Yet, the idea that considerable change will occur in higher education

192

during the sixties has wide acceptance. Yeast-like rises predicted for both costs and enrollments portend enforced, if not planned, change. Clearly, student personnel programs will be among those affected. In fact recent literature contains frequent references to the need for student personnel administrators and counselors to prepare for working with a far greater number of students per staff member. Additional pressures identified include: proliferation of student personnel functions which increase communication, human relations, and efficiency problems; demand for more intensive "pursuit of excellence"; decreasing time of teaching faculty for advising students; depersonalization caused by the "mass" approach; and the need for more and better evaluation and research with less time and money. The elements of planned change outlined in this article, while directed toward a student personnel program, may also prove useful if applied to other aspects of the college program.

Changes in college student personnel programs are typically brought about in diverse ways—through administrative fiat, staff turnover, financial ups and downs, recommendations from faculty and student committees, marshaling of data from local, regional and national research, or pressure groups from students, faculty, administration, alumni and surrounding community. Planned change involves carrying out a decision to effect improvements in a given setting by means of a systematic methodology. In student programs, as in other phases of higher education, it seems that little attention is given to planned change. However, it is possible that more planned change is taking place than appears in the literature.

In any event it is likely that most student personnel workers would agree that more could be done about the nature and direction of "change" in the college student personnel program.

Force-Field Analysis

One useful scheme for thinking about change has been proposed by Kurt Lewin [4]. He described it as a level or phase of behavior within an institutional setting, not as a static "habit" or "custom," but as a dynamic balance of the institution. An example would be a production level of work teams in a factory. This level tends to fluctuate, but, by and large, the pattern persists at a given level over a period of time. The reason, according to Lewin, is that the forces which tend to raise the level of production are equal to the forces that tend to depress it [4].

Examples of forces which might raise the level of production are: (a) pressure by supervision on the work team to produce more; (b) desire of some team members to "look good" and therefore get ahead individually; (c) the desire of team members to earn more under the plant incentive plan; and so on. Lewin called these *driving forces*.

Forces tending to lower the level of production might be: (m) a work group standard that a team member should do no more than a certain amount of work; (n) team resistance to accepting training programs which would increase productivity; (o) feelings by the workers that their product is not important; and so on. These are *restraining forces*. When these sets of forces balance each other a certain level of production is established which Lewin called quasi-stationary equilibrium. This equilibrium may be diagrammed as follows:

Force-Field Diagram

Restraining forces	(m)	(n)	(o)	. . . (etc.)
	↓	↓	↓	↓

Present level of
    production   Quasi-stationary Equilibrium

	↑	↑	↑	↑
Driving forces	(a)	(b)	(c)	. . . (etc.)

Change takes place when an imbalance occurs between the sum of the driving forces and the sum of the restraining forces. Such an imbalance "unfreezes" the pattern and the level changes until the opposing forces are again brought into equilibrium. An imbalance may occur through a change in the *magnitude* of any force, a change in the *direction* of a force, and/or an *addition* of a new force.

Suppose that members of the work team join a new union which is challenging the over-all wage structure of the company. This may heighten dissatisfaction with current policy and increase workers' suspicion toward management motives, including supervisors. The results may increase restraining force (n); the equilibrium is unfrozen and the level of production moves down unless increasing driving forces also take place. In the present illustration as the production level falls, supervisors increase their pressure toward greater production and driving force (a) tends to increase. Thus, the increased counterforce brings the system into balance again somewhere near the previous level. These are changes in *magnitude* and may create problems. An increase in magnitude of opposing forces may heighten tension and make the situation less amenable to rational control.

A war situation demanding greater productivity may convert restraining force (o) from a feeling that the product is not important to a feeling that the product is important and that one should work harder to assist in the war effort. The level of production will rise as the direction of force (o) is reversed to help elevate production until a state of equilibrium is reached at a higher level.

Suppose a new driving force is added when a supervisor wins the trust and respect of the working team. The new force motivates the working team to make the well-liked supervisor look good. This force may operate to offset a generally unfavorable attitude toward management. Or the work team, by setting their own standards of production as a result of a different supervising approach, may significantly reduce restraining force (m) [2].

Force-Field Analysis in a Student Personnel Program

The force-field model has been used by researchers and practitioners in various organizational settings during the past dozen years. Can this conceptual approach be utilized in helping with planned change in a college setting? One aspect of a student personnel program may serve as an affirmative illustration:

Suppose one of the goals of the student personnel program is to stimulate and assist student leaders more closely to identify the student activities program with the intellectual objectives of the university. The force-field situation is described in the accompanying diagram.

Table 1
Force-Field Diagram of Degree of Identification of
Student Activities with Institutional Intellectual Objectives

Restraining forces	(m)	(n)	(o)	(p)	. . . (etc.)
	Feeling of student leaders that present student activities program is adequate	Counter dependence: against idea because faculty and administration are for it	Student feeling that intellectual activities should be confined to the classroom	Faculty disinterest in spending time with students outside the classroom	
	↓	↓	↓	↓	↓
Present situation		Quasi-stationary equilibrium			
	↑	↑	↑	↑	↑
Driving forces	(a)	(b)	(c)	(d)	. . . (etc.)
	Efforts of faculty advisers, personnel deans, residence hall, union, and other personnel staff members	General faculty and administration concern that student activities are busy-work and anti-intellectual	Group of student "intellectuals" have requested such a program	Community reaction against student emphasis on social life and "college escapades"	

These sets of forces are in quasi-stationary equilibrium. It is recalled that change takes place when an imbalance occurs between the sum of the driving forces and the sum of the restraining forces.

Suppose a student-faculty committee appointed to develop a new honors program attacks student activities as anti-intellectual and a waste of time. Their report is circulated among faculty and printed in the student newspaper. The committee action increases driving forces (a) and (b), thus tending to move the situation toward intellectually oriented programs. But the attack on student activities as being inadequate is responded to strongly and defensively by the student leaders, thus increasing restraining force (n). The result would be the force field system coming into balance again, somewhere near the previous level.

These opposing changes in magnitude, as in the factory example, may increase tension and stress, thus making the entire situation less stable and predictable.

Suppose a series of exploratory seminars is arranged for the student leaders with several articulate and highly respected faculty members discussing the nature of a university. This may convert restraining force (m) from a feeling that the present student activities program is adequate to a feeling that it is inadequate. Thus, a restraining force becomes converted to a driving force. Hence, concern for the role of student activities becomes more closely identified with the objectives of the university and raises the student activity program to a new level. In addition, faculty satisfaction with participating in the seminars may result in reducing restraining force (p).

Finally, suppose a new driving force is added. As a result of an in-service training program student personnel staff members acquire new skills and insights in working with student leaders. This new force may result in strengthening driving force (a) and reducing restraining force (n).

In brief, the three major strategies for achieving change in a given situation are: (a) increasing the driving forces, (b) decreasing the restraining forces or (c) a combination of the two. The strategy of increasing the driving forces, as pointed out earlier, creates higher tension. It is therefore better to initiate a change effort with the second or third strategy listed as these are more stable, more predictable, and less threatening [5, 8].

The examples utilized suggest that change takes the form of unfreezing—upward or downward movement—refreezing. In planned change, forces must be arranged or refrozen to prevent backsliding. Change in any human situation is often followed by a backward reaction toward the "old ways" after the pressures toward change are relaxed. For example, following a survey, a college puts into effect recommended changes under pressure of the board of trustees. As vigilance relaxes, old patterns creep in. Whenever change is effected it is important that the "refreezing" at a new level will be stable. Not only must the forces "for" change be analyzed, but the new restraining and/or driving forces which will exist after the change must be anticipated as clearly as possible.

In planning for change it is important to identify all relevant driving and restraining forces impinging upon the given situation. Of equal importance is the taking into account the many neutral, uncommitted, or unknown forces. Changes in one force field situation are likely to affect others directly or indirectly related to it. For example, a change in student activities toward more intellectually oriented programs might result not only in other student activities being discarded but might also mean involving many more faculty in student activities than anticipated. Some of the faculty involved might as a result of their experiences with students in these settings experiment with new approaches in their classroom teaching. Moreover, the identification of these uncommitted forces might make possible their utilization as driving rather than restraining forces. For example, in the foregoing illustration the student newspaper may be uncommitted. Whether the newspaper becomes a driving or restraining force might be crucial as attempts are made to unfreeze and refreeze the situation.

A Case Illustration

The following case example of a force-field situation on a state university campus is a further illustration of the use of such a model as a way of analyzing and effecting change. One of the goals of the University student personnel program has been to help the fraternity system become more closely identified with the University and its educational objectives. The force-field situation as it appeared in 1954–1955 is diagrammed in Table 2.

Among the more important driving forces were (a) pressure on fraternities by the fraternity dean and the administration to produce more meaningful chapter programs and to become more closely identified and cooperative with the University; (b) some fraternity leaders recognized the need for a closer fraternity identification with university objectives and were attempting to get the fraternities to change in this direction; (c) the need for new fraternity houses meant developing closer ties with the University, since the only land available for such houses was owned by the University; and (d) some faculty members and townspeople were attacking fraternities as anti-intellectual and were advocating their abolishment.

Major restraining forces were (m) fraternity suspicion and distrust of

Table 2
Force-Field Diagram of Degree of Fraternity Identification
with the Educational Objectives of the University

(m)	(n)	(o)	(p)	... (etc.)
Suspicion and distrust of university motives based on fact and fiction of past dealings with the administration	Feeling of fraternity members that the present situation is adequate, due in part to lack of understanding and concern with university educational objectives	Traditional counter-dependency: desire to be free from university "control"	Tendency to become defensive and withdraw further when criticized	
↓	↓	↓	↓	↓

Quasi-stationary equilibrium

↑	↑	↑	↑	↑
(a)	(b)	(c)	(d)	... (etc.)
Pressure on fraternities by dean and administration to produce better chapter programs	Some fraternity leaders recognize need for closer fraternity identification with the university	Need for new fraternity housing means closer ties since only land available is owned by university	Some faculty and town people attack fraternities as anti-intellectual and advocate their abolishment	

University motives based on factual and fictional reports of past dealings with the administration; (n) the feeling among fraternity members that the present fraternity situation is adequate, coupled with an unwillingness to evaluate current programs and face their problems; (o) the traditional counter-dependency of fraternity members: their need to be aggressively resistant to parental and other authority symbols, which is reflected in their desire to be free from University "control"; and (p) the tendency of fraternities to become defensive when criticized, thus withdrawing further from the University orbit.

An initial strategy directed toward heightening fraternity identification with University educational objectives was to reduce restraining force (m), fraternity suspicion and distrust of University motives. This could be initiated by reducing driving force (a), thus lessening pressure on fraternities by the administration. The appointment of a new fraternity Dean, who was skilled in human relations and experienced in working with fraternities, implemented the reduction of driving force (a). Thus within a year restraining force (m) was considerably reduced, making it possible for driving force (b) and restraining force (n) to become the next leverage point. Having developed new fraternity confidence and trust in the administration, it became possible to add a new driving force, consisting of a series of workshops and conferences with individual fraternities, fraternity leaders, and the interfraternity council. These were directed toward evaluating individual fraternity programs heightening understanding of fraternity and university objectives, and planning programs of improvement. Hence driving force (b) was augmented by increasing the number of fraternity leaders and members who recognized a need for a closer fraternity identification with the University. The result was the reduction of restraining force (n), from the feeling of satisfaction to dissatisfaction with the present fraternity situation on the part of many members. Restraining force (n) therefore became converted in part to a driving force.

Meanwhile an additional new force was introduced by the creation of an alumni interfraternity council, whose major objectives included facilitating mutual understanding between the University and alumni groups and working toward the acquirement of University land for the construction of fraternity houses, thus increasing driving force (c). Shortly thereafter, however, the University administration made public its priority list for the long-range building program on campus. The "campus of 1970" projection did not include provision for fraternity houses. These announcements brought about a resurgence of fraternity suspicion and distrust of the University administration, which increased restraining force (m). Hence the quasi-stationary equilibrium was pushed down somewhere near its original level. In 1957 a survey of fraternity housing needs by the alumni interfraternity council was reported to the board of regents. The result was the passage of a resolution by the board of regents, recognizing the urgent need for fraternity housing and favoring fraternity housing on campus when land became available. This increase of driving force (c) tended to reduce restraining force (m) and raise the quasi-stationary equilibrium level. More recently a fraternity study committee, consisting of faculty members, fraternity members, other students, administrators, and regents was appointed by the president. Outcomes of the study would be to define University and community goals and expectations for fraternities, to anticipate potential developments and needed changes, and to plan accordingly. It is hoped that the fraternities themselves will become deeply involved with the project. The appointment of the study committee as a new driving force may reduce driving force (d) and convert restraining force (p) from defensiveness and withdrawal to honest self-criticism and willingness to collaborate towards improved programs.

In five years the level of fraternity identification with the educational objectives of the University has heightened somewhat. There have been ups and downs, and there are likely to be additiional set-backs in the future. An understanding of the forces at work in the situation will help in the minimizing of restraining forces, and by bringing the right forces into play at the right time it is hoped that the level of equilibrium will continue to rise as more meaningful programs are developed.

Force-field analysis can be utilized in other college areas where the need for planned change is indicated; for example, to facilitate communication among expanding departments as enrollments mount; to establish more effective articulation with high schools directed toward stimulation of gifted students; to help departments find and take the time for continuing research and evaluation; to get teachers and counselors to collaborate toward the total education of the student; or more simply, to help personnel workers and instructors relate more effectively and productively with each other.

Additional Guideposts

The problems which have been summarized exist in most if not all colleges and universities. Usually there is motivation to bring about improvements—to effect "planned change." It is difficult, however, to come to grips with the complex human and organizational forces within a college setting. A force-field analysis, one systematic method of diagramming situations in which organizational change is desired, has been described. Regardless of what approach is used, it is clear that the rate of change will be strongly accelerated in the years ahead. Controlled or planned change will come about only by means of some type of systematic methodology. Force-field analysis is the core of an approach which colleges and universities may find useful.

Administrators, instructors, or personnel workers desiring to collaborate in effecting planned change will have in mind further guideposts or principles as they develop their approach. Some of these can be briefly noted.

The processes of change within an institution can be constructive only if conditions permit reassessment of goals and the means to their achievement. If a college is to function in relation to the changing needs of faculty, students, and community, it must provide for an objective evaluation. A responsibility of each staff member is to help build the climate within which he and his associates can think and act upon facts in a manner different from the usual norms. Such a climate would encourage both academic and student personnel departments to make periodic self-studies which may lead toward change as results are analyzed and acted upon.

A most powerful barrier to organizational change is the resistance which persons can express when a projected change seems threatening to roles in which they have invested considerable security. The process of change is facilitated by the following conditions suggested by Coffey and Golden [3]:

a. When leadership is moving as far as possible in the direction of participative action and group members have optimal freedom to participate in decision-making.

b. When norms have become established which make changing (innovating, inventing, experimenting) an expected aspect of institutional development.

c. When change can be brought about without threatening the individual's membership in a group.

d. When the group concerned with a change or trying to change has a strong sense of belongingness, is attractive to its members and when it is concerned with satisfying members' needs.

e. When group members actively participate in the leadership functions, help formulate goals, plan the steps toward goal realization, have the freedom to "try out" new roles, and to participate in the assessment of these functions of leadership.

A change within a given group must be supported by the organizational structure or the group will become a target of mistrust by other groups in the organization. Therefore, communication must flow from one authority level to another, and proposals for change must be legitimatized within the organizational authority structure.

Changes in one part of an organization produces strain in other related parts which can be reduced to toleration only by eliminating the change or by bringing about adjustments in related parts. As in the earlier illustration, if the student activity program is changed toward more intellectually oriented activities, then greater demands upon faculty time and energy would result. Either the faculty would adjust to these increasing demands or the new program would fail.

A change attempt is most likely to be successfully introduced through an experimental approach [7]. This approach includes the continuous cycle of diagnosing a problem situation in the organization, planning action steps, taking these steps, and studying their results [6]. In this way, the process of planned change becomes an integrative force in an institution's developmental program.

References

1. Cartwright, D. Achieving change in people: some applications of group dynamics theory. Hum. Relat., 1951, 4, 381–392.
2. Coch, L., & French, J. R. P., Jr. Overcoming resistance to change. Hum. Relat., 1948, 1, 512–532.
3. Coffey, H. S., & Golden, W. P., Jr. Psychology of change within an institution. Fifty-sixth yearbook, National Society for the Study of Education. Chicago: University of Chicago Press, 1957.
4. Lewin, K. Frontiers in group dynamics. Hum. Relat., 1947, 1, 5–42.
5. Lewin, K. Group decision and social change, Swanson, G. E., Newcomb, T. N., & Hartley, E. L. (Eds.), Readings in social psychology (2nd Ed.). New York: Henry Holt, 1952.
6. Lippitt, R., Watson, Jeanne, & Wesley, B. The dynamics of planned change. New York: Harcourt, Brace, 1958.

7. Miles, M. B., & Passow, A. H. Training in the skills needed for inservice training programs. *Fifty-sixth yearbook*, National Society for the Study of Education. Chicago: University of Chicago Press, 1957.
8. National Training Laboratories in Group Development. *Reports of summer laboratory sessions*, twelfth, 1958: thirteenth, 1959. Washington, D.C.: National Education Association.

Perception and Perfection

Melvene Draheim Hardee

Directives and Directions

Presidential addresses show a singular affinity. If you were to examine them, you would find interlocking themes, recurrent ideas, as well as implied—if not outright—parting directives. In a very real sense, an outgoing president structures the life and times of the incoming officer.

Through the Lenses

By way of initial charting for these remarks, I shall cite my perceptions of ACPA at several levels—national, regional, state, local and global. Thereafter I shall make editorial comment about our professional image, commenting upon perfections which influence perceptions.

At the outset, may I describe the lenses by which I perceive? Throughout, I am defining *the place of student personnel work in higher education*. First, I am speaking of higher education as a field of specialty   a disci pline worthy of scholarly study in its own right. Currently there are some 93 graduate institutions which offer coursework in higher education—courses in the history of higher education, in organization and administration, in student personnel work, in curriculum and teaching, practicum and internship—these preparing candidates for positions of president, dean, controller, student personnel administrator or counselor, development officer, teacher, or researcher in junior or senior colleges and in universities and professional schools. This view of higher education (as a discipline worthy of scholarly study) is dramatized by the rapid growth not only of courses but also of full-blown departments of higher education. The inclusion of the major in student personnel work as a contributing area can be seen in the graduate programs of higher education.

Second, I regard student personnel work as an integral part of the educational enterprise in the 2,100 collegiate institutions of the country. My concept is one of a *comprehensive* program with the efforts of student personnel workers integrated as closely as possible with the instructional program and the curricular process. Those engaged in the total educational endeavor—including student personnel workers— must understand and thereafter articulate—(1) what they want students to learn, (2) what personal qualities they expect the college experience to include and, (3) as Ordway Tead affirms . . .

What kinds of adults with what kinds of competences they would like to be able to point to with pride in their graduates. . . .[1]

I believe that student personnel work must take its rightful place among the forces—instructional, administrative, managerial, noninstructional—that combine on a campus to effect this educational product of singular quality.

The National Scene

My visits to Washington in the past twelve months have been four— all of them "side saddle" trips for other main missions. It does not take long, in visiting thirty or more offices and agencies, to discover that the most powerful voice in Washington with respect to American higher education is that of the American Council on Education, composed of 1,000 member *institutions* and 175 member *organizations*. Currently our organization, ACPA, has a separate membership in the American Council, but it also holds another one-sixth membership by virtue of its Division I status in American Personnel and Guidance Association which is a constituent member of ACE.

1. Ordway Tead, *The Climate of Learning*, Harper and Brothers, New York 1958, p. 30.

You will recall that our association has enjoyed several decades of good working relationships with ACE, as can be seen in the impressive list of student personnel publications which began with *The Student Personnel Point of View* and continued with more recent releases, *They Come for the Best of Reasons* and *Spotlight on the College Student.*

At the bidding of our own Executive Council, I conferred last May in Washington with Dr. Logan Wilson, President of American Council on Education, inquiring about the way in which ACPA could figure in the work of the newly re-organized American Council. Dr. Wilson was quick to affirm that the work of our association was related to that of the newly designated Commission on Academic Affairs. He suggested we begin negotiations with the about-to-be-appointed chairman of this Commission, Mr. Lawrence Dennis.

As a result, conferences have taken place during the year both in Washington and Chicago. Mr. Dennis' participation in our program this week is testimony of the fact that negotiations have been mutually profitable, and thus, I share the first perception.

Perception 1: I have abiding confidence in the ability of ACPA to contribute meaningfully, through designated representatives, to the important work of the Commission on Academic Affairs of the American Council on Education. This meaningful participation, however, is dependent upon other perceptions to follow—a baker's dozen of them, twelve-plus-one, separate but inter-related.

Now, to keep the muscle of its ambition from atrophy, ACPA must be at the cutting edge of competence with respect to study of the profession of student personnel work, to the centrality of its philosophy and practice with respect to the whole of higher education. Both *intensive study* and *extensive participation* of members would seem to be two inseparable requisites.

Perception 2: The twelve commissions, activated in Summer 1961 for the designing of the Boston program appear to offer a convenient vehicle for continuing study of our profession. Some 250 persons have been attracted to the commission activity prior to Boston. For this convention the commissions have designated sixty-eight programs, utilizing 372 participants. The product of these permanent commissions would be reflected in convention programs in the future, in issues of the *Journal of College Student Personnel* and in the *ACPA Monograph Series*, the latter recognized as two communications media of growing excellence.

At your places, you will find a veritable blizzard of paper. From time to time, I shall refer to one or another item in this Easter gift packet. The first reference is to a copy of *Higher Education as a National Resource*. This booklet, made available to you through the offices of Mr. Charles Dobbins, Chairman of the Commission on Federal Relations of the American Council, bears the date of January, 1963, and urges the federal government to take early and definite action. This same information has been reprinted in the *Congressional Record* of Tuesday, January 19, 1963. In Section I, p. 5, you will note the proposal for student housing. In Section III, pp. 8–10, there will be found consideration of student loans, student grant assistance and international student exchanges. In Section IV, pp. 10–11, you will note the proposal, anticipated a year ago in our Chicago conference, relating to extension of guidance institutes to include college student personnel workers. Finally, on p. 12, of the brochure, it is stated that:

The American Council on Education is convinced that it speaks not only for organized higher education but also for a much broader American consensus when it asserts that the opportunity for quality education beyond the high school should be widened and deepened through Federal action.[2]

I am concerned with this statement. If ACE speaks for organized higher education, then it purportedly speaks with knowledge of what we in ACPA think, but how *does* our organization think with respect to student housing, student loans, grants and international exchanges, as well as in the matter of extending NDEA institutes to college personnel workers? Are the opinions of this association transmitted with clarity and force to key personnel who in turn speak with clarity and force into legislative ears?

There is, among the twelve study commissions of American College Personnel Association, one designated as Commission V, Student Financial Aids. This commission has drafted goals for working with recently appointed financial aids officers—surveying their functions and assisting in their professional upgrading. However, by affirmation of its chairman, Rexford Moon, Commission V plans *not* to enter into discussions which will attempt to influence legislation in this area.

Therefore, of the moment, ACPA must look *outside itself* for both initiating and implementing legislative goals in the area of financial aids. There are two possibilities visible—(1) through the parent organization, American Personnel and Guidance Association and (2) through the efforts of a newly-organized Joint Commission on Financial Aids under the sponsorship of the Inter Association Coordinating Committee.

Permit me to backtrack, as best I can, to recall the record of legislative activity affecting higher education in the past few months. On the tables you will find copies of the bill which has been under study by the House Committee on Education and Labor. (These publications have been contributed through the kind cooperation of Dr. John Russel, Chief of Faculty and Student Services, Division of Higher Education of the U.S. Office of Education.) Note, please, Title I covering college student loans and the college student work program. I have been asked by a number of you to reply to the question: *Has ACPA been heard with respect to particulars of this bill?*

Now, if you will re-cast your persisting question to read: *Can ACPA be heard with respect to the particularities of Title I,* I shall respond with a perception.

Perception 3: As of this moment of time, I should adjudge the IACC Joint Commission on Student Financial Aids as the best medium by which ACPA can figure in federal legislative action affecting student financial aids. I see the possibility of an uninterrupted conveyor-belt operation, with the ideas of ACPA being moved (1) to the IACC Joint Commission on Financial Aids and thereafter (2) to the ACE Commission on Legislative Affairs, the U.S. Office of Education, the House and Senate Committees on Education or other.

For those of you who resist Perception 3 and the two to follow, possibly on the grounds that lobbying is unbecoming to student personnel workers, I would urge that you acquaint yourself with the fine differences between *lobbying* and *leading.* Decisions affecting each of us will be made regardless of our activity or inactivity. It would seem to be the better part of wisdom for us to give constructive assistance to those who will make the decisions ultimately.

There are other legislative concerns—student housing, international student exchanges, and extensions of NDEA institutes to include college personnel workers. On the last-named, I would speculate as follows:

Perception 4: Assuming the IACC Joint Commission on Financial Aids provides a voice in federal legislation that *is* heard, we would do well to lend support to another established IACC sub-committee which can, in conveyor-belt escalation, take our ideas on NDEA institutes for college personnel workers to appropriate Washington receptors. I refer to the IACC Committee on Preparation and Education of Student Personnel Workers which has, with vigor and purpose, begun to explore its relationship to offices and agencies in Washington.

Perception 5: There is likely an intermediate or enabling step needed which is that of naming an ACPA Committee on Omnibus Legislation which I suggested last May without any knowledge of an "omnibus bill" in education in the offing. Such a proposed committee, with strong regional ramparts which I shall discuss shortly, would determine association posture on particular issues in order that our designated IACC representatives be informed spokesmen for the Association.

Last June, I selected from the Directory of Higher Education some seventy associations which centered their work on higher education. Believing the way could be paved for conference, I directed a letter to the executive officer of each association inquiring whether our two organizations could work together along these five lines: (1) in reciprocal programming through seminars, work conferences joint committees, consultations, and similar; (2) in exchange of personnel in convention or conference programs; (3) in exchange of journals or other professional materials; (4) in joint research activities; and (5) in effecting legislation at national, regional, state and local levels.

What has come of this overture? By mimeographing 100 copies of our Boston program early to send key personnel, and by follow-up in conference or letter, we have at this conference representatives from many educational associations, both as observers and participants, who have hitherto not met with us. The exchange of materials of mutual interest before the convention has been spirited. All this amounts to an observation long overdue.

Perception 6: ACPA resides in a professional-educational world with many centers of power. Our Association must find its place—and with some haste—among the alphabetically souped-up groups of recognized associations in higher education. Personnel from these groups must be encouraged to continue their communication with us. In addition, ACPA must send official observers to conventions like this of other associations. Convening in the next few weeks are national meetings of the American Association of Collegiate Registrars and Admissions Officers, the American College Health Association, and the National Association of Foreign Student Advisers, to name but three deserving of our cooperation.

Other Than Washington Operations

May we turn our attention now to the cruising of regional, state, local and global areas? I am convinced if we build only on a Washington base, we will demonstrate a singular myopia.

Among the letters I alluded to earlier were three directed to the trio of regional compacts: (1) the Southern Regional Education Board (SREB); the New England Board of Higher Education (NEBHE); and the Western Interstate Commission on Higher Education (WICHE). I call attention to the reprint at your place, WITHIN OUR REACH, which summarizes the Report on the Commission on Goals for Higher Education in the South. (This brochure was sent to us through the kindness of the Southern Regional Education Board in Atlanta.) On p. 2, column 2, item 4, please note the Committee's citation of student counseling, actually a reference to comprehensive student personnel programs. That this is no counterfeit nod is seen in the continuing assistance provided by the Southern Regional Education Board to the Southern College Personnel Association—assistance in the form of three summer work conferences dealing with student personnel programs, in service education, the contemporary college student, and a fourth workshop on institutional research productive of data on student characteristics.

You of the West know of WICHE's sponsorship of institutes on college student characteristics and the assessment of the campus climate. NEBHE, operating in the area in which we are meeting, is moving to sponsor institutes on admissions, the profile of the college student, and the organization and administration of housing programs.

Perception 7: There are about us benevolents in the guise of regional Dutch uncles. ACPA should familiarize itself with the work of the regional compacts in higher education, for there is much to be shared in ideas for research and programming, facilities, publications and grants which can effect change in the climate of learning on campus.

Attendant upon this move is the need to take inventory of numbers and activities of the regional college personnel associations. The pink Quick-Check sent to ACPA members in the recent mass mail-out brought replies indicating (1) that many knew of no regional or state associations where, in actuality, they existed. (2) More regrettable is the indication that regional personnel groups seem to be peculiarly incommunicado.

Perception 8: Regional *encapsulation* weakens a profession. There is a common market of ideas in our profession that stretches country-wide. A mutual upsurge of strength would surely be felt if—at this convention—there were called a meeting of the representatives of the various regional college student personnel associations, the gains being these: (1) *coordination* of ACPA's program with that of the regions—but not superimposition of program; (2) communication of regional groups by newsletter or other media; (3) identification of competent officer and committee personnel for ACPA and (4) research and/or legislative activity-in-combination among the regional groups and ACPA.

Perception 9: ACPA's friendly handclasp must, on occasion, form a fist for our Association has not spoken out firmly on the adequacy of regional—or national—accreditation criteria. Before ill-conceived criteria are applied to the detriment of good programs and the plaudit of poor ones, our association must investigate and act!

Other grassroots and tidelands areas to which ACPA must look are the 50 individual states and the 2,100 individual college campuses. There are rapid triggerings of statewide studies of higher education in New York, Michigan, California, and Louisiana. In the past 15 months, we in Florida have been confronted with facts from three major studies authorized by the State Board of Control and spelling out the future of higher education—and of student personnel work—in our warm peninsula. I am gratified to find in the most recent report a fact-packed chapter on college student characteristics.[3]

Perception 10: This association must effect a means for the study of

3. *The Setting for Higher Education in Florida* edited by Charles M. Grigg and Charles N. Millican, Role and Scope Study Project, University System of Florida, Board of Control, Tallahassee, Florida, 1963.

statewide surveys of higher education, for they not only prescribe minimal to model programs in student personnel for existing institutions but also for colleges and universities now only on the drawing boards. Likewise, ACPA must find a means for collecting and disseminating data derived from self-studies and similar appraisals of both the private and public institutions to obtain barometic readings on the status of student personnel work in respect to the total educational endeavor.

Perception 11: ACPA, somewhat like the fabled Rip Van Winkle, is awakening from a deep sleep in the hills, aroused but recently to its responsibilities relating to the international dimensions of the institution. This association must seek to work increasingly with the Programs and Services unit, Cultural Affairs Section, U.S. Department of State; with the U.S. Office of Education; with the Institute for International Education and other agencies whose global program demands more than we have hitherto given. ACPA must concern itself increasingly with what in student personnel work is readily exportable—that is, with what is packaged to carry abroad by scores of our colleagues in overseas assignments, long term and short. What does the basic philosophy and current practice in *American* college student personnel work presage for faculty and staff in Nigeria, India, Afghanistan, Ecuador? What kind of *image* goes overseas in our professional name—beneficent, benign, impressive, or superficial?

And thus, the time has come to face *the image* we portray to those who observe us. That there are some distortions in this collection of perceptions will be obvious. In Washington, we appear to some to be riding *piggy-back* with student personnel work in higher education balancing on the shoulders of counseling and guidance which stretches K through G—kindergarten through graduate school.

Then, it is thought that personnel work is chiefly regulatory—that, in fact, student personnel workers are, in the words of one thoughtful colleague, "wild life managers" who relieve members of the teaching faculty of onerous out-of-class activities. A member of the budget commission in my own state adjudges student personnel work to be the supervision of student recreation—of fun and games which detract from the real educational mission.

Finally, we have been viewed in the literature as parent surrogates, substitutes for mother and father, in *loco parentis*, and—say the wags—mostly in *loco*!

In my judgment, the length and breadth, width and depth of student personnel work has not been sufficiently well enunciated for at least a decade and a half during which time a whole new generation of college presidents, development officers, controllers, members of governing boards, and teaching personnel have assumed their posts on campuses of the land. These coworkers lack a carefully delineated picture of us.

But, I prefer NOT to speak of *building* an image but rather of *restoring* one. Madison Avenue, of certainty, has no claim on restoration. This is a delicate, old-world craft that we, as professionals, can effect if we but flex our memories and exercise our faculties.

There needs to be recalled to life the image of student personnel work NOT as a gilded dynasty; NOT as an island in splendid isolation cut off from the mainland of activity; NOT as a string of service stations stretching over academic acres; and NOT as a student welfare state. Rather, the likeness should be one reflecting our earned place in the mainstream of purposeful education which, in an era of automation, effects a precision product, well-tooled in competence, insight, and morality. Ours is a proud profession with a durable heritage. *This organization represents that profession well.*

Our task—one to test our skill and patience—is that of stripping or peeling off the accumulated film of years masking the touch of true genius beneath. If the image of student personnel work in higher education *is* to be renewed, it will come about in the multiple ways enumerated: (1) active participation in policy formation in the committee-rooms of American Council on Education; (2) active participation in legislation affecting student financial aids, student housing, institutes for preparation of student personnel workers and other; (3) collaboration with the multiple associations whose work, like ours, is higher education directed; (4) cooperation, at appropriate levels, with the regional compacts and the regional accrediting associations; (5) planning in combination with regional, state, and local college personnel associations; (6) analysis of state-wide studies of higher education as well as local campus studies, and (7) a grasp of the international dimensions of our work in acknowledgment of the fact that the *local* and the *global* are closer than we think. The weight and extent of all this endeavor to restore an image leads to a twelfth perception.

Perception 12: It is my considered judgment after these years of service in the executive eschelons that no president of this association nor any executive group scattered about the country can do all of this. To try would be to emulate what industry terms "moonlighting"—that is, extending the working day beyond sundown or the working week to encompass both Saturday and Sunday. Too many of us in leadership roles in education are "moonlit"—more of shadow than real substance in our fulfillment of the expectations of our rapidly growing constituencies. The Self Study Committee suggests a means—the naming of an Executive Secretary within the existing APGA framework, which idea has already been under discussion with APGA headquarters staff.

Perfection—and Conclusion

We have been talking of the renewal of the image of student personnel work in higher education. Last week, the truth was again apparent to me. In the basic class in student personnel work on our campus, twenty students, ages varying from twenty to fifty, presented in a two-platoon system their end-of-course project—a model student personnel program for our newest state institution, the Florida Atlantic University at Boca Raton, for reasons of class anonymity designated as The College of the Clouds.

To the best of knowledge, only one of these twenty students had ever been a college student personnel worker. The other nineteen were department heads or teachers of such subjects as music, public health, business administration, nursing, mathematics or psychology. They were retired from the military service or they were homemakers recalled to academic life.

The performance of these students in roles assumed by them—deans of students, deans of men or women, directors of admissions, counseling, placement, health, financial aids—is indelibly etched on my mind, for they reflected *their* image of *our* profession in *their* decorum. These students in their dual performances last week declared the goal of student personnel work was one shared with all forces on the campus aiming to

. . . assist the student in effecting an understanding of himself and his studies in relation to the culture, creation, and the Creator.

Listening—and learning as I always do from students—I found the question cited earlier turning in upon me. What kinds of graduates of programs of student personnel work, with what kinds of competences would we like to point with pride?

I believe they are graduates who possess a significant and profound quality—a sense of what is specifically human in human beings—a sense of the heart which accompanies the sureness of science—behavioral, physical, biological. In the book, *Personnel Services in Education*, a spokesman for our Yearbook Committee reiterated the importance of integrity of each man's personality, of mercy which overrides facts, of love as a positive quality of existence—those attributes residing in Judaeo-Christian idealism.[4] I do not find it difficult to talk of these qualities with the advent of this very special week in which we meet each year in convention, for Holy Week is themed with renewal, restoration, and resurrection. And thus, I would conclude.

Perception 12-plus: The real renewal of the image of student personnel work—as well as the renaissance of this Association—will come about through the ideas and energies of highly motivated young professionals crowding the field and seeking our affiliation. This, in turn, will exact of us "old pros" a singular performance in both practicing and professing in the area of student personnel work.

Phrased as you heard it . . .

to assist the student in effecting an understanding of himself and his studies in relation to the culture, creation, and the Creator . . .

ours is a simple yet extravagant assignment. It is, I think, to seek to accommodate *the spirit of the learner* in *the climate of his learning.*[5]

To this pursuit—that of perfection in performance to *restore a latent image*—I would commend this association.

4. C. Gilbert Wrenn, "Philosophical and Psychological Bases of Personnel Services in Education," in *Personnel Services in Education*, 58th Yearbook of the National Society for the Study of Education, Part II, edited by Nelson B. Henry, University of Chicago Press, Chicago, Illinois, 1959, p. 77.

5. A basic theme in *Comprehensive Counseling in College*, a manuscript in process of publication, by Melvene D. Hardee,

Reflections of a Troublesome But Hopeful Rip Van Winkle

W. H. Cowley

Washington Irving's Rip Van Winkle, you'll recall, took a swig from the keg of a stranger before the American Revolution and woke up twenty years later burdened with years and bewildered by the wonders of the new age in which he found himself. I liken myself to that fabled Dutchman because in 1938 I too took a swig from an intoxicating keg and left the ravines of personnel work which I entered as a neophyte forty years ago this coming September.

Washington Irving portrayed Rip Van Winkle as troubled by the fantastic changes that had occurred during his long absence but I'm not a bit troubled. On the contrary, I'm delighted with the enormous growth of student services as epitomized by such facts as these: the numbers of men and women engaged in these services has multiplied at least 25 times; the institutional budgets for your programs have grown from a few thousand dollars to more than a million in a number of universities and have increased proportionately in most small colleges; and the membership of this Association has grown from 91 in 1934 to 3,200 last year.

These and other advances "pleasure" everyone who has been or is now engaged in your area of higher educational activity; but, it seems to me, the debit side of the ledger very considerably outbalances the credit side. For example, this Association and the three dozen or so others devoted to student affairs in colleges and universities are currently struggling with the same crucial problems that afflicted them 25 years ago. Here and there a bit of headway has been made, but in the main the confused and vexatious situation of the past continues to prevail.

For example, Bill Craig's presidential address of two years ago listed and discussed much the same congeries of problems over which the

217

Association perspired during my day; and an article in the June, 1963 issue of your journal once again goes over the same ground that I traversed in a still relevant article of 1936[1] and which a score of other writers have explored meanwhile.

I became aware of a very recent development about which I had not previously heard. Its tremendous importance and potential led me to the decision that I should throw off the mantle of self-chartered prosecuting attorney and instead become an advocate for the alluring plans now maturing in the just organized group known as Council of Student Personnel Associations in Higher Education or, for short, COSPA.

Suffice it here to say that it is the latest and by all odds the most promising of the many efforts made to develop cooperation among the national associations concerned with the extra-instructional student affairs of American colleges and universities. Ed Williamson has called it "the most auspicious development in the student affairs field that has occurred during the past 30 years." I agree heartily with his judgment, and in this paper I want to do my bit to help convert its high promise into buoyant reality.

Toward that end I began with a postulate, namely, that the activities or functions of colleges and universities fall into three categories: first, teaching and research which constitute their *core* functions; second, the extra-instructional services performed to facilitate education, denominated in my paper *complementary* functions; and third, the maintenance and promotional activities which institutions undertake in order to continue in operation and to prosper which I labelled *continuity* functions. The members of this Association all give their attention to activities in the second of these functional categories. That is to say, they perform complementary functions.

Some members of this Association—counselors in particular—believe, I know, that their activities should be considered core functions; but may I make a distinction that will perhaps help them to agree with designating them complementary, namely, the distinction between formal and informal teaching. As a one-time counselor I yield to no one in the value I put upon it; but the fact remains that many students learn more from counseling than they do from some of their formal courses.

1. "The Nature of Student Personnel Work," *The Educational Record*, April, 1936, pp. 198–226.

What functions do you and your fellow workers in related associations perform? You do many different kinds of things, but all of them have one distinctive characteristic, namely, they occur outside the formal curriculum. Some of you, of course, teach courses; but those who do wear two hats—one donned occasionally as a faculty member, the other worn most of the time as a student service officer. Mark well the designation *student service officer* because in operational fact all of you do work that directly serves students and indirectly the institutions in which you live.

These activities appear to me, as remarked earlier, to be complementary to the core teaching and research functions of colleges and universities; but regardless of whether you like or dislike the term complementary functions, the fact stands out clearly that the distinguishing characteristic of all the members of all the groups in your field is this: you serve students in various non-curricular ways. In short, you are student service officers.

I submit three reasons why you should not only accept this fact but also, welcome and, indeed, broadcast it. First, if the terms guidance and personnel have been obstacles to consummating the urgently needed cooperation among your associations and among their members on college and university campuses, then it seems essential that a generally, acceptable name be found. Second, since not a few administrators and universities grant credit toward degrees from learning acquired through classroom instruction and do not grant credit for learning resulting from counseling. In short, regardless of the enormous importance of counseling and other student services, faculty members and administrators consider them to be supplementary to curricular teaching and hence complementary functions of colleges and universities.

It will be recalled that counselors and their student-service associates perform functions historically handled by faculty members. In addition, colleges and universities today serve their students in numerous new ways. For example, not until about the time of the Civil War did chaplains appear on college campuses, presidents and faculty members being the preachers and religious advisers of students. Not until about the same time did any American college give direct attention to guarding the health of their students, but today rare are the institutions which do not have at least a part-time chaplain and a part-time physician.

The kinds and numbers of the extra-instructional officers on American college campuses multiplied slowly and unobtrusively during the last half of the nineteenth century, and either before or immediately after the First World War their growth and self-awareness led several groups of them to organize associations for mutual assistance.

1. The deans of women who first began to meet annually in 1903.
2. The directors of student unions, seven of whom met at Ohio State University for the first time in 1914.
3. The teacher placement people who met informally soon after the establishment of the first appointments office at Harvard in 1898 and formally organized in 1924.
4. Several deans of men who similarly conferred as individuals created the National Association of Deans of Men in 1917.
5. College physicians whose roots go back to 1861 and who organized the American College Health Association in 1920.

You'll observe that these groups appeared upon the scene before or soon after the introduction of two new terms, namely, *guidance* and *personnel.*

As most of you know, the so-called "guidance movement" began in secondary education in Boston about 1905. Some of you also know that for a quarter of a century a vigorous debate went on concerning the meaning of the term, one group led by Harry Kitson emphatically insisting that its meaning should be limited to the *vocational* advisement of students. Kitson and his fellow thinkers lost the debate. Thus they substituted the term *counseling.*

Soon after the Boston Vocational Bureau put the word *guidance* into circulation, Ernest Martin Hopkins, who later became president of Dartmouth College, helped establish the word *personnel* in English by introducing it as the Hawthorne plant of the Western Electric Company. He had just been appointed to help improve employer-employee relations there, and against considerable opposition he suggested that his unit be called the personnel department.

I've been unable to discover how rapidly American industrial organizations adopted the word, but everybody knows that the U.S. Army employed a phalanx of psychologists to test and assign First World war draftees and that they became known as personnel officers. The head of the psychology department of Northwestern University, Walter Dill Scott, headed the group with the rank of colonel; and one of his associates, Major Clarence S. Yoakum, appears to have been the first individual to bring the term over into higher education.

When in 1927, I became director of the Board of Vocational Guidance and Placement at the University of Chicago, three clusters of student service people had become well established in American colleges and universities: first, the special service officers such as chaplains, deans of men and women, directors of health services and student unions, etc.; second, counselors sometimes referred to as guidance people; and third, psychologists primarily concerned with testing.

Like many of you, I believe that APGA has been a boon and that the bridge it has built between school and college people needs to be widened and lengthened. I also believe that the present energies of this association (ACPA) and of other higher educational groups should at this juncture be primarily devoted to promoting cooperation among the organizations whose interests center in post-high school institutions. Toward this end COSPA has already taken the initial steps, and because of its impressive prospects I shall make bold a bit later to submit some suggestions to it through you. I heartily wish that I had had a part in its launching; but since I didn't, perhaps I can help its and faculty members look upon you with something less than enthusiasm and even on occasion call you by such epithets as obnoxious upstarts and wearisome do-gooders, you need an appellation that will win you friends among your institutional colleagues. Third, the concept of service chiselled in your name will continuously help to illuminate and to enrich your day-to-day activities.

This brings the discussion back to COSPA which has for its prime purpose the enrichment of the day-to-day activities of the approxi-- mately 25 thousand men and women who work with students outside the confines of the curriculum. They hope to initiate a number of programs which will do for all groups what no one of them can do for itself. These include, I've been told, publications, upgrading seminars, a central placement office, and a united front in dealing with organized groups of presidents and with governmental agencies.

I can perhaps be useful to both ACPA and COSPA by reviewing a concept which I believe, will help in mapping the road ahead.

• The concept goes by the name of "the centric triad." It has evolved from the efforts that my students and I have made over the years to describe the components of crafts, professions, and other foci of human interest as they advance to and achieve maturity. Consider the application of the triad, for example, to medicine. In preliterate societies families looked out for the well-being of their members. Then primitive specialists in the persons of medicine men appeared, and gradually in more advanced societies these specialists began to study the causes and cures of diseases and to pass on their findings to disciples. Later—much later—some of these specialists dropped the daily practice of medicine and devoted all their time to teaching and research. Others in turn took on the task of educating people at large about how to keep well.

Today all three of these kinds of medical people flourish and interact. One group centers its attention upon the practice of medicine and are, in the terminology that my students and I use, practicentrists. The word derives from the Greek noun *praxis*, meaning practice, and the adjective *centric* which means centered in. Those who teach esoteric medical knowledge and who undertake research to expand it we call logocentrists from *logos*, one of the Greek words for knowledge combined with *centric*. The third group, the democentrists (from *demos*, as in *democracy*, meaning people in general), inform the general public about medical progress and problems. They include not only physicians and surgeons but also those who teach courses in physical and health education and laymen who write about medicine.

By means of the centric triad the maturity and status in social esteem of any field of human activity from bricklaying to nuclear physics can, I believe, be gauged.

At the outset probably most of you will agree that the great majority of student service people are practicentrists, that is, specialists in various kinds of functions ranging from counseling students to administering overall programs. Some of you will probably also agree that you have had insufficient training for your work and that therefore you somewhat resemble the rule-of-thumb medicos who have been denounced by well-trained members of the medical profession since Hippocrates' day. This, may I observe, isn't your fault. Rather, you are handicapped in your activities because as yet few logocentrists have emerged in your field to create a solid body of knowledge upon which you can draw.

In support of this generalization about the scarcity of logocentrists among you, I submit a series of observations. First, over the country only three or four professors have been appointed to date who give all their attention to student services in *higher* education. Many scores of courses typically including the phase "Guidance and Personnel" in their titles have been offered for several decades; but I've been able to discover, as I say, only three or four professorships focused upon college and university problems. The paucity of such professorial specialists chiefly accounts, as I see it, for the relative dearth of fundamental knowledge in your field and also for the limited training of so many of its practicentrists.

Second, among the 30 writers who contributed chapters to Nevitt Sanford's volume of two years ago, *The American College*, which everyone I've talked with acclaims as the most important logocentric book yet published in your bailiwick, only one—I repeat, *only one*—belongs to this or any interrelated association.

Third, the letters that I've recently written to deans of students and others who work with students asking them about the number, size, and affiliations of the groups championing student participation in social and political demonstrations and other direct-action activities have given me practically no help at all. My requests for the names of others to whom I might write for such information have also been largely fruitless, my respondents almost all replying that if they needed such data they would write or telephone colleagues in other institutions, Ed Williamson in particular. None of them referred me to a definitive source, and this situation also strikes me as a justification of my conclusion that your craft lacks and badly needs a corps of logocentrists to help carry it beyond its present trial-and-error stage.

I'd also like to importune COSPA to take steps to facilitate the emergence in your ranks of gifted democentrists. You urgently need a group of gifted speakers and writers to elucidate your activities to your academic colleagues—both faculty members and administrators—and, further, to clarify for trustees, alumni, and the general public the characteristics of present-day students and the raging ferment of student life. My reading may be limited, but I've come across very few such elucidations and clarifications bearing the names of members of student service associations. Those I have encountered have chiefly, instead, been produced by psychologists, sociologists.

• By means of this quite incomplete exposition of the centric triad I've sought to sketch some of the problems with which I imagine

COSPA will be dealing, and now I'd like briefly to discuss ACPA per se. I doubt that any of you—including such old hands as Esther Lloyd-Jones and Ed Williamson—know that in 1931 I collaborated in converting the National Association of Placement and Personnel Officers into the ACPA and, in fact, proposed its new name. I recall this ancient history only to record my long if also sporadic concern for its well-being, a concern which accounts for my being here today. I'd like, in short, to be helpful to the Association which I helped launch; and toward that end I'll rapidly sketch some pertinent background and then make a suggestion about the future.

The National Association of Placement and Personnel Officers became ACPA because a handful of its members saw the need of a national organization to interrelate all segments of student services and affairs. The most evangelical members of the group included F. F. Bradshaw, A. B. Crawford, J. E. Walters, and me. Francis Bradshaw, Dean of Students at the University of North Carolina, believed that his fellow deans and also the deans of women could be induced to join such an association or at least to integrate with it. On my part, like Crawford a psychologist, I contemplated an influx of measurement people, of more placement officers, and of the educational and personal counselors then being appointed in fairly large numbers—at least these looked like reasonable prospects from my new post at Ohio State where my work criss-crossed with that of everyone engaged there in extra-instructional work with students.

I can't recall all the efforts we made to convert our hopes into actuality, but at all events we failed. Thus the groups we hoped to entice into our visionary consortium continued to go their independent and generally uncooperative ways and, to boo, the placement people, whose organization we had commandeered, broke away from us and established a number of structures of their own. These circumstances side-tracked our conception of ACPA and converted it into an organization largely made up of people interested in counseling and psychological testing, of individuals who performed functions for which no specialty society had yet been established, and of earnest souls who still wanted to help create an all-encompassing confederation of associations whose nucleus would be the ACPA.

Since the war, as everyone knows, you have grown helter-skelter; but most of your leaders with whom I have been in correspondence seem to be uncertain about what ACPA ought to be and what it should seek to become. I gather from other sources that an undetermined proportion of your membership also ponders the Association's place in the sun, and these ambiguities pose two questions: first, how large a proportion of your membership is puzzled about your activities and direction? Second, if the aggregate is sizable, what should be done about the situation?

I suggest that answers to these questions should promptly be sought and that your new officers immediately upon taking over their duties petition one of the foundations for a grant to investigate not only your own situation but also, in conjunction with COSPA, the whole sweep of the student service undertaking with a view to making an inventory of it and determining the most practicable methods of capitalizing its potentials. Now as never before, you are ripe for such a full-dress self-study, and I earnestly urge that it be undertaken as soon as possible.

• Throughout this paper, I have been annoyingly critical, and you may well reject my avuncular nagging. Before you do, however, may I tell you that as one who during recent years has been engaged in the task of mapping all sectors of the higher educational terrain I believe to the depths of me that the activities you perform—although I consider them complementary to the core functions of teaching and research—have incalculable significance in maintaining and improving the health of student life, of colleges and universities, and moreover of the nation. Thus this troublesome but hopeful Rip Van Winkle prays that you'll tirelessly exploit the opportunity created by the establishment of COSPA and that you'll make your compartment of higher education as vital, impressive, and influential as it should and can be.

The College Student Personnel Leader of the Future is an Educator

Dennis L. Trueblood

The development of functions in our society into an identifiable career area or professional identity area would be within itself an interesting study. The evolvement of the student personnel function has been one in which there has been on-going conflict between those who perceive themselves as procedural technicians, service station attendants so-to-speak, and those who perceive the student personnel leader as an educator whose special interest is the college student and the environment which affects him both as a whole person and as a scholar-student.

The definition of function has been further beclouded by the failure of college faculty and student personnel staff to properly understand that there need be no basic conflict between an interest in the "whole" student and the scholar-student. Certainly what happens in any facet of a persons life affects other aspects of that "whole" person including frequently his ability to perform as a scholar-student. The human factor being that which it is, there is little question that there are student personnel staff who perceive themselves in direct conflict with the faculty and his concern with the scholar-student in the classroom; and therefore program and otherwise behave with an improper understanding that, historically, society has assigned to the institution of higher education the function of preparing the intellects of its young. On the other hand, there are those faculty who fail to recognize that the student's out-of-class behavior is obviously going to influence his ability to perform as a scholar-student. Furthermore, with the increasing pressure to publish or research, the faculty member may be tempted in the future, at least in the next two decades and in the larger institution, to be even less concerned about good teaching which includes an understanding that the student is a "whole" person.

226

The void which appears to be developing in the higher education scene because of the pressure for publication, research, increasing larger classes, and the ever widening base of knowledge seem to force more and more faculty to be less concerned with teaching and more concerned with academic discipline matters, and the attention to the student as a "whole" person must be filled by the college student personnel leader who perceives himself as an educator. This role for the student personnel leader is a multiple one involving reinforcement of classroom activity, programming for other learning needs of the "whole" student, and behaving in his relationships with students, with the primary attitude of an educator-teacher. The challenge is a great one, but nevertheless one which must be accepted if the student is to gain the utmost from the college attending experience.

The implications are many to the development of the college student personnel leader:

1. He must be selected as a person with the intellectual capacity to comprehend the educator-student personnel leader role.

2. He must develop his skills and knowledge to be able to become the administrative leader with the information about student behavior, environmental factors which affect student behavior, the context of higher education, and the necessary channels to keep communication about matters affecting the student with students, administrative staff, and faculty.

3. He must have the necessary commitment to a way of life which includes an understanding of and a willingness to implement those basic values which are important to a humanitarian way of life. In many ways the student personnel leader and his staff play the role of "ethical counselors" as described by Chief Justice Earl Warren,[1] "I can conceive also of lay scholars who, having mastered the ethical thought of the study of the modern world and its problems, could helpfully suggest courses of action and alternatives which might prove helpful to the modern business man, politician, academic executives and other professionals who wish to discern the right." Or to place in the context of student personnel, to quote E. G. Williamson,[2] "I firmly believe that, in order to be a practical counselor, one must think out his value orientation and commitments to the big philosophic questions about human beings and the culture they have developed."

4. He must be committed to accept the personal implications of the effective college student personnel leader's unique function in the university community. The student personnel leader of the future must not be apologetic for not being a member of the "teaching faculty" nor in any sense feel insecure in his contribution to the learning of the scholar-student.

5. He must be committed to the inherent importance of the professional position that he is willing to aggressively recruit to the career young people with the intellectual interests, mental ability, personal values, and motivation to work to develop and succeed as a college student personnel leader.

The implications to the American College Personnel Association of the evolving role of the student personnel leader as an educator seem many. Primarily and most important we must again recognize that ACPA has been and must continue to be an organization which must set the standards for research on students and the professional functions of student personnel staff and for the intellectual development of the student personnel staff. Our every effort in the future should reflect this emphasis.

The recent meetings of IACC, (Inter-Association Coordinating Committee), now COSPA (Council of Student Personnel Associations in Higher Education), showed a continuing concern with cooperation among the various student personnel associations. The content of the pre-COSPA meeting was high level showing that there is ability to attack the difficult problems which face the student personnel leader as an educator—it was in three areas: (1) the implications of equal educational opportunity to all youth, especially the Negro, (2) the implications of the year round calendar for programs of higher education, (3) the implications of academic freedom and student rights. The business meeting of COSPA showed a continuing developing base for cooperation among student personnel associations in higher education—the Joint Commissions on Financial Aids and on Professional Development are continuing, Lillian Johnson of NAWDC has succeeded to the chairmanship of COSPA, and two annual meetings were set with an all COSPA meeting just following the annual ACE meeting (usually October) and the Executive Committee to meet at the time of the annual AHE meeting (usually March or April).

This is my last message to you as ACPA president. Let me again share with you my enthusiasm for the development within ACPA and student personnel in the past two years. The evolvement of COSPA seems to be the long range base for real significant progress for the student personnel field—the progress may not be as rapid as all would want but if we in ACPA can be patient there is excellent potential development in COSPA. The resolution of ACPA-APGA relations has been healthy. For ACPA there is a bright future within APGA if we can and will continue to see the unique opportunity that the "bridge" function of ACPA for APGA to the higher education scene contributes to all of education. It is a difficult role and one where tensions are undoubtedly bound to occur, but challenging, and I would hope that all 3,400 of ACPA'ers will continue to work hard to implement this role.

1. Warren, Earl (Chief Justice of the Supreme Court), "Address before Louis Marshall Award Dinner of the Jewish Theological Seminary of America," New York, New York, November 11, 1962 (mimeographed).

2. Williamson, E. G., "The Societal Responsibilities of Counselors," *IGPA Newsletter*, Winter 1963.

Identity Crisis—1965

Barbara A. Kirk

It is a great pleasure for me to be together with so many of you today. For us to meet in Minneapolis, the home of the University of Minnesota, has especial significance. The college student personnel field, and student personnel work, are deeply rooted in the philosophy, the research, the practice, and the training that emerged, beginning several decades ago, on this campus. Its influence has been widely felt, wherever universities and colleges have been concerned with their students as individuals who have ongoing personal lives, even while they engage in the struggle to learn. I am sure that if I should ask any of you here today to rise who has studied or worked at the University of Minnesota, or studied or worked with someone trained at the University of Minnesota, we would have a very considerable shuffling of chairs, including those at these head tables, notably that of our President-Elect.

I trust you are in a mood to forgive personal references, because I feel some coming on! I, too, have my student personnel roots in Minnesota's soil. When I came many years ago to the University to work in the Institute of Child Welfare with Florence Goodenough and John Anderson, I found myself migrating in every spare moment to the then very young and novel Student Counseling Bureau. I have never ceased to be grateful to Ed Williamson, extraordinarily busy as he then was (and still for that matter is) for giving me the opportunity to learn to counsel students, and taking the time and great pains to read and review every single case record I produced that year.

It is of the growth and development, and present status, of our profession that I want to talk with you today. I suppose I should at the outset disabuse you of the expectation that today's title refers in any direct way to the events that have taken place on my campus this year! As a matter of fact, however, *they* are illustrative of some of the problems of our era,

230

and its changing times, in which many young adults, and some not so young adults, are unsure at many times of who and what they are.

A *New Yorker* "Talk of the Town" item recounts attendance at a lecture of Dr. Leonard J. Duhl's at the New York Academy of Medicine last July:

"The lecture was billed as being addressed 'to the laity,' but, like most psychiatrists, Dr. Duhl, who is chief of the Planning Staff of the National Institute of Mental Health, in Bethesda, Maryland, began by diagnosing the problem in professional terms: 'The most prevalent disease of our time [is] urban man's loss of self-identity.' *Unlike* most psychiatrists, however, he quickly switched to a more personal vocabulary, and in a chat with us after the lecture he explained what he meant.

" 'In the past, when people grew up in closely knit communities, there was seldom any problem about making independent value choices. The community had its own ways of coping with the world, its own stable system of values, which it passed along to the child. In relation to these, one's self-image was clear. But these reinforcing factors have broken down, just as the individual is being handed a tremendously increased fund of information through radio, television, and travel—other people's, if not his own. So, instead of four or five variables, let's say, he's suddenly faced with thousands. And no one has trained him to make the choices. It's like sending an astronaut into space without preparing him for a weightless environment.'. . . the loss of self-identity is the most prevalent disease of our time."

With changing times, the nuclear age and the insecurities it brings, so even our diseases vary! Cultural complexity, lack of structure and stability cause us to respond in different ways. And, indeed, for several years psychiatrists and psychologists, notably Rollo May, have been reporting what purports to be considerably more than a semantic shift in diagnosis: considerably fewer neurotic and hysteric manifestations are observed, many more character disorders and identity difficulties, essentially problems of growing up and maturing.

Because so many young people are suffering from diffusion and uncertainty, Harvard and other universities to follow came to the adaptive policy of permitting students to take a leave of absence when and as required to "find themselves" before forfeiting the precious opportunity for education. Indeed, we are all cognizant of the hordes of students arriving at our campuses with no clear idea of their reason for being there, who they are or what they wish to become, and lacking, in varying degrees, the "readiness" for college, as I choose to call it.

And even as the growing complexity of our culture and its resulting uncertainties and anxieties is having its impact upon the identity formulation of the individual, so I submit it is equally true for our profession of student personnel work whose identity crisis in 1965 no less is a product of rapid and major social and sociological change, change in economic, industrial and occupational structure, change in ideologies, rapid growth in technology and knowledge.

This growth and change may or may not have the value of "progress" attached to it at this time, depending upon your own personal views, but change it all is, I suspect you will admit, and fast, and in the direction of complexity rather than simplicity. Thus it is movement rather than status quo which we as a profession are attempting to meet, and it is little wonder that we are searching and questioning, rather than being firm from our antecedent "closely knit families and communities."

What has happened to the community in which the student personnel profession has grown—higher education, the university and college campus? With the well publicized "population explosion" following the World War II, coming to a peak for higher education in the sixties, very few university or college campuses have been able to hold the line and retain their smallness, or on the other hand accommodate fully their rapid expansion. State universities especially are bound to provide education to the children of citizens of their state; private institutions have attempted to do their share. New institutions also come into being, new campuses, new junior colleges. It is not only the population explosion which has caused the crowding of our institutions of higher learning; it is also the space age's concept of how to get along in this world —get an "education," whatever that may be, but specifically obtain a "degree." Several decades ago, four per cent of our population went to college. Currently it is 40 per cent or more. A national survey sample of parents of high school pupils a year or two ago tells us that over 80 percent of parents expect their children to attend a college or university.

The "stable system of values" of higher education has indeed been subject to change. There has been insufficient faculty of high calibre to go around. Faculty student ratios decrease. Classes become larger. Faculty loads become heavier, permitting less faculty time or opportunity for contact and exchange with students. Student housing becomes crowded and inadequate. Because uncertainty exists regarding the definition of who is qualified for a college education and for a particular institution, admission requirements frequently become more stringent. Grading practices may not be revised as the calibre of student capacity increases. With the ever-greater need for more and more specialized education there is the need to maintain grades for admission to graduate school, and, indeed, for very many pressured students there is the desperate struggle for academic survival itself in the increasingly competitive atmosphere. There is also, in this generation of students, a keen interest in the social and political forces in the broader community.

So our young profession is groping. The symptomalogies are evident. There is incomplete agreement about whether we are a profession at all, or several professions.

How do we prepare those greatly needed recruits for student personnel work? Some of us believe that a broad base in social and behavioral sciences is our best approach, some believe that the focus shold be on the field of higher education as a discipline, some in a more specific practical address to student personnel administration, others in an emphasis upon counseling, adapting secondary counselor education or counseling psychology preparation to the generality of student personnel.

Let us take a specific example, that of financial aids administration. Rapid expansion of provision of federal funds for financing students' education has caused a lag in adaptation of the counseling approach to the individual student's confusion about financing himself through college. Nor has the student personnel point of view been incorporated in many instances where business and financial concerns have been predominant.

We are also unresolved as to role. To what extent are we policy makers or policy executers? Am I an educator or an administrator? Whom do I represent? Do I stand in *loco parentis*? If I am a parent, what kind of parent am I? Am I a parent or someone else? If someone else, who?

Beside uncertainty as to role, there is uncertainty as to functioning. How do I function? Am I a consultant to the institution or part of its administration, or separate? To what extent do I work with groups or with individuals? What methods, approaches, techniques can I use which will be most fruitful?

What do we mean by identity? Erikson[1] says, "the conscious feeling of having a personal identity is based on two simultaneous observations: the immediate perception of one's *selfsameness* and *continuity in time*; and the simultaneous perception of the fact that others recognize one's sameness and continuity. . . . Ego . . . identity is the *awareness* of the fact that there is a salfsameness and continuity to the ego's synthesizing methods and that these methods are effective in safeguarding the sameness and continuity of one's meaning for others" (p. 23).—that is, his social role. This description of individual identity seems, as we examine it, to apply to a profession: our *awareness* of a consistent, continuous inner organization, which is recognized and perceived by others.

Attending to the ways in which identity is formed for the individual should have meaning for us also. Self-esteem is a basic attribute upon which such development depends. Without adequate and appropriate self-esteem, confirmed at the end of each major crisis, grows to be a conviction that one is learning effective steps toward a tangible future, that one is developing a defined personality within a social reality which one understands" (p. 89).

"Ego identity develops out of a gradual integration of all identifications," in our case role models, and values, if you will.

• For our purposes, a strategic point in development in the "relation of the final adolescent version of the ego identity to economic opportunities, realizable ideals, and available techniques" (p. 41). "In general, it is primarily the inability to settle on an occupational identity which disturbs young people." "The young individual is forced into choices and decisions which will, with increasing immediacy, lead to a more final self-definition, to irreversible role pattern and, thus, to commitments." While identity *formation* is a lifelong development, identity *crisis* occurs at the end of adolescence.

We who work in the field of vocational counseling deal with this stage as our most common undertaking. Choices and decisions must be made before there is the readiness to make them. The ways which we have learned to help the individual to accelerate his development, to

1. Erikson, Erik H. Identity and the Life Cycle. *Psychological Issues*, 1959, Vol. 1, No.

resolve his crisis, to come to know who and what he is, have relevancy and form an analogy, it seems to me, for the resolution of our profession's identity crisis.

First of all, an adolescent needs to embark upon his undertaking with the desire to move ahead, the motivation to progress, attain maturity. Having, or acquiring this, he needs to have or acquire the belief, faith, confidence—self-esteem, if you will—in its attainment. Enough desire needs to be present to get him started, going; it will augment itself as he moves forward.

We encourage him to explore, to investigate, to sample experiences, to try things out, but not to experience in the behavioral sense alone. He needs to *think* about what he experiences, to wonder, consider how it may fit him and his needs—how he feels about it, how right it seems, how it relates to him. And so by broadening his context, extending his operational and experimental behavior, espousing and rejecting, he comes gradually to establish for himself stable values, the image of the admired performer with whom he wishes to identify, and thus evolves his knowledge of who and what he is.

How can our student personnel profession move toward its identity? For, as President Johnson said in his State of the Union address in January, "Progress must be the servant, not the master, of man," and we must have command over the complexities that change has brought about, and surely we want to, and believe that we can.

• *We* can explore. We can try new methods, we can innovate, we can be attentive to what others are doing, are studying, are trying. We can *look at* and *think about* what we and others are doing, what their studies mean to us, investigate, find out what is effective and why. As T. R. McConnell at our ACPA luncheon in San Francisco last year so well put it, in winding up his address: "Student personnel work will become less and less the practice of a mystery and more and more the practice of a profession as its methods take root in relevant basic research and sound clinical evidence."

• We can examine our values. In writing recently of the growing shortage of college teachers, John W. Gardner, President of the Carnegie Foundation, refers to what he calls the current "crisis in values" that has infected a generation of young scholars with "the crassest opportunism in grantsmanship, job hopping and wheeling-dealing." Traditionally, student personnel workers are thought to be other-oriented, devoted to student welfare and student growth and development. Are we free from infection and likely to remain so? Surely we can determine our common ideals, our beliefs, and our positions and so arrive at those "stable values" that give us identity and purpose.

Let us consider the image of the "admired performer" with whom we wish to identify. Here comes into play the standards which we set, and adhere to, that degree below excellence for which we will settle. There are many facets to the performance of our profession as a profession. What standards do we set and how can we raise them for professional preparation, for the calibre of person we recruit and employ, for the kind and quality of performance within the profession? At present surely we can utilize to the full all that we have which is high quality and work ever more actively towards improvement and advancement. We can also recognize and accept our current limitations and, as is true in any good profession, work within our competences and not in disregard of their borders.

● I should like to suggest just one more of the ways of overcoming our identity crisis. This is to look inward, seeking that which is internally consistent. We have many special functions, many different aspects of working with the student among us. What is the central core? We can synthesize, taking the best from one another, conceptualizing our similarities in objectives and approach. Furthermore, we can supplement and complement one another in practice, finding identity in the common effort to which we contribute our specialty. This means sharing, team work, pulling together rather than apart. Partly this comes from attitude, partly from communication. Clearly we can increase communication within our profession, and without: to have identity you remember, it must be recognized and perceived by others. Our "others" include chiefly our academic administration, our faculty and our students.

We are busy putting our puzzle together. You may remember the story of the young child who was trying valiantly to fit together the many tiny fragments which together would make a picture of the *world*. But he was too small, too frustrated, too unsuccessful. And so he turned to his elders, and his father said, "Have you forgotten that the other side of your puzzle is a picture of a man? Turn it over, put it together, and when you turn it back you will have your world put together."

● Consideration of the ways in which we may achieve identity is not to be taken by any means as saying that we are *not* moving forward. Let us remind ourselves of Gesell's psycho-biological concept of "equilibrium and disequilibrium." You remember, a child moves from an integrative to a disintegrative phase to an integrative. While he is in a state of disequilibrium, he is growing, changing, moving. *Then*, temporarily, he is sunny, easy, at peace with himself and the world—until again he is in a state of disequilibrium—difficult and incomprehensible, while change and growth takes place. That this occurs in adults, too, as they experience change or movement, was attested to by Freud. Just as there is symptomatology of our identity crisis, so are there many evidences of vigorous and constructive efforts on our parts to attain our identity. Here, today, we should speak of the American College Personnel Association, our organization which serves as an instrument of the profession, and works in close co-operation with other organizations of student personnel workers in higher education. The viability of our organization is a sign of our energy. Our organization has grown by a thousand members this year. It is past, it seems to me, its earlier and then necessary preoccupation with its own organizational structure. Now its attention is turning to substantive areas of ideas, research, programs, activity. It is getting on with a number of the infinite fascinating concerns which surround us and what we do. Remain for our Divisional Meeting and you will have abundant evidence as you review the year that was. Throughout this week's program, also, will be highlights of what we have been doing, not to mention what has been done to us! The American College Personnel Association has the prospect of being the unifying force through which we may become the profession we want to be.

A *personal word, in concluding*. As you know, I am a counselor. Counselors have a number of organizations where they talk with each other, rewardingly, about what they do. I joined the American College Personnel Association in order to have the unique opportunity to get to know the majority of student personnel workers and what *they* do. I hoped to broaden my perspective, to be able to help students better by understanding better the others on my campus team, what they offer the student and how. I hope all of you, as I am, are richer for the association with our membership. It cannot help but be so, it seems to me, with the people who make up our organization.

I want particularly to thank you for the honor and privilege of being

your President. The expansion of my horizons could not have been so
effectively accomplished in any other way. The learning has been im-
mense. I want to express, also, my appreciation to all of you who have
had the interest and taken the trouble to communicate with me, and in
so constructive a fashion; my appreciation of the devoted services to
the association of those, so many of you, who have been active in it;
and most especially of the officers, and committee and commission
chairmen. It is a wonderful experience to have close working relationships with so fine, congenial, and helpful a group of people. It has been
a real pleasure to be associated with our President-Elect, in whom we
are very fortunate, and under whom we should have a most productive
year. Thank you very much.

Student Personnel Work: Definition and Redefinition
ACPA Presidential Address

Ralph F. Berdie

The years I have been associated with ACPA have contributed to my knowledge and awareness of student personnel work and higher education, but more than that, these years have shown how important it is, and how difficult, to recognize the important questions that face us. What is student personnel work? What is its place in higher education? What are its purposes and how do we achieve them? What are and should be our relationships with students, instructors, and administrators? What is our scientific heritage? How do we use our professional associations to attain our educational goals? Almost every report I see from an ACPA committee or commission, almost every letter I receive from a member, almost every article and book I read, implies or directly asks some of these questions.

A person's sensitivity to questions such as these depends in part on the intellectual curiosity of his associates, and certainly I must acknowledge the influence others have had on me and attribute to them the credit but certainly none of the blame for what I say today. First, Ed Williamson, through his constant search in higher education, has provided all student personnel workers with a continuing dissatisfaction about the little we know and much of our urgency to explore is due to him. Donald G. Paterson and E. K. Strong provided me, as they provided to many of you, with a need to be hardheaded. Many of our questions were faced earlier by W. S. Miller and T. R. McConnell and the latter has had at least two opportunities to present his questions to you directly. Barbara Kirk and Leona Tyler are two of the wiser women in our generation and they bring many old questions into new focus. The people with whom I have worked directly at the University of Minnesota, although they do an excellent job of providing answers, are even better at discovering questions and among these I should name Martin Snoke, Lavern Snoxell, Don Zander, Theda Hagenah, Vivian Hewer, Forrest Vance, Ted Volsky, Dave Campbell, Bill Layton, Jack Merwin, and many others. What I say today comes out of the atmosphere which these friends have provided and the questions I raise are theirs as well as yours.

Let us attempt to define and redefine. Let us approach the question, "What is student personnel work?" and examine its purposes. Let us look at the avenues through which we achieve our purposes and review our methods.

Each student personnel worker has arrived at his own tentative definition of student personnel work. Some define it in terms of its purposes, some in terms of its relationships with other activities, and some in terms of the persons engaged in the activity. My own definition is oriented more toward the activity itself and certainly it reflects a background of psychology and research. Student personnel work is the application in higher education of knowledge and principles derived from the social and behavioral sciences, particularly from psychology, educational psychology, and sociology. Accepting this definition, student personnel work is different but not apart from other persons and functions in higher education. Neither is it the exclusive responsibility of any one or several groups of persons in colleges and universities. The student personnel worker is the behavioral scientist whose subject matter is the student and whose socio-psychological-sphere is the college. Student personnel work is effected by any person in the college applying knowledge and skills derived from the behavioral and social sciences to further the education of students.

Purposes

If this definition reveals the values and biases of the speaker, his list of purposes of student personnel work is nothing but the reflection of his own value system. A primary purpose of student personnel work is to humanize higher education, to help students respond to others and to themselves as human beings and to help them formulate principles for themselves as to how people should relate to one another, and to aid them to behave accordingly. This is a purpose implicit in higher education, particularly in liberal education, but the student personnel worker carries it a step further. The traditional assumption is that as a person has increasing experience with the story of man's development, as he gains appreciation of the arts and humanities, and as he learns more of man and his world, this knowledge will have a humanizing impact. The student personnel worker accepts this assumption but contends that this is not sufficient. More is needed.

When we help fraternity members to respond to prospective pledges on the basis of interest, merit, and personality, and not on the basis of race or religion, we are humanizing their education. We are doing this when we help students express their charity and compassion in social service programs, or when through our counseling, they learn that parents are people, too.

Another purpose of student personnel work is to individualize higher education. We recognize the presence and significance of individual differences and hope to structure the education of each individual accordingly. Many educational patterns are required if the needs of most students are to be met and the student personnel worker is concerned not only with helping each student discover what his needs are and make appropriate choices but also with helping the college develop the alternatives and resources from which students can make wise choices. We are doing this when we discuss with students their abilities and interests and attitudes, and help them select from the many available resources. We are doing this when we encourage the development of new educational programs.

Student personnel work also has as a purpose to bring into balance the world of the student, that of the university, and the enveloping "real" world that encompasses all. Students come from families, high schools, and communities that share many of the values of the University but that also are unaware of or perhaps rejecting other values. From the college, the student moves into a world of work, family, and community that again in many ways is different from his alma mater. While in college, the stresses and demands of the curriculum and college life are balanced against those of social problems, religious conflicts, racial discrimination, civil rights, and a society out of joint. The purpose of the student personnel worker is to facilitate movement into and out of the institution and to keep the student an effective member of the college and at the same time a real member of the community.

Another broad purpose of the student personnel worker is to implant, nurture, and extend students' drives, interests, and motives, so that college and community resources will be used maximally by students to achieve their educational purposes, both in and after college. Institutional atmospheres are developed and individual student attitudes fostered, and I might even say *manipulated* to arouse and maintain intellectual curiosities and to develop habits of searching and learning that will last long after college. We do these things when we arrange seminars for entering students, when we bring visiting scholars into dormitories, when we have special camps for talented students, and when we admit students into the mysteries of institutional decision-making.

Finally, a purpose of the student personnel worker is to increase the immediate satisfaction and enjoyments experienced by students so that higher education is perceived as a pleasantly productive experience. Learning, and the hard work required to learn, should be seen by students as providing satisfactions outweighing almost all others, and the extent to which this goal is achieved provides one means for us to appraise our success. Perhaps we best do this by exhibiting to students the satisfactions to be derived from our own intellectual pursuits.

Avenues

Through what avenues does student personnel work function? Sometimes we tend to regard ourselves as mainly concerned with face-to-face contacts with students, either individually or in groups. Certainly, one of our most effective and frequently used avenues in education is our relationship with students and the primacy we assign to our counseling function attests to that.

However, our relationships with many other individuals and groups provide us with additional avenues. For example, the work done by student personnel workers with college and university administrators does much to establish the atmosphere within which our objectives can be attained—the relationship between the student personnel worker and the president, the dean, the assistant and associate deans, the admissions officers. Another important avenue is provided by the faculty and the curriculum, and here I refer to the people who actually teach classes and to the teaching they do, their actual classroom and classroom-related activities. The curriculum and the instructional program of a college, along with the people who are primarily responsible for it, provide a means for the attainment of our goals.

As college student personnel workers with our origins in psychology and the behavioral sciences, we are imbued with the fact of psychological individual differences. We are so aware of the variability among persons that we tend to forget a fact that Strong (1943) repeatedly emphasized. Persons are more similar than they are different, and the similarities among persons are larger than and as equally significant as the differences between persons. The classroom teacher and the college instructor are mainly concerned with the commonalities of their students. Students share certain abilities, competencies, and needs, and the college professor sees as his main purpose satisfying these common personal and social needs. We student personnel workers, in our concern that individual differences be recognized, sometimes overlook the importance of common objectives, group programs, and mass instruction. Perhaps our respect for our teaching colleagues, and their respect for us, can be increased through mutual recognition of the significance of both these similarities and differences among students.

Increasingly, college student personnel workers are finding opportunities to work effectively with high school counselors and principals. The problems of high school and college relationships often are viewed in terms of curricular continuity, but equally important are the attitudes of students as they move from high school to college, and the problems they bring with them, along with the habits for solving these problems. ACPA's involvement in the National Council on School-College Relations is evidence of this concern.

Increasing also is the student personnel worker's involvement with other persons in the community, particularly those in local, state, and federal government, and private industry and foundations. NDEA Institutes, graduate fellowships, research grants, funded conferences, all result from these relationships.

Methods

The definition, purposes, and avenues of student personnel work all are dependent on the methods we employ. If any one tool is basic in our kit, it is counseling. Counseling is a means of establishing and maintaining an individualized and personalized relationship with students, and in colleges, the primary purpose of counseling is an educational one. That is, the relationship with which we are concerned has as its purpose the development of the student as an educated person.

My own view of counseling presents it as a discussion between a counselor and a student where the topic of the discussion consists of the characteristics and behaviors of the student within the framework of his social setting and with the purpose of helping the student understand and realize the implications of the ways in which the student differs from and resembles other persons. Counseling can be a part of the classroom teaching process, but it must be a part of almost all, if not all, student personnel work. It is a kind of teaching, a kind of therapy, and perhaps, according to Schofield (1964), a kind of friendship.

Advising is a method of student personnel work somewhat related to counseling. The immediate purpose of advising is to help a student make a decision, and the advantage of advising is that it provides a vicarious experience to the student which can save him both time and effort and at the same time increase his knowledge concerning the probable outcomes of various alternatives. Advising is one of the means adopted by society so that each individual does not himself have to recapitulate the painful history of mankind. Advising, or providing to students, opinions, previous experiences of one's self or others, or explanations of probability, is a basic educational function of the student personnel worker.

The student personnel worker also uses many of the teaching methods used by the classroom instructor. Although usually he employs a different terminology in a different setting, he may at times refer students to publications, advocate library research, suggest laboratory and research approaches, organize and present information and skills to be learned, and even examine the student's mastery of what is expected. He must rely as much as the classroom instructor on the little that is known about the psychology of learning as it pertains to the development of the college student.

Persuasion is another procedure important in the personnel worker's repertoire. The student personnel worker, like most persons in education, is concerned that the student incorporate into his behavior and personality those conformities that constitute civilization. Persuasion is defined as demonstrating or proving that something is true, credible, essential, commendable, worthy of belief, adoption, practice; bringing about by argument, the doing, practicing, or believing of a desired action or condition (*Webster's Unabridged Dictionary.*) Surely, much of education consists of persuasion, and the student personnel worker uses persuasion to aid students to become honest, truthful, reasonable, compassionate, and tolerant. In a sense, persuasion consists of counseling, advising, and teaching, but perhaps there is a difference insofar as the persuasion process requires that both the persuader and his subject be well aware of the objectives or behavior change the persuader has in mind.

A fifth essential method of the student personnel worker can be encompassed under the term "research." By this I do not mean only experimental designs, laboratory research, or statistical analysis, but the constant study of problems and search for new answers. The research about which I am speaking is an attitude as well as a behavior. The research perception or orientation of the student personnel worker is one of his most important tools. It is what allows him to listen to a student and while listening, consider the reasons why he is not able to better help the student. It is the perception that shows him the gaps in his knowledge and urges him to explore new avenues, develop new procedures, and perhaps as important as any of these, examine the impact he has on the student and the institution. The recent publication by Volsky, Magoon, Norman, and Hoyt (1965) provides an excellent example of how student personnel workers ask themselves the question, "What are we doing when we counsel students?", and then determine if they really are doing this. They found, as many of you know, that they were not doing what they thought they were doing, but in fact they were doing other things that were equally, if not more, important.

I also include among the methods of the student personnel work, administration. Apparently, people regard administration in many ways. Recently I had an opportunity to discuss the administrative aspects of a position with a couple of candidates being considered for employment and they told me they did not like administration. They meant they did not like spending hours on maintaining and reviewing budgets, preparing reports, and supervising and reprimanding employees. All of this is essential in the management function of administration but the student personnel worker's concern with administration is primarily in terms of organization, staffing, programming, policy determination, and relationships within and outside of his institution that facilitate all this. All the responsibilities involved in program development and operation are included in administration and like other methods discussed here, administration encompasses counseling, persuasion, advising, teaching, and research.

Implications

From what I have said, it should be obvious that student personnel work in higher education is of a piece with higher education and is not a separate function, part, or segment of the college pattern. It is an integral part of the whole educational process and everything encompassed in student personnel work is found in some other aspect of higher education; nothing is unique. Obviously, the purposes of the student personnel worker are the purposes of higher education. The avenues of student personnel work are those of higher education. The methods of student personnel work are not unique to it. The student personnel worker is a behavioral scientist employed in higher education to help achieve the goals and purposes of higher education through means of whatever knowledge and skills his background provides.

We have heard speakers at these sessions in the past more effectively discuss relationships between student personnel work and higher education. In Buffalo and again in San Francisco, Dr. McConnell showed us what student personnel work looked like to at least some other people in higher education. He asked the question really of *why* we were outside the college door. President Craig (1962) asked a similar question several years ago and essentially raised the question as to whether student personnel workers in higher education really belonged in a professional organization of guidance workers.

Following the questions and reasoning presented by these persons, and the introduction I have made, let me raise the following questions. Is there and should there be a profession of student personnel work? Or should we who are concerned with the objectives, purposes, and methods of student personnel work cease considering ourselves as student personnel workers and begin to regard ourselves as educators with particular competencies in the behavioral sciences, working with college and university students and institutional programs to further the ends of higher education? Should we cease attempting to train persons for a profession that may not exist and make sure that we are training persons to work in higher education with broad backgrounds and skills that can be employed to meet institutional and student demands? Should we resist attempts to standardize professional preparation programs, to define curricula, and even to accredit training programs? Should we say that we want instead good psychologists, sociologists, anthropologists, and political scientists, who know a lot about higher education and a lot about students and who are willing to place themselves in situations where they can apply their knowledge and learn more through such application?

Let me restate Bixler's comment directed to the Association for Counselor Education and Supervision (1963)—

If those now active in the counseling and guidance movement refrain from standardizing training at this point and instead frankly experiment on a wide range of approaches to the problem of directing youth to goals, then they will retain their leadership in this area.

His warning, given only three years ago, is still most relevant.

Currently, I am reviewing texts in guidance, including my own, to select one to use in a course I will teach this summer. Do you realize how little the authors of these texts refer to research, how little verified information they cite? Do you appreciate the extent to which such texts assemble and discuss opinions instead of research, the extent to which authors pontificate and how little they demonstrate? In guidance and student personnel work perhaps we have too few principles and too little systematic knowledge to constitute a discipline, and perhaps we are committing a fraud by introducing specialized student personnel work courses and seminars into the curriculum. Should courses and seminars be devoted to more disciplined knowledge, and should students learn how to improvise to handle dormitory riots and union programs through practicums and internships?

If we attempt to alter the current trend toward professionalization in student personnel work, what are the implications of this for our relationship with the American Personnel and Guidance Association? Currently, APGA increasingly defines itself as a professional organization concerned with the development of professional programs in government, schools, and community agencies. In a sense, the high school counselor faces the same dilemma we do in student personnel work in higher education and the wise counselor is concerned with the relationship between himself and the rest of elementary and secondary education. How will he solve his dilemma? Both our colleagues in secondary education and we in higher education have much to gain through our associations with APGA and we must do all in our power to see that it is a strong organization.

Perhaps, however, our future lies as closely to other associations in higher education—the American Council on Education, the Higher Education Association, the Council of Student Personnel Associations and its affiliated organizations, the American Association of University Professors, the United States National Student Association. Perhaps we have as much in common with organizations such as these as we have with the various professional associations explicitly defined in terms of guidance and counseling.

I am not proposing here that we have the answers. They will not be found within the next year or few years. Constantly, we will be faced with these problems, and I am concerned that we always remember our primary commitment to higher education and that as student personnel workers, we are educators who share with our colleagues in higher education responsibility for the transition of the student into a citizen.

References

Bixler, R. H. The changing world of the counselor II. Training for the unknown. *Counsel. Educ. Supv.*, 1963, 2, 170.

Craig, W. G. The student personnel profession: an instrument of national goals. *J. Coll. Stu. Personnel*, 1962, 3, 162–168.

Schofield, W. *Psychotherapy: the purchase of friendship.* Englewood Cliffs, N.J.: Prentice-Hall, 1964.

Strong, E. K., Jr. *The vocational interests of men and women.* Stanford: Stanford University Press, 1943.

Volsky, T., Magoon, T. M., Norman, W. T., & Hoyt, D. P. *The outcomes of counseling and psychotherapy.* Minneapolis: University of Minnesota Press, 1965.

Three Dilemmas of the Student Personnel Profession and Their Resolution

Kate Hevner Mueller

On whatever campus he may find himself, any personnel worker will face three dilemmas which other faculty and administration workers are able to escape. The first of these grows out of the contrast between the goals that his profession embraces and the functions that higher education assigns to him. The second dilemma stems from the inadequacy of the personnel worker's methods for achieving either his own objectives or those that the faculty and administrative officers expect of him. The third dilemma involves the paradox of developing student individuality in the increasingly bureaucratic structure of the campus.

I. Professional vs. Assigned Goals

In 1937 the goals embodied in *The Student Personnel Point of View* were expressed as follows:

> One of the basic purposes of higher education is the preservation, transmission, and enrichment of the important elements of culture—the product of scholarship, research, creative imagination, and human experience. It is the task of colleges and universities so to vitalize this and other educational purposes as to assist the student in developing to the limits of his potentialities and in making his contribution to the betterment of society.[1]

1. American Council on Education. *The Student Personnel Point of View: A Report of a Conference.* (Series 1, No. 3.) Washington, D.C.: the Council, 1937.

In 1961 Nevitt Sanford and others stated more explicit goals in modern psychological terms:

> Education means openness to change. It means that we help the student shed the conventional wisdom and enable him to make rational choices by the use of information, insight, and sensitivity. It means, first of all, that we generate the willingness to change. We communicate excitement about the worlds of knowledge and of the arts, so that our students will want to expose themselves to unaccustomed experiences . . . . For the student, too, education is self-revelation. He must be able to expose himself to the teacher and to other students so that he may be helped better to realize his own potential.[2]

Sanford also mentions such traits as freedom in the expression of impulse, independence of pressures toward conformity, sense of social responsibility, and sensitivity to ethical issues. Reports from research at Berkeley and elsewhere show that these same traits are also those that distinguish the creative from the non-creative personality, the freshman from the senior.[3]

Since the original 1937 statement, however, it has been pointed out that this "personnel point of view" is an imprecise basis for theory and there has been an emphasis on the importance of social interaction in development and on the larger society as the milieu in which personal development must take place. The personnel profession seems to have accepted these criticisms with little or no dissent.

The first dilemma appears when the personnel officer finds himself actually on the job. He knows that his job is to offer services to all students—including the foreign student, the financially needy student, and the entering student; but all too soon the personnel officer learns he is also responsible for the *control* of the student, the supervision of the student's activities so that they will provide satisfactory developmental experience for him, and the provision of a residential life that fosters the kind of socialization process which the student *needs* but does not *want*. The studies of Pepinsky and Correll have exposed this dilemma with great clarity:

2. Sanford, Nevitt, editor. *College and Character.* New York: John Wiley & Sons, 1964, p. 277.
3. *Ibid.*, p. 286.

Personnel people, as agents delegated by the institution to perform institutional functions, must administer and control in order to do their jobs efficiently—indeed, in order to survive in the institution. They must, on the other hand, be benign and ever attuned to the needs of individual students in order to meet the demands of their own self images, as well as those of the students, the institution, and society alike. How to resolve this dilemma?[4]

"Control" and "supervision" are key words in this dilemma. Control may be elaborate and ingenious, understated and casual, or kindly but firm; supervision may be comprehensive or superficial and welcome or resented. Each campus has a spirit and method of its own. Student rebellion against either control or supervision has been demonstrated in every decade of educational history, and the present *seeming* increase in student antagonism may actually represent a decrease in view of the smaller proportion of the student body which becomes actually involved in campus demonstrations and the disproportionate attention given by newspapers to this aspect of college life.

Qualitatively, however, there is a difference between the student rebellions of 100, 50, or 25 years ago and today's rebellions. Today there is a larger proportion of youth in the total population and a much larger proportion of these young people attend colleges.

Education is now the chief business of the college student, his occupation. The college student is as mobile, as affluent, and as independent as most citizens; and he is encouraged to be as well organized as any other citizen in our democratic society. He has observed the easy, dramatic, and effective civil disobedience methods. From the faculty, the only voices he has heard are those that use the magic word *freedom*.

The profession of personnel work is not without its own methods of attack on these dilemmas. The primary approach for the professional is always research, and in this case more research is needed on students' precollege expectancies and postcollege behavior. More research should be done on the attitudes of parents, alumni, and the general public who

4. Correll, Paul T. "Student Personnel Workers on the Spot." *Journal of Counseling Psychology* 9:232–37; Fall 1962.

See also: Correll, Paul, and Pepinsky, Harold. "The Overt and Covert Control of Students." *American Psychologist* 17:409; July 1961. (Summary statement only.)

Snoxell, L. F. "Counseling Reluctant and Recalcitrant Students." *Journal of College Student Personnel* 2:16–20; December 1960.

might be educated to other expectancies and to more sympathetic support for whatever degree of supervision the administration expects. Research is also needed on social control and communications but especially on the process by which administration in higher education can promote an environment for individual development.

In addition to research, two kinds of action are needed to solve the first dilemma: First the study of group counseling, of communication, and of social control must share the emphasis on individual counseling in the training of future personnel officers. Counseling concepts and techniques as rigidly defined in their purest form will prove of limited use to the campus personnel officer whose assignment is control and whose goal is maximum self-development in the campus milieu.

The second needed action is more difficult but more important: The old-fashioned concept of supervision and control and its exclusive assignment to the personnel division must be recognized for the impossibility that it is, and this responsibility must not only be modified but distributed more equably among other administrative officers and faculty.

II. The Authority Behind Personnel Practices

The second dilemma stems from the inadequacy of present personnel methods for achieving either the stated goals of the profession or those usually assigned to it. In other campus disciplines the student is treated as a client, not as a customer. He cannot present himself to the health service and say, "I have decided that it would be a good idea to have my appendix taken out this semester." He accepts the physician's right to guide him in such a matter. Likewise, the student accepts the authority of the professor to say, "If you do not learn these rules of French grammar, you will not be understood," but what authority can the counselor invoke to convince the student that it is to his best interest to conform to certain standards and practice certain behavior patterns?

In today's society, authority, the basis of all professionalization, is largely based on scientific proof, on a model found in nature itself. Science is the darling of the public; and research, the rock upon which it rests, is conceived in terms of experimentation, laboratory work, apparatus, basic elements, and logical structures. We are a science-oriented society. We believe that progress is made in terms of scientific endeavor, and we demand proof for any course of action and a soundly supported hypothesis for any adventurous departure.

The student, as any other citizen, feels therefore that it is his right to demand proof from the personnel worker that the education in living he teaches and the process of maturing he promotes are exactly the right ones to achieve the goal that the personnel worker envisions, namely, full realization of all individual potentiality and the fullest development of individuality and creativeness. However, it is clear to the personnel worker and, unfortunately, to the student as well that he cannot produce proven methods for reaching his goals in the same way that the classroom teacher can invoke the authority of his discipline. Psychology, sociology, philosophy, economics, and anthropology have taught the counselor a great deal; but they have not given him proven methods and results.

There is hope that the residence hall director may eventually be able to say as a professional: "We have searched the literature, made experiments, surveyed the field, and analyzed the problems. We now know that our present method is the best possible way to manage group living." But he would also have to add in all honesty, ". . . on this particular campus, in order to meet the stated goals of this institution and the needs of its students, within the prices charged, and in the present world situation."[5]

Personnel has always hoped that its basic sciences—psychology and sociology—would give the data and hypotheses about attitudes and behavior, communication, and human development which would be useful for interpreting the post-adolescent youth and the nature of the campus society. But this hope has now grown dim because unlike the natural and physical sciences, the social sciences have no model in nature to serve as a criterion for the ultimate truth.

What reasons are behind the student's refusal to accept extraclassroom learning with the same deference to authority that he generally assumes toward the teaching of the faculty?

5. Useem, Ruth Hill. "Professionalizing an Academic Occupation: The Case of Student Personnel Work." *Journal of the National Association of Women Deans and Counselors* 27:94–101; Winter 1964.

The first reason, a psychological one, is that the student is at an age when freedom from authority means most to him. He is breaking away from the restraints of family authority and family living. He feels the responsibility that goes with taking a large share of the family income for education. The departure from the old neighborhood to another where he must make his own way as an independent person is the most significant milestone he has yet encountered in life. He has long anticipated this freedom and will resist any inroads into it. Naturally, many students abuse this new freedom. Indeed, for many students it is only through this abuse of time, effort, and feeling that self-discipline will be acquired.

The second reason, a sociopsychological one, is that there is a clash between the student's growing awareness of self-potential and the many frustrations and complexities of modern life. The student is asked to assimilate too much in too little time. He is confronted simultaneously with new ideas, new personalities, and new opportunities but also with stiff competition, unaccustomed rebuffs, and disappointments in himself and others. Half of this clash is his own fault because of his own prejudices, bad habits, and ignorance. He recognizes some of these deficiencies, although not always accurately or fully. This lack of recognition is a healthy trait at this stage of his life. He must maintain a balance between self-confidence and humility to allow for the growth of a self-identity that can adapt to both success and vicissitude. The other half of the clash comes from the pressures of new knowledge which challenge old habits of thought and pressures from the total society, especially from its characteristic bureaucracies which require adaptation and conformity.

Conformity in and of itself is not unacceptable to youth. The student practices it willingly each day of his life. Some of it is of his own choosing—as dress, manners, and entertainment. Some of it is forced upon him—as payment of tuition in designated amounts at set times and following the requirements of classroom learning. Conformity offends him when it interferes with his natural desires and habits in regard to pleasure. Conformity also offends him when it touches his pride, his ideals, his faith in justice and other virtues, and his dignity as a human being with individual rights and privileges.

In seeking the answers for this second dilemma of authority and professional autonomy for personnel's special kind of teaching, much useful research has already been done on campus subcultures, their goals, and their characteristics.

It would help a great deal if some scholar would gather all this research together; discard the insignificant locally limited pieces once and for all; place it in historical perspective so that some of it would be eliminated and some enhanced; classify the materials in large-small, selective-nonselective, and other categories; translate the diverse philosophical, psychological, and sociological concepts into one unified vocabulary; separate the hypotheses from the empirical evidence and the management factors from the learning elements; and organize the whole around some feasible theories. We could then identify the researchable problems and the significant questions; carry on more useful research; and probably arrive at some operating principles that our clients, the students, could more readily embrace.

Reasonableness is the best basis for authority in most phases of management of group living and student activities. This would mean having insight into and sympathy with student needs and behavior and having regular revisions to meet changing fashions in manners, dress, and recreation.

III. The Individual Student and the Campus Bureaucracy

The third dilemma arises for the personnel worker because in recent decades higher education has inevitably been caught up in the bureaucratic trend characteristic of many other aspects of modern life. So long as the student may be dealt with in an individual, face-to-face relationship, the training and skills of the dean or counselor are adequate and his work can be joyful, challenging, and rewarding. Students are intelligent, ambitious, often troubled, sometimes reluctant, but, on the whole, eager and responsive.

But the personnel worker is no longer able to deal in a face-to-face, primary relationship and not always in the individual-to-group, or secondary, relationship—except on the smaller campus or with the relatively few student officers or in the groups which he serves as adviser. Rather, he must deal with the student in a tertiary relationship as a part of a complicated bureaucratic structure, a man-to-organization confrontation and process which is a new relationship still to be learned by both student and counselor.[6]

As preparation for dealing with the organization world—that tertiary, man-to-management relationship inescapable in our society—America's youth has had no specific formal education and a great deal of informal miseducation via observing the current adult folkways. In the family the child learns how to deal with human beings as individuals—how to please, cajole, defy, manipulate, and so forth. But between the ages of 18 and 22, the student has his first significant experience in one of the many large organizations with which he will find himself dealing all the rest of his life. It is a new and difficult experience for which he is totally unprepared.

The bureaucratic structure that stands between the counselor and the student is obnoxious but inevitable. It may be elaborate or simple, efficient, or wasteful, but every campus has *some* of it. The president cannot deal with the student directly in teaching him his culture, in developing his potential, or in offering him the services of his everyday life. Between the student and the president then stands the personnel division, that bureaucracy of people and function designed to mediate the extraclassroom activities and opportunities that develop student potential and foster individuality.

As the student meets the bureaucracy of any large campus, the very mechanisms designed to expedite, equalize, and protect his interests will irritate him. For example, if he wishes to schedule a social event, he must register two weeks in advance in triplicate; to charter a bus for an off-campus game, he must guarantee the number of riders, take out insurance, and finance in advance. The closer he comes to the hierarchy which pyramids human beings for their interlocking operations, the more disillusioned he may become.

The faults of the bureaucracy itself—the ineptitude or downright viciousness of the adults within it and its lumbering impertinence—aggravate the clash of the individual with campus organization. On the campus the student begins his lifelong experience with disappointing agencies and personalities in society. In this postadolescent period, the youth's own individuality is of prime importance to him. This trait is

6. Coleman, James S. "Research in Autonomy and Responsibility in Adolescents." *Journal of the National Association of Women Deans and Counselors* 28:2–9; Fall 1964.

psychologically acceptable to his elders although it is not his most admired or most ingratiating trait. Can we teach him that there are useful methods and a "due process" for dealing with bureaucracies and that it would be rewarding for him to study and practice them for their value to him in later life?

It is exactly at this point that the student's lack of training in such methods is critical for his self-esteem. He sees only two possible actions: either to submit and let the bureaucratic structure take its toll of his ego strength or to rebel and suffer the role of outlaw to the "good" society. But he *could* learn how to brace for significant inroads on his freedoms and shrug off the insignificant ones, how to count the cost of resistance and organize in accordance with what he can afford, how to circumvent impossibilities, or how to follow necessary routines with the least expenditure of his emotional energy.

No other bureaucratic structure seems so obnoxious as that which touches group living and student activities. Even within the personnel division some specialties escape. But in housing, student government, activities, fraternity relationships, and discipline, the personnel worker is definitely the front man on the firing line.

The student finds it much more natural and easy to embrace the classroom bureaucracy because he views it as the eventual entrée into his chosen profession. He can, for the most part, tolerate the conformity that his curriculum requires because of the authority of the discipline itself. The student is also reconciled to the unfeeling bureaucracy of the business office, to fee payments, to meal tickets, to library rules, to parking fines, and to half a hundred other routine restrictions. He accepts them as extraneous to his learning, as not pretending to be other than they are: pure management processes developed to the highest possible degree of efficiency for the structure and its workers.

IV. A New Theory and Role for the Personnel Division

The three dilemmas of the student personnel worker call for a new perspective on student personnel goals, functions, and methods. Suppose that we begin with the third all-embracing dilemma and realize that the student needs to learn how to meet this tertiary relationship, how to deal with organized society and all its institutions, including its bureaucratic ones. Why not emphasize that we are student personnel *administrators*, demonstrate that we are good ones, and teach the students how good administration works and what it can mean to them now and in the future. We can streamline our efficiency procedures for the benefit of the student rather than for our own benefit.

Each teacher, each personnel worker, and each student has his part to play in the total campus structure. To be a whole person, to achieve full personal and intellectual maturity within a modern, industrialized, democratic society, is one of the student's major developmental tasks. It is not easy to achieve this in a world made up of hundreds of organized and bureaucratic structures. Actually, the campus is a wholesome and benevolent organization, the best possible place to learn how to deal with other, perhaps vicious and difficult ones.

Certainly, by teaching students how to deal with organizations in general and campus hierarchy in particular, it is the personnel worker who has the most to gain: He should show the student that he is himself a part of and a full member of the campus bureaucracy and that there are accepted functions and roles which go with this status.

Could not the student government become an important part of the campus administrative and bureaucratic structure on its own under the sponsorship of the personnel division?

The student then will understand that he has no rights of "citizenship" or vote in somebody else's organizational structure but that he does have the right to the expression of his opinion, to a voice which can be heard in the making of any policy which may concern him— along with all the other voices to be heard by those campus officers to whom authority for general policy and action is delegated by the trustees. Granted, to be effective the "voice" may sometimes require "action." But riots, demonstrations, and civil disobedience techniques are not the appropriate means of communication between the individual and the university administration.

Students, parents, and counselors are now well aware of the "due process" that any offender can claim in the implementation of policy in his own individual case. Likewise, a "due process" must be observed in the opposite direction: When the student finds it necessary to deal with the bureaucracy, there are channels for the proper approach, protocol, and authority—all of which call for careful observance and must be set up as the first responsibility of the student body and the personnel division.

The student should understand his own carefully prescribed part in the process by which campus policy is made and implemented if he is to accept the authority behind the counselor. The student would learn that although the larger society has become oriented to research and scientific proof in the accepting of authority and in the bestowing of prestige, there are several other bases on which to accept authority and to bestow prestige and that there are several other kinds of authority practiced and acceptable in the organizations of modern society. Law has been developed out of precedent, which is in turn the product of reasoned evaluation of both sides of any problem. Precedent serves for a while in a dynamic society until it is eventually changed. Policies often are also based on consesus after careful consideration for individual and group differences, responsibilities, and rights. Reasonableness will also serve as the basis for authority and can be arrived at satisfactorily after proper study. These are the democratic traditions. Law and policy must be clearly stated and closely followed; deviations will call for vigorous protest.

This new perspective then helps solve the dilemma of authority by invoking new sources. Some experiments are available, and there are many useful precedents in the traditions and history of higher education. Consensus, reasonableness, and due process are all appropriate and available to be carried on always by dialogue, never by negotiation. This will not be easy, for society itself offers students only the wrong examples.

Among other things, students need to learn that much patience is required in any man-to-organization relationship, that delegation of some rights and responsibilities makes life simpler, that one chooses his conformities as carefully as his freedoms, and that tolerance for ambiguity is the quality that distinguishes the sophisticated from the naive.

The student learns all of these by many methods: by direct communication, by formal study in orientation, and, most especially, by experience and by observing such campus models as junior and senior students, counselors, and faculty members. Of special importance for students would be the working out of a code of behavior which would help an individual student solve his own moral problems. Students need to learn that in a power-and-status-conscious society, there are many forces at work that might undermine the intelligent approach to problems and the maintaining of general behavior standards and outlook.

In the various campus departments there should be codes of behavior for the student to observe at first hand, not fragmented or invisible codes, such as those for athletics, for hiring and firing the faculty, and for freedom of speech, but a code for the total university as a leading institution in our society.

The entering freshman's orientation to his new status and responsibilities should also be thorough and formal, his behavior code adequately taught. The organization of his affairs to his own best advantage and by the best management principles will be a joint project but certainly a major project for the student personnel administrator. This is the new and appropriate "assignment" of function to replace the former "control" and "supervision"; but only as a bona fide assignment from highest authority with the concern and cooperation of all campus adults can it succeed.

Some Unsolved Problems in
Student Personnel Work

E. G. Williamson

I turn now to one of the fundamentals of my resurging harmonic theme: Students are human beings. At least they are human beings in their potentialities of becoming motivated and humane persons. Some of them have not yet achieved eligibility, but one always lives in hope.

And one fundamental theme needs constant restatement. I recall Professor John Anderson's *obiter dictum* that a "good" doctoral thesis is one that raises more questions than it answers. Thus, as educators, we must constantly reformulate both our purposes in seeking to motivate and educate all students to their full potentialities, as well as seeking to reforge the means to that objective.

Our efforts to aid more students achieve higher learning discloses increasingly and definitively what we do not know, as well as what we have already learned. I happen to believe in the theory of education as essentially a matter of mapping out one's areas of ignorance, in the hope that one can reduce those areas. My concept of education is essentially *knowing as endless learning.* And this kind of education is not restricted to "inert knowledge," as Whitehead described much of classroom exercises. Rather is education a style of living characterized as progressive search in learning of the not-yet-known.

And in the spirit of learning as living and living as learning, I suggest that the unity, or the essence of our profession as student personnel workers is not so much its current *corpus* of technique (often mere *ad hocism*) or even its foundation *technology* of program development and maintenance. For me, the essence of our professional mission, as deans of students, is rather a restless and eternal quest for answers, often provisional, to the "great" queries about what has traditionally come to be defined as our own sphere of concern—our mission: The facilitation of humane maturity.

To be sure, we professional educators, usually denoted as deans, are reconciled to the fact that most of the time our efforts to achieve humane maturity produces *paradoxes* rather than *definitive answers* of a simplistic type: such as either-or, yes or no, true or false. We have come to empathize with our colleagues in cognate disciplines who must labor with paradoxes and uncompleted and provisional "conclusions" in their search of understanding and unknowns of human existence.

With these efforts at mood-setting and thematic backgrounding, let me etch some unfinished questions—problems which may worry us well into the next century. From this " old guard" I gladly and cheerfully bequeath these unanswered queries (perhaps unanswerable?) to the new generation of deans!

1. Is student personnel work a profession in its own status, or is it "popularity" with students? Or are the professor's assent and students' acceptance the ultimate criteria of the relevance of our profession to the higher learning?

It is about time we began to emerge in our own right as a relevant part of higher learning, not as an adjunct or even as a repair station for something gone wrong. You know, we began that way, "something went wrong," that is a squeaky axle, and we specialized in repairing and re-greasing squeaky axles ever since. One is entitled to ask the question whether or not we have anything unique, or whether or not we are merely a little more relevant in the hierarchy of the academic environment just a bit above the janitors and the groundsmen.

2. Within the accelerating urbanized and impersonalized American culture, what can and should we deans do to avoid losing the student in complex organization, processes and massed numbers?

This is a horrible nightmare when you think of all the forces that make for impersonalization of our urban culture. Shall we give up, and deal only with the few, particularly the discipline cases, who are the squeaky axle, or shall we innovate and invent new ways of personalization in the midst of large numbers?

The essence of student personnel work has from its very beginning centered the emphasis upon individualization. As my mentor used to say, "It is the individualization of mass education." And little did he anticipate what mass education would mean today.

3. Why do we persist in assuming that individualization is necessary or desirable in education? As one dean said to me one time, why not

just give up and just process students, one every 10 minutes? That was before the computer made it one every nine minutes. Should we rather be reconciled to the possibility that alienation of some individuals is inevitable in our education and society?

4. Is personalization of the educational experience—Kindergarten through College—necessary? In what ways, if any, does personalization facilitate human development, via education? Is the personalized relationship an outmoded concept of the 19th century and no longer relevant or appropriate in these days of mass congestions of humans in urban centers of population?

5. What can we do to live with the paradox of "authority" within the "democratic" educational experience and with benign concern for the individual student's development according to external criteria of the good life? Are we justified in "imposing" *external criteria* of excellence upon the "free" individual within our form of democracy?

Some day you may want to read a very interesting book on this topic by Levine, in which he uses the phrase "imposed posture" which seems to be contradictory to the concept of freedom and certainly is contradictory to the concept of self-chosen criteria of the good life so prevalent in adolescents today.

6. What, if anything, can we deans do with the paradox (often conflict?) of formal classroom learning (memorization) of fact, concept, theory in contrast with the informal development of motives, internalized criteria of the good life? How can we become, and how can we aid our students to become socialized persons through the interpenetration of each other—in sharp contrast with the established American doctrine of autonomy of the individual?

7. Are there conflict and mutual exclusion between the intellectual mission of American education and the post-Freudian assertion that man is also irrational and impulse-dominated? Hutchins is fond of referring to a university as a sort of intellectual monastery where one cerebrates, but does not viscerate. Have we exhausted the possibility of mediating between these two paradoxical and conflicting models of man, as a rational animal and as an irrational animal? How can we reconcile these conflicting points of view to achieve our mission of humanizing the maturity of the individual student?

8. What do we do with the paradox of privation (often the resultant

of excessive autonomy of self) and the requirements (opportunities) of membership in groups within school, community and society?

9. How can we survive the paradox of uniform, or even unitary, ideology in contrast with the proclaimed virtues of cultural pluralism, producing as it does diversity and often fragmentation of our campuses and, indeed, our society? Which is relevant and appropriate within our democracy—or are both possible and desirable or necessary? What degree of ambiguity or divergence of individual or subgroup efforts and activity is possible and desirable to maintain some measure of unity within our student culture? Too much fragmentation obviously destroys unity. Too little produces standardization. What is our role, as personnel deans and student personnel workers to aid in seeking some centripetal force to stabilize the forces of disruption, disunity, and autonomy of individuals?

10. Should we continue to serve as agents to aid each individual to seek and serve his own ends and purposes and thus abandon the search for unity or some degree of commonality within our campuses? Has the half century of efforts to organize and maintain "services" for students experiencing "problems" proved to facilitate maturity of student clientele, or have we merely patched them up? Are we now searching for new and hopefully more effective student personnel services beyond those inherited from our professional founding fathers and mothers who never faced a Berkeley of this proportion and diversity?

My own prediction is that in the years ahead we need to innovate new services for a new kind of clientele and new kind of society. We are going to find alternatives to the old services instead of merely reshuffling them. And one of the reasons is that we are in the midst of a revolution in morality, and have been for the past three decades. And it may be to the end of the century before we find some stabilized way of helping individuals adopt satisfying moral commitments with regard to sex, drug addiction, honesty, and LSD.

We need to invent new forms of services. One of the ones that I am advocating now is that we go back to school and learn how to help students organize revolutions. Every time I say that, my fellow deans shudder because they grew up in the tradition of trying to maintain a midcity operation, a Pandora's box, a calm campus. And I say that the decades ahead will demonstrate that conflict is natural and is of the very essence of the higher learning.

11. What have we personnel workers accomplished in our efforts to reduce scholastic failure, human misery, and withdrawal from college? Do we have any professional obligation to seek to innovate new and more effective services to reduce or alleviate these forms of "waste" in manpower utilization in our urbanized and technological society? Or should we conclude that such "wastes" are inevitable in Western civilization, and indeed within education itself? Many of our faculty colleagues have reached that conclusion, that those who are doomed to failure are doomed to failure, and there is not very much you can do about it, so spend your time on those who are going to become professors.

12. Has our assigned mission within education continued to be efforts to "control" students through "lid-sitting" and punishment? To my way of thinking, controversy is at the very heart of 20th century education, "lid-sitting" is an operation of the 1920's, doomed to failure, and our efforts to maintain orderliness and calm and decorum are middle class virtues that need to be re-examined.

13. Should personnel deans seek to insulate the campus from the disruptive forces of the surrounding community? I glory in the fact that students have really sought to do what John Dewey sought to do, but never succeeded completely, and that is to bring the disorder and disruption of the 20th century on to the campus and to apply reasoned inquiry in the search for innovations of those new kinds of services which will aid students to deal with unsolved problems. I glory in the fact that the bearded ones are among us. I agree with their objective to bring the 20th century into the campus.

14. In addition to our services supportive of the educational mission of the college (financial aid, counseling about choice of curricula, remediation of study skills, and the like, which are all relevant personnel services, just as relevant today as when they were invented) what can personnel workers do to create a campus and residence climate and mores, indeed even an environmental stress of standards conducive to significant learning outside of the classroom? The whole extra-curriculum is ours. The faculty does not care about it, and does not believe that it really contributes much except distraction to what they consider to be the main mission of the institution, namely, intellectualism. Hundreds and hundreds of opportunities to saturate the extracurriculum with learning that is worthy—not worthy of credit, heaven forbid, but worthy of esteem and respect.

What a topsy-turvy world this is. Only Alice in Wonderland would have understood it. Professors are entitled to due process before dismissal and students are now claiming the same inalienable right. But a college president was dismissed ungraciously without due process, and so allegedly was a dean of women at Stanford. When will deans of students come next in line for La Guillotine? Have you thought about that? Do you have due process? No. No, you don't even have rights. You only have obligations.

We are several decades retarded in our efforts to apply rationality and reasonableness to university problems of control, restraint, and academic freedom both for students and faculty, and now for presidents—hopefully soon for deans of students. Our profession's traditional posture, nationally, of non-involvement in controversy has done much to produce our image as campus agents of resistance to contemporary, current, unsolved problems of our urban culture. But professional problems continue to arise from these unsolved societal problems of our decade. What will we do to seek solutions or at least resolutions?

Without in any way diverting our *expertise* in programs of necessary services to students in need of assistance, we must add to our mission as a profession, research on these and other unsolved questions and problems. And in a prevailing spirit of experimentation and innovation, I suggest that we deans and all of our staffs turn ourselves into researchers and thinkers concerning these unsolved problems of the higher learning, conceived as the releasing and cultivation of motivations of striving to become one's full potentiality of humane being. This is our categorical imperative as deans and student personnel workers in the higher learning.

How Others See Us

Elizabeth A. Greenleaf

Each year, members of the American College Personnel Association assemble at a national meeting and each person comes with his own anticipation of the event. For some this is an opportunity "to get away from it all"; for others it is a fulfillment of a professional responsibility to keep in touch with major concerns in specialized areas. Although it may be a vacation time for some, many still have their minds on the Dow Chemical interviewers due on campus, the student body elections, the problem of budgets and the need to hire staff while in Detroit, or on the officers of the Black Power organization whom you couldn't see until next week.

A study made two years ago to determine the effectiveness of conventions indicated that our members come to convention to share ideas with one another, to become aware of current practices on other campuses, and to hear papers presented on the major research and innovative practices of colleagues and leaders in our professions (Hoyt & Tripp, 1967). These opportunities will be available this year in more than sixty programs planned by ACPA commissions and the 1968 program committee.

The tradition of these national conventions has been for the president of ACPA to present a luncheon address. These addresses have centered around the presidents' speciality areas or have dealt with major student concerns of the day.

As I have visited various college campuses, and read the current literature—including our *Journal* and *The Chronicle of Higher Education*—as one actively engaged in preparing young men and women for entering positions in the student personnel field, as one actively involved as a student personnel administrator and educator, as the problems of accreditation for the preparation of student personnel educators have been considered, one question comes to mind: *What is the future of student personnel administration?*

There is much concern today for what one sees and hears. Few if any persons with experience in student personnel administration or counseling have been promoted to top level student personnel positions on any major college campus during the past two years. During the past few years, there has been a major reorganization of student personnel services on campus after campus. When this takes place, most often a major problem is how to reassign the Dean of Women. She is left either as Director of Women's Education (and one questions how women's education today differs from men's) or she is given an undefined job as a general administrator. Rarely are women in our profession given a real functional responsibility. The concern is strong enough that many in our profession are asking whether women should be encouraged to earn advanced degrees or strive for top level positions.

On campus after campus the chief student personnel administrator has become the "whipping post" for students, faculty, and other administrators. The dean is seen as responsible in some way for the Student Power movement, for the image of the university as seen by the public. Outstanding senior members of our profession are leaving administrative responsibilities and going into teaching positions in Higher Education or in a Counseling department, where the emphasis is placed on the preparation of student personnel educators.

As I myself view the eight-hour teaching load of a faculty member and as I consider the possibility of having time to do one task well, I am faced with the question, "For what are we preparing the young men and women who will enter our field? What will be their role on the college campus in the 1970's?" I remember a question raised by one of our own members at a recent accreditation meeting: "Will there be any student personnel workers in the years ahead?"

It appears to me that at this time, Spring, 1968, if there is any one thing we need to do as a professional group, it is to define our role in the contributions we are to make in the institutions of higher education which we represent. Are we seen as student personnel educators, or as babysitters, managers, operators on our college campuses? Are we administrators with real responsibility for determining and interpreting policy, for making decisions and budgets, or are we to carry out the orders of the students, the faculty, and the general public? *How do others see us?*

I'll begin by defining the *us* as student personnel educators, as those on the campus of an institution on higher education who traditionally, and in many cases *still* have job descriptions which indicate that their responsibilities include the setting of an environment in which the community can meet its academic objectives, the counseling of young adults to the end that each person becomes more self-directive and can secure the widest possible benefits from the college expeiences, and teaching in the out-of-class curriculum; a curriculum to better prepare the young adults as a citizen with skills in human relations.

Titles such as Director of Residence Halls, Director of Financial Aids, Dean of Men, Dean of Women, and Vice President for Student Affairs, may be new, but their functions long have been performed within the American college campus. Leonard (1956, pp. 106–114) best describes these early functions and beginnings:

One of the strengths of the American Higher Education system has been the freedom to develop institutions that expressed the specific educational aspirations of many groups of people. This freedom gave our educational structure an unparalleled vitality and flexibility, but it also made necessary the assumption by the institutions of learning of certain responsibilities that are not carried by similar institutions in other countries.

One such responsibility has been overseeing the general welfare of students which was first assumed by Colonial academies and colleges brought about in part by the compelling urge of the colonists to have their children learn the principles of their particular religion that led to the establishment of the early academies and colleges and to the housing, boarding, and disciplining of students in accordance with their sharply defined standards of conduct.

Thus from the early days, governments and institutions assumed the responsibility "not only for the intellectual development of the youths but also for the aspects of their lives that in the Old World had been carried by families. As a result, in most of the Colonial academies and colleges the students were housed or boarded. Their recreation, manners, morals, religious life, and general welfare, in addition to their studies were closely supervised. Personnel services were a constituent part of the program and the [reason] for the founding of the institution . . . The colleges sought to extend supervision to include every hour of the day and every activity of students. The rules governing student conduct were numerous and detailed. Punishments for even minor infractions were severe.

The first personnel officers in an American college were the colony overseers at Harvard and the members of the Boards of Trustees in other colleges. Later presidents and members of the faculties shared the responsibilities and were assisted by tutors, ushers, stewards, and student monitors. They acted "in loco parentis" and were required to patrol the dormitories frequently and report all absences and misdemeanors to the boards of trustees, which determined the punishments.

During the early 19th century colleges gradually began to recognize that the positive approach to behavior was preferred. Students were even "permitted" to assist the administration in meeting the current problems of the college, financial aid in the forms of scholarship became available and there was a clear concern for health and general welfare of students.

Are these historical responsibilities still seen as the major function of student personnel educators, or are the students responsible for their environment? Is counseling performed only by a clinically trained counselor in a central counseling office? Is there any education outside of the classroom? How do others accept these as our functions and responsibilities? When I say others, consider four groups: the students; the faculty; other administrators; and the parents and citizens of the community responsible for our institutions.

The Students

Much space is given in current publications and news releases to the strength and importance of Student Power. As defined at the August, 1967 meeting of the National Student Association, it is a "movement designed to gain for students their full rights as citizens, their rights to democratically control their non-academic lives, and their right to participate to the fullest in the administrative and educational decision-making process of the college or university." In all the years that I have attended meetings of this association I have heard much talk among the activity advisers as to how we could secure the involvement of students in responsible student government, be it the Union Board, the Residence Hall Council, Judicial Boards, or the many committees on our campuses. Are we seen as opposed to Student Power?

I'm reminded of a panel I heard a few years ago at a Southern College Personnel Association meeting. A panel of students were asked to describe what they considered to be their relationship with the Dean's office and the students' role in influencing their college or university. These were officers of campus organizations on various types of college campuses—a student body president at a small Catholic men's college, an AWS president on a large residential college campus, a Panhellenic president from a liberal arts college, etc. The students were most perceptive in describing the actual situations on their campus. A student body president said that the average student never saw the dean except when he welcomed the freshmen or as he dealt with students who had seriously violated rules or regulations. This student felt that they as students had a responsibility for activities, but that it was not real involvement. Another student felt that they really made the rules on their campus which affected them, and that they as students had a great deal of influence.

Are we, as student personnel educators, seen as really available to students, and do we have responsible, well prepared, intellectually sharp staff available to students? What students do you really know on your campus? With whom do students see you eating in the student commons or at a fraternity or sorority house? Do they see you talking to the "Green Bagger," the man with the long hair and earrings; the couple not married but living together in the off-campus apartment, the person or persons challenging the right of the university to be responsible for students' out-of-class activities? Do students see you at a meeting with those who advocate "Black Power," and can you really understand what our Black students are saying? Are you seen as spending your time only with the "elected" officers, with the Dow Chemical violators, or do you sometimes see "Mr. Average College Student?"

Students are saying, "Trust us, take us as adults; we are capable of and willing to be responsible for our own way of living." *Are* we trusting them, taking them as adults, giving them responsibilities for their way of living, and then, as educators, are we holding them responsible for their participation?

Those of us who are becoming gray, who are over 30, are often seen by the average young adult as the authoritarian they left at home. They want no help until the time they need it. I'm reminded of a young man who won the presidential election in a residential community on our campus. With 800 of a possible 1100 votes cast, he had won by 25 votes and had won on an anti-staff campaign. Students were to have no "interference" or assistance from the dean of students' staff in that community. As director of residence hall activities, I received a call from this independent student leader about nine o'clock one evening. Without proper scheduling of either space or event, an elaborate installation program had been planned and many campus leaders were in attendance for the ceremony. The inter-residence hall judicial board had issued an injunction against his installation because of election campaign violations. Would I tell the board that he was to be installed? How tempted would one be to remind him that he had won on an anti-staff campaign, that he had followed no university regulations in scheduling his event, and that now it was up to him! No, as an educator, he was showed the functioning of student government, assisted to understand what an injunction was, and then student government was held responsible for evaluation of his actions.

How can we be seen as responsible for helping students find a balance where they can have real involvement and concern for their in- and out-of-class life? This should mean self-direction brought about on the part of students, with a realization of what real responsibility they can take in terms of time, and in terms of legal and financial responsibilities. Do students see us as helping, or are they hiring us? Do they view us as persons with a joint concern for the total environment of our college campuses?

Do students see us as concerned about world affairs, concerned with the scientific wonders of today's world, concerned with the political issues of the day? Do they see us at campus lectures, do we carry on conversations with them about anything academic or about concerns of today's world? Are we seen as encouraging a learning in the free University discussions and lectures held outside the classroom, held in our residence halls, in our sorority and fraternity houses, and in our student union buildings?

Are we still seen as serving "in loco parentis," or are we, as indicated in *Goldberg versus the Regents of the University of California*, responsible for the regulation of "conduct and behavior of the students which tends to impede, obstruct or threaten the achievements of [the college's] educational goals." Are we seen as providing an environment in which free inquiry and learning can take place?

Do students see us as available and helpful, or have enrollments increased so rapidly that today we are only managers? Have we given students their due respect? Are we so busy sitting in meetings that we are no more help to students than the faculty member who puts first and foremost his research and writing? Have we taken our strongest personnel into administrative posts and failed to reward financially those who will work regularly with students? How many campuses are developing student personnel preparation programs in order to have staff in residence halls, and thus are placing persons to work directly with students who are no different than the teaching assistants we have complained about in the classrooms? Are we giving students real responsibilities and respect for their capabilities, and are we as educators holding them responsible for their actions?

The Faculty

How does the faculty view us? How many times can you walk into a faculty gathering and have someone say, "Well, are the students all under control today," "Guess you'll have all the students out of classes next week to work on homecoming floats," or "I wouldn't have your job for anything!"?

Each year as a part of the practicum seminar for second year student personnel interns some time is spent with representatives of our Indiana University faculty council. I'm reminded of two recent incidents. A distinguished senior member of our faculty, a member of the University's Faculty Council and the Student Affairs Committee, a Faculty Associate in one of our residence halls, made the statement to our future colleagues that "the dean of students' staff is an arm of the faculty council." He pointed out that on our campus, as is true on many others, the responsibility for student affairs belongs to the faculty and that they have delegated this to the dean of students. At about the same time another distinguished member of our faculty was asked by a young member of our residence hall staff how the faculty viewed the role of the residence hall staff. Without hesitation, the faculty member replied, "Oh, most of them don't even know you exist."

Are we seen only as an arm of the faculty, or are we partners with the faculty in helping to meet the needs of our educational community? As we have become more and more specialized in our jobs, as we have added many new staff members, are we seen by faculty as making a contribution to the campus, or are we seen as taking away from the budget money that might go for more adequate teaching staffs? Having grown up in a faculty home, I'm conscious of my father's colleagues asking, "Who are all those new counselors over in the dean's office? What are they supposed to do? They had better not begin to advise my students!"

It appears certain that no members of ACPA would question the fact that the first objective of our institutions is an academic one. Many student personnel educators may accept the fact that they are an arm of the faculty, but there must be an acceptance of student personnel staff as professional persons with knowledge and skills to help meet the needs of students. If we have educated, professionally prepared, experienced personnel and are specialists in working with students, how are faculty who are specialists in academic disciplines seen as prepared to move in and make decisions on policies affecting student life? How adequate is our data seen when we are called on to present to faculty committees information to serve as basis for their decisions? Are we really seen a having done our research and shared this adequately with one another? In a meeting before a faculty-student committee discussing visitation in our residence halls, I was asked for evidence from other campuses on the effects visitation had on the educational environments. Have we the answers?

How do we interpret our role to the faculty? How do we prove that we are more than policemen and disciplinarians? Do we go to faculty meetings and are we seen sitting only with members of our own division, do we go only with our colleagues to the faculty room for lunch, do we take the opportunity to attend faculty functions? Not just the dean, but is the dean seen as making it possible for assistants to have the opportunity and take advantage of faculty contacts?

Are we seen taking the leadership in suggesting ways in which faculty may become more involved with students? Have members of the dean of students' staff been included when residential colleges or special scheduling of classes by residential areas have been considered, or has the dean's office been informed that a hall was being taken for an academic program? What are we doing to work with the commuter student to the end that he has faculty contacts? When we hear students complaining because they cannot secure academic advising, when we hear that a faculty member is failing to meet his classes, are we seen as responsible for pointing out these problems? Do we have free access and do we take the opportunity to suggest corrections needed in the teaching field as the faculty through AAUP have indicated to us how we should handle discipline? Have we as a professional personnel organization effectively reacted to the AAUP *Statement on Rights and Freedoms of Students?* Why are we not, like librarians, seen as eligible for membership in AAUP? Are we not seen as having a teaching role?

Administrators

Thirdly, what is our relationship with fellow administrators? As one considers responsibilities fundamentally a part of administration, one would expect student personnel administrators to have a major role for determining policy, interpreting policy, enforcing policy, decision-making, selection and supervision of staff, and budget making.

Does the President, the Dean of Faculties, the Board of Control of your institution consult student personnel educators on your campus on matters concerning students? Does the student personnel staff keep them well informed on problems which may affect the campus? Can the student personnel educator tell them about the demonstration to take place, or what type of reaction might be expected from various groups of the campus community when a new policy is announced? How often do the student personnel divisions recommend possible actions to the board of control or to the administrative committee on campus?

How realistic are the student personnel educators in defending their budgets? There are many concerns today as to whether money is effectively used to meet the objectives of the institution. The student personnel budget easily can be seen as going a long way in paying for a great number of new teaching faculty.

In terms of the relationship of our role to students and faculty, is it our role to co-operate with the Dean of Faculty to shape the direction of the educational experiences of students? How can student personnel educators serve as catalysts to bring all forces of the campus together to the end that there is a joint direction given to educational experiences?

How do the President and the Board of Trustees view student clashes with the Dean? Is it best to just reorganize and get the problem out of his hair? How does the president view the basic philosophy of the student personnel services on your campus? Are student personnel educators seen as so idealistic and so dedicated to their work that they are unable to view situations realistically in terms of today's world? We must not be defensive as societal changes bring about many changes in our responsibilities.

How does the budget officer look at the request from the dean of students office for travel to meetings of ACPA, APGA, ICPA, IPGA, NAWDC, IAWDC, NASPA, Midwest NASPA, ACUHO, ACU, NASFSA, Financial Aids Officers, AAHE, ACE, etc.? Do we today have any professional organization to give us direction as we work with the college presidents? A majort concern for all of us should be what is happening during a one week period which may end this afternoon. Within a week NASPA, NAWDC, and ACPA will each separately have passed resolutions on *The Statement of Rights and Freedoms of Students*, and we will have jointly or individually acted upon other areas of mutual concerns. How can we be seen as working together for a common goal?

A last question as we look at how other administrators view us: How do our own staff view us? Do we give real responsibility to staff who work with us and who come into contact day by day with the students, and at the same time do they keep us informed on student feelings and student needs? Many of us need to take an honest look at our student personnel structure, responsibilities of various members of the staff, and to be certain that we are dealing with one another in a respected way.

Parents and the General Public

We are often responsible for the first contacts with parents and students as they come to visit campus. Members of the student personnel division are most often the ones to prepare the orientation materials which go to parents and send out the rules and regulations which parents often *do* read. Have you taken a real good look lately at the types of materials which go into the homes of your students? On our campus it took a conference on the Negro in Higher Education before most of us were aware that we had no pictures of Negro students in any of our student orientation materials. Are we seen as realistic in extending expectations to parents for what we can do or are we seen as placing certain educational responsibilities squarely on the shoulders of their daughters and sons?

How does the student personnel educator interpret the college to the taxpayers of the community who see more and more property going off the tax lists? What are your institution and your student personnel services doing to bring about new experiences for students in realistic community projects? As we move towards the day when the students on our campus will have a right to vote, will we be taking a lead in the involvement of students in political affairs of the wide community? Do we as student personnel educators have any concern for the way the draft law is currently operating? If so, have we done anything about it?

I expect that all that has been done in this presentation is to raise questions, but that is what I intended to do. I have no more of the answers than each of you has. More important, each of us on our own campus must evaluate how others see us in relation to the goals and the objectives of our colleges. Each of us must evaluate ourselves as real educators. If our role is to set an environment in which the academic process can take place, is to provide counseling to the end that each student sets effective goals for himself, is to serve as an educator in out-of-class education, are we seen doing this effectively on each of our campuses?

Is there a future for student personnel educators? My answer is *Yes!* The functions are there to be performed, but the way these functions are to be performed are changing and must change. It depends on how others see us as effective in carrying out these functions that we may become real educators taking a leadership in the world of today's students. We must take a lead in bringing together faculty, students and other administrators to the end that each contributes to the education of the leaders to the future.

References

Hoyt, D. P., & Tripp, P. A. Members' evaluation of ACPA programs and services, *Journal of College Student Personnel*, 1967, 8, 40–45.

Leonard, E. A. *Origins of personnel services in American higher education.* Minneapolis: University of Minnesota Press, 1956.

Received April 4, 1968

Student Personnel Workers: Student Development Experts of the Future

Philip A. Tripp

If our object is to predict trends in student personnel work for the next 30 years, we must hypothesize what our country will be like 30 years from now. The forecast of 300 million people in the United States in the year 2000 indicates that space will be an acute problem. Most people will live in megalopoli; society will be more complex and will depend on sophisticated problem-solving skills. Power in all its forms will be available to all competent to use it; physical energy will be harnessed to perform most work. A cup of sand, we already know, contains enough energy to run a city for a day.

By the year 2000 psychological and social knowledge will be vastly expanded. We will have detailed knowledge of how to foster, prevent, and manipulate learning through teaching. We will be able to transform life itself. All the world will be immediately accessible to many people, and increased leisure will make men increasingly mobile. Probably the most stiking change will be the disappearance of the Protestant work ethic as a basic paradigm for organizing Western society.

There will be a new perception of what it means to be a human being, and that perception will be invested with a new respect for humanness and for the individual worth of human beings. Because we are beginning to see their value and necessity, we will see openness and greater honesty in interpersonal relations. We have been sensitized since World War II to the social hypocrisy in our society. Student personnel work has been accused of some of this hypocrisy and, in efforts to answer the charges, has made some real progress in the recent past. The twenty-first century may see a new era characterized by greater sensitivity and deeper qualities of love between and among people generally.

We have lived in our own times, and perhaps even throughout our country's entire history, in an adversary society. Adversary relations will shift to more wholesome ends in the future. There will be increasing awareness of the need to compete for everyone's benefit instead of exclusively for individual benefits. This is what is meant by deeper qualities of love among men. We, as a people, will develop greater sensitivity and a national set of values with deeper roots in moral and ethical concerns.

We will develop a more profound understanding of life as a continuous process of change. This will replace the search for a Holy Grail of knowledge that is, by implication, static, permanent, and unchanging. The promise of leisure is that it will give men time to fulfill themselves in all realms of their beings, both cognitive and affective.

All of these predicted changes have either direct or indirect implications for student personnel work and higher education in general. Students will require more individualized attention, and instructional patterns will become increasingly tutorial. Education will continue to be highly cognitive, but more attention will be paid to developing emotional and affective capacities. There will be more concern for self-awareness and development of warm and fulfilling interpersonal relations as significant objectives in the educational experience. Although education will continue to become more technical, curriculums will be highly individualized, and there will be no concern for credit hours or quality points or the kind of formalized mechanics now used in an attempt to quantify what is essentially a qualitative experience. Much of the future will fall to a new generation of *student development experts.* They will be responsible not only for integrating the intellectual experiences of the individual but also for assisting students in their study and treatment of moral and ethical problems. They will consult in the development of life styles and on the affective and aspirational aspects of student development.

To accomplish these educational goals, a new type of institution will be required. There is much evidence already that the multiversity is something of a dinosaur, an anachronism that must be replaced by a more viable social organization. The multiversity is the logical conclusion of our old conception of what education is about. There is an obvious need for a new mode of operation with more concern for primary groups and individualized instruction. Since many of the functions that the university-educated man now performs, such as engineering and middle management, may well be performed by machines, the university will turn to a different kind of task, i.e., making man more person-ally effective and a more fulfilled human being.

It is difficult to conceptualize the new forms of preparation for stu-dent personnel work. The old mission is obsolescent, and the new mis-sion is not quite in sharp focus yet. As a result we have many disloca-tions, many disruptions, and a sense of anxiety about what seems sensible to do to bring about some stability, some order, where it no longer exists. It is to be hoped that all of the solutions of problems cre-ated by the "new mission" will not be administrative solutions, but rather that social phenomena of the kind that I discussed earlier would be brought to bear in rethinking these problems. The future role of the student development person must be an increasingly professional role in the sense that he will be a qualified scholar in student development. He must have clear-cut status in the academic community, and this mission must be supported or at least accepted by all quarters of that community.

Rather than merely transmitting the stable, enduring facts from the past, we will learn to live in a world of change. Our mission is basically phenomenological. We are presumably prepared to deal with the idio-syncratic materials of the individual student's life. We are presumably competent to take process and to turn it to educational ends in a way that traditionally prepared scholars are not. This has not been their mission, and we have not specified it as our mission in these terms. But that is what we are talking about when we talk of ourselves as agents of change and when we talk of ourselves as instruments for promoting the effective use of the facts of change in achieving educational ends. We must prove ourselves in the coming decades.

Student personnel work is in a primitive stage of development. Many of our forebears and many of our colleagues have been motivated by a "good Samaritan" instinct. We have been applied persons who tend to regress to immediate needs and to settle for practical solutions to prob-lems, without any philosophical anxieties, because we think we are do-ing what situations require. This is no longer adequate. In fact, it is a passé conception of what it means to work to help young people grow up and to grow up ourselves. In the future, the student personnel worker will be much more knowledgeable than his present-day counter-part. He may even be more sophisticated than his traditionally trained disciplinary brethren, inasmuch as he knows that process has as great a force in life as content. If he is skillful in the use of process in promoting educational ends, he can substantially change the face of higher education.

In preparing professionals to be effective, as higher education evolves into a new form, we must prevent being caught in the old paradigms. It is easy to be captured in these because they are forced on us by history, custom, and tradition. We have a style of academic life now that is pretty rigid and formal. The first thing that must be done is to look at those rigidities and formalities with a very, very critical eye. We must begin to raise suitable questions about the techniques of teaching and learning in colleges and universities, in terms of a new mission of education. We have evidence of the beginnings of a new approach in group sensitivity training and dynamics programs. We have yet to deal with the area of teaching people generally to understand their feelings. Our society has been disposed against people admitting they have any feelings. Here is a zone where we must be pioneers and the precursors and the showers of the way.

In the development of an environment that is conducive to the kind of growth in students that we might strive for, the use of technological advances within the university must be carefully examined if we are to prevent machines from being disadvantageous to our mission. The reliance of student personnel workers on technical hardware can be a form of professional regression. These devices, improperly used, identify us as adversaries of the students. Our machines seemingly become our swords against them. A student saying, "Please do not fold, bend, staple, or mutilate me," is, in fact, saying to us, "You are trying to dehumanize me and I resist you." We should be glad for that affirmation and use technology only insofar as it clearly serves developmental purposes.

Student personnel workers have an unprecedented opportunity to point the way as higher education undergoes a major transformation in the next 30 years. If they become qualified student development experts, they may be major partners in the reformation of this social institution. They can help make it better able to treat matters of love, knowledge, and wisdom and thereby to foster the growth of persons.

Student Personnel Work:
A Profession Stillborn

James F. Penney

In half a century, student personnel work has not achieved professional recognition on campuses. As evidence, basic literature is cited both quantitatively and qualitatively. Preoccupation with housekeeping functions remains a major reason for the field's low esteem. The personnel point of view provides an inadequate base for professional organization. Fragmentation into a growing number of specialties characterizes current developments. The early dreams of a profession of student personnel work cannot be realized.

Few occupational entities have devoted as much energy to self-examination and attempts at self definition as has the amorphous body calling itself student personnel work. The specialty is roughly half a century old—surely time enough to achieve whatever degree of recognition and maturity the academic community is likely to allow. It is certainly time enough for it to establish itself as a profession among professions, if it is ever to do so. In that same half-century or less, a score or more new specialties have been born, matured, and become professionally established in the world of academe.

Student personnel work has not achieved professional recognition in the community of professionals operating on campuses. While it has sought to establish a position among the dominant power centers—faculty, administration, students—a realistic assessment of campuses in the 1960's can lead only to the conclusion that the effort has failed. Student personnel workers, their philosophy, and their goals are not among the major influences today in colleges and universities.

Basic Literature: Quantity

An attempt to identify causative factors may begin with an examination of the literature in the field. Analysis suggests several characteristics, each of which contributes to the conclusion that the occupation is not truly a profession and is not moving toward becoming one. Striking is the observation that there is a paucity of basic literature in the field. Though disconcerting to practitioners inundated by a plethora of journals, research reports, convention proceedings, position formulations, and policy statements, the observation remains supportable.

Where, for instance, are to be found basic writing that trace in their conceptualizations the development of a field of endeavor? Where are the rival statements of thesis, antithesis, and synthesis that have provided the crucial methodology through which knowledge has developed in the West? Where are the fundamental descriptions of the occupation and its practitioners that can serve to identify for it a place in the sun?

The student personnel specialty has produced surprisingly little of this sort of writing that endures. What are the basic textbooks in the field? Arbuckle (1953), Lloyd-Jones and Smith (1938), Mueller (1961), Williamson (1961), and Wrenn (1951) constitute the core. Included as historically significant might be the pamphlets in the American Council on Education Series on Personnel Work in Colleges and Universities, produced sequentially between 1939 and 1953. While each dealt with a specific topic, it is not unreasonable to consider the series as an entity that provided basic textual material representing the activities, rationales, and objectives of the field in an important period of its development. Altogether, the list is not quantitatively imposing as to represent a half-century of effort.

In contrast, problem-centered writings abound: Journals, abstracting services, and monographs multiply *ad infinitum*. Quantity, however, may be misleading. The fact of its timeliness implies that a journal article, research report, or monograph is likely to be of short-term value. Further, it has probably been developed upon already available principles nad accepted concepts instead of having focused upon the production of original formulations. In this context, the problem-centered literature of a field, appearing in periodical publications, may not be a valid index of the field's strength, endurance, or professional status. Student personnel work has not historically produced, and is not currently producing, a body of permanent, fundamental literature by means of which the specialty can be identified, evaluated, and its progressive development calculated.

Basic Literature: Quality

A qualitative assessment of the literature in student personnel work leads to other observations. The contents of the seminal books fall generally into three groupings. In the first is a large quantity of material taken over wholesale from the social sciences, chiefly psychology. Included is information on counseling, vocational development, group processes, the subculture of the campus, human development, and learning. The implication is that these materials have direct relevance to the activities of the student personnel worker. The inclusion of a major emphasis on counseling, for example, suggests that he is a psychological counselor. But is he also to be a test administrator-interpreter? A group dynamics leader-trainer? A manager of residences and food services? A manipulator of environments to enhance their contribution to learning? The student personnel worker, by implication, must be a multi-specialist. Can one individual be adequately prepared to do all the things that student personnel workers are supposedly competent to do? In an age of specialization and expertise, it seems unlikely. Perhaps, then, he should be considered not a specialist, but a generalist.

The value of the generalist and the point of view he can bring to administrative and managerial tasks is an important concept in the era of the specialist. Is there a place for the generalist in student personnel work? Can the student personnel worker, "broadly educated," expect to be accepted as competent when he performs tasks that overlap with the operations of more "specialty-educated" colleagues? The hope has historically been that generalist preparation plus good will and the "personnel point of view" will enable the student personnel worker to perform student-related tasks in ways that "experts" could or would not do. Three results may be discerned currently:

1. The student personnel worker has not been accepted by academicians as competent in some areas where recent developments have produced highly trained specialists with whom the student personnel worker competes. This is especially true in counseling, where the specialty of counseling psychology has developed; other areas where parallel trends are visible are housing administration, union programming and management, foreign student advisement, and financial aid administration.

2. Student personnel workers tend to be relegated to subordinate and peripheral positions as middle- and lower-level administrators who are seen by academicians as essentially uninvolved in the real-life issues of campuses in the 1960's.

3. When given the option, students, having learned to value expertise, will turn to "fully qualified" specialists rather than to generalists whose role and qualifications are less clearly identified.

Personnel Work as Housekeeping

A second category of textual material is concerned with administrative, organizational, and coordinating matters that may appropriately be called housekeeping activities. To so designate them is not to deny their urgency, but to suggest that they are hardly matters about which a learned, academically based discipline or profession will be fundamentally concerned. Indeed, the student personnel specialty's long-time preoccupation with such how-to-do-it issues as admissions, orientation, housing, financial aid, student activities, and campus discipline has been a factor that has encouraged campus colleagues to denigrate the student personnel worker and to reject his aspiration to equality in a world dominated by teaching and research.

The fact that current thinking continues to focus on housekeeping and technique-centered matters is evidenced by the subject matter of the monographs in the Student Personnel Series of the American College Personnel Association. Eight booklets have appeared since 1960; included are considerations of financial aid, housing, health services, discipline, testing, and group activities. While in most cases the contents represent careful thinking about some functions of student personnel work, it is quite possible to read the entire series without recognizing that the field under consideration is one that should, by its nature, be at the center of campus life and activity. Discussion of the matters with which students are centrally concerned in the 1960's is conspicuously absent in these publications. One wonders how the publication series of a major student personnel group could appear so irrelevant and prosaic in a decade of monumental change.

The Personnel Point of View

A third portion of the texts in the field is devoted to elaborations of the personnel point of view. The authors are unified in urging that not

only workers in the specialty but all members of the academic community embrace what is essentially a value orientation. The personnel
point of view may be characterized by three postulates: (a) Every student
should be recognized as unique; (b) Every individual should be regarded
as a total person; (c) The current needs and interests of individual
students are the most significant factors to be considered in developing
a program of campus life. Concern with particular values, of course, is
not uncommon among professions. Medicine, law, and the natural
sciences—all, in their devotion to objectivity, are committed to humanly derived values. But in contrast to the established professions,
student personnel work has developed primarily as an enterprise defined
by a point of view rather than by its content or the services it provides.
Indeed, as Shoben (1967) pointed out, most of the services that represent personnel functions are not distinctive to student personnel
work, but fall also within the province of other professions and occupations. The things that make such activities part of a student personnel
program are the outlook, the assumptions, and the general philosophy
of those who participate in them. The concept of a single professional
entity, student personnel work, is therefore abortive.

Emergence of the Council of Student Personnel Associations
(COSPA)* in the 1960's indicates that in reality there are several
readily identifiable specialties (together with organizations representing
them). All of them may be seen as falling more or less within the
province of student personnel work, while at the same time each provides a service reasonably distinct from the others. Are there, then,
enough common interest, activities, and objectives to provide a base
for any sort of shared professional identification?

Parker (1966) proposed that it should be possible to identify a student
personnel worker as one whose occupational tasks enable him to find
membership in one of the COSPA organizations. His approach rests

---

*The Council of Student Personnel Associations includes the following organizational
members: American College Personnel Association, Association of College Unions,
American Association of Collegiate Registrars and Admissions Officers, Association of
College and University Housing Officers, Association of College Admissions Counselors,
Association for Coordination of University Religious Advisors, College Placement Coun-
cil, Conference of Jesuit Student Personnel Administrators, National Association of
Student Personnel Administrators, National Association of Women Deans and Coun-
selors, National Association of Foreign Student Advisors.

on the assumption that counseling is the one common aspect of all student personnel jobs. It follows that each student personnel worker should be educated primarily as a counselor who includes in his preparation some peripheral study of other aspects of personnel work. Parker's rationale includes the observation that there are five critical skill areas possessed by the counselor that are basic to virtually all student personnel functions. They are: (a) the counselor's sensitivity to others, enabling him to develop effective working relationships; (b) the counselor's skill in objectively analyzing the strengths and weaknesses of individuals; (c) the counselor's skill at interviewing; (d) the counselor's awareness of the nature and extent of individual differences in those with whom he works; (e) the counselor's ability to identify learning difficulties and his expertise in knowing how learning takes place.

No one is likely to disagree that these would be distinct assets for student personnel workers to possess. This is not to say, however, that they are *uniquely* valuable to student personnel workers. On the contrary; they would be invaluable to *anyone* who deals directly and professionally with human relationships. To conclude that education in counseling should be the basic preparation for student personnel work, therefore, is to say very little. The question is whether such preparation is enough to identify a professional group, or to serve as the foundation for membership in professional organizations. Obviously, it is not.

Organizational Fragmentation

The COSPA phenomenon represents a proliferation of so-called professional organizations. Several of these organizations are of quite recent origin: More than half the COSPA groups have been organized since approximately 1960. Examination of the literature, activities, and job titles represented suggest that several of the organizations have quite specific and unique interests that are shared only peripherally—if at all—by the others. For other members who attempt to be more general in their interests and global in their constituencies (i.e., ACPA and NAWDC), the literature suggests a major concern with unresolved matters of identity, purpose, and role. Such observations lead reasonably to the conclusion that the field of student personnel work is in the process of becoming increasingly fragmented and diversified as time goes on and new specializations develop. The longer this process continues, the less likely it will be that common interests, activities, and a universal core of training can be possible or relevant for all.

Conclusions

The issues raised here lead to a fundamental conclusion. No longer viable is the hypothesis under which the early writers of the 1930's and 1940's operated—namely, that there was an identifiable point of view and an occupational entity that might be recognized as the student personnel work profession. The field is now composed of a number of relatively separate and distinct specialties linked largely by organizational contiguity (i.e., they all involve working with students out of classrooms) and, to a lesser extent, by the sharing of a common philosophical view of their tasks. The long-sought "profession" of student personnel work has not been, is not, and will not be recognized or accepted as a vital aspect of the academic world.

References

Arbuckle, D. S. *Student personnel services in higher education.* New York: McGraw-Hill, 1953.

Lloyd-Jones, E. M., & Smith, M. R. *A student personnel program for higher education.* New York: McGraw-Hill, 1938.

Mueller, K. H. *Student personnel work in higher education.* Boston: Houghton Mifflin, 1961.

Parker, C. A. The place of counseling in the preparation of student personnel workers. *Personnel and Guidance Journal,* 1966, 45, 254–261.

Shoben, E. J. Psychology and student personnel work. *Journal of College Student Personnel,* 1967, 8, 239–245.

Williamson, E. G. *Student personnel services in colleges and universities.* New York: McGraw-Hill, 1961.

Wrenn, C. G. *Student personnel work in college.* New York: Ronald Press, 1951.

IV

The Emergence of Student Development

As the 1960's were characterized by change, so the decade of the 1970's is generally associated with labels such as process orientation, transition, developmental and student-centered. Confrontational politics, sit-ins and student activists were less evident. College and university educators turned their attention toward questions of relevance and human values, placing a new emphasis on the process of learning as well as on the acquisition of content. Increasingly, value was placed on skills and competencies in the areas of problem-solving and career development.

New roles for student personnel professionals incorporated the concepts of instruction, consultation and milieu management while realigning these roles as partners to faculty. The goal of the student development educator became facilitation of human growth and development rather than control of student behavior. Relationships with students and faculty, heretofore based on an hierarchical arrangement were now marked by a more democratic attitude. All individuals within the academic community were viewed as colleagues.

The literature of this period is rich with theoretical contributions to our understanding of student growth and development, noteworthy for its varied perceptions of the changing nature of student affairs, and significant for its authors' orientation toward the next twenty years.

Describing student-to-student personnel administrator and student-to-faculty relationships as confrontational, Ivey and Morrill (1970) develop an encounter model to provide more meaningful and productive interpersonal interactions. Basic assumptions identified became cornerstones for the emerging philosophy of student development later articulated by Brown (1974) and COSPA (1975). Ideas forming this philosophy are: 1. There should be a new emphasis on problem-solving as a generalizable process rather than a problem-centered approach to issues; 2. student personnel professionals must become more concerned with creating an educational environment on their campus; 3. student personnel practitioners must assume a consultative role with faculty; and 4. student affairs functional area personnel should design programs that are preventive rather than remedial in nature.

Hurst and Ivey (1971) offer an assessment of fundamental concerns of students. The significance of their article lies in its suggestion for a new direction or a new student personnel point of view to be characterized by an emphasis on human development. To be more effective in future decades, the authors suggest that student personnel professionals must serve as colleagues to students and as facilitators/consultants to their own institutional learning environment. In addition, future professionals must be involved in teaching human relations skills and helping to increase awareness of the importance of the philosophy of body-mind relationships. A new term, "proactive posture," appears in this piece of literature. Hurst and Ivey also predict that student personnel work and counseling will disappear as professions as we realize "our true objective: the elimination of the field as it now exists." (p. 303)

In what may very well be the first article to compare the traditional student personnel orientation and the emerging developmental approach termed "student development," Crookston (1972) reminds the reader of concepts and principles found in the earlier writing of Cowley (1936) and Lloyd-Jones (1954). He believes the growing movement toward student development has been accelerated by the demise of *in loco parentis*. Presenting arguments that a bureaucratic system is contra-developmental, Crookston proposes an organizational model incorporating the concepts of encounter, egalitarianism, collaboration and competency as a means of achieving the goals of student development.

Addressing herself to professional preparation program educators, Dewey (1972) believes that the serious problems confronting the profession can be laid at the doorsteps of existing graduate preparation programs. Identifying curriculum and course selection as two issues recurring in the literature from 1927 to 1970, she recommends that graduate programs be revised to offer substantive areas heretofore lacking: organizational theory, dynamics of institutional and societal change, futuristics and strong research components. In contrast to earlier authors, Dewey concludes that the student personnel function will not become extinct. Instead she challenges us to consider the question of who will perform its functions.

Recognizing that the field of student personnel, grounded in the student personnel point of view, is involved in a significant period of transition, Chandler (1973) advocates an organizational model for vice presidents of student affairs as a means of initiating student development attitudes and programs. Overall supervisory responsibilities could be categorized according to three major functions: managerial, student development and judicial control.

Shaffer (1973), citing the need to integrate elements of the organizational development process used in the corporate profit making sector, proposes that student personnel work assume a new role designed to enhance overall institutional effectiveness. Among the steps advocated by Shaffer to mobilize the student personnel division for change and the implementation of a systems approach are: initiation of self-studies, development of position papers, and the establishment of a power base to influence institutional decisions and behaviors.

Lewis (1973) places an emphasis on accountability and describes the lack of progress made in the professionalization of student personnel work. He identifies the variety of societal factors influencing the changing context of higher education. To achieve a greater degree of effectiveness in the future, student personnel administrators must initiate staff evaluation procedures based on accurate job descriptions, apply behavior modification techniques to current student problems, reduce one-to-one counseling contacts and increase their own involvement in teaching functions.

Representative of the emerging body of literature depicting the evolving philosophical perspective known as student development is Parker's "Student Development: What Does It Mean?" (1974). The selection of developmental stage theory and its application to the four-year undergraduate experience focuses our attention on the potential benefits to be derived from the interconnectedness of student affairs programming with the rest of the academic community.

Harvey (1974) portrays one educator's view of the changes that lie ahead for the student personnel field. Predicted trends include an increased use of the term "aruncularity" to describe the relationship between the institution (students) and student personnel professionals, the merging of student personnel with educational administration and the need for the role of environmental administrator to "orchestrate institutional resources for the total benefit of students" (p. 381). Implicit in the profession's future will be a central focus on intentional human development as preparation for both work and life. Life-long learning has become a tenet of the evolving field of college student personnel.

The Commission of Professional Development of COSPA produced a competence based curriculum for graduate preparation programs (1975). Beginning with a reformulation of the student personnel point of view, the authors integrate a developmental dimension with the assumptions underlying the student personnel field. Three roles are prescribed for the future student development specialist: administrator, consultant and instructor. Future practitioners and graduate students are encouraged to be cognizant of the continuous process of self-assessment, goal setting, allocation of resources and application of behavioral change strategies.

Support for the application of eco-system models to the campus environment and for the new role of the student personnel practitioner as a milieu manager can be found in the writings of Crookston (1975). Regardless of the conceptual framework selected (Erikson, Maslow, Chikering), Crookston believes that a supporting framework for student development must be established on each campus and be tailored to particular needs and goals of the institution. On the basic assumption that the relationship between the goal of actualization of an individual and society must be symbiotic, Crookston discusses community governance as a means to marshall institutional resources for the benefit of all human beings within the campus environment.

Reacting to pressures of accountability, fiscal reductions and an increasing sense of identity crisis among student personnel professionals, the American College Personnel Association developed the Tomorrow's Higher Education (T.H.E.) Project. Phase I consisted of Brown's reconceptualization of the role of student personnel as student development education and his predictions and recommendation for the future growth of the field. Because of the availability of Brown's work entitled *Student Development in Tomorrow's Higher Education: A Return to the Academy* excerpts from the monograph are not included in this volume. Phase II of the T.H.E. Project is represented by the 1975 article resulting from the Phase II Model Building Conference. The model described incorporates student development competencies (goal setting and assessment) with strategies for creating change intentionally (instruction, consultation and milieu management). Inherent in the model is the belief that collaboration among students, faculty and student personnel staff is required.

Perhaps the most frequently cited article by Crookston is his "Student Personnel—All Hail and Farewell!" (1976). The purpose of this work is an examination and comparison of previously developed vocabulary associated with traditional student personnel work and that of the contemporary movement of student development. Passionately, he calls for future nomenclature to be predicated on an understanding of and commitment to the assumptions of student development. Crookston advocates changing the names of professional associations and professional journals, retitling course offerings and defining new graduate preparation programs. We are encouraged to consider student personnel work as deceased in much the same way as we have come to understand the demise of *in loco parentis*.

Confrontation, Communication, and Encounter: A Conceptual Framework for Student Development

Allen E. Ivey and Weston H. Morrill

Recently, a student leader on a college campus stood up in a demonstration against a university regulation and said, "To H—— with the administration. We'll force them to give in." This type of feeling and approach is not uncommon on university campuses today. Students are *demanding* to be heard, and their demands are placing administrators in a bind such that even if they wanted to, they could neither hear nor communicate with these students.

The task of relating with students on a meaningful level is one of the most pressing issues facing higher education today. Few administrators and faculty reach students in any depth. Clearly, there is a need for new approaches. This paper discusses a conceptual framework for more meaningful interactions on a university campus. Further, a new developmental model is suggested for the student personnel worker and for the university. The university has too long been a static institution which has had difficulty involving students in the process of their own education.

The master teacher learned long ago that his most productive teaching resulted from an active interchange and involvement with his students such that both he and his students grew. This meant that the teacher was both a teacher and a learner and that the learner was both a learner and a teacher. The dialogue resulted in growth for both the student and the teacher. The willingness for the one to grow and change produced growth and change in the other. This process of education has important implications for administrative personnel in higher education. It is now recognized that the classroom is no longer the only vehicle of education. The total university environment with various personnel and management experiences is an important part of the educational process.

A crucial goal for higher education in this time of change is that of helping individuals and groups on campus (e.g. faculty, administrators, student leaders, activists, dormitory residents) start talking with one another in such a way that a process of growth for all is possible. Administrative planning should aim to create a climate of mutual understanding and respect. In the past college administrators and student personnel faculty have tended to be content with smoothing the troubled campus waters and intervening between conflicting groups. In the future, we must be more concerned with promotion of meaningful interaction among many viewpoints on the college campus.

College students are in a stage of development which is typified by efforts to establish independence and develop a personal set of values which they can consider to be their own, rather than values which have been imposed on them by parents, by society, and by authority. Universities need to provide a climate which allows students to examine issues critically and develop values based on a thoughtful and meaningful investigation of the issues rather than permit situations in which students assert their self-direction and independence by opposition.

As the master teacher found that his teaching was most effective when both he and his students were actively involved in a process of seeking answers, that both learned in the process, and that both were involved together in seeking these answers, universities need to provide the kind of climate which will allow students, faculty, and administration to concern themselves about issues in such a way that all parties involved are free to learn, to grow, to change, and to develop.

Confrontation, Communication, and Encounter

Confrontation was demonstrated in a press conference in Washington (October 25, 1967) when National Student Association President Edward Schwartz denounced the use of force in dealing with student demonstrations. He said, "If college administrators continue to rely on their unrestrained, even brutal, use of police force to disburse these demonstrations, we are heading for the most serious crisis higher education has faced in this century." This represents the ultimate in *confrontation* by both parties—attempting forceful imposition of a point of view upon an opposing individual or group. Confrontation is defined as the meeting or confronting of viewpoints with relatively little regard to the ideas of the other party. Confrontation too often occurs between administrative officials and students in regard to rules and regulations. Neither group makes an effort to see what the other is really saying.

Another approach, perhaps representative of the "modern" student personnel point of view, is that of *communication*. Recent movements in counselling, psycho-therapy, and student personnel labeled as client or student-centered approaches perhaps best typify the communication model. Under a communication model, the college administrator would meet with student leaders and student activists. He would attempt to understand and demonstrate to the students that he understands their point of view. As is implied in the term student-centered, the focus is on the student and the message that *he* is attempting to articulate.

Communication is an effort to "smooth the waters" and provide points of contact and understanding between different groups. An effort is made to communicate to student groups that administrators in the university understand their point of view and understand their feelings and concerns. Emphasis is usually placed on positive aspects of the relationship between or among groups. Communication is often concerned with just talking to "see if something can develop." In the typical communication model, student personnel tries to understand the other person or group and start a dialogue which aims for "understanding." This theory implies that content is not relevant. Values and personal commitments are too often missing: there is nothing to communicate about . . . we simply aim for an exchange of views.

When the confronting activist student meets the confronting student personnel staff members, an automatic tension point is established and an inevitable power struggle will follow with neither party growing. If confronting students are met with "understanding" student personnel "communicators," student personnel staff may find itself laughed at or ignored at best. A third, and possibly all too frequent occurence, is a student personnel staff which alternates between communication and confrontation approaches and ends up with respect and trust of neither students nor faculty and administration nor themselves.

Encounter is suggested as the basic model for student personnel and for higher education. Encounter as used in this paper is perhaps best typified by the methods of the master teacher in which both parties bring their points of view, their knowledge, their frame of reference, and their feelings to bear on issues of common concern. To better understand and better cope with the issues and problems involved, the teacher and the student jointly attempt to seek solutions, to broaden their own understanding, to change their perspectives or set, and to view problems from a different perspective. Encounter could be defined as "confrontation with communication" in that each party constantly confronts the other, but at the same time makes a constant attempt to "break his own set" and see the viewpoints of the other. Encounter concepts imply that the administrator or personnel worker would not hesitate to speak for what he feels is correct, but would never retreat into his viewpoint to the point that communication is denied. Neither party attempts to forcefully impose his viewpoints on the other. Further, constant self examination of values and awareness of possible changes in one's set and one's point of view is required.

The college administrator takes a value stand, but at the same time attempts to involve himself with the students in the process of seeking solutions to problems and concerns. He attempts to see other alternatives or viewpoints. Key in the concept of encounter is awareness of one's own "set" and willingness to examine the tenets on which that set of values, opinions, and ideas is held. It could be stated that the values, opinions, and ideas are basically predicated on emotional loadings underlying intellectual concepts. Thus, in any meaningful encounter, the student personnel worker must not only look at other views, but also understand his own fully. The personnel person who takes encounter as his model will sometimes find himself "stirring things up" and providing new points of tension between groups or individuals. On the other hand, encounter concepts will serve as the best vehicles for developing *real* communication and positive action.

Encounter Concepts for Student Development

Instead of traditional methods of confrontation and more recent communication efforts represented by the "student personnel point of view," student personnel workers must move increasingly to the use of encounter concepts. Administration must become more concerned with developmental aspects of college youth and not be willing to limit their interests to "keeping the lid on" or helping students plan programs to solve campus problems.

Student personnel is becoming increasingly involved in the question of the meaning of higher education to the individual person. The future role of student personnel should be that of maximizing the student's ability to learn and, at the same time, working with the college and university to enable it to change and meet the needs of today's youth in a changing world. The totality of these concepts imply that a completely new definition of student personnel is now necessary. *Student development specialist* is suggested as the title for a new professional who may need to be a combination of psychologist, administrator, human relations specialist, and educator.

Basic to the encounter and developmental framework is the need for a major change in administrative emphasis. Focus should be on the *process* of planning and the organization which goes into the development of an activity or resolution of an issue. As such, the task becomes one of helping the students learn to ask important questions instead of the traditional one of helping them find *the* right answer. In the past the tendency has been for student personnel to assume that they can solve all problems. As such, student personnel has maintained a problem orientation to students and has ignored the process of problem solving. It is suggested that this basic process, which can be more easily generalized to settings other than the activity in questions, is the "content" of the new profession of student development. Goodman (1964), Friedenberg (1959), and Holt (1964) all approach this issue when they imply that "learning how to learn" is far more important than the learning itself.

As an example, residence halls offer a vital and unique setting for implementation of encounter and developmental concepts. The typical residence hall program is too frequently centered on problems which students may face in the residence hall. An examination of the orientation for head residents or student counselors generally reveals an emphasis of *what* one should do in each anticipated problem situation. There is little emphasis on the process of problem solving in which the person encounters all aspects of himself and others. Residence halls should focus on the processes of human interaction in small and large groups. Viewed from this perspective, residence halls actually do become "laboratories" for student development. The old concept of university residence halls also mentioned laboratories, but the implication was that the laboratory was a production unit; somehow the residence hall was to produce the "well-rounded student." The encounter concept implies a process orientation which suggests that the residence hall may better aim its interests toward helping the student face the important questions of responsible group living.

Student development workers should become more involved with faculty consultation and in improving the educational climate of the institution. Korn's (1966) use of television at Stanford to help faculty view their teaching is but one example where student personnel can make a change in educational planning. The principle of faculty consultation is not to tell faculty members to refer their problem students to student personnel, but rather to help the faculty themselves work with the students. Faculty members are not necessarily open, socially skilled individuals. A program of consultation could provide much to help them learn to use the untapped talents they possess. It should be possible, for example, to interest faculty in students through calling the faculty in as "consultants" and requesting them to help student personnel study student development. Danskin at Kansas State (1966) asked faculty to join him in studying a small group of students over an extended period of time. In addition to new insights about students, he found that faculty can be introduced to how interesting students can really be and this experience tends to generalize to the classroom.

It should be possible to run an experimental sensitivity training course in which a student development counselor and a supervising master teacher from the education department meet weekly with returning practice teachers to discuss feelings and attitudes toward student teaching instead of the traditional methods emphasis. It should be possible to establish a "Friday Afternoon Controversy" on a weekly basis with a different faculty member each week interacting with the same group of students. A psychologist could be present to help interpret the students to the faculty and the faculty to the students. More traditional programs could include "T-groups," pre-marital groups, and vocational groups. In as many programs as possible, we would hope to influence not only the participating students, but also the faculty member participating with the student development counselor.

Traditional counseling concepts would not be dismissed within such a concept. Individual counseling, information programs, and group therapy all are relevant to the developmental concepts. These programs have, in the past, been too oriented to problem solving, rehabilitation, and remediation. Counselling must become more developmental in nature. Students should not be counselled to solve problems, but should be counselled in such a way that they learn the techniques involved in problem solving. Vocational counselling, then, should center on how a person makes occupation decisions. Therapy with the disturbed student should center on how the student relates with himself and others and how he faces key developmental tasks of human growth.

Financial aids should be focused on how to plan finances rather than on solving specific problems; placement should be centered on how a person obtains a job rather than on the end result of finding a job. Placement offices, in addition, might wish to emphasize a career approach more developmental in nature in which the student is helped to see his life as consisting of many jobs and locations instead of one final choice. The recent trend to alumni placement seems to be one example of this type of approach. Student health services might move from their medical repair model to a preventive and developmental health point of view. In short, encounter and development concepts seem to have relevance throughout the many areas of student personnel.

Summary

Today's university is typically established within a confrontation or problem-solving model. Relatively little attention has been given to the process by which problems are solved. It is suggested that the challenge which activist students present is in reality a basic questioning of the method of higher education. Unfortunately, these students have clouded over the basic issues as they too have used a confrontation, problem-solving approach.

As an alternative approach to confrontation, the "student personnel point of view" will often be found. Here we find student personnel workers attempting to communicate with students. Unfortunately, too often there is nothing to communicate about as the student personnel worker is simply interested in the communication process itself. This method of dealing with campus problems too often results in student personnel workers finding themselves irrelevant and ignored.

It is suggested that a deeper concept of *encounter* be considered as an alternative approach. Encounter, the process of "confrontation with communication," implies that the process of solving problems may be as important or more important than the solution achieved. Student personnel workers may be better defined as student development faculty who are concerned with bringing more process and encounter into the total university community.

References

Danskin, David, Personal Communication, 1966.

Friedenberg, Edgar Z. *The Vanishing Adolescent*. Boston: Beacon Press, 1959.

Goodman, Paul, *Compulsory Mis-Education*. New York: Horizon Press, 1964.

Holt, John C. *How Children Fail*. New York: Pitman, 1964.

Korn, Harold A. "Counseling and Teaching: An Integrated View." *The Journal of College Student Personnel* 7: 137–140.

Toward a Radicalization of Student Personnel

James C. Hurst and Allen E. Ivey

The university and society are today facing radical attempts to seek either the abolishment of institutions or a complete change of the philosophical basis on which these institutions have been founded. McLuhan (1964) and Skinner (1953) clearly foretell the possibilities of radical changes in society by the year 2000. Futuristics, the science of futures, is becoming an essential adjunct to the planning process for the university and society in general.

In contrast to this dynamic situation which demands complete renewal and reconceptualization, student personnel, once again, appears to be *responding* to the crisis. The traditional role of student personnel has been reactive rather than proactive. Even some of the current student personnel efforts which emphasize prevention in place of remediation are still responding to crisis situations with little thought for determining what should or can be existent in the university community.

If student personnel is to be fully relevant to the evolving mission of the university, it must devote more of its energies toward planning for the future. Such planning may eventually call for a complete radicalization of the foundations on which student personnel has rested for the past 50 years. For example, it is suggested that student personnel should devote more of its energies to diagnosis of the *nature* of crisis, which is in itself only a symptom of deeper student discontent. Diagnosis of student discontent, in turn, must be followed by imaginative programs designed to make students more fully mature participants in the educational process.

This article is an attempt to diagnose basic issues of concern to students and to suggest new alternative programs for the future of student personnel based on the needs suggested by this diagnosis. If the pre-

304

sented diagnosis is valid, it would appear that a viable future for student personnel may require a complete radicalization of our present point of view.

The Diagnosis of Students' Major Concerns

The report of the Commission on Current and Developing Issues of COSPA (Straub & Vermilye, 1968) identified six prime issues relating to students which are relevant to the university's functioning. Important among these issues was the suggestion that the university reconsider its mission to include the three functions of social critic, implementer of social change, and the provision of *associates* for students as they develop critical facilities through the process of disciplined reflection. The remaining issues centered on implementation of this primary concern: the question of how the university can effect this aim through policy action.

It is our contention that careful diagnosis of student concerns is essential before action is prescribed. Students have forced issues on university faculties and administrations for a variety of reasons, but several themes are being voiced consistently by activist students throughout the country. First among these is the student's feeling that he is insignificant in the scheme of things; that he feels like an object rather than a person. The university communicates this message of insignificance to students implicitly through large classes, restricted contact with faculty and administration, lockstep degree programs, and rigid policies that fail to take into account the uniqueness of the individual. An ever-growing group of students has now become sophisticated enough to recognize these implicit messages and are in the process of making them explicit through actively seeking to modify the very practices and policies responsible for communicating insignificance and impersonality.

The second theme is a result of the first, for when the modifications are attempted, students find themselves *impotent!* Frustration is experienced with the institution's unwillingness to listen or, after listening, with the unwillingness to share responsibility for the governance of student life. Students have become sufficiently sophisticated to recognize their impotence for what it is and become even more dissatisfied with the university. Students are communicating their absolute unwilling-ness to remain in an impotent role and have set about finding ways to manipulate their environment, change their circumstances, and con-trol their own destinies. They shout in ways that the institution cannot ignore, "I am a man!" The parallels between student unrest and the Black Power movement are indeed noteworthy.

A third theme is that students are unwilling to submit to an authority with an unimpressive record in nontechnical areas of human existence. Students suggest that they could play a teaching role in addition to a learning role in the university and in society in some technical and nontechnical areas if only they were allowed. Related to this theme is the perceived irrelevance of much of the educational process today. A perceived preoccupation with words when there is such a critical de-mand for deeds reduces respect for formal education. Students for the most part have looked in vain for action-oriented coursework dealing with the issues of civil rights, Vietnam, overpopulation, drugs, en-vironmental pollution, poverty, and their roles in society.

The result of this upheaval in the educational establishment is re-ports such as that of the COSPA Commission. The identification of the relevant issues is, however, only a first step if student personnel ser-vices are to play a meaningful role in shaping the direction of higher education. Many of the revolutionary demands being made are such that a viable creative student personnel services organization is in the enviable position of being the best qualified and organized to help effect the desired modifications. If this role is to be assumed, however, imme-diate steps must be taken to modify present attitudes and practices and adapt and adopt procedures for filling it.

Directions for a Viable Future

If student personnel is to meet the demands of a complex and chang-ing university scene, radical new approaches need to be considered. Following are some possible future directions for a new student person-nel point of view—that of Human Development.

1. Student personnel workers will be most effective as colleagues of

students sharing in a learning experience. At times, he will give students advice; at other times he will learn from students. Primarily, however, student personnel, in order to survive the wave of activism, must join hands and participate *with* students in reforming higher education. In a time when students ask for participation in determining the direction of the university, student personnel should not abdicate their own responsibility for educational reform.

2. Facilitators instead of controllers of counselors

The student personnel worker will become a facilitator or consultant to the college campus. He will be an expert in applied educational psychology and will teach students how to be helping agents (Carkhuff & Truax, 1965; Ivey, Miller, Morrill, Normington, & Haase, in press), how to run groups (Whalen, 1967), and how to be more effective "people." He will work with faculty to help them improve and change the structure of the curriculum and their teaching habits, (Korn, 1966). Eventually, he will teach faculty how to relate to students on more than an intellectual basis. Equally important, he will show faculty how to use affective learning to advance cognitive goals. We will work toward the day when a professor can run a personal growth group on a weekend with his class, then use the students the following week to help him restructure his course. In such activities as this the student personnel worker will constantly serve as adviser and consultant to administration, students, and faculty, helping them to maximize their own growth potential, (e.g., Brown & Gaynor, 1967; Garfield, 1966; Raths, Harmin, & Simon, 1966).

3. Training in student personnel

Training in student personnel will move increasingly to applied educational psychology and to experiential learning such as human interaction training and microteaching in human relations skills (Ivey, 1967). Students will be increasingly given the opportunity to participate in developing their own unique curricula through the identification of behavioral deficits and selection of behavior change goals. Student personnel trainers will begin to see their students as junior colleagues who can give as well as learn in this process of development.

4. Teaching human relations skills instead of administering

A major emphasis on teaching skills of effective human relations will be found within student personnel. Instead of counseling students, the student personnel worker will be teaching college students how to be helpers to each other, how to listen, and how to understand. Techniques such as teaching via television in human relations (Higgins, Ivey, & Uhlemann, 1969), T-groups (Berzon, Reisel, & Davis, 1968; Rogers, undated; Schutz, 1967), programmed texts (Berlin, 1965; Smith & Smith, 1966), and computers will be just some of the vehicles used by student personnel workers to teach students and faculty how to experience life more fully together. Some traditional therapists and counselors will still be needed, but the new emphasis on teaching people directly the skills of effective behavior will greatly reduce this need.

5. Recognition of physical activities as a province of student personnel

Relaxation training, Yoga, Zen meditation, psychoanalytic bodily exercises, and related techniques will take their place in student personnel as supplementary activities (Gunther, 1967; Jacobson, 1938; Kamiya, 1968; Lowen, 1958; Oetting, 1964). The importance of body-mind relationships is being recognized, and student personnel would help implement this recognition.

6. Systems analysis and cybernetics will be applied to the university setting in relation to the community

The concepts of systems analysis will demonstrate to the university the interrelationship of knowledge and the importance of all parts working together in harmony (Buckley, 1968; Cole & Oetting, 1968; Miles, 1965; Miller, 1965). Along with this trend will come awareness of the artificiality of boundaries between the university and the community and the nation. As such, people will move in and out of a university more frequently and easily. As degrees and grades will have been deemphasized, students and faculty alike will concentrate on developing new and improved skills and on eliminating behavioral and intellectual deficits. Competitiveness will for the most part disappear and be replaced by new models of cooperative behavior.

7. A new model for the university

Personnel workers will help the university to become completely restructured so that degrees will be deemphasized and perhaps eventually abolished. Instead the university will offer a set of development tasks which have been planned or specifically programmed to lead to specific behavioral skills (Oetting, 1967). A student in consultation decides what skills he wishes to obtain from the university and proceeds through programmed steps to achieve these skills through a contract with the university.

One important possible emphasis for all students will be on the structure of knowledge. Behavioralism, gestalt psychology, psychoanalysis, humanistic and existential psychology, and other theoretical models will be recognized by the field as just that—"models" of human experience. Similarly other fields will increasingly realize that model-building is a useful art, but that different models offer different pictures of "truth." A major goal of education in the future in sciences, social sciences, and humanities will be to help students to develop their own unique models. Distinction between academic fields will become increasingly blurred.

8. Student personnel and counseling as professions known to us now will disappear

Although the profession will be important in developing the procedures to implement these ideas, once the system is started it will be self-perpetuating, and a professor of chemistry or a student in English literature will also have sufficient skills (in concert with others, of course) to redesign and update the total educational system, thus finally helping us realize our true objective: the elimination of the field as it now exists. In its place will be an office of campus consultants for ongoing training and the continual modification of the evolved campus community in the direction of Human Development.

The best of student activists have a critical message for student personnel to hear. The time for insignificance, impotence, and docile submission to authority is past. The time for interaction as colleagues in teaching, training, planning, facilitating and radically modifying is here. If student personnel is to survive, its traditional reactive stance must be replaced with a proactive posture for Human Development of all people implemented through the university environment.

References

Berlin, J. I. Management improvement program. Atlanta, Ga.: Human Development Institute, 1965.

Berzon, B., Reisel, J., & Davis, D. P. Peer: Planned experiences for effective relating, an audio tape program for self-directed small groups. LaJolla, Calif.: Western Behavioral Sciences Institute, 1968.

Brown, G., & Gaynor, D. Athletic action as creativity. *Journal of Creative Behavior*, 1967, *11* (2), 155–162.

Buckley, W. *Modern systems research for the scientist: A sourcebook*. Chicago: Aldine, 1968.

Carkhuff. R. R., & Truax, C. B. Lay mental health counseling: The effects of lay group counseling. *Journal of Consulting Psychology*, 1965, *29*, 426–431.

Cole, C. W., & Oetting, E. R. *Measures of stress and concept evaluation: The experimental modification of factor structure*. Technical Report No. 2, Colorado State University, Contract RD-2464-P, U.S. Department of Health, Education, and Welfare, January 1968.

Garfield, O. Human relations in the classroom. Paper presented at the Annual Conference of the American Personnel and Guidance Association, Washington, D.C., April 1966.

Gunther, B. *Sensory awakening and relaxation*. Big Sur, Calif.: Esalen Publications, 1967.

Higgins, W., Ivey, A. E., & Uhlemann, M. *Media therapy: Programming human relations skills*. Amherst: University of Massachusetts School of Education, 1969.

Ivey, A. E. Confrontation, communication, and encounter: A conceptual framework for student development. Unpublished manuscript, Colorado State University, 1967.

Ivey, A. E., Miller, C. D., Morrill, W. H., Normington, C. J., & Hasse, R. F. Micro-counseling and attending behavior: An approach to pre-practicum counselor training. *Journal of Counseling Psychology* (separate monograph), in press.

Jacobson, E. *Progressive relaxation*. Chicago: University of Chicago Press, 1938.

Kamiya, J. Conscious control of brain waves. *Psychology Today*, 1968, *I*, 57–60.

Korn, H. A. Counseling and teaching: An integrated view. *Journal of College Student Personnel*, 1966, *7*, 137–140.

Lowen, A. *Physical dynamics of character structure*. New York: Grune & Stratton, 1958.

McLuhan, M. *Understanding media*. New York: McGraw Hill, 1964.

Miles, M. B. Planned change and organizational health: Figure and ground. In R. O. Carlson, A. Gallaher, Jr., M. B. Miles, R. J. Pellegrin, and E. M. Rogers (Eds.), *Change process in the public schools*. Eugene, Ore.: Center for the Advanced Study of Educational Administration, 1965. Pp. 11–34.

Miller, J. G. Living systems: Basic concepts. *Behavioral Science*, 1965, *10*, 193–411.

Oetting, E. R. Hypnosis and concentration in study. *American Journal of Clinical Hypnosis*, 1964, *7*, 148–151.

Oetting, E. R. A developmental definition of counseling psychology. *Journal of Counseling Psychology*, 1967, *14*, 382–385.

Raths, L., Harmin, M., & Simon, S. M. *Values and teaching.* Columbus, Ohio: Charles E. Merrill, 1966.

Rogers, C. R. *The process of the basic encounter group.* LaJolla, Calif.: Western Behavioral Sciences Institute, undated.

Schutz, W. C. *Joy: Expanding human awareness.* New York: Grove Press, 1967.

Skinner, B. F. *Science and human behavior.* New York: Macmillan, 1953.

Smith, J. M., & Smith D. E. P. *Child management: A program for parents.* Ann Arbor: Ann Arbor Publishers, 1966.

Straub, J. S., & Vermilye, D. W. Current and developing issues in student life. *Journal of College Student Personnel*, 1968, *9*, 363–370.

Whalen, C. K. *The effects of a model and instructions on group verbal behaviors.* Ann Arbor, Mich.: University Microfilms, 1967.

An Organizational Model for Student Development

Burns B. Crookston

As they view introspectively as well as retrospectively the turbulent, often traumatic past decade of dramatic, accelerating change, student personnel administrators must face up to the practical realities and consequences of such changes. Deans of students, deans of men and women, trained in the nuances and skills of applying in *loco parentis*, are now consequently, with its demise, looking for new ways and means to function effectively in a new ball game in which the rules appear to be made up as one goes along. Many are becoming intrigued, if not enamored with the rhetoric of student development. Discussions and writings extolling the virtues of a "new" developmental approach began as a small trickle early in the sixties. Now, there is widespread support for the idea. Draft statements articulating student developmental philosophy have been under preparation by COSPA and other student personnel associations.

This paper is directed toward the problem of building an organization to fulfill the goals of student development. While accepting student development as a theoretical concept aborning, certain assumptions concerning student development are discussed as applied to problems of organization. Arguments are presented that assert bureaucracy as a system of organization does not support the goals of student development. An organizational model for student development is presented together with operational suggestions.

312

Contrasts in Student Personnel and Student Development

An examination of assumptions around student development as a concept compared to the old student personnel point of view indicates some critical differences that warrant discussion. Although for approximately twenty years, culminating at the end of World War II, most authorities in the field accepted Cowley's view that student personnel work consisted of all non-instructional activities in which the all around development of the student was of primary concern,[1] for the past two decades increasing support has developed for the view that it was erroneous to speak in terms of a dichotomy between student personnel work and instruction. Student personnel was to include not only those processes and functions that emphasize intellectual, social, emotional, cultural, and physical development of the individual, but also those which help build curricula, improve methods of instruction, and develop leadership programs. In sum, it was held student personnel work complemented as well as supplemented the instructional program in the total development of the individual.[2]

The principal differences between the student development idea and the old student personnel philosophy rest in (1) doing away with the term "student personnel," which has always been a descriptive anomaly, and (2) asserting that student development is not merely complementary or supplementary to the instructional program, *it is a central teaching function of the college.* Thus, while Lloyd-Jones wrote in the mid-fifties that the student personnel worker should no longer be viewed as a technician or specialist but as an educator collaborating with the teacher in the development of the student as a whole person in a democratic society,[3] the student developmental view makes no such educator-teacher distinction. According to student developmental theory the entire academic community is a learning environment in which teaching can take place, whether it produces academic credit or not; hence, the teacher in multiple development teaches in multiple situations, including the classroom.[4]

Student Personnel Orientation. As indicated by Figure 1, there are contrasting behavioral orientations descriptive of the student developmental and student personnel approaches. Under the student personnel approach staff behaviors tended to be passive. Staff would wait, usually in their offices, and as a problem developed, react, applying counseling,

Figure 1

Contrasting Behavioral Orientations Descriptive of Student Personnel and
Student Developmental Methodologies

Student Personnel	Student Developmental
Authoritarian	Egalitarian
Reactive	Proactive
Passive	Encountering
Remedial	Developmental
Corrective	Preventive
Controlling	Confrontive
Cooperative	Collaborative
Status oriented	Competency oriented

mental health, or advising skills as appropriate to correct or ameliorate
the situation.

In the general area of student activities, advising student personnel
workers took a service approach, providing the means by which the students could do their thing. The style was to be helpful but only rarely to
get involved. In the areas of student behavior and welfare, student personnel administrators exercised traditional *in loco parentis* control prerogatives. Rules and expectations were established. When students
broke the rules staff reacted by punishing, imposing sanctions or conditions, or by utilizing paternalistic counseling or various rehabilitation
efforts.

Staff generally stayed clear of issues, rarely took a stand and were tim-
orous to test whether they had, or were entitled to faculty prerogatives
of academic freedom. After all, as Shoben exhorted, student personnel
workers had long since allowed themselves to be sucked into the administrative establishment.[5] The battle for academic freedom of administrators is only now in a state of preliminary skirmish.[6]

Student Developmental Orientation. In contrast, perhaps in response to
the student revolt of the sixties, perhaps in recognition of the inadequacies of the old student personnel approach, there developed a movement at a few institutions, which has since spread rapidly, of moving
toward a proactive, developmental, preventive, collaborative model.
Counseling psychologists were discovering that seeing students on a
one-to-one basis in their office was not the locus of the action. Adapting earlier community mental health approaches, they developed a new
style of training and acting as mental health and student development

educators.[7] They moved out onto the campus, into the residence halls, off campus, into the drug scene, actively seeking out, encountering, confronting or otherwise influencing students toward more effective solutions of their developmental and maturational problems.[8]

The move toward a developmental approach was accelerated by the demise of *in loco parentis*. Deans of men and women and others trained to function and apply their knowledge and skills under the protective umbrella of control over students with power to impose sanctions discovered that with the loss of control, upon which they built their relationships with students, they were unable to function with confidence and effectiveness. A number have not been able to make the adjustment of functioning from a status-based relationship with students to a relationship based on competency and collaboration. The result has been a methodological and staff skill retraining problem of first magnitude for many persons in the field.

Of course the inference should not be drawn here that the student personnel methods described above are all to be abandoned in the student developmental approach. Some—like the status behaviors and control functions—should be abandoned, while obviously remedial and mental health functions should continue. The difference is the latter become secondary in thrust to proaction, collaboration, and other student developmental technologies. Success in developmental approaches should result in less need for remediation.

Bureaucracy is Contradevelopmental

The dramatic changes during the past decade in the conceptual development of learning outside the classroom that culminated in the redefinition of student personnel work into the student developmental model have not been accompanied by organizational schemes to achieve the new goals set forth by modifying the system. Most writers and practitioners in the field still appear to be assuming that these changes can be accommodated to the existing bureaucratic organization of the institution.

Admittedly it may be a bit early. New concepts need a period of incubation and testing before any radical organizational modification.

Having worked in no other system than a bureaucracy, most staff cannot conceive of another model that could possibly work. Consequently, the logic persists: all that is needed is to make modifications *within* existing bureaucratic line-staff structures. Is it not merely a question of being more effective and efficient, perhaps reorganizing here and there, perhaps setting up another department or subdivision, perhaps firing a department head or hiring new people? The trouble is these old organizational bromides no longer work.

Bennis and Slater identify four principal conditions that are making bureaucracy obsolete as an effective twentieth century organization: rapid and unexpected change, growth in size of organizations, increased diversity, and change in managerial behavior.[10] During the past twenty-five years many of the larger industries have exhibited a rather dramatic shift in philosophy. A growing awareness and sensitivity has developed: the old push button idea of man must be replaced with the concept that man has needs, aspirations, and problems that transcend the mechanistic view of him as part of a production machine. The self actualization formulations of Abraham Maslow and the concerns for human values expressed by behavioral scientists such as Douglas McGregor, Rensis Likert and Chris Argyris have profoundly influenced the thinking of the leaders of many industrial organizations. Consequently business and industry have moved much further toward humanizing their organizations than have the universities. In many leading companies concepts of power have shifted from the autocratic model based on coercion and threat to one based on rational processes and collaboration.

The old student personnel approach was nicely suited for the bureaucratic model that has been utilized by higher education for more than a century. The passive, reactive, correctional, control modes of student personnel staff behavior described in Figure 1 (above) were congruent with a bureaucratic reward system which emphasized conformity, control, stability, punctuality, predictability, evolutionary change, and behaviors that strengthen the institutionalization of the bureaucracy. Bureaucracy is based on a power and status hierarchy and fosters the notion of a career line to the top through promotions and good work. Thus, with the possible expection of counseling, a successful "career" in student personnel meant getting promoted to the top of the organization.

Bureaucracy generally demands a relatively high degree of conformity in its membership. Uniform standards are common and seen as desirable in the hierarchy. A junior staff member, for instance, is assigned a small office and a small desk. A bigger and better office, dictating equipment, travel budgets, and other emoluments of status come with promotions or with seniority in the system. Such preoccupation with acquiring status symbols works against goal achievement.

Rewards inherent to student developmental theory go counter to the rewards built into a bureaucratic system. Student development emphasizes creativity, flexibility and innovativeness, egalitarian rather than authoritarian concepts; it emphasizes planned, often rapid, if not revolutionary change rather than evolutionary. It builds its organization on the basis of symbiosis between individual and group need satisfaction and goal achievement and organizational goal attainment. It rewards taking reasoned positions, commitment, risk taking and action in support of legitimate issues in contrast to what appears generally to be an unwillingness in student personnel administrators to risk being on the "wrong" side of an issue in the face of administrative censure or other coercive power within the academic bureaucracy. This tendency is also illustrated by the high degree of faculty and student abstention from participation in political processes noted by Wise in his study of small colleges.[11]

The contemporary university is a striking example of how bureaucratization is preventing the flexibility and adaptibility needed to respond to needs of students and of society. Developing means and skills to bring about modifications in the system through planned, systematic change in higher education must head the priority list for the seventies.

The Student Developmental Model

What kind of system, then, should be invented that will be futuristic enough in concept and function to serve the interests of a changing institution within a rapidly shifting world scene? Let us begin with reiterating the behaviors we have already identified as descriptive of the developmental methodology: egalitarian, proactive, encountering, preventive, confrontive, collaborative, and competent. An organization that would foster and reward the expression of these qualities should include the following:

A. *Shared power and decision making.*

Evidence suggests that the most effective decisions are those made by those at, or close to the source of relevant data needed for the decision. Decision making authority for most operational matters should therefore be distributed to those closest to the data sources. Influence should stem from competence and knowledge rather than "the vagaries of personal whims or prerogatives of power." [12] In a modern organization no human being is so omniscient as to possess the knowledge and technical competence needed to make all decisions. The selection of administrators and managers should be based on their human management capabilities rather than technical competence. In the old days the man chosen to run a railroad supposedly knew more about it than anyone else. Societal and technological change and organizational complexity are modifying this image to one who knows how to mobilize human resources and deal effectively with human problems of work, interaction, communication, decision making, and actualization.

Paradoxically studies have shown both the military and industry have developed more democratic ways of functioning than has the university. Bennis and Slater think it is because increasingly they have come to rely on science for the furtherance of their objectives, the reason being that *science methodology is based on and geared for change.*

The new professionals in and outside higher education are therefore more likely to identify initially with the adaptive values of science-democracy than with establishment bureaucracy. Witness the drive toward change manifested by many young college professionals before they yield to the bureaucratic status and power pressures of the establishment. The rise of faculty power during the past fifty years has been motivated in part at least toward achieving and protecting scientific-egalitarian values. There is evidence that individual support of organizational goals accompanies an opportunity to participate in their establishment. [14] Thus "we-ness" becomes the feeling of members who share in decisions and who consequently become identified with the organization, rather than the "they-ness" that expresses an attitude of non-identification with a centrally controlled organization where decisions flow from the top.

A developmental system should require full representation and participation in all major policy decisions, including selection of principal leaders. In a university this means that trustees would represent the public interest in decisions that are made but that they no longer should have the sole power to make such decisions. The academic community government, including representation and participation from all segments—administration, faculty, student and public—should make major policy decisions.

B. *Flexibility.*

To keep ahead, or at least abreast of the demands of accelerating change, the developmental organization must have built-in ability to adapt and adjust quickly and painlessly to meet changing situational demands or data modifications. For the moment a combination management by objectives-action research-systems model of functioning (action$_1$—data collection$_1$—analysis$_1$—new goal and priority setting$_2$— reorganizing for action$_2$—action$_2$—data collection$_2$, etc.) appears suited for such flexibility. This model requires continuous reorganization as needed to place people and resources in ways to carry out the objectives most effectively. It is in marked contrast to the bureaucratic model which assigns priorities in such a manner as to disturb the existing structure as little as possible.

Such a flexible, free-wheeling system admittedly has greatest appeal to competent professionals secure in their relationships and confident of being able to meet their personal needs in temporary systems. Individuals dependent on the security offered by an authoritarian bureaucracy would be threatened, if not immobilized by such shifting organizational and group boundaries, role expectations, and interpersonal relationships. They would need help in developing the necessary confidence and skills.

C. *On open communications system.*

It is essential that the developmental organization permit maximum communication between and among individuals and groups as well as with other elements of the academic community. An open system is possible only if a high degree of acceptance and trust exists among group members and among groups within the system.[15] Free flow of data leads to realistic goal setting and sound decision making based on adequate information. In contrast is the restricted communication resulting from fear and distrust often typified in bureaucratic organizations where the "news is managed," games are played and strategies employed. An open communications system is, of course, difficult, if not impossible to achieve in a bureaucracy where the power and control over communication channels emanate from the top.

A prominent feature of an open system is that it not only permits, but encourages reorganization of the system as needed to achieve most efficiently the goals set forth. With a high degree of confidence and trust, there is little need to build in any substantial organizational controls, rules and regulations that restrict individual behavior. Rules are made because group members do not trust others. If trust exists few rules are needed—which, of course, fosters the flexibility required (B above) to make a developmental system work.

D. *Term leadership.*

Student development should be based on the belief that there is no such thing as a career leadership position. No one should assume that once he achieves a position of top leadership that he is to remain on indefinitely. Enough competence within the organization should allow for rotation through leadership positions. Rotation may be greatly facilitated by the presence of organization development specialists within the system to train leaders, administrators and managers to function effectively during their tenure.[16]

Thus term leadership functions like the other elements of the organization that shift, modify, adapt to changing goals, needs and priorities. Leadership by this definition sheds the aura of status and power and becomes viewed as another set of competencies needed for effective organizational functioning and should be rewarded on that basis, not in terms of span of power or responsibility. Consequently, pay differential between a leader and members of a team should not be significant. Salary should be based on competence, professional preparation and merit. Professional people committed to egalitarian principles should have a built-in expectation that those who are inclined towards administrative and leadership positions through abilities, interests and capacities should expect to assume their share of responsibility for taking leadership where needed. There should be no assumption that higher pay is a necessary consequence.

In those positions embracing sensitive public relations areas there might be some justification for "hazard pay," but even here, since one expects to remain in the position only for a specified period before moving into another area, or back into an original area of interest, there should not be that much of an argument for "hazard pay."

E. *Individual and organizational symbiosis: the developmental contract* *

An organization member is more likely to experience personal and professional growth if he shares in the development of organizational goals, and consequently becomes committed to their achievement, while at the same time is able to work toward the attainment of personal and professional goals that coalesce with those of the organization through the process of the developmental contract. Putting it another way, each individual within the organization shares in the development of a plan that will allow him to grow and develop as a person and professional while at the same time maximizing the use of his talents and energy in furthering the goals of the organization. Thus the relationship of the individual to the organization is symbiotic: living together in a mutually beneficial way—a "developmental contract" between the individual and his organization.

How does the developmental contract work? It can be summarized in the following steps:

1. *Organizational goal and priority setting.* On an annual basis (or more frequently if needed and manageable) the organization proceeds to reassess its goals and set action priorities on the basis of evaluation of current efforts and new data emanating from within and without the system. The procedure:

a. *Initial goal setting.* Each individual and each subgroup within the organization evaluates what has been accomplished, looks at intervening events and other data, including future projections, and sets objectives for a quarter or semester or an entire year. Immediate and long-term targets are included with the understanding that the long-term targets can be modified as needed. Within this context, for example, it will not be enough to plan and execute a student-faculty conference to modify student attitudes unless an evaluation is built in and the attitude change ascertained.

b. *Organizational goals and priorities decision.* The behavioral objectives of each individual and group within the organization are collated

---

* The author is indebted to Allen C. Ivey for a number of ideas considered in this section.

centrally by a "goals and priorities" team. The collated data are fed into a decision making process, the outcome of which is to establish goals and priorities for the next time period together with any modifications in the long range goals. The decision, which is determined through a process of involving the entire community, should take into account any externally imposed priorities or conditions, recent events, evaluation of current programs, and future projections.

c. *Organization modifications to best achieve goals and priorities.* Modifications in the organization are made as needed for most efficient and effective goal achievement. The elimination of some activities, addition of new tasks or projects along with the continuation of certain high priority functions with or without modification would be likely consequences.

d. *Individual goal reassessment.* Once the goal and priority setting exercise is completed and the decision on organizational modifications is made then each individual reassesses his own goals in the light of these modifications and puts forth a proposition that would best achieve his own objectives as well as best utilize his talents to help meet the goals and priorities of the organization.

e. *Negotiation with individuals.* Once the entire picture can be presented according to individual and organizational goals, an attempt is made to match the total institutional expectations with the objectives of each individual. Appropriate negotiations at several levels make as congruent as possible individual behavioral objectives with organizational goals and expectations. Upon completion of negotiations there is a written developmental "contract" articulated between each staff member and his unit head and with each head and his organizational head according to each person's goals, how they are related to the organizational goals, how they are to be accomplished and within what time frame, and how they are to be evaluated and measured as products. This contract is used as a measure for merit salary increases and a basis for organizational goal and priority modifications during the next period of developmental contract negotiations.

2. *Organizing for the task.* A hallmark of a developmental organization is its flexibility and adaptability. Unlike the bureaucracy which adapts goals and priorities to its existing structure with as little discomforture to the system as possible, the developmental organization modi-

fies its organization as needed to best achieve the goals and priorities. Putting it simply, in the developmental organization you put the people and the resources where the priorities are. This means the likely utilization of work teams, task forces, and other common goals and interest groups that are constructed to do a job, evaluate it, dissolve, or reconstitute in modified form depending on the settling of new goals and priorities. Leadership focuses on coordination and management of the human resources and providing communication linkage within and without the system.

3. *Allocation of resources.* These are allocated centrally or by the goals and priorities group in accordance with developmental contracts agreed upon. No individual or subunit can assume that the receipt of a fund allocation means automatically receipt of a like or increased amount for the next period of negotiation. In this way vested interests over control of funds cannot be established, nor "squatter's rights" on equipment or facilities obtained, but must be based on priorities on a continuous basis.

How would it work? One possibility is to start with a "seed money" approach. Each individual is given an allocation to spend as he sees fit, the sole stipulation being that he must make an accounting for the manner in which all his funds are spent. The individual may wish to pool his resources with another person to buy equipment or to develop a special project. Under such circumstances travel is likely to become of lesser importance, particularly if travel has been viewed as a status symbol. As master of their own funds staff might well reorder their priorities and use the money in other ways.

It is important that resources be allocated in accordance with goals and priorities. It makes no sense to continue to fund or maintain programs that have little or no value and are not evaluated as significantly contributing to the overall goals of the organization. To do so is to fall into the bureaucratic trap of justifying work to keep people on the payroll.

In summary, the developmental contract idea has the singular advantage of systematically establishing for each individual, as well as the total organization symbiotic objectives for a specific time period. There is a built in system for a regularly evaluating and rewarding performance on the basis of merit and not on the basis of bureaucratic criteria.

References

1. Cowley, William H. "The Nature of Student Personnel Work," *Educational Record* (April 1936), pp. 3–31.

2. For a review of the early literature on philosophical development see Blaesser, Willard W. and Crookston, Burns B. Student Personnel Work—College and University. *Encyclopedia of Educational Research*, Third Edition, 1960, pp. 1414–1427.

3. Lloyd-Jones, Esther. Changing Concepts of Student Personnel Work. In Esther Lloyd-Jones and Margaret R. Smith (eds) *Student Personnel Work as Deeper Teaching*. New York: Harper & Bros., 1954.

4. Crookston, Burns B. "A Developmental View of Academic Advising as Teaching." *Journal of College Student Personnel* 13:1 (January, 1972), pp. 12–17.

5. Shoben, Edward Joseph, Jr. "The New Student: Implications for Personnel Work." *CAPS CAPSULE* 2:1 (Fall 1968), pp. 1–7.

6. For example, see statement of desirable conditions and standards for maximum effectiveness of the college administrator, adopted by NASPA Executive Council, *NASPA Journal* 9:1 (July 1971), pp. 3–5.

7. Oetting, E. R. "A Developmental Definition of Counseling Psychology." *Journal of Counseling Psychology* 14, (1967), pp. 382–385.

8. For a discussion of the concept see Ivey, Allen E. and Morrill, Weston M. "Confrontation, Communication, and Encounter: A Conceptual Framework for Student Development." *NASPA Journal* 7:4 (April 1970), pp. 226–243. For application see Crookston, Burns B. "Coping with Campus Disruption." *Student Development Staff Papers* 1-2, Colorado State University, 1969. For background theory see Morrill, Weston, Ivey, Allen E. and Oetting, E. R. The College Counseling Center—A Center for Student Development. In Heston and Frick, *Counseling for the Liberal Arts College*. Antioch, Ohio: Antioch Press, 1968, pp. 141–157.

9. Bennis, Warren. "Organic Populism." *Psychology Today* (February 1970), p. 48.

10. Bennis, Warren and Slater, Philip E. *The Temporary Society*. New York: Harper and Row, 1968.

11. Wise, Max W. *The Politics of the Private College*. New Haven, Conn.: The Hazen Foundation, 1968.

12. Bennis and Slater, *op. cit.*

13. *Ibid.*, p. 6.

14. See the early studies on human motivation by Allport, F. H., *Social Psychology*. Boston: Houghton Mifflin. 1924. Also see Gordon, Thomas. *Group Centered Leadership*. New York: Houghton Mifflin, 1955. For application see Crookston, Burns B. and Blaesser, Willard W. Planned change in the college setting. *Personnel and Guidance Journal* 49:7 March 1962), pp. 610–616.

15. Gibb, Jack R. Climate for trust formation. In L. P. Bradford, J. R. Gibb and K. D. Benne (eds), *T-Group Theory and Laboratory Method*. New York: Wiley, 1964.

16. For a discussion on organization development theory and practice see Beekhard, Richard, *Organization Development: Strategies and Models*. Reading, Mass.: Addison-Wesley, 1969; also see Bennis, W. G., *Organization Development: Its Nature, Origins, and*

Prospects. Reading, Mass.: Addison-Wesley, 1969; additionally, Buchanan, Paul C. "The Concept of Organization Development, or Self-Renewal, as a Form of Planned Change," in Watson, Goodwin (ed.), *Concepts for Social Change.* Washington: NTL IABS-NEA, 1967.

   17. Mager, Robert F. *Preparing Instructional Objectives.* Palo Alto: Fearon Publishers, 1962.

The Student Personnel Worker of 1980

Mary Evelyn Dewey

To plan appropriate professional preparation for the field of student personnel work for the future realistically, we must place the topic in its larger setting, namely, the life situation of the field of work. We must also have some knowledge of what has gone before, in order to know what has or has not been successful. Some attempt must be made to project into the future, both on the basis of what we can learn from the first two elements and on what we are told portends for society in the post-industrial world to come. Obviously, time does not permit a full and comprehensive development of the task so defined; however, one may, using such an outline, attempt a condensed coverage, a précis, that will seek to identify major issues, questions, and suggestions for further discussion and/or exploration. Actually, this discussion can be condensed in a telegram based on the three factors and, of course, appropriately spiced with interrobangs:

1. THE FIELD IS IN SERIOUS TROUBLE.
2. THE FIELD HAS ALWAYS BEEN IN TROUBLE—AND DOES NOT SEEM TO HAVE LEARNED MUCH ABOUT RESOLVING ITS PROBLEMS.
3. UNLESS THE FIELD TAKES SOME ACTION, THE STUDENT PERSONNEL WORKER OF THE EIGHTIES MAY WELL BE EXTINCT.

That, in essence, is the message this writer would send, and I would address it to all professional preparation programs, to practitioners, and to all our various national associations. I very much fear, however, that in that form it would promptly be placed in the circular file as being nothing new, and life would proceed as usual. Therefore, the message must be fleshed out a bit for emphasis, underlining, and highlighting.

326

Most important, new focuses to the argument must be introduced, lest the message be received as merely another alarm call—the 1971 version of Chicken Little.

Hence to Point 1: THE FIELD IS IN SERIOUS TROUBLE. There is no doubt that the identity crisis of student personnel work appears to grow only more acute with each passing month. The trickle of works in earlier decades now more resembles an avalanche, the boulders of which typically signal the same basic problems: the field has no clear definition of function acceptable to the educational field at large; there exists no clear status or reward system; there is little recognition or acceptance of the field by the students it presumably serves, or by faculty and administrative colleagues. The Hodgkinson data reported in the July 1970 NASPA *Journal*[1] tell the story—and it is a painful one—of a national study confirming what our critics have said for years: we have not made it in the central arena of the institution. This, coupled with the acute financial distress facing higher education (indeed, this emerged as the central theme of the AAHE conference in Chicago in March), causes increased apprehension in student personnel circles, as indeed it should, and we see in the field an ill-defined but increasing malaise characterized by defensiveness, anxiety, and frustration. The frustration that develops under these circumstances leads to cries for unionization, demands for recognition and for tenure or other forms of job security, and calls for control over working conditions. There is a hope that unionization will provide the strength necessary to force the field's will on the academic community and that organization will establish the field as a bona fide profession. New attempts at role definition appear periodically, as do new constructs for services, and new pleas for activism, relevance, and effectiveness emerge as deans are urged to "stand up and be counted," to get on all those policy-making committees, to do a better job of publicizing their activities and accomplishments on their individual campuses, to obtain and retain faculty status (if you can't beat 'em, join 'em), to work for faculty status for members of their staffs (apparently whether or not they may qualify), to contribute to research knowledge, and so forth. Old arguments are resurrected and restated: e.g., counseling is or is not the major function of the field; there is or is not a body of knowledge that may be defined as a discipline known as student personnel work; there is or is not a role for the generalist; the field is or is not going to establish itself as a profession. All in all, a serious reader of the literature is given the impression of vaulting idealism alternating with discouraged despair, interspersed with horrifying periods of becalmed inertia and startling complacence. If any pattern is to be discerned in this, it is a circular one. As the arguments repeat, the suggested solutions recur, while the issues remain constant.

Why is this? Doth the lady protest too much? Surely if good work is done, it will be recognized. Surely if the work is truly educational in nature, someone will notice and will give due credit where credit is due. Surely if the professional expertise warrants it, the top professional title will go to a "professionally trained" person, rather than a faculty member from an unrelated but respected academic discipline. . . . surely, but apparently not so.

Can so many effective personnel workers be wrong in this matter? Can they, honestly believing in their efforts, knowing their function is vital, sensing intuitively (if in no demonstrable way) that they are close to the matter, be so mistaken? There is evidence that such might be the case, despite the paradoxical fact that in all the years of development of this field, there has been a constant and abiding faith (now well supported by research) that student personnel work's realm of operation is situated closer to the truth of educational growth and development than is standard classroom learning.

How are we then to resolve this dilemma, this frustrated defensiveness, this apparent inability to break through to the matter successfully, with confidence and with appropriate recognition??

Let us move to Point 2: THE FIELD HAS ALWAYS BEEN IN TROUBLE AND DOES NOT SEEM TO HAVE LEARNED MUCH ABOUT RESOLVING ITS PROBLEMS. The argument over the decades has singled out many villains: the recalcitrant faculty, safe in their academic security and self-respect; the overbearing administrator who hands out policies to be enforced by personnel lackeys who are presumably incompetent to contribute to the formulation of those policies; practitioners endowed with goodwill but short on effectiveness; the "anti-intellectualism" of the applied fields; overidentification with the custodial-control role; lack of sound theory in which to ground the field; et cetera, et cetera, et cetera. It is likely that all of these elements contribute to the problem, but it is also apparent that they do not totally encompass it. Without denying the necessity of working toward the solution of the many problems extant or without claiming that there is one approach to a grand solution, I would direct attention to what seems to me to be a more culpable villain. In the many analyses of issues, there is too little *pertinent* discussion of the role and responsibility of professional preparation programs in this state of affairs. An intensive examination of the literature indicates two major themes, which in my view are questionable and therefore stand as unresolved issues: curriculum and selection of students.[2]

First point, *curriculum.* Examination of typical programs reveals just that—"typical" programs, involving human relations skills, some counseling, some overview of practice, some internship experience (M.A. level). One sees an awesome similarity of approach; one sees a recurring sameness in the periodic attempts to develop guidelines for professional preparation; one sees "new" formulations developed that always seem to be based on surveys of existing practice; and one wonders if it is too simplistic to suggest that this approach tends to perpetuate the problem rather than solve it. Within these programs one does *not* typically see much emphasis on organizational theory, dynamics of institutional and societal change, American studies, sociology of student life and culture, futuristics, heavy research components, or the like—indeed, one does not even see a great deal of the field of higher education as a major social institution and as a discipline in its own right in the typical curriculum. The focus is too much on the specificity of student services and much too little on the institution as a whole, an organism, a system—of which student personnel work is but a part, albeit, one hopes, a vital one. We have not educated professionals to see the institution whole. Worse than that, we have not done a good job of educating people to see the field itself in its entirety, but have tended to look at counseling as the be-all and end-all. We have not done a good job of listening to some of our best friends and most severe critics—as, for example, Wrenn saying in 1948:

I'd also relegate "counseling" to its appropriate position as one of a *number* of the personnel functions and not have it substituted in people's thinking for the entire personnel program.[3]

Or Barry and Wolf saying in 1959:

By our overuse of the word counselor, we have identified ourselves with a single phase of our activities.[4]

Too often graduate programs launch into the field neophyte professionals who have been led to believe that their function will not only be central to the educational process, but that in all probability it will be the most significant—a concept supported by aspiration, stated goals, and supportive counseling tools than by clear methodologies for achievement. Too often the neophyte's program has perhaps unintentionally shielded him from the realities of the situation by not including in his professional preparation certain elements which would, at the very least, provide him a more comprehensive and realistic knowledge base from which to operate.

Second point, *selection*. Just as there has been too little challenge of the typical curriculum, there has been an ongoing simultaneous belief that the real problem in professional preparation was *selection*. If we could but develop the right instruments to assess personalities, we could admit that ideal type to our graduate programs. *That* would be the answer. And we *knew* over the years what we were looking for. The pattern recurs and recurs: we wanted as primary factors in candidates for admission sincerity, warmth, loyalty, enthusiasm, ability to relate to others, interest in people—in short, counselor-types as they are known. (Some lists advocated a sense of humor as desirable—perhaps to enjoy the irony of the situation?)

Is is not paradoxical that this field which above all others has proclaimed a belief in uniqueness has made its graduate programs so similar? Is it not paradoxical that this field, with its time-honored adherence to belief in individual differences, over the years has sought to identify *the* ideal personality type to work with all those different, unique, individual students? Critics of the field have pleaded for more research on the part of its practitioners, yet we have not made serious efforts to recruit individuals who will do this naturally and by inclination. We recognize specific needs within the field, but we do not widely promote varying plans for recruiting and developing people who have the needed skills. We recognize the need for the comprehensivist mind applied to higher education, but we do not know how to develop it or how to recruit it in its raw state. We have continually sought the mellow and the smooth rather than the abrasive, the critical, the one-sided, the questioning—we have sought the cooperative, the loyal, the enthusiastic (in its narrow sense) and have avoided the individualist, all the while proclaiming to be the champion of individualism. We have assumed that warmth of personality correlates with good research ability, with mental acuity, with individuality of approach, with interest in change and innovation. We have sought and honored good intentions over realistic achievement—and none of us can doubt that the resulting holier-than-thou syndrome has done extensive damage to the field's aspiration for recognition as a profession, not to mention its effectiveness in working with students.

Thus we have a field in serious trouble, and the trouble has been of long standing. I have attempted to argue that professional preparation programs have contributed heavily to this condition by being too limited in design, too repetitive, too reluctant to question themselves, too unimaginative, too committed to fitting the field into psychology instead of vice versa. I submit that professional preparation programs must bear much of the onus for the harvest we are reaping and that the effective practitioners of artistry and skill may be successful in spite of and not because of their professional preparation. We know, for example, from the very provocative study by Blackburn[5] in 1969 that—

both preparation and experience contribute to perceptions of student personnel work in unique ways. Preparation in student personnel work contributes emphasis upon the individual, counseling, educational reform, models for behavioral learning, and the use of behavioral science techniques to create an environment for learning. Experience in student personnel work contributes an emphasis upon research, needs of students, interpretation of the nature of education and experiences to achieve personal developmental tasks (133).

After ten or more years of experience, the chief student personnel officers with academic preparation and the chief student personnel officers without specific training tend to view the purposes of student personnel programs more similarly. Those with academic preparation, after ten or more years of experience, place less emphasis upon counseling and the individual student. Those chief student personnel officers without specific preparation, after ten or more years of experience, embrace many of the philosophic foundations on which counseling is based (136).

The implications of this are fascinating and bear further discussion and investigation.

At any rate, as we move to Point 3: UNLESS THE FIELD TAKES SOME ACTION, THE STUDENT PERSONNEL WORKER OF THE EIGHTIES MAY WELL BE EXTINCT. Obviously, it is my argument that it is the major responsibility of professional preparation programs to effect necessary change if they are to help avoid extinguishing the field. Some of the suggestions naturally grow out of what has gone before, some will grow out of what we have seen predicted as coming in the future. To look briefly at the first category:

Professional preparation programs must begin to supply our effective and experienced practitioners with the variety of individuals they need to meet the complexities of today's campuses—individuals to fill a variety of roles—research, communications, residence personnel of the highest order, group specialists, comprehensivists. Programs must recruit for diversity, for interdisciplinary orientations, for individuality as well as for persons whose strength lies in the counseling methodologies and interest. And, dare I say it, in a time when so-called "elitism" is in disfavor, for intellectual excellence. We need some unique types, some powerful brainpower, some doers instead of maintainers, some questioners, some thinkers—perhaps some people who do not like to work with people, but who are fascinated by institutional processes, decision-making patterns, research questions, etc. Programs need to distinguish between the pros and the pseudo-pros of the future. Let me explain: currently, it seems to me, we have a clear distinction in the field between the real "pros" (the "all-rounders" by virtue of their ability, leadership, and experience—those people "in spite of" and those people from other fields who came in because of their commitment) and the "pseudo-pros." My point is that we must start the *real* pros in our professional preparation programs, for there will be no positions for pseudo-pros in the future. Financial stringency may be the initial reason, but one hopes the better reason will be that the professionalization of the field will not allow it.

Professional preparation programs must be reconstructed to offer preparation heretofore lacking in substantive areas. Flexibility, individuality, a genuine "exploitation of the institutional resources" available, crossing disciplinary lines, creating new degree structures, new approaches to the study of that ill-defined "personnel function" in higher education—all these will be necessary.

The curriculum will reflect and respond to and contribute to what educational processes will exist in the future. Personnel professionals will perhaps operate on the modular pattern that is being forecast, in specialty teams on short-term bases, in a variety of situations. We are told that linear thinking will not be the mode of the future—nor will it define the future. Just as undergraduate curriculums of the future will be modular, restructuring itself, redesigning itself, reapplying itself in new formulations—an exciting prospect, wild in its possibilities and demanding the very finest professionals. May I conclude by reiterating my third point about the extinction of the field: I did not say the personnel *function* would be extinct. In my view, that is not in question. The question lies in *who will perform it.* Professional preparation programs in higher education have no small responsibility here: If they (professional preparation programs) choose McLuhan's description of the average person's approach to the future—that is, happily driving forward looking into the rearview mirror, it will be all over in the year 2000.

References

1. Hodgkinson, Harold L. "How Deans of Students Are Seen by Others—and Why?" *NASPA Journal* 8: 49–54; July 1970.
2. Bibliography available from the author.
3. Wrenn, C. Gilbert. "The Greatest Tragedy in College Personnel Work." *Educational and Psychological Measurement* 8: 413; Autumn 1948.
4. Barry, Ruth, and Wolf, Beverly. "Guidance-Personnel Work: The Near Look and the Far Vision." *NAWDC Journal* 12: 175; June 1959.
5. Blackburn, J. L. *Perceived Officers as a Function of Academic Preparation and Experience.* Doctor's thesis. Tallahassee: Florida State University, 1969. 194 pp. (Available from University Microfilms, Inc., Ann Arbor, Mich.)

Student Affairs Administration in Transition

Everett M. Chandler

There is a transition stage in the organization of student affairs involving student personnel work as defined in the period following World War II and a newer concept of student development. An organizational model is proposed for the transition along with a proposed approach leading toward a student development goal.

Recently there have been articles indicating interest in overall administration, organization and what might be labeled the philosophical basis of student affairs work (Crookston 1972; Rickard 1972; Sandeen 1971). One can detect a state of doubt, sometimes confusion, and occasionally despair over the present condition of the profession and its place in higher education in such articles. Perhaps this state of feeling reflects a transitional period in the profession.

Since World War II, there appear to be two identifiable trends relating to the administration of student affairs. The first is exemplified by the writings of such authors as Wrenn (1951), Mueller (1961), and Williamson (1961) which set forth a framework for student personnel work based on the student personnel point of view. Three assumptions regarding students are the foundation for this viewpoint: (a) individual differences among students are anticipated: (b) the student is conceived of and treated as a functioning whole person; and (c) teaching, counseling, activities, and other organized educational efforts start from where the student is and not where the institution would prefer the student to be in development.

It is believed that few would take exception to these concepts. In translating these concepts to the job, it appears that these assumptions may not have been worked into the practice of student personnel as

334

fully as originally conceived. During this same time period, administrators responsible for student personnel work identified a series of from 10
to 15 different functional services to students such as counseling, testing, placement, health, cocurricular activities, and financial aids.
Skilled practitioners were developed for these various areas of service.
These services are frequently remedial or controlling in nature; these
functional areas operate somewhat independently of one another. Neither students nor faculty were or are involved to any extent in planning, organizing, staffing, or evaluating them.

A second trend is of more recent origin and is frequently labeled student development. The entire campus is involved in facilitating the behavioral development of the student. The student is assessed as to
where he is in terms of his goals. There is emphasis on the meaningful
involvement of the student in the educational activities affecting him.
The concepts are not so basically different than found in the student
personnel point of view, but the emphasis on more intensive involvement of both student and faculty in cooperative efforts is. This emphasis requires new thinking and new attitudes about what is being done
and how to do it.

Student personnel work often finds itself in a service station role
with the staff waiting for customers and reacting to their declared
needs; whereas student development is viewed as a preventive, proactive, collaborative role with the staff moving outward. The two approaches are not only separated by the nature of the duties performed
but also by an attitude about why and how the work is done. The difference is not so much concept as it is practice.

Roles in Transition

It would appear that the student affairs profession may be in a state of
transition. What are some of the indicators of transition and how do we
operate in a transitional period? A few examples from recent literature
indicate aspects of this transitional state. The NASPA research report
on "Assumptions and Beliefs of Selected Members of the Academic

Community" (Dutton and others 1970) shows differing role expectations for the Vice President for Student Affairs (VPSA) on the part of various members of the academic community. Students prefer an advocate role but are confronted often by an adversary relationship. The presidents feel that maintenance of control and order is the major responsibility of the VPSA and that this should not detract from other duties. The faculty appear to view student affairs as an academic civil service.

Sandeen (1971) declares that "college student personnel workers have not adequately defined their roles," adding that "too often there is a discrepancy between the educational goals of the institution and the goals that the dean and his staff may share [p. 223]." Thus, the role of the VPSA and his staff can be one of confusion. Rickard (1972) wisely warns the profession to be aware that the mere adoption of the title student development in a "frenetic search for relevance without examining and updating what the staff do is merely a semantic exercise [p. 222]." He states that the title *student development* without proper groundwork may cause both faculty and students to react unfavorably. There are faculty members who are unaware, uncaring, and sometimes unsympathetic to the work done by student affairs. The words student development imply only instructionally related development as viewed by some faculty members. A change in title to student development by student affairs may be seen by this type of faculty member as a real or implied threat to his real or assumed prerogatives and may draw a hostile reaction which may infect others not ordinarily involved in such matters.

It appears clear that the full scale implementation of a student development program requires a nearly complete acceptance of the concept by the vast majority of the entire academic community. It involves more than a reshuffling of departments in student affairs; attitudinal changes by the staff of student affairs, key administrators, and faculty leaders are necessary. It is not likely that all parts of the academic community will accept the concept at an equal pace. It appears that the student development concept will evolve on campuses in differing rates and by different means. There will be a transitional state of undetermined length and depth. This creates a situation in which the VPSA must consider organization in a transitional setting. If the goal of student development is desirable, both organization and attitudinal steps should be taken.

Implementation of Goals

First the attitudinal situation is of utmost importance. The VPSA needs to create an attitudinal environment favorable to the development of the program. To do this, he can begin by establishing objectives and strategies relating to student development. Among these can be a plan to use staff members to present ideas to the various parts of the academic community. Perhaps using a low profile, they can begin to gain understanding from those with whom they are in frequent contact. To accomplish this satisfactorily, the VPSA should establish a staff training program to provide his own staff with adequate insight into the student development goals and processes. The staff should collaborate in setting objectives related to student development in accordance with the degree of acceptance by the academic community of collaborative work by students, faculty, and student affairs at any given time. One facet of such training should be to teach patience in reaching the goals. As the program gains acceptance, other members of the academic community should be involved in the collaborative processes and the setting of objectives.

The effort expended by the staff to explain student development should not be so self-righteously done as to create a counterforce. There is a decided difference between defeating enemies and winning friends. After all, the student development concept does not seek to change the basic character of the institution, but it seeks to provide a more effective process to help students achieve within that institution.

Second, there are organizational responses that may be made within student affairs which would assist in heading toward the goal. Undoubtedly there are a number of organizational models that would work well. One model is suggested that would appear to work in institutions in the 7,500 to 20,000 enrollment range. Both smaller and larger institutions may have special needs and situations making the model less valid for them. Of course, individual institutions may have special characteristics, including particular types of presidents, deans, and others, and even curricular offerings that would invalidate this model.

It is also obvious that various institutions are in different places on any scale measuring the state of transition in student development. However, it is likely that there is a grouping together at some modal point indicating that a plan of organization will evolve that has similarities among the institutions.

Implementation of a Model

In considering this model the first premise is that student affairs is one of the major components of the university organization. As such it should report to the chief executive of the campus. This means that the VPSA should be an administrator. Occasionally, a desire can be detected among some colleagues not to identify fully with the administration. In fact, Hedlund (1971) in his article on the preparation for student personnel, foresaw a cleavage between administrative functions and student development functions. He forecasted a separation of the two, with administrative functions being assigned to an area consisting of persons who are professional administrators but not necessarily expert in the educational process. He indicated that an administrator needs managerial talent not required by an educator and that an educator needs human development talent not required by the administrator. The inference is made that these areas of expertise clash and cause problems for current administrators of student affairs. Sometime in the future the cleavage may occur, but it is believed that the presidents and the trustees who establish the administrative organization of the institutions will continue to expect the VPSA to perform both administrative and educational functions for some time to come. It is also believed that a good administrator can absorb both functions and perform them well. Presidents, academic vice presidents, and many corporate executives satisfactorily administer a number of varied activities.

As a major component of the institution, student affairs requires an administrator as its head. Such functions as planning, organization, communication, control, and evaluation are as essential to student affairs as to any other administrative organization. If the VPSA does not perform these functions, someone else in the institution will do it. It is suggested that the VPSA accept his role as administrator as the one best prepared to understand and support the desired objectives of the student affairs program as delineated by the president and as agreed on by student affairs staff, faculty, and students where collaborative efforts are employed.

Second, from the standpoint of organizational structure, it is believed that differing concepts of the student affairs program can be accommodated together in one organization. A portion of the work done in student affairs is strictly management. These services are needed and will continue to be located in the administrative structure. Another portion of the work can be closely related to the student development concept, and a third is the judicial-disciplinary control function.

The three areas named would be administered by professional staff members under the general direction of the VSPA. The first area should be directed by a person who has managerial skills. He might have business administration skills, education, and experience. His function would be to provide services such as admissions, records, placement, housing, and financial aids efficiently and well.

The second area should be administered by a human development consultant (Morrill, Ivey & Oetting 1968). Since the student development approach lends itself to the use of project, task force, and team approaches, the person taking the lead in this area may be rotated according to current needs and the collaborative interaction of students, faculty, and administration. Any given project agreed on through collaboration might call for the special skills of a specific staff member. This person would take the lead in administering this particular project. Another project might require a different project team with a different leader.

The third function of discipline-control would preferably be run by a person who is primarily educationally motivated but is able to perform the necessary control and discipline tasks as required by any given institution.

The three areas—managerial, student development, judicial control—would have subfunctions grouped under them. These subfunctions would vary from campus to campus according to the outlook and expectations of the functions in the eyes of the campus at large. Although it is recognized and hoped that each function would have a student development outlook, it is not realistic to expect everyone in the organization to have it in the same degree.

Managerial

There are many student personnel professionals who have performed their work ably and who hold tenured positions in their job. The tenure may be legal, or it may be a moral obligation to those who have served well for many years. Consequently, those whose outlook is more managerial than student development may be grouped together for this reason.

The general campus community, including students and faculty as well as administration, may expect certain functions to operate in relatively fixed ways. These ways may even be bound by statutory requirements. Such functions as records and placement may be located in the managerial section. Crookston (1972) pointed out that it should not be inferred from his strong advocacy of a newer student development approach that all student personnel methods should be abandoned, because some remedial and mental health functions as practiced under the student personnel point of view should continue. It is hoped that effort in leading these functions toward a proactive and collaborative approach would be ultimately successful and lead to less need for remediation. One organizational model suggested for the transitional stage is shown in Figure 1.

It is realized that the Figure standing alone reflects a hierarchical organization or a bureaucratic structure which is not intended. This form should be understood to portray location of functions: the assignment of functions in the chart is not meant to be arbitrary. For example, placement may not emphasize career development but may perform the essential managerial task of bringing employer and student together efficiently, providing an accurate available system of files and resumes. Most financial aid programs following detailed guidelines established by federal, state, and institutional agencies perform largely managerial operations. A large portion of the decision making in admissions work on many campuses involves application of state dictated entrance requirements. It is recognized that there is room for collaboration with faculty and students in some aspects of these services but not to the degree found in such functions as counseling or cocurricular activities. Obviously student and faculty collaboration is not barred in the managerial services, but the fact is that in practice it just has not occurred to any great extent for the past twenty years or so. Certainly managerial services should not be performed in a cold punched-card manner calculated to cause student and faculty antipathy and even rejection. This is a matter of emphasis. It is believed that efficient service from this type of managerial function is the expectation of presidents, faculty, and students.

Student Development

In examining the functions listed under student development, it should not be thought that efficient service is to be forgotten—every office should strive for such a goal. However, the emphasis is not managerial. There is much more room for student and faculty input in the decisions which affect the student. The functions suggested for inclusion in this area are those which appear to be in a state where the initiation of a student development approach will be more readily understood and accepted, not only by the staff but also by the rest of the academic community.

An example of the team effort in student development might be the following hypothetical case. Residence hall students working with members of the counseling staff, health center, cocurricular activities staff, and the housing office might establish a team project for making the residence hall a more effective instrument for education through experiential learning in a living environment. Key faculty members in certain disciplines might also be involved. The group would establish behavioral objectives and an agreed-on means of achievement. The group would establish evaluative procedures and measures to ascertain progress toward the goal.

It is recognized that there are agreed-on objectives and, in addition, certain routines prescribed by law or by administrative direction that must be accomplished by various offices or positions in the student development area. Although some persons might assume that any managerial functions would compromise the proactive, collaborative approach necessary for student development, the fact that such work is

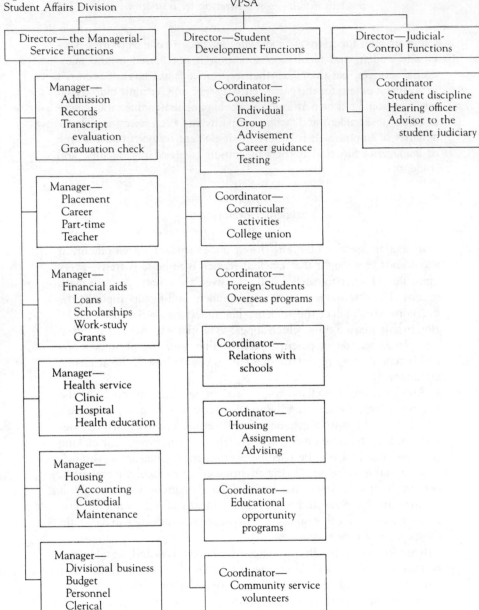

Figure 1
Student Affairs Division

done does not negate the student development approach and attitude, which is key to the success of student development. These assignments should be included in the administrative objectives. The procedure for accomplishing them should be done with a proactive collaborative approach, including staff of the department, students, and faculty where possible.

Judicial-Control

The judicial-control functions are not as extensive in terms of offices or personnel. Because of their influence (positive or negative) they have an importance beyond mere numbers. It is particularly important to separate out of counseling, housing, and cocurricular activities the functions relating to discipline and control. Such functions assigned to these other areas can impede a proactive collaborative student development effort because judicial-control functions are essentially an adversary relationship which creates communication barriers.

The disciplinary and control functions can be combined in a small office. The advisorship of the student judiciary, performance of hearing officer tasks at lesser levels of discipline, gathering of evidence, arranging for judgmental hearings, and implementation of necessary due process procedures are tasks requiring professional leadership.

As a matter of fact, there are many student government leaders who prefer a legalistic role in dealing with the institution in regard to application of rules and regulations. The establishment of an office to carry out the function in an orderly, legalistic manner may meet a real need. In addition, the courts today are requiring a more legalistic approach in order to avoid having cases overruled.

Conclusion

The need for a transitional state comes about because there is an ongoing program of student personnel services on the majority of campuses. The present system is based on a traditional hierarchical administrative organization structure of authority and responsibility. In large part, student personnel work consists of a series of remedial services and the application of rules and regulations in control functions. The staff is usually passive, waiting to serve those who find their offices or apply corrective measures to those presumed to have erred.

Recently a strong trend is developing which is leading toward a student development approach. This approach requires both a change in attitude toward service to students and a change in the way of providing it. The staff is expected to move outward from their offices and to interact collaboratively with staff and students toward a common goal of aiding each student in his behavioral development. The emphasis on rules and controls is decidedly decreased.

On many, possibly a large majority of campuses, the total academic community is not ready to accept a full scale student development program emanating out of the student affairs area.

It is believed that the proposed transitional model is one way to enable student affairs administrators to initiate a student development program on campuses where the complete change to a student development concept would be difficult to achieve in the near future. Understanding of the program by an entire academic community may take time. Evidence of smooth working of the student development program in certain specific areas may hasten the day of full acceptance.

References

Crookston, B. B. An organizational model for student development. *Journal of the National Association of Student Personnel Administrators*, 1972. *10*, 3–13.

Dutton, T. et al. Assumptions and beliefs of selected members of the academic community. *A special report of the NASPA division of research and program development.* Bloomington, Indiana: National Association of Student Personnel Administrators, April 1970, 6.

Hedlund, D. E. Preparation for student personnel: Implications of humanistic education. *Journal of College Student Personnel*, 1971, *12*, 324–328.

Morrill, W. H.; Ivey, A. E.; & Oetting, E. R. The college counseling center: A center for student development. In J. C. Heston and W. B. Frick (Eds.), *Counseling for the liberal arts campus: The Albion symposium.* Yellow Springs, Ohio: Antioch Press, 1968. P. 141–157.

Mueller, K. H. *Student personnel work in higher education.* Cambridge, Mass.: Riverside Press, 1961.

Rickard, S. T. The role of the chief student personnel administrator revisited. *Journal of the National Association of Student Personnel Administrators,* 1972, 9, 219–226.

Sandeen, A. Research: An essential for survival. *Journal of National Association of Student Personnel Administrators,* 1971, 4, 222–227.

Williamson, E. G. *Student personnel services in college and universities.* New York: McGraw-Hill, 1961.

Wrenn, C. G. *Student personnel work in college.* New York: Ronald Press, 1951.

An Emerging Role of Student Personnel— Contributing to Organizational Effectiveness

Robert H. Shaffer

To remain a significant force in higher education, the student personnel field must contribute to the total organizational development of colleges and universities and not just focus on the development of the individual student. This article suggests some needed steps to this added role.

Improving organizational effectiveness is a complex challenge to all colleges and universities. Novel demands and even threats to their very existence face all institutions of higher education. Current literature in the areas of organizational development, systems analysis, and administrative evaluation suggest some bases for improving the effectiveness of organizations in responding to future shock, the greening of America, or the plain, old fashioned budget crunch.

This paper is intended to suggest an emerging role of student personnel as a field—that of contributing to institutional effectiveness. First will be explored some of the reasons it was not as effective as it might have been during the past decade in helping colleges and universities respond more creatively to student unrest and other tensions, and then some steps student personnel staff members can take to strengthen their collective contributions to institutional effectiveness will be suggested.

Problems

Rigidity, lack of sensitivity, inadequate feedback, and cumbersome institutional response mechanisms are among the factors that have been identified as elements in situations which have escalated into violent confrontations from relatively innocent looking beginnings (Braungart

& Braungart 1972; Foster & Long 1970; Sampson & Korn 1970). The inability and unwillingness of institutional machinery and personnel to respond swiftly and effectively enough to prevent misunderstandings and emotions from contributing to flaming conflict has frequently been cited as a failure on the part of the student personnel field.

Student unrest was construed by many faculty members and administrators to be a phenomenon of little concern to the total organization, until students and their faculty sympathizers started disrupting the total institution. Prior to disruptions, many academic and administrative members of the campus community viewed student protest with amused condescension as a problem for the student personnel dean and his staff. Once dragged into conflicts, however, these detached segments of the campus community frequently took unto themselves the handling of student issues demonstrating little confidence in the student personnel system or its component parts. Once attuned to student complaints and charges, many faculty members and general administrators saw student personnel as essentially irrelevant, if not actually detrimental, to effective response.

Regardless of the wisdom of past actions on various campuses, the student personnel field is challenged to analyze the behavior of their institutions and their various components with an eye to the future. Failure to do so is an abdication of professional and institutional responsibilities. The student personnel organization is usually the sub-system within the total system of higher education charged with understanding and providing for individual needs and for serving as liaison between the formal institution and its students.

Why was its contribution, actual or potential, so often considered ineffective or inadequate? The explanation may be found in the traditional orientation of student personnel administrators and their counseling colleagues.

The orientation of some student personnel has been toward institutional stability, preservation of order, establishing procedures, and insuring compliance with rules. The orientation of counseling has been toward individual behavior and the resolution by individuals of their problems. Both operated in many cases without perceiving themselves as being responsible for input into the organizational pattern for meeting stress, predicting tensions, and facilitating resolution of differing perceptions of the operational environment characterizing the campus.

Administrators and faculty members in colleges and universities are not the only individuals alleged to be rigid, inflexible, and self-centered. However, to the extent that these adjectives apply to student personnel their causes must be analyzed and removed if the field is to be more effective in the future.

In retrospect it is clear that some of the very qualities reinforced most by student personnel offices caused institutions during the past decade to respond to student unrest and militant activity in a rigid, defensive manner. Institutional response often was basically designed to express its authority and to discourage militant behavior rather than to remove its causes. Even more significantly, many institutional policies and procedures were in direct conflict with their verbalized goals and statements of desired outcomes. Many goal statements emphasized the encouragement of student expression, development of concern for world affairs, and personal involvement in the resolution of social problems. Harried administrators and institutional policy makers responded on a day-to-day basis with little insight into the institutional posture they were presenting.

Just as the counseling process with individuals stresses insight into basic motivations, feelings, and goals, so could student personnel have assisted the leadership of institutions in realistically seeing themselves and understanding their behavior. This is a fundamental element of the organizational development process (Beckhard 1969; Bennis 1969; Lawrence & Lorsch 1969; Schein 1970).

For the same reasons, student personnel as a subsystem of higher education could also have been more aggressive and more effective in encouraging institutions to see themselves and their behavior objectively. Many student personnel workers understood what was happening, attempted to explain to their colleagues the need for understanding and insight, and argued for responsive institutional behavior in the form of dialogue with student militants, changes in rules, and opening more effective communication channels. However, all too frequently institutional and social lethargy, resentment, and prejudice blocked effective positive action. Clarification of goals, building of cooperative relationships, gaining insight into organizational behavior, and establishing integrating forces within the institution are fundamental elements of the organizational development process which would have contributed significantly to effective institutional behavior (Beckhard 1969; Bennis 1969; Lawrence & Lorsch, 1969; Schein 1970).

Many of the stands taken by institutions under stress grew out of established traditional roles and relationships. More often than not their actions were not based on conscious review of their stated goals and objectives. This failure of administrators and faculty governing bodies to translate generalized goals into operational guidelines has been frequently cited as the cause for the wide gulf between students and administrators, a gulf which frequently neither side could understand. As a result, ill feeling and actual duplicity were imputed by both sides to the other. The campus credibility gap often arose from vagueness of goals, ignorance of the reciprocal nature of intrainstitutional behavior, and the complex nature of organizational response to challenge and stress. In current terminology, goals and desires were not internalized into meaningful behavior (Gross & Grambsch 1968).

Not only were basic motivations not recognized and clarified, but procedures and policies were frequently followed which had predictable outcomes at variance with verbalized desires and reasonable expectations. It is precisely at this point in analyzing institutional behavior that student personnel can play a significant role in the future. To be effective this analysis must not be limited to crisis situations.

The student development point of view has a significant contribution to make in evaluating existing policies and procedures on the basis of their impact upon individual student development. Student personnel oriented administrators should have been more effective in pointing out the disparity between some custodial policies and societal expectations. If they had been, the debilitating, wasteful arguments over dress regulations, women's hours, and parietal rules would have been reduced to a minimum. With a clear orientation to institutional goals and student development, there would have been a sound basis for discussions, confrontations, and resolution of differences (Brown 1972; Kaufman 1968).

Student personnel can play a significant role in institutional policy making by insisting on a consideration of fundamental goals and objectives as the basis for decisions and actions. Thus, if the institution states that individual development is one of its primary concerns, student personnel workers need to assist administrators and faculty members to translate this generalized goal into operational practices exemplifying it. The failure to define individual development specifically enough to make the concept applicable to practice has resulted in meaningless generalizations about educational goals while actual operating policies and practices have often continued on traditional bases.

The problem of many colleges and universities in contributing most effectively and consistently to students' achievement of autonomy is one example of the failure of student personnel to contribute to a reformulation and updating of personnel practice. The concept of defining student growth as the achievement of the various developmental tasks is accepted by most student personnel administrators. However, the specific policies and procedures most effective in contributing to this goal are debatable and are the source of much campus tension. Some campuses until very recently treated upperclass women students practically the same as freshmen women with respect to housing regulations, curfew hours, and other custodial policies. When this situation was challenged during the past few years by students and faculty alike, many campuses just as illogically swung to an opposite position and treated freshmen women students as seniors. From a developmental point of view, neither position can be sound.

For effective resolution, issues such as the above can best be decided by careful consideration of the complex nature of educational institutions and the interdependency of their subsystems. Knowledge of complex organizations prevents any office or agency from thinking in simplistic terms. Further, application of the procedures used by businesses and public agencies to clarify organizational understanding of feedback and control mechanisms reduces tension, minimizes personal animosity, and provides greater security during change. Failure to follow such practices results in increased fragmention of the organization, nonproductive internal competition, and compensatory reactions (Etzioni 1964; Perrow 1970; Schein 1970; Schmidt 1970).

Mobilizing for Change

Before the student personnel subsystem of higher education can make the needed contribution to colleges and universities, it must clean its own house by clarifying its roles, reassessing its basic assumptions, and establishing an open relationship among its component parts. This process of renewal involving clarification, reassessment, and security shattering challenge can be implemented in a number of ways.

Improving Staff Meetings

The most commonly used channel has been the staff meetings of the division of student personnel. However, this device has been so misused by being limited in scope and effectiveness, burdened with administrativia, and being narrowly conceived that it is often handicapped by cynicism and latent resistance. One of the first tasks of a staff director or the staff meeting agenda committee is to establish a new tone or perception of staff meetings. This can be achieved in a number of ways but needs to be consciously approached, otherwise a new approach will be viewed as only another agenda item.

Another obstacle to the effective use of staff meetings for changing attitudes as well as securing broad-based input into policy formulation and decision making is the all too frequent resistance to the introduction of theory in staff discussions. Individuals who perceive the meetings as problem or task oriented often look on the efforts of those who attempt to introduce theory into the discussion as an affectation or at least as being unrealistic and time consuming. When staff members are rebuffed in their attempts to contribute greater substance to staff discussions, they tend to retreat into amused or derisive silence or even carping criticism of administrative and action-oriented considerations. This further widens the gulf between personnel, solidifies preconceived positions, and defeats efforts at openminded consideration of issues.

Contributing Position Papers and Research Reports for Internal Institutional Use

Position papers and research reports represent another type of frequently neglected input device. During the past few years, discussions concerning changes in institutional posture regarding custodial and welfare responsibility for students have occurred on almost every campus. In many cases, a well prepared position paper by the counseling staff, for example, would frequently have provided the theory and information needed to raise the consideration to a professional level. All too often such considerations have been based on a mixture of personal preferences, prejudices, blind traditions, and individual perceptions of others' feelings. Effective handling of the complex issues in the student personnel field in the years ahead requires input from every relevant source.

The student personnel staff in an institution will often perceive the rise of a problem or indications of needed changes before pressure forces consideration of the issue on the crisis-oriented administrator or onto the cumbersome agendas of student-faculty committees. By recognizing and defining impending issues, necessary research can be begun and fact finding procedures initiated in time to head off poorly considered, emotionally motivated, expedient actions and decisions.

Memorandums exemplify another device for placing discussions of issues on a higher plane. By having to verbalize their positions and the reasoning underlying them, staff members are encouraged to rise above personnal bias and defensiveness. Many staff discussions can be turned from time-consuming, nonproductive has sessions by tabling issues until a formal memorandum can be prepared.

Memorandums, positions papers, and research reports are important devices for securing student personnel input into institution-wide decision making. All too often student personnel staff members stand by waiting for their opinion to be sought when an administrative office, student-faculty committee, or other agency is considering a change in college rules or policies that affect individual student growth or the degree to which the institution achieves its goals. It is professionally negligent for them to refrain from becoming involved in such considerations. It is even worse for them to wait until policies have been adopted, rules promulgated, or other action taken and then engage in second guessing or carping criticism. Student personnel professionals should feel as compelled to make their opinions considered by institutional agencies as a public health official would feel if the institution were considering a practice or procedure affecting health conditions in the environment.

Initiating Self-Studies and Conferences for Institutional Uses

Still another approach by which the student personnel staff can initiate self-study, policy review, and goal clarification is that of initiating conferences specifically oriented to institutional problems concerning student development.

Such conferences need to be no more than the student personnel divisional staff meeting augmented by faculty and administrative colleagues representing various relevant agencies and functions. Involving them with the student personnel staff in a non-crisis-oriented discussion will not only provide a broader basis for student personnel discussion but will also serve an educational function for those not immediately involved in student personnel functions. By emphasizing an analysis of institutional matters and their impact on student development regardless of specific roles and functions, staff participants grow individually, and the institution as a whole becomes more coherent.

Using Consultants Effectively

Off-campus consultants as an objective or neutral force are often valuable in keeping discussions of issues from being actual or latent confrontations. Visitors can often see and say things which on-campus personnel cannot. Staff members are enabled to see themselves and their hangups more clearly when a consultant or visiting professional reflects or interprets them. Unfortunately the traditional use of consultants in many situations has been to reinforce preconceived positions or to convince others about a particular view.

Encouraging the Institution to Respond Creatively to Greater Off-Campus Involvement and Programming

Another aspect of institutional effectiveness of particular concern at this time involves off-campus relationships through student volunteer activities, services to the nontraditional student, public interest research groups, and student political activity in the community.

Conceptually, these and similar activities involve much more than merely rewriting old rules pertaining to student organizations, admissions, etc. On the typical campus, the student personnel staff needs to resolve and clarify its posture vis à vis such off-campus, community centered matters and then lead its institution in doing the same. Waiting until problems in these areas are formalized into proposals or demands handicaps the institutions in responding to problems innovatively. Constraints posed by off-campus relationships are often more complex because of the involvement of governmental, community, and other educational agencies.

Sensitizing the Personnel Staff to the Institutional Governance Structure

The nominal governance structure is rarely the operational or functional one (Baldridge 1971). Yet all too often student personnel as a subsystem has relied on input through some typically cumbersome formal system. such as the student affairs committee of a faculty council, when in fact operational decisions having significant student personnel and education development implications were being made on an ad hoc basis elsewhere in the institution in response to challenges and crises. Therefore, it is important that the personnel staff become aware of and skilled in initiating input into all governance, because the staff usually has information, perceptions, and skills needed by the institution for most effective behavior.

Building a Realistic Power Base for Significant Input into Institutional Behavior

The fact that student personnel as a field is not considered one of the most significant or powerful subsystems in the general system of higher education has been commented on frequently. Many student personnel professionals reject the concept of power because of their orientation to human relations and their commitment to individual development and behavior. Baldridge (1972) particularly has emphasized the operational difference between the human relations and political systems approaches. He has further emphasized the importance of the latter in changing institutional behavior. The human relations approach, so often the basis for student personnel work, tends to regard bureaucracy as a significant obstacle, if not the actual enemy of personalizing the educational process. Complex institutions by their very nature are bureaucratic, and the student personnel organization is an important segment of that bureaucracy. Therefore, for student personnel to be naive or unaware of political functioning approaches sheer negligence. To be effective in the future, the student personnel staff will have to understand and be skilled in participating in the political subsystem of its institution and be able to use it as a power base for significant input into institutional behavior.

Summary

Student personnel has often neglected to fulfill major responsibilities during the past decade. It has rendered significant services to numerous individuals, groups, and offices. However, as a field or subsystem of higher education, it has failed to mature in its self-perception as the total system became more complex. Much of this failure must be attributed to the lack of awareness by student personnel workers of advances in understanding and conceptualizing the nature of organizational development, in applying current knowledge of complex organizations to operational behavior, and in adapting the systems approach to student personnel work. By viewing itself in such a limiting role as "student services," it is now often viewed, at the worst, as an expensive luxury with insatiable appetite for funds and staff, and at the best, as a difficult-to-evaluate function which needs to clarify its roles, inputs, processes, and results.

In most institutional settings, budget restrictions, new evaluative procedures, and cost benefit analyses prohibit the continued addition of staff members with narrow perceptions of their roles and limited estimates of their value. However, by perceiving the entire organization as a client and by vigorously reallocating expenditure of energy to contribute maximally to institutional goal achievement, the worth of student personnel functions will be visible, their contributions and achievements recognized, and their role in organizational effectiveness enhanced.

References

Baldridge, J. V. *Academic governance.* Berkeley, Calif.: McCutchan Publishing, 1971.

Baldridge, J. V. Organizational change: The human relations perspective versus the political system perspective. *Educational Researcher,* 1972, *1,* 4–10.

Beckhard, R. *Organizational development strategies and models.* Reading, Mass.: Addison-Wesley, 1969.

Bennis, W. G. *Organizational development: Its nature, origins and prospects.* Reading, Mass.: Addison-Wesley, 1969.

Braungart, R. G. & Braungart, M. M. Administration, faculty, and student reaction to campus unrest. *Journal of College Student Personnel,* 1972, *13,* 112–119.

Brown, R. D. *Student development in tomorrow's higher education—A return to the academy.* Washington, D.C.: American College Personnel Association, 1972.

Etzioni, A. *Modern organizations.* Englewood Cliffs, N.J.: Prentice-Hall, 1964.

Foster, J., & Long, D. (Eds.) *Protest! Student activism in America.* New York, N.Y.: Morrow, 1970.

Gross, E., & Grambsch, P. V. *University goals and academic power.* Washington, D.C.: American Council on Education, 1968.

Kaufman, J. F. et al. *The student in higher education.* New Haven, Conn.: Hazen Foundation, 1968.

Lawrence, P. R., & Lorsch, J. W. *Developing organizations: Diagnosis and action.* Reading, Mass.: Addison-Wesley, 1969.

Perrow, C. *Organizational analysis: A sociological view.* Belmont, Calif.: Brooks/Cole, 1970.

Sampson, E. E., & Korn, H. A. *Student activism and protest.* San Francisco, Calif.: Jossey-Bass, 1970.

Schein, E. H. *Organizational psychology,* (Rev. ed.) Englewood Cliffs, N.J.: Prentice-Hall, 1970.

Schmidt, W. H. *Organizational frontiers and human values.* Belmont, Calif.: Wadsworth, 1970.

College Student Personnel:
A Current Estimate

Charles L. Lewis

Educators in general and college student personnel practitioners specifically seek and receive criticism and evaluation—almost to a masochistic level. A recognition of this need on my part, coupled with several months of freedom to read, reflect, and visit practitioners across the land after 20 years of engagement in all levels of student personnel services and leadership, prompted this article.

The opportunity to review without line responsibilities is an ambiguous position. It is pleasant to reflect free from day-to-day pressures, decisions, and the derisions of ubiquitous second-guessers. However, this quiet perch presents the handicap of impractical reactions—old soldiers too often have selective sensory connections.

Student personnel professionals are highly compartmentalized both in their on-campus administrative hierarchies and in their off-campus professional life. In this they are similar to their faculty colleagues. This compartmentalization of student personnel work and workers requires definition before criticism. Relatively long experience, both pragmatic and vicarious, causes me to favor a broad general definition of student personnel. The titles and services I define as part of student personnel include: the generalist offices (deans of men, women, students, programs; and vice-presidents), conduct regulation, orientation-admissions articulation, student financial aid, counseling and testing, international affairs, research, placement and career advising, remedial and skills assistance, religious activities, unions and centers, housing and food services, and psychiatric and medical services.

This list was checked against a more precise and concise list prepared by Kamm in 1950. In 20 years, little has changed, if change may be noted by comparing service lists, except for separate identification of religious and international divisions and steadily changing senior-most titles.

The professional literature on evaluation is of limited help in setting a framework for this current estimate. The efforts of Hoyt (1971) and Kamm (1950) are sufficiently unique to merit separate mention. Hoyt developed user-satisfaction indexes and made some inter-institutional comparisons. Kamm attempted to identify, label, and assess availability and to assign weighted values for specific services or policies. Aside from checklists, satisfaction surveys, and technique comparisons, our effectiveness is estimated by tabulating users and soliciting opinions. In a period of reallocation of declining financial resources, our limited success in developing sound evaluational methods or criteria will prove troublesome.

The Changing Context in Higher Education

In 1970 Niblett wrote: "Since the middle of the sixties there have been smoke signals that we are not going to be allowed as easily as in the last thirty years to go our ways unchallenged and unmolested, or even in the state of 'incorruptible indecision' natural to academics." Two relatively recent publications by the American Council on Education reflect the tenor and tempor of today's collegiate environment. The volume entitled *Perspectives on Campus Tensions*, edited by Nichols (1970), assembles papers prepared for a special commission on campus tensions which catalog perceptions of the power struggle among faculty, students, and trustees-administrators. The 1971 American Council on Education conference background papers were published with the theme "Universal Higher Education—Costs and Benefits." Only one-third of the papers adhered to the theme; the remainder centered on finances and cost effectiveness. The location, effective use, and best allocation of funds is receiving priority attention by trustees, administrators, and providers of funds.

Student personnel receives strikingly little attention in two current publications by Mayhew (1971) and Newman and others (1971). Mayhew, for example, wrote: "However, as compared with the 1930's, when a rather comprehensive literature about academic deans appeared, or the 1950's, when much was written about counselors and deans of students, the present period has not been productive."

These selected references support three trends for higher education: changes are forthcoming, finances are critically short, and tensions will continue. A deemphasis on students is also evident in recent literature. Recent conferences and conventions have decidedly reduced the participation of student speakers, panelists, or critics. There is a sharp increase in participation by economists, labor experts, and financial managers.

Governance

Conflict over authority, responsibility, and power extends beyond campus constituencies to include trustees, alumni, trade unions, systems offices, public agencies, legislators, and elected public officers. Clear trends are not discernible; however, it is likely that external voices will demand more administrative authority and accountability and that student government will continue to decline in potency in inverse proportion to increased student representation on institutional committees and boards.

Finances

Analysis of the universal shortage of funds in higher education is not simple, since many factors must be considered. These include: source of funds, who should pay, public funding for private institutions, tax base for support, local-state-federal funding and distribution, student aid and fees, direct institutional aid, voucher systems, cost benefit analysis, accountability, planning program budgeting systems, and cost effectiveness analysis.

Budget or program cuts are routine on most campuses. Any salary increases occur at a cost of positions and program deferrals. To date, college student personnel services are not experiencing disproportionate cuts, in spite of expectations to the contrary. However, a colleague [1] wisely admonishes that student personnel budget growth has not been proportionate to general budgetary increases, thus causing an indirect decline in services.

Collective Bargaining, Representation, and Negotiation

Support workers (clerical and crafts), graduate students (to a degree), faculty (at a rapid rate), and undergraduate students (by confrontation, not representation) are all in line or at the bargaining table. Student personnel practitioners are usually considered to be administrators and occasionally are seen as "shop stewards" for undergraduate students. The emergence of bargaining for employee benefits and a voice in governance has placed student personnel in an undesirable or untenable position. Professionals will be compelled to decide whether to seek representation separately, with faculty, or with supportive staff.

The type of tension between the American School Counselor Association and the American Personnel and Guidance Association, partially created by the collective representation question, will spread to colleges, and tensions between the American College Personnel Association and the American Personnel and Guidance Association will probably increase. Many student personnel leaders have changed opinion on representation and joined the American Association of University Administrators which, like AAUP and AMA, is trying to assure constituency prerogatives.

College Population Changes

Whether popularly accepted or not, the origins of college student personnel reside in the concepts of vocational guidance and in loco parentis. The age range of college students has changed, as has enrollee mobility. Adjustment of services and techniques for the new populations has not kept pace. Astute presidents will press for a justification of student personnel staff as the expectation of student conduct control and

1. Alice Thurston 1972: personal communication.

management disappears. The humanistic and existentialist attitudes of newer practitioners are shifting counseling from its traditional role of educational and career assistance. As cost effectiveness pressures grow, this change will be noted and is likely to be challenged on the grounds that the newer approaches do not adequately relate to education.

Leadership Changes

College presidents are replaced as frequently today as were preachers in small towns in earlier days. Since student personnel senior officers are traditionally identified with the president's policy, turnover is equally evident for them. Having recently experienced this phenomenon, I was able to understand my colleague's remark: "For deans and vice-presidents for student affairs, a new president's arrival is analogous to looking at the single card drawn to four cards low probability inside straight."[2] Clairvoyance is not required to see the implications for people, policy, and representation.

In summary, innovation and change are expected and are sought during a period of tight finances, shifting enrollment patterns, and demands for more power, authority, and representation from many sides. Student personnel practices and people will inevitably change. The important question is, "How?"

Some Specific Comments on Student Personnel

After a review of college counseling services, I facetiously suggested a report title, "The Unchanging Counselor in the Changing World"—a parody on C. Gibert Wrenn's book title. For a person to be able to catch up with counseling literature and practices in a few weeks after reduced involvement for 10 years is an alarming indication of slow change.

We have struggled through a period of confrontation and legalistic infusion with little clarification of our role in institutional policy for-

2. John Truitt 1972: personal communication.

mulation. We practically retreated, one bunker to the next, while students, faculty, and some colleagues casually and even scholastically observed our dilemma of being tightly squeezed between students and other forces, community constituencies, and agencies. Yeoman service was performed, but at a severe cost in respect, prestige, and confidence.

We have clung to our devotion to individual differences and rights while being compelled by manifold pressures to try to hold students down or at least steer their thrusts. The cleavage created by a casual shift to groups with reduced attention to testing and career educational assistance without a carefully designed philosophical base is provocative. We too often talked innovation and research and adopted cliches to cover our slowness in systematically changing our approaches to relating with students.

We have enthusiastically discussed and endorsed student development, human development, and facilitator-consultant roles without really critically laying the new labels side by side with the older labels of individual difference and learning based concepts. The casual use of phrases and labels that are not understood by our presidents and faculty colleagues is not likely to be productive. It is urgently suggested that a thoughtful look be extended to the "quietly gossiped" colleges who lost staff and departments after taking a plunge of commitment to these "innovative and creative models."

We have not really moved far in meeting the two requirements of professional status identified in the 1940's: (a) a discrete body of knowledge and a transmittal system and (b) self-policing of professional standards.

Too much energy and too many dollars have been expended on fragmented professional organizations. We have indulged too much discussion about our inadequate voice in the national, regional, and state policies affecting us and, more importantly, the students, and have failed to find new ways.

Despite these criticisms, all is not bleak. Most of the discussion I hear is searching, sincere, and candid. A comparison of reactions among three professionals on evaluative missions similar to mine last year revealed forward movement. At least two and often all three agreed on these trends:

1. General uneasiness exists about how the area of student personnel services will be modified in its relationship with students, faculty, and

other administrators; however, this uneasiness is accompanied by a consistent optimism about continuance, an optimism shared by others than student personnel specialists.

2. New roles will develop surrounding our apparent expertise in applied group work, consultation, conflict management, and joint participation with faculty and students. This will involve coupling and combining of ideas.

3. The use of relatively untrained people (peers and paraprofessionals) is a clear trend, and expanded use of these helpers is under way. This use of peer and paraprofessional helpers in residence halls, orientation activities, and miniority programs has merely scratched the surface of potential.

4. Talk about innovations and service decentralization is largely talk, as revealed by a deliberate check for specific models. The eagerness of effort shown in searching for new approaches is encouraging in its anxious pace and extensiveness.

5. Student governance gains have not as yet resulted in effective student roles. Student personnel staff are the most likely prospects to design and operate programs to help prepare students (and for that matter faculty and staff) to handle complex change processes in our institutions.

6. The interest in and emphasis on psychotherapeutic and sensitivity groups is "peaking out." A return to direct, career-related educational assistance is likely in this period of cost effectiveness evaluation and declining reliance on college education.

7. The present intense interaction of presidents, academic deans, and faculty leaders with students will not continue. Student personnel staff will be expected to return to traditional interaction roles, and, hopefully, this will be accompanied with restored colleague confidence and a little more tolerance.

The Future

Any estimator faces accountability. Where does it lead us? What steps must be initiated by our campus level leaders? Some of them are listed below:

1. Initiate a thorough staff evaluation procedure and set up a formal

means for regularizing it. It is distressing to consider how few professionals receive evaluation or even supervision and regular salary increases as evaluation is disappearing. Evaluation will indicate that some should be encouraged to retool or relocate. Some savings gained as a result can be used to strengthen staff appointments for individuals who can motivate and organize others, and the rest of the savings can be used to add student paraprofessionals in expanded roles.

2. Reestablish leadership retreats, skill development programs, and programs creating human interaction opportunities. Modern behavior modification techniques should be adapted to attitudinal problems with study, drugs, and sex. Use of new information storage, retrieval, and transmittal devices is long overdue, or at least is underused.

3. Reassessment of residence hall programs should be started and have as a goal the establishment of a 10-year plan to keep them filled and staffed. Minimum policies should be established and vigorously sold to all who will listen—particularly senior administrators and trustees.

4. A reduction of one-to-one counseling and general sensitivity groups should be encouraged, but task-oriented groups should be stressed. Our highly trained and skilled counselors should develop materials and projects to be packaged for repeated use. Teamwork with faculty paraprofessionals and administrators is necessary now.

5. More staff should engage in classroom teaching (not only student personnel and counseling courses) since accountability or formula-type reimbursement will increase. Such classroom efforts have proven quite useful when formula justification arose in some community college situations.

6. Formal job descriptions with performance expectations should be set up for each staff member. Our roles have been too kindheartedly vague, allowing everyone else to define them and to project unrealistic demands upon us. The "boss" should be educated about the issues and problems concerning which we cannot be expected to make or hinder progress.

7. Our potential contributions to the directions set forth in recent Newman and Carnegie reports must be delineated and debated quickly.

8. Budgets must be reviewed for funds which could be foregone if necessary. A historical study of budget growth and expansion to identify areas of softness and weak justification should be privately initiated as a precursor to corrective action.

The future is not grim if the legitimate need for careful reappraisal is faced squarely. Most encouraging are the many indications that students desire to rejoin student personnel professionals in efforts to maximize their own and fellow student's development.

References

American Council on Education. *Universal higher education—Costs and benefits.* Background papers to annual meeting of ACE. Washington, D.C.: Author, 6–8 October 1971.

Hoyt, D. P. *An evaluation of student personnel services at Kansas State University.* Research Report No. 16. Office of Educational Research, Kansas State University, July 1971.

Kamm, R. B. An inventory of student reaction to student personnel services. *Educational and Psychological Measurement,* 1950, *10,* 537–544.

Mayhew, L. B. *The literature of higher education 1971.* San Francisco: Jossey-Bass 1971.

Newman, F., et al. *Report on higher education.* Washington, D.C.: U.S. Government Printing Office, 1971.

Niblett, W. R. (Ed.) *Perspectives on campus tensions.* Washington, D.C.: American Council on Education, 1970.

Student Development: What Does It Mean?

Clyde A. Parker

Three different uses of the term student development—humanism, complexity, and developmental stage theory—are reviewed. The latter is thought to be the most fruitful for the use of student personnel work. Two examples of the use of stage or hierarchal developmental theory for making changes in student personnel structures are described.

In recent years the field of student personnel work has been in search of new moorings. The field has never had a clear identity, and the student protest movement of the 60s intensified the feelings of identity diffusion amongst those on campus responsible for student welfare. One solution to the diffusion has been student development. To date, however, there have been very few attempts to translate the construct into operational structures or programs. Part of the difficulty has come from the rather vague, non-specific meanings attached to the term; another part has come from the inertia involved in changing organizations and institutions. In this article we will examine student development as a psychological construct and then illustrate the use of the construct in shaping the programs of two different institutions.

Student Development as a Psychological Construct

Development as the new humanism. Some writers equate student development with providing a rich environment productive of growth. There are no clear indications of what should result from such growth, but terms such as self-fulfillment, self-actualization and self-realization are used. The programmatic implications of such terms are unclear. An example of such a position is O'Bannion and Thurstone's (1972) recent book on student development in the community college. They did not define student development per se, but they did describe the student development worker on the one hand and a student development course on the other, as follows:

One way of describing the model that needs to be developed is to present an idealized prototype of the student personnel worker as a person. . . . [a] person who is needed has been described by Maslow as self-actualizing, by Horney as self-realizing, by Privette as transcendent-functioning and by Rogers as fully-functioning. Other humanistic psychologists . . . described such healthy personalities as open to experience, democratic, accepting, understanding, caring, supporting, approving, loving, and nonjudgmental. . . . They believe that every student is a gifted person, that every student has untapped potentialities, that every human being can live a much fuller life than he is currently experiencing. They are not only interested in students with intense personal problems, they are interested in all students, in helping those who are unhealthy to become more healthy and in helping those who are already healthy to achieve yet even greater health [p. 204]. . . .

Such a course is a course in introspection: the experience of the student is the subject matter. The student is provided with an opportunity to examine his values, attitudes, beliefs, and abilities and an opportunity to examine how these and other factors affect the quality of his relationships with others. In addition, the student would examine the social milieu—the challenges and problems of society—as it relates to his development. Finally such a course would provide each student with an opportunity to broaden and deepen a developing philosophy of life. Such a course would be taught in basic encounter groups by well-prepared human development facilitators. In many cases sensitive instructors can work with student personnel staff to develop and teach such a course [p. 208].

Brown (1972) is another example of use of the student development construct in place of humanistic language. In his ACPA monograph he uses the term student development interchangeably to mean either holism, humanism, "affective" or "personal" development as opposed to intellectual development.

In general, student development theories of such "humanistic" or "affective" bent consist mostly of goals rather than propositional statements that tell us how such goals are reached by students. Although such end goals may be worthy, they are statements of final states rather than processes of development. The "developmental" is applicable only in the sense that growth occurs toward some goal.

Development as cognitive and behavioral complexity. Sanford (1966) has discussed developmental communities in a more general sense and higher education as a specific illustration of such a community. His construct of development can be more easily understood in the context of what it prescribes as characteristics of a development-promoting community. He said that there are three such characteristics. The first is the capacity to upend or disturb a person's equilibrium, so that new learning must take place before equilibrium can be restored. Although he felt that movement to complexity represents the desirable direction of change, even "regularity of change," he said that this movement had to be stimulated or provoked to counter the natural tendency toward equilibrium. This assumption directly contrasts the humanistic assumption of self-growth potential. He recognized that such upending experiences could have destructive as well as constructive effects.

Therefore, the second characteristic of such a community is the capacity to assess with high accuracy the capability of the individual to withstand stress and to make use of the upending experiences. Even in a fairly accurate assessment, there are bound to be mistakes. Therefore, it is necessary to have supportive resources available to sustain persons through precipitated crises. Examination of these characteristics revealed a construct based on a notion of development that occurs when the person is caused to analyze experience and discriminate between options; in effect he must take his previously organized self apart and reorganize it in a more complex way, which enables him to cope more effectively with new situations. Sanford says, for example:

. . . A high level of development in personality is characterized chiefly by complexity and wholeness. It is expressed in a high degree of *differentiation*, that is, a large number of different parts having different and specialized functions, and a high degree of *integration*, that is, a state of affairs in which communication among parts is great enough so that the different parts may, without losing their essential identity, become organized into larger wholes . . . [1962, p. 257].

Thus development and growth for him are distinct processes, the latter having to do with enlargement, the former with differentiation and integration. The advantage of the complexity theory is that it does suggest a process for promoting development, but the content and end goals (intellectual competence, universal morality, affective freedom) are unspecified.

Development as stages. In contrast to the ambiguities of the humanistic theories, there is a group of developmental theories that are best described as stage or hierarchal theories. Such theories differ from those that have been described above in that stage theories postulate a regularity of change and form that is built into the organism, rather than simply change in form or feeling or complexity such as are involved in either the humanistic or complexity theories. Examples of such stage theories are presented by Erikson, Piaget, Kohlberg, and Perry. Some theorists would differentiate between true stage theories such as those of Piaget (1970) and Kohlberg (1972) and hierarchal theories such as those of Erikson and Maslow in that the former have invariant structural properties in the person, while the latter refer to the sequence of developmental tasks which must be mastered if normal development is to occur. Kohlberg describes the essential characteristics of structural theories as a "series of stages from an *invariant developmental sequence.* The sequence is invariant because each stage stems from the previous and prepares the way for the subsequent stage [p. 4]." In somewhat greater detail Piaget (1960, pp. 13–14) outlined the criteria as follows:

1. Stages imply distinct or qualitative differences in . . . modes of thinking or of solving the same problem at different ages.

2. These different modes of thought form an invariant sequence, order, or succession in individual development. While cultural factors may speed up, slow down, or stop development, they do not change its sequence.

3. Each of these different and sequential modes of thought forms a "structured whole." A given stage-response on a task does not just represent a specific response determined by knowledge and familiarity with that task or tasks similar to it; rather it represents an underlying thought organization . . .

4. . . . stages are hierarchal integrations. Stages form an order of increasingly differentiated and integrated *structures* to fulfill a common function.

Although Piaget made specific reference to cognitive developmental stages, his formulation is applicable to other stage theories that might be applied to the development of the college student, such as Erikson's constructs of identity and intimacy or Super's constructs of vocational development. Since most research within the development frame has been done with children or young adolescents, we have little data available for appraising the usefulness of a stage developmental theory in the understanding of college students.

One exception to this is the work that Perry (1970) has done in the area of cognitive and ethical development. From his interviews with students, he was able to identify nine stages that seemed to fit the criteria cited above. They ranged from a basic duality of right and wrong, good and bad on the one end, to developing commitments, after a resolution of the available data is made, on the other. The exciting thing about Perry's scheme is that it is central to what the college experience is about and opens the way for relating other schemes of personality development to it.

We are not concerned here with the finer distinctions between stage and hierarchal models. The important consideration for our purposes is that stage theorists, because they deal with direction, level, and content of change, seem to offer greater possibilities for psychologists and others in higher education who are looking for ways to set directions for the processes of higher education. This makes it possible to prescribe what an educator should do.

In the case of the humanistic theorists we have some global virtues (Sprinthall 1972) that are to be attained, but little that is prescriptive of what a student personnel worker should do. In effect, they present slogans, some new some old, but few that suggest what programs should consist of. And we have had enough of that. The complexity theorists are more helpful in that they are able to show that by a series of upending and disquieting experiences an individual can be forced to reconsider his existing resolution of evidence, analyze his experiences, and reintegrate them into a more complex whole than existed before. However, what is lacking in that formulation is a consideration of the content of the experience.

In contrast, most stage theorists, by specifying the particular behaviors that are characteristic of particular stages, are able to specify what tasks must be mastered in order to make progress. In this way a curriculum can be devised that includes both the content and the necessary processes for mastery. We have not often thought along these lines about such matters in higher education and, particularly, in student personnel work.

Two examples have been selected to illustrate the usefulness of student development theory for student personnel work. In one case, the structure was not set, and a committee was given an institutional problem to solve. They applied developmental theory and evolved a program that has wide, institutional implications. In the second case, an organizational structure was imposed and a developmental theory was used to help define both organization and program. In this way the new organization would have unity of purpose, working relationship, and program.

Theory—Then Program

Augsburg College is a relatively small liberal arts college located in Minneapolis, Minnesota. It is church-related and has maintained an excellent reputation over the years. Like most private schools, it has been challenged by current changes in higher education to build a program that will attract a student body of sufficient size to make the institution viable. Recognizing that one of the crucial factors we have to cope with in our modern society is rapid change, particularly as it affects the relevance of the curriculum, steps were taken to evaluate and update the total program of the college as it relates to the employability of the graduates of the college. A committee was formed called The Committee on New Career Preparation (Augsburg College 1973) and given the following charge:

The Executive Committee of the Board of Regents requests the faculty of Augsburg College to strengthen the college's enrollment potential by identifying those new careers for which Augsburg College may appropriately prepare students to serve in society, and to design whatever curricular programs that will support such career preparations, at the same time indicating what programs, if any, are no longer essential to the growth and strengthening of this college and ought to be eliminated. . . [p. 1].

There was a liberal sprinkling of staff from the Center for Student Development on the committee. They had been giving serious thought to how the philosophy underlying that Center could be implemented. Rather than limiting the work of the committee to the specific charge from the Board of Regents, they began to ask some fundamental questions such as: What is a career; what is the relation between a career and one's life style; and how is all this related to the curriculum of the college? They came up with some answers that did not make the work of the committee easier and did not leave the college feeling very comfortable.

For example, they concluded that career preparation had to be approached as a much broader concept than vocational training. According to them, a career included much of what others might refer to as life style, involving vocation, avocation, leisure pursuits, aesthetic interests, and so on. In this way they saw a liberal arts college in interface with vocational preparation. They recognized that the demands of the limited job market required specialized preparations in at least one area of competency, but that the impact of the liberal curriculum was a necessity in preparing a person for a career in the larger sense.

More specific to our concerns here is the following statement from the committee:

Career preparation is a four-year process which begins with building realistic pre-college expectations with potential students and continues through regular advising and career development services in each year of the student's college education [p. 4].

This is the nucleus from which their theory or career development began to take shape. The theory has not come from extensive empirical research or rigorous structural stage theory, but rather from close observation of students in that setting and from careful reasoning leading to logical conclusions about the sequence and kind of help students need. It is developmental in that it is sequential, in that the steps are qualitatively different, and in that the steps represent a hierarchal integration. Further, it has heuristic value in that it allows one to make deductions about potentially helpful interventions and curricular modifications. In addition, the committee has begun to hypothesize about how this development is normatively related to the four year liberal arts college experience.

The following statements explain the sequenial steps shown in Figure 1 and are quoted from the Augsburg report (p. 35).

BUILDING EXPECTATIONS

The first step in career development starts during the admissions stage. Augsburg has a responsibility to promise only those things which can be delivered. We feel that the college must help the student preassess what experiences he can expect to have during his college days and the benefits a liberal arts degree may accrue.

SELF ASSESSMENT

The first task for the student at college is to assess himself. To be able to select appropriate career goals, a student must first know himself . . . his particular interest, abilities, values and background. Through the curriculum, personal and group counseling, vocational tests, life planning labs, and interaction with faculty and staff, the student can clarify values and explore tentative major areas.

HYPOTHESIS FORMATION

On the basis of his self assessment, he gathers information about the real world, forming career hypotheses, which are tentative ideas of where he can fit into the real world. Academic advising is crucial here as the student solidifies major plans.

REALITY TESTING

If self-assessments are valid, the student must confront the work world as a participant. Such encounters can be accomplished through field experiences, Metro Urban Studies Internship Program (MUSIP), Conservation of Human Resources (CHR) classes, and "Stop Out Career Day," which provides for one-to-one experiences for part of a day with resource people in the community.

SELLING SELF

When the student has made a career decision, the next step is to "sell himself" to an employer. He needs to know about appropriate job-seeking techniques and behaviors such as writing resumes, correspondence, and interviews. Seminars, job seeking groups, workshops, role playing and on-campus mock and real interviews with recruiters provide him with these learning experiences. This culminates in placement into graduate school, work, military or other alternatives.

Figure 1
Augsburg College Career Development

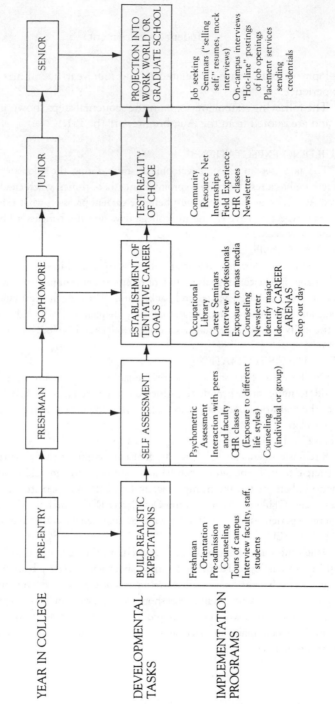

YEAR IN COLLEGE	PRE-ENTRY	FRESHMAN	SOPHOMORE	JUNIOR	SENIOR

DEVELOPMENTAL TASKS	BUILD REALISTIC EXPECTATIONS	SELF ASSESSMENT	ESTABLISHMENT OF TENTATIVE CAREER GOALS	TEST REALITY OF CHOICE	PROJECTION INTO WORK WORLD OR GRADUATE SCHOOL
IMPLEMENTATION PROGRAMS	Freshman Orientation Pre-admission Counseling Tours of campus Interview faculty, staff, students	Psychometric Assessment Interaction with peers and faculty CHR classes (Exposure to different life styles) Counseling (individual or group)	Occupational Library Career Seminars Interview Professionals Exposure to mass media Counseling Newsletter Identify major Identify CAREER ARENAS Stop out day	Community Resource Net Internships Field Experience CHR classes Newsletter	Job seeking Seminars ("selling self," resumes, mock interviews) On-campus interviews "Hot-line" postings of job openings Placement services sending credentials

HUMAN EFFECTIVENESS—ULTIMATE GOAL

The humanly effective or self-actualized person is always in the process of growing. He knows himself and is consciously competent, creative, flexible to change, sensitive to others and is characterized by dedication to something "bigger than himself" [p. 35].

Most of the interventions that are shown in Figure 1 are interventions that have been developed and tried in other settings or are part of the more traditional student personnel operation. The theory assists in putting a package together and in identifying the gaps in programming. It also shows how one type of program is related to other programs so that overlap can be eliminated or one program substituted for another. In other words, having a theory that guides program development helps to prevent a "grow like topsy" approach to student personnel work.

In this case, as mentioned earlier, the staff from the Center for Student Development through their work on the New Careers Committee was able to go even further by showing how the concern for career development could be implemented through the curriculum as well as assisted by the Center. These recommendations were based on a theory of learning that included didactic, experiential, and practical components; they thus suggested that the curriculum be arranged to reflect opportunities in all three modes of learning, using the Center for Student Development heavily for experiential and practical components. These recommendations bridged traditional student personnel work with traditional curriculum.

Thus, we have a case where a practical, expedient concern of the Board of Regents is translated into a well-integrated program fusing the work of the faculty with that of student development experts so that students might have the opportunity to progress systematically toward careers that allow self-expression. One may ask: Will it work, or is it operationally sound? These are empirical questions by which the theory may be tested. The point is that without the theory there would be neither a systematic program nor the opportunity to test it.

Program—Then Theory

Although it is much neater if an institution can take time to develop a rationale or a theoretical structure from which programs and organizations can emerge, it is not always possible. Frequently, decisions are made on an expedient basis; too often they are left that way, and we have to "just make the best of it." It is, however, possible to do more than that: If one is operating from a solid base of theory, he can always bring programs and organizational structures into a reasonable "best fit."

The University of Minnesota like most major institutions of higher education has been subjected to major reductions in its total operating budget. One of these budget revisions is reviewed here because it illustrates how theory can be applied to a set decision and how a program can be developed in line with that. In the College of Education there has existed for some time three separate units, each with its own special function, budget, and administration. The Student Personnel Office started as a counseling office with two counselors in 1946. Since then it has been given the responsibility for admissions, coordination of advising, scholastic progress administration, and institutional research-type information processing. More recently they have taken on the additional functions of conducting "growth groups" and doing some faculty consulting, particularly with student teaching supervisors.

The Bureau of Recommendations has had the responsibility for the placement of pre-service teachers and graduate students, and has maintained a placement file for all former graduates who chose to file with them. The Office of Clinical Experiences has coordinated and administered the student teaching experiences of the college, providing direct supervision of students and supervising teachers.

As part of the retrenchment and reallocation program, the Dean of the College announced that the Student Personnel Office and the Bureau of Recommendations would merge into a single office. In doing so he provided a general explanation as follows (University of Minnesota 1972):

. . . I had seen things moving in from several different directions that indicated maybe that we had come too far in thinking about our students as being the responsibility of some of us part of the time. One of the reasons had to do with finances . . . We were running into deficits in some of these operations which were being made up from various sources. Those sources are drying up. I think also, there was a serious need for information. As I saw it, some of the operations being conducted by one office were needed in the other office [p. 1].

With that general rationale, representatives of the two offices beg: in early fall 1972 to make plans for the merger that would take place th. following summer. In early spring, after a considerable amount of planning had occurred, the dean announced two further decisions. One was that the Department of Clinical Experiences would also be merged into the new unit and that the entire unit would be moved into a separate building, becoming the sole occupant of the former University YMCA. As might be expected, this shift in organizational components and location upset previous plans. A decision was then made to invite an outside consultant (the present author) to assist the group in what was thought might be some difficult decisions regarding both staff allocation and programming. This consultant was interested in employing student development theory to such problems and took that opportunity to see what could be done in a situation where the limiting structures, staff, and general functions had been prescribed.

The realities of the limitations imposed by the merger were immediately apparent. There was the physical constraint of a new building, the space of which had to be allocated so that it would be possible to carry out whatever functions the new unit ascribed to itself. There was the constraint of three existing staffs experienced in carrying out responsibilities of their former units. And there was the constraint of the existing functions themselves. All of these things had to be unified within a finite period of time, while at the same time keeping the units functioning so that their clientele were not abused. Since this required the intricate coalescing of many factors, it was recommended that a flow chart be created showing how all of the separate tasks had to flow together in order that the overall task be accomplished on time. These functions in planning were then overlaid with a timeline so that each function had a deadline and those staff members assigned to that planning function would know when their work was due.

A central concern of all staff members was to find out what were the common goals of all three units. The following is a partial answer given by the task force assigned to answering that question (University of Minnesota 1973, p. 1):

1). "Student development," "career development," and "student services" are three concepts which have been mentioned as potentially fruitful for organizing the efforts of our merged units.

    A. Responsibilities of the Bureau of Recommendations go beyond student development. (The population served by the Bureau is much larger and more varied than that served by student personnel and clinical experiences.)

    B. While service to students is a primary function of each of our units, "student services" appears to be too limiting and unfruitful as a unifying concept.

    C. Career development does have potential for housing the functions of our merged units.

2). Career development can be viewed from several perspectives:

    A. Career development may have as an object of central concern each or all of the following.

        1) Students in the College

        2) Staff in the College

        3) Teachers in the Profession

It was agreed that the construct of career development was something that all units had in common, and that a useful unit of the College could be built around it. There was less understanding along programmatic lines of exactly which functions would be involved and how they would be carried out. A preliminary formulation is shown in Figure 2 where one can see that the sequence of steps required in the career development theory is derived from the logical progression one makes through an educational institution. They are assumed more from the structure of the institution than from any empirical research on personality development or from any careful consideration of the alternatives. There is also a strong possibility that they were derived from the existence of the particular structures and personnel that were being formed into the new unit. Nevertheless, it was possible for the staff to see their interrelatedness and to give a meaning to the new unit which went beyond the expediency of a budget squeeze.

It is also clear that some of the programs necessary to carry out the sequential steps of induction, training, and placement might be relevant in several or all of those steps. For example, counseling might be useful in each of those steps, whereas decision making might play a major role at the time of induction and at the time of initial placement. Supervision seemed most crucial during the training phase. What is less obvious is that the staff that had been identified primarily with one

Figure 2
Education Career Development "Stages" and Supportive Functions

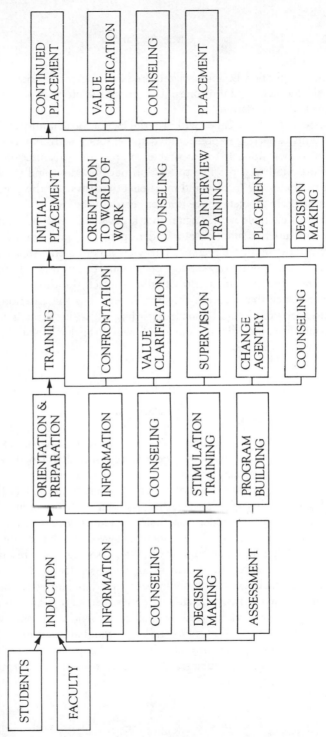

agency might now be appropriately used in a number of functions which would cut across old unit lines. This raised the problem of staff allocations and organizations.

One reality to be coped with was the fact of the administrators of the old units expecting responsibility commensurate with that asked for in their former units. It was desirable to create an organization with as much flexibility as possible to take on new functions and to carry out the old functions in new and more effective ways. At the time of this writing these problems have not yet been solved.

In this example we see again that a developmental view can shape the structure and function of a student personnel program, even when many of the limits are present. This view is both a philosophy (a set of values) and a psychology (a set of operations) of education. In this case, it formed the unifying construct around which the three offices could merge. Once that direction was set, it served as the criterion against which decisions could be made regarding which functions were to be retained from the old units and which were to be developed and carried out by the new one.

Conclusions

The trend in the past several years to change the language of student personnel work into what may be a more respectable language of student development may only be a mirage and a subterfuge if, in the process of changing titles, we only opt for what Sprinthall (1972) has called a "new bag of virtues" rather than a new theory of what should and does happen to students in the collegiate environment. The position taken here is that a developmental stage theory has greater potential than other developmental theories for assisting in the resolution of curricular decisions and for structuring those services and learning experiences which have traditionally been called student personnel work. In the examples cited, the stage theories used were weak when compared with more solidly based psychological theories, yet they were instrumental in shaping programs and organizational structures, and they had some relevance for curricular decisions. Future work in the student personnel field should concentrate on the creation and testing of sociopsychological theories that can be applied to higher education for the furtherance of student development.

References

Augsburg College. The Report of the Committee on New Career Preparation, Minneapolis, Minn., Augsburg College, Spring 1973. (Mimeograph)

Brown, R. D. Student development in tomorrow's higher education: A return to the academy. Washington, D.C.: American College Personnel Association, 1972. (Monograph)

Erikson, E. H. Identity, youth, and crises. New York: W. W. Norton, 1968.

Grant, W. H. A student development point of view of education. A proposal presented and accepted by the Council of Student Personnel Associations in Higher Education, Ithaca, N.Y., October 1971.

Maslow, A. H. Motivation and personality. (2nd ed.) New York: Harper & Row, 1969.

O'Bannion, T., & Thurstone, A. Student development programs in the community junior college. Englewood Cliffs, New Jersey: Prentice Hall, 1972.

Perry, W. Intellectual and ethical development in the college years. New York: Holt, Rinehart, & Winston, 1970.

Piaget, J. The general problem of the psychobiological development of the child. In J. M. Tanner and B. Inhelder (Eds.) Discussions on child development. Vol. 4. New York: International Universities Press, 1960. Cited by L. Kohlberg. The concepts of developmental psychology as the central guide to education: Examples from cognitive, moral and psychological education. In M. C. Reynolds, (Ed.) Psychology and the process of schooling in the next decade. Minneapolis, Minnesota: University of Minnesota, 1972.

Sanford, N. Developmental status of the entering freshman. In N. Sanford (Ed.) The American college. New York: Wiley, 1962.

Sanford, N. Self and society. New York: Atherton Press, 1966.

Sprinthall, N. S. Humanism: A new bag of virtues for guidance? Personnel and Guidance Journal, 1972, 50, Pp. 349–356.

University of Minnesota. Minutes of Student Personnel Office and Bureau of Recommendation Merger, College of Education, University of Minnesota, November 1972.

University of Minnesota. Report of Committee on Unifying Concepts for Student Personnel Office, Bureau of Recommendations and Clinical Experiences Officer Merger, College of Education, University of Minnesota, April 1973.

Some Future Directions for Student Personnel Administration

Thomas R. Harvey

This author sees the field of student personnel administration taking on significant changes over the next 25 years: It will begin to merge with educational administration; it will have to help higher education in general to accept the concept of avuncularity in place of "in loco parentis"; and it will have to conceive of functions and paradigms—particularly counseling, curriculum, ombudsman, bureaucracy, and environment—instead of offices.

The field of student personnel administration is currently deluged by volume after volume describing the current crisis: Is student personnel dead? Has it ever been alive? What is its future role? Where is it going from here? These are all frequent and important questions that are being raised about the future role of student personnel administration. The last five years have seen a major identity crisis descend upon the field of student personnel administration. This crisis, however, has been a healthy one, for out of it are emerging new visions of appropriate personnel functions.

These new visions do not evolve out of a vacuum, however. Student personnel administration has been and will continue to be a function of societal and institutional redefinitions. Many additional factors and imperatives will reshape and redirect the field.

In the first place the role of undergraduate education in preparing students for vocational roles in society is being questioned. Well over 50 percent of all students graduating from college enter professions for which they received no professional preparation (Mayhew 1969). Furthermore, achievement in college, as measured by grades, bears little significant relationship to achievement in postacademic situations. Factors such as motivation, socioeconomic background, and self-concept bear much stronger relationships to success (Hoyt 1968; Spaeth & Greeley 1970). And college graduates are finding that the knowledge they acquired as undergraduates quickly becomes obsolete (Berg 1970; Carnegie Commission 1973b).

Related to these points is the current crunch in the labor market and the increasing disregard by many youth for material accumulation (Carnegie Commission 1973a). Finally, it is becoming increasingly clear that in the future leisure and quasi-volunteer services will become more time consuming than employment. Along these lines, the National Association of Business Economists (NABE) projects some interesting statistics. Hypothetically, let us assume that you all work a 40-hour week and began employment at age 21. According to the NABE you will retire at age 38, after essentially 17 years of vocational life. This does not mean that there will be less societal work, only less employment needs. People will become more fully involved in leisure and quasivolunteer social services. All of these factors combine to suggest that undergraduate education may need to get out of the business of professional or vocational preparation and back into the business of human development.

The second major factor contributing to the redirection of student personnel administration is that the concept of "in loco parentis" is now obviously dying. Increased student independence and expectations have made this quite clear. The problem, however, as to what should appropriately replace it still exists. The university still needs to establish some sort of explicit relationship with students.

The third important factor is that the faculty boom is now over. Faculty will be afforded much less autonomy as their mobility becomes more limited. One of the effects of the past boom has been that individual faculty members could become highly specialized and parochialized. They have been able to ignore a number of institutional functions by turning them over to other specialists instead (Honey 1972). One set of these functions has concerned the extracurricular and personal development of the students. With the PhD labor crunch at hand, faculty members may be much more interested in reassuming some previously specialized student personnel functions.

These fundamental reconsiderations within higher education will cause major shifts in the role and nature of student personnel admin istration. Obviously, it is impossible to foresee what these consequences might be; but it is possible to make some predictions. For example, over the next 20 years there will be less of a distinction between educational administration and student personnel administration, with the two concepts probably merging; this has already happened in many places. In the past, a functional necessity has been personnel specialization and separation, but in the future such specialization will be neither functional nor possible. As the purposes of higher education begin to shift back to student development and as faculty members reassume personnel functions, student personnel administration will have to merge into educational administration within the university.

This does not suggest that the field will disappear. On the contrary, it will become increasingly important for future institutions to have articulate administrators whose primary concern is for students, those who use students as the keyhole through which they view the rest of the imperatives of the institution. It is just that these administrators will no longer be separated or isolated from the mainstream of educational administration.

Another consequence of the changing nature of student personnel administration might be that the concept of "avuncularity," borrowed from Hefferlin (1969), who uses it in a somewhat different context and meaning, will emerge in place of in loco parentis. "Avuncular" is drawn from the Latin word avunculus meaning "uncle." The uncle figure serves a distinctly different familial role from the parent. The uncle is available for advice, guidance, even protection, when the individual needs it. However, he does not exercise control or constraint upon the student. In essence, he gives the student large measures of freedom, while defining the student's heavy burden of responsibility. This is perhaps the ideal role for institutions of higher education to take at present. They would be available to render to students a large measure of freedom for trying out new ideas and conceiving new life styles. At the same time they are there to initiate the student slowly but surely into a concern for responsibility.

This concept does not argue that responsibility is an unimportant element, but rather that it is an element that when too fully introduced to human beings in an adolescent period may limit their ability to experiment and use freedom most fruitfully. Responsibility must be defined for the individual so that he can take full advantage of it. He grows into responsibility; he is not thrown into it. The avuncular institution gives him a maximum amount of freedom with limited but increasing degrees of responsibility.

In avuncular institutions, faculty and administrators alike must be prepared to give up their paternalism and custodial care. They must accept the dilemmas and inconveniences that student freedom brings and share the burden of educating human beings for taking on responsibility. Faculty and administrators must learn to become uncles or aunts instead of parents.

A third direction that seems to be emerging is that personnel services are becoming defined less by offices and more by functions. Undoubtedly there will always be some need for office designations but probably to a far smaller degree than currently assumed. At this point some suggestion of possible alternative paradigms of personnel functions might be appropriate. These paradigms are not necessarily mutually exclusive, and none of these is more appropriate than any other for any individual student personnel administrator. The match must include the personnel administrator, the institution, institutional purposes, and the individual whom he is serving. Five possible paradigms can be suggested.

The counseling paradigm. In this model most of the administrator's concern is for a dyadic relationship with students, that is, the relationship between himself and one student. In this context some administrators may be more concerned with the hygenics of counseling, others with the pathology. Some may be more concerned with strengthening the essential health of individuals, whereas others may be much more concerned with finding the essential illness of individuals and then curing them. Both are legitimate functions in a counseling mode, but each has different kinds of orientations and concerns.

This administrator's essential belief is that the institution needs to be humanized and that the most effective way to humanize it is by dealing with students as individuals. He also believes that the institution currently is not functioning as a humanitarian institution and that his role is to serve that function. He sees paper work as a necessary evil and committees as terribly time consuming and wasteful. The creditability of the administrator's role rests on his personal creditability with his students on a one-to-one relationship and his ability to personalize the institution. Most programs of student personnel administration put heavy emphasis on this paradigm.

The curriculum paradigm. This student personnel administrator directs most of his attention to affecting curriculum development in favor of the student. He attempts to determine student needs and then interacts with faculty and administrators to design curriculums that reflect those needs. A great deal of his time is spent dealing with the faculty. He sits on curriculum committees; he submits proposals and suggests ways of integrating the curriculum with the cocurriculum. He recognizes curriculum as a central thrust within the institution and sees his role as one which creates an effective curriculum that reflects the needs of the students. In essence he is the student advocate in curriculum development. His creditability is essentially based on his ability to create student-centered curriculums. Many newer programs of higher education and instructional development prepare such personnel administrators.

The ombudsman paradigm. Most of this administrator's concern is for dealing with student problems. He is the arbiter and mediator between the institution and the individual. This paradigm does not suggest that he directly serve the role of the ombudsman, but rather that he fulfill the type of function that the ombudsman would serve in an institution. In fact, an effective student personnel administrator in this paradigm obviates a need for ombudsmen on many campuses. This administrator does not solicit student problems, but he gladly accepts them and acts to facilitate their resolution. He knows the institution extremely well and is well respected as a problem solver by all the constituencies. He is seen as not aligned to any constituency but as a free agent and problem solver within the institution. His creditability rests on his ability to solve problems.

The bureaucratic paradigm. This administrator recognizes the importance of an efficiently operating university. His concern is for balancing the budget and maintainaing facilities. He realizes that if he fails to do this the institution may no longer remain solvent and therefore might not exist. The majority of his time is spent dealing with administrators. He usually is socially mobile within the institution and has a high degree of loyalty to it. He understands concepts of administration, management, and decision making, and to him bureaucracy is not a bad word but the reality of the formal organizational pattern by which the purposes of the university are achieved. He delegates all necessary student contact to subordinates because his time is limited and he prefers to spend it dealing with bureaucratic needs. Most programs of higher education currently focus on this paradigm.

The environmental paradigm. The concern of this administrator is with his relationship to groups. Rather than working in a one-to-one relationship, he works on the one-to-groups relationship. He recognizes that he does not have enough time to deal with all students on a one-to-one basis, so he concentrates on helping individual student development by establishing an effective and potent educational environment within the institution. He considers curriculum too confining a concept for institutional concern and focuses instead on a variety of functions that exist within and beyond the curriculum. He must by necessity have a strong knowledge of the research done on college students and an understanding of its implication for his college or university.

This paradigm is probably the most demanding and all inclusive of the paradigms and calls for the most skilled administrator—he must have concern for counseling relationships, for the imperatives of the institution, for individuals' problems, and for the nature of the curriculum in higher education. His essential concern is with creating an educational environment that no longer needs him. He attempts to work himself out of a job by having the other major constituencies within the university assume major responsibilities for an effective educational environment. Although in all probability he will never fully reach his goal, he strives to bring all other major constituencies into a concern for the student.

No one of these five paradigms is correct; and no one of them is incorrect. Each one of us is probably best represented by a combination of these. Higher education, however, is most in need of the environmental administrator, the one who can orchestrate institutional resources for the total benefit of students. This paradigm is far more synoptic than the others; yet it is not in itself sufficient. An institution that does not have some individuals distinctly concerned with counseling, curriculum, student problems, or institutional maintenance can not be entirely beneficial to its students.

The choice of model depends fundamentally on the kind of talents and predispositions of the person who is the administrator. In choosing his model, however, the administrator must also take into account the needs of his institution and the needs of the individuals whom he seeks to serve. In addition, he must be sure that when he chooses one model, the other paradigms and paradigmatic needs are in some way dealt with and incorporated into the current institutional structure. He shares a responsibility for seeing that all five functions are fulfilled within the institution.

In summary, this author feels that the field of student personnel administration will take on significant changes over the next 25 years: It will begin to merge with educational administration; it will have to help higher education in general to accept the concept of avuncularity in place of in loco parentis; and it will have to conceive of functions and paradigms—particularly the five paradigmatic functions of counseling, curriculum, ombudsman, bureaucracy, and environment—instead of offices.

If such a regeneration of the field is to be successful, three things must occur. First of all, those who are established practicing professionals in the field must be open to redefining the role of student personnel administration in higher education. Second, those who are accepted and valued counselors, supporters, and scholars of college student personnel administration must share with all a responsibility for both maintaining that valued link with the heritage of the field and helping to create desirable alternative futures. Third, programs of higher education must attempt to anticipate future needs of higher education and create scholarly practitioners who can use insights of knowledge to inform their actions. In concert, the practitioners, scholars, and students of higher education can create a very exciting and significant system for the year 2000.

References

Berg, I. *Education and jobs: The great training robbery.* New York: Praeger, 1970.

Carnegie Commission. *Graduates and jobs.* Hightstown, N.J.: McGraw-Hill, 1973. (a)

Carnegie Commission. *Purposes and performance of higher education in the United States.* Hightstown, N.J.: McGraw-Hill, 1973. (b)

Hefferlin, J. B. L. *Dynamics of academic reform.* San Francisco: Jossey-Bass, 1969.

Honey, J. C. Will faculty survive? *Change Magazine*, 1972, 4(5), 24–31.

Hoyt, D. P. Criterion problems in higher education. In O. Milton and E. J. Shoben, Jr. (Eds.), *Learning and the professors*. Athens: Ohio University Press, 1968. Pp. 125–135.

Mayhew, L. B. *Contemporary college students and curriculum*. Atlanta, Ga.: Southern Regional Examination Board, Monograph #14, 1969.

Spaeth, J. L., & Greeley, A. *Recent alumni and higher education*. Hightstown, N.J.: McGraw-Hill, 1970.

Student Development Services in Post-Secondary Education

Preface

This document describes the ideal roles for the student development special-
ist. While the committee acknowledge a gap between theory and practice, they
are very conscious of practitioners whose behavior now models some of the
basic concepts. The philosophy in this document is operational in a significant
number of institutions. It now becomes appropriate to set forth lofty though
obtainable goals for staffs to move toward with varying speeds and degrees of
success.

It should be further noted that the Phase II document, "A Student Devel-
opment Model for Student Affairs in Tomorrow's Higher Education" (JCSP,
July 1975), makes assumptions about roles and urges competency develop-
ment in terms similar to those of this document. This instance of mutual re-
inforcement should be a matter of satisfaction and encouragement to the
committees responsible for each statement.

GERALD L. SADDLEMIRE

Introduction

The Commission on Professional Development of the Council of
Student Personnel Associations in Higher Education (COSPA) was
given the task of revising "A Proposal for Professional Preparation in
College Student Personnel Work." However, after reading the state-

390

ment, the commission members saw that the basic formulation of an operational philosophy (*The Student Personnel Point of View*) would have to be reviewed before any attempt could be made at a statement on professional preparation.

The commission, after reviewing the *Student Personnel Point of View* documents of 1937 and 1949, began a free-floating brainstorming discussion from which concensus began to emerge.

Certain points of view emerged as keystones of the commission's thinking:

1. The orientation to student personnel is developmental.
2. Self-direction of the student is the goal of the student and is facilitated by the student development specialist.
3. Students are viewed as collaborators with the faculty and administration in the process of learning and growing.
4. It is recognized that many theoretical approaches to human development have credence, and a thorough understanding of such approaches is important to the student development specialist.
5. The student development specialist prefers a proactive position in policy formulation and decision-making so that a positive impact is made on the change process.

The commission then prepared a working paper on the philosophy and subsequently one on professional preparation. This was submitted to the COSPA Council and distributed to its constituent groups for reactions. It was also presented at a program session of the American College Personnel Association Convention in Chicago in spring 1972 and published in the January 1974 issue of the *Journal of College Student Personnel*.

This paper reflects reactions, criticisms, and suggestions received. The title, "Student Development Services in Post-Secondary Education," should be viewed as an inclusive term for the areas usually included in student personnel programs. Harold Grant (ACPA), George Jones (ACURA), and Gerald Saddlemire (ACPA) drafted statements that became the basis for this document. King Bradow ACURA), Alva Cooper (CPC), Virginia Kirkbride (NAWDAC), Jack Nelson (ACUHO), Robert Page (ACUHO, former chairman of the commission), and Harold Riker (ACUHO) contributed to the development of the paper from its inception to its final form.

The commission hopes that this document will be used for the professions as a point of departure for assessment, innovation, and development.

ALVA C. COOPER, *Chairman*
Commission on Professional Development
Council of Student Personnel Associations
in Higher Education
July 14, 1972

Student Development Services in Post-Secondary Education

The purpose of student development services in post-secondary education is to provide both affective and cognitive expertise in the processes involved in education. The specialists providing these services function in a cooperative-integrative role with the student who seeks development toward self-direction and interact with the faculty members who are concerned with the academic content to be acquired in this development. The student development specialist bears a responsibility toward the broad spectrum of persons who can profit from post-secondary education.

Collectively, we use an educational institution to structure behavioral development so that it occurs in the most effective and efficient manner. Education includes the content of behavior (what is to be developed by a person) and the process of development (how and when it is to be acquired). Educators include experts in content and process. In general, faculty tend to emphasize content, and student development specialists tend to emphasize process.

Assumptions of Student Development Specialists

Human beings express their life goal as becoming free, liberated, self-directed, and they seek it through a process variously called self-actualization, individuation, ego integration, full functioning, and behavioral development.

The student development specialist believes that the potential for development and self-direction is possessed by everyone. Education is a way of assisting in developing these potentials.

The student development specialist believes that acceptance and understanding of persons as they are is essential. Since human potential cannot adequately be measured, a person's possession of unlimited potential may be assumed.

Clientele

The student development specialist deals with human relationships among individuals, groups, and organizations. To do so, the specialist should be familiar with the dynamics of social structure and should be able to utilize this knowledge in facilitating student growth.

The individual. The student development specialist will draw from various conceptual models available from philosophy, psychology, theology, physiology, and other disciplines in dealing with individuals. It is further recognized that an individual's behavior is affected by involvement with other people. The expression of behavior by an individual, however, may be public or private.

The group. Groups may provide a powerful learning environment to promote individual development. Involvement or participation in a group contributes to individual growth. Groups also provide a structural unit for facilitating and promoting collective experience and normative behavior.

The organization. Organizations comprise varied components of groups and individuals. As social systems of differing sizes and relationships, they enable individuals to strengthen and/or learn additional coping behaviors such as cross-cultural understanding, methods of conflict management, skills in problem-solving, decision-making, and other leadership approaches.

The educational institution is composed of individuals, groups, and organizations that may provide a complete and balanced environment for human development.

Competencies

The student development specialist provides expertise in the following:

1. Assistance in establishing goals for development based upon an appreciation of the unlimited potential of human beings. The goals are not only ultimate, but also intermediate, leading sequentially toward completeness.

2. Assistance in the assessment procedures necessary for any individual, group, or organization to progress toward defined goals.

3. Use of various methods of change such as organizational development, systems theory, intervention theory, futures intervention to facilitate behavioral development within the individual, the group, the organization, and the institution.

The competencies of each student development specialist are used in functions categorized as administrative, instructive, and consultative. These functions are integrated according to the particular responsibilities that are assumed. One may be primarily an administrator in the morning, use instructor competencies later in the day, and then participate in an evening event requiring consultant competencies. The likelihood of having a role exclusively as administrator, instructor, or consultant is minimal.

Administrative function. Titles applicable to this function are vice-president, dean, and director, along with staff members such as associates or assistants.

Instructor responsibility. When this responsibility is emphasized, the student development specialist usually carries the title of dean or professor, with staff members having the rank of associate or assistant. The staff is organized into schools or departments emphasizing staff relationships rather than the line relationships of the administrator role. As a result, evaluations and participation in decision-making among colleagues are more highly valued.

Consultant responsibility. Major titles are counselor and consultant, with the staff associated with the counseling center serving the entire institution.

Functions

Administrative function. The function is based on the premise that a systematic approach to human relationships helps to achieve continuous growth. This is gained through organization emphasizing coordination, communication, supportive services, rules, and regulations established and maintained through the personal competency of the leader, whose commitment is primarily to the educational goals of the institution. Typical administrative concerns are for clear definition of rights and responsibilities, for means of accountability, and for program development.

In this function, achieving goals efficiently and effectively and the concept of doing are valued as the bases for movement toward continuous growth.

Instructor function. This function emphasizes exploration of knowledge and integration of experience as the primary means by which the student moves toward full development. Knowledge is gained through investigation, research, and experience and is disseminated through various forms of teaching. Academic competencies, including the ability to teach and to do research, are elements of the instructor function both inside and outside the traditional classroom. The interdisciplinary and applied field of student development is paramount.

In this function, knowing oneself and one's environment is valued as the basis for movement toward continuous growth.

Consultant function. This function is based on the premise that the student has personal responsibility for individual development. The consultant helps the individual focus on relationships that foster self-achievement and that encourage personal initiative, involvement, and responsibility for further progress. Professional competence to counsel, consult, intervene, and collaborate with individuals and groups is basic to the consultant function. The consultant works with other educators to help provide the necessary physical, social, financial, and intellectual resources for student development.

In this function, the concept of becoming is an essential source of personal satisfaction and fulfillment.

Table 1 summarizes the major elements of the three functions. A change in any of the items affects and changes each of the other aspects

TABLE 1
Major Elements of the Three Functions

	Administering	Instructing	Consulting
Approach	Structure Objectives	Knowledge	Personal responsibility
Process	Organization	Teaching & Research	Counseling & collaboration
Staff qualifications	Leadership/ Management Objectives	Scholarship Leadership Research	Facilitation
Context	Primary commitment to the institution	Primary commitment to the discipline	Primary commitment to students
Titles	Vice-President or Director	Dean Professor	Counselor, advisor, or consultant
Structure	Division	Dept. or School	Counseling center
Modes	Doing	Knowing	Becoming

because of the interrelatedness of functions and the various elements of functions.

The elements of the three functions are listed in separate columns, but the functions must come together in various combinations for each practitioner. For example, the vice-president for student affairs will spend a substantial amount of time administering but will also be instructing and consulting to the extent appropriate to the particular task to be performed.

The ultimate goal of all three functions is to contribute to continuous, positive self-development. Major attention is thus given to relationships that respect existing self-direction and encourage initiative, involvement, and responsibility for further development.

In all three functions research plays an integral part.

Implementation

The organization of Student Development Services may vary, depending on the unique purposes, functions, and changing aspects of a particular institution. It may also be influenced by the performance and integration of respective functions. The staff may be organized around functions with relationship to clientele and use of competencies contained in each area, around competencies, or around clientele. At present, no single structure seems superior.

Professional Preparation

Strong grounding in and commitment to student development purposes and assumptions, development of the competencies required, practicing and performing the respective functions, and consideration of various approaches to organization should be included in any preparation program. The emphases, sequences, and methods of instruction can vary from program to program; yet each can prepare professionals of excellence.

Program of studies. Curricular innovation is necessary in graduate programs preparing persons for student development services during the last third of the twentieth century. A critical need exists for professionals who give assertive leadership regardless of changing job title, excised organizations, declining budgets, diversifying student bodies, and often hostile public opinion. At the same time these professionals must be open, warm, optimistic human beings. Comfortable conformity to guidelines based on traditional patterns of graduate education will not suffice. The following recommendations are general approaches to professional preparation consistent with the purposes and practices recommended in preceding sections.

Since student development is seen to be the process by which individuals gain increasing mastery of their own self-direction and fulfillment, this process should be the basic means of professional education for the student development specialist. The goal of a professional program should be the preparation of persons who, in addition to having a high level of self-development, have skills to collaborate with others in their self-development. They must be able to use their competencies in assessment, goal-setting, and change processes as appropriate in implementing the roles of consultant, administrator, and instructor in relationships with individuals, groups, and organizations.

General goals should be translated into the specific competencies needed for functioning in the professional role of the student development specialist in the processes involved in education. These objectives should be stated in measurable terms in order that performance criteria can be developed for evaluation. The following is an example of a listing of program objectives.

Objectives are categorized according to three competencies: (1) helping students move toward goals; (2) assessing status, abilities, and progress; (3) using strategies of change to facilitate human development. Within each category of competency, objectives are listed that illustrate the three possible functions of the student development specialist: administering, instructing, and consulting.

The essential features of these functions are as follows: (1) Administrative—organize, coordinate, communicate, support, write and enforce rules and regulations, be accountable, assume and protect rights and responsibilities, and emphasize staff relationships in departments. (2) Instructional—know individuals, groups, and organizations through investigational research in order to teach. (3) Consultative—be available for student and faculty member collaboration for policy determination and problem-solving that relates to improvement of student learning and environment modification.

The student development specialist is expected to master the following behavioral objectives:

I. Helping clientele move toward goals
   (These behaviors are necessary professional competencies to help students with their goals.)
   A. Be able to apply various aspects of personnel management.
      1. Write job descriptions.
      2. Administer salary schedule.
      3. Recruit professional staff.
      4. Evaluate staff.
      5. Administer inservice training.
   B. Draw up and justify a budget showing fiscal management that follows planning, programming, and budgeting principles.
   C. Be able to apply legal decisions and legal processes to the collegiate institution and to all of its constituents—faculty, students, administrastion, and nonprofessional staff.

    D. Identify and assist undergraduate students who are underprepared for higher education learning experiences.

       1. Describe elements of an academic-assistance program.

    E. Identify the characteristics of critical thinking and problem-solving so they may be applied to improved self-understanding.

    F. Demonstrate how to assist students in developing comprehensive career planning and implementation.

    G. Demonstrate the ability to establish a productive counseling relationship with individuals and with groups.

II. Assessing status, abilities, and progress

    A. Write a report describing the emerging style of governance on the campus and describe the political and social matrix: student, faculty, and administration.

    B. List and describe the opportunities for learning in the external community so that student development may take advantage of the complete resources of a region.

    C. Construct and apply a model for measurement of the effectiveness of the student development program.

       1. Identify quantifiable outcomes of such functions as counseling, financial aids, residence halls, academic assistance, student activities.

    D. Be able to state the purposes, values, competencies, and roles of a student development specialist.

    E. Assess behavior of the college population using clinical and objective methods.

       1. Write a comparison of life styles and cultural differences of student subgroups.

       2. State the principles of growth and development patterns of the student.

    F. List the general characteristics of American institutions of higher education and compare them with the specific characteristics of the local institution.

III. Using principles and techniques for change to facilitate human development

    A. Act in accordance with the list of values (based on professional assumptions) in dealing with students from diverse backgrounds.

    B. List strategies of conflict resolution on campus.

      1. Demonstrate conflict strategies of management in the power models and the collaborative models of administration.

C. Conduct personal growth seminars and discussion groups for improvement of self-understanding.

D. Write out a program of requirements for use by architects.

      1. Describe student needs to the designer of specific educational facilities.

E. Seek solutions to student-related problems, using fact-finding and analysis, given an attitude of serving as defender and interpreter of student concerns.

F. Critique research studies in human behavior in order to describe the application of the findings to the campus population.

G. Complete a research project that tests a hypothesis related to student behavior or institutional characteristics.

The general final objective for a preparation program is this: Given a real or simulated situation where the student development specialist will emphasize one of the three roles—administrative, instructional, or consultative—the specialist will demonstrate specific competencies in three areas: goal-setting, assessment, and the process of change applied to the individual, group, and organization.

The criteria for the list of objectives are derived from the concept that the student development specialist performs so that clientele are able to (a) achieve goals, (b) manage conflict, and (c) become more self-directed and self-fulfilled.

The student development specialist should be able to be perceived as a resource of personal satisfaction and fulfillment. Students should be involved in an ongoing process of self-assessment, goal-setting, use of resources, and behavioral change. Professors of student development, student development specialists, and graduate students should continually relate as full collaborators. Internships and other supervised practice should be available as needed in pursuance of particular objectives. Graduate students should be adequately compensated for the professional services they provide during their program of professional preparation.

The administrative organization of the program should clearly identify the student development program as a graduate program in its own right. Representatives of related departments should be consulted regularly to insure an adequate multidisciplinary base for the curriculum.

To continually improve the program, feedback should be obtained from the field on the performance of graduates.

A master's degree program should be directed toward the preparation of the beginning professional who holds basic humanistic values and evidences potential for facilitating student development. Specialist or sixth-year programs should provide resources for acquiring more sophisticated levels of competence and functions in specific settings of student development. Programs at the doctoral level should give particular attention to values, compentencies, and functions needed for leadership in higher education. Programs at this level require a commitment to scholarship and human development.

Admission, Evaluation and Professional Endorsement

Students seeking admission to programs of professional preparation should be assessed on the bases of values, competencies, and functions. They will be required to perform as student development specialists.

Continuing evaluation during the professional preparation program should be based on the same criteria. Those endorsed by the graduate program for admission to professional practice will thus exhibit behavior most consistent with the professional purposes, values, competencies, and functions stated in this document.

Milieu Management

Burns B. Crookston

Presentation of an emerging key role of the principal student affairs officer

This paper is in large measure an outgrowth of a week-long conference on student development sponsored by the American College Personnel Association in June, 1974 in which a small group, including this writer and John Blackburn, chairman of this program, were invited to conceptualize a model building phase of ACPA's Student Development in Tomorrow's Higher Education project. The result was the publication of a conceptual and operational draft model (Miller and others, 1974) that is now under active consideration by that association. The statement included an articulation of theoretical and methodological foundations for student development in higher education. Among the conclusions reached by the drafting group was that in order to achieve the goals of student development certain basic competencies should be developed by all members of the academic community, but, depending on the nature of the division of labor, each person should develop at least one of these competencies to a higher degree, as suggested by the following chart:

CHART I
BASIC COMPETENCIES NEEDED TO FOSTER STUDENT
DEVELOPMENT IN THE ACADEMIC COMMUNITY

Academic	*Student Development*	*Administrative*
INSTRUCTION	Instruction	Instruction
Consultation	CONSULTATION	Consultation
Milieu Management	Milieu Management	MILIEU MANAGEMENT

The academic community is subdivided into three basic functions: academic, student development, and administration. The drafting group agreed that in order to maximize the achievement of the goals of student development and of the college, which ideally should be one and the same, individuals should possess the same basic *competencies* in instruction, consultation, and milieu management, but with expertise in one or more of them. Thus, those whose functions are primarily academic should be experts in *instruction* (teaching and research), but they also should know how to *consult* with students, staff, and colleagues and others, and be familiar with the concept, scope, problems and functions of *milieu management*. Those whose functions are primarily student developmental should be experts in *consultation*, but with competencies in instruction and milieu management. Finally those whose functions are primarily administrative should be experts in *milieu management* with competencies in instruction and consultation that are also utilized at appropriate times. This commonality of competencies possessed by all facilitates collaborative efforts within the community toward human development goals. At the same time it reduces the likelihood of conflict and misunderstandings that often take place under the usual sharp distinctions drawn among traditional functions in the academic, student affairs, and administrative sectors.

Milieu Management

Our focus here is on milieu management both as a concept integral to student development and as an emerging key role of the principal student affairs officer (PSAO), whom we believe is the most logical person in the central administration to whom the primary responsibility for milieu management (MM) should be designated.

Definitions

What is our milieu? For our purposes it is more than the physical environment in which the institution is located; it includes the intellectual, social, esthetic, creative, cultural, philosophical, emotional, and moral environments as a totality; it includes the interactions among the individuals in all such groups. Milieu involves the interface between and among all those groups that comprise the institution and the interface of these groups with outside groups and environments. And it involves the impact of outside or inside forces on the milieu, whether enhancing or retarding, whether interaction or oppressive, whether collaborative or competitive.

What is milieu management? It is the systematic coordination and integration of the total campus environment—the organizations, the structures, the space, the functions, the people and the relationships of each to all the others and to the whole—toward growth and development as a democratic community. In furtherance of human development theory the relationship of the whole milieu with all its parts, and vice versa, must be symbiotic, or mutually enhancing or growth producing.

Implicit in this definition is goal directionality, the uses of power, influence, skill, and technology toward the creation of a milieu in which optimum conditions for human development prevail; a power that ideally must be derived from the community served and is, as a consequence, an expression of the common will.

Why should MM be the responsibility of the principal student affairs officer? In a recent study of 627 colleges and universities (Crookston and Atkyns, 1974) the principal student affairs officer has in the past decade clearly emerged as a major administrative office on the same level as academic affairs and business affairs at 86 percent of the institutions. Five functional areas are now identified for student affairs: (1) all teaching, counseling, consulting, evaluation, and research functions related to, or labelled as student development that are either institutionally assigned to student affairs, or which function in collaboration with the academic sector; (2) all administrative or para-academic functions assigned to student affairs, such as discipline, scholastic standards, admissions, registration, orientation, records, and student leaves of absence; (3) all other programs and services provided for students by professional or paraprofessional staff that fit into the conventional historic definition of the functions of student personnel work; (4) all activities, programs, and functions generated by, run by and/or controlled by students, or run by students under the control of the institution (even when there is no direct administrative control there is an implicit coordinate or consultative responsibility in student affairs); and (5) all management functions assigned, including housing, college unions, food services, bookstore, and other auxiliary services as the case may be (Crookston, 1975). Thus, the PSAO is the one officer who not only has direct concerns with the students on a 24-hour basis, but has many functions and connections that are academic or feed into the academic sector, business management functions, and functions that lead off campus into the larger community. All this places the PSAO in a strategic position to effectuate milieu management.

Thus, next to the president, who, of course, has to be concerned with the total milieu, the principal student affairs officer is the most logical choice, in terms of preparation (training and experience), span of administrative and program responsibility, and philosophical perspective and who by definition must look upon the campus in its total environmental and ecological perspective. Ideally the entire leadership of the college should be possessed of such perspective, but as a practical matter the burdens of instruction and research and fiscal management and accountability are likely to fall too heavily on the principal academic and business officers respectively for them to give priority to MM.

The Need for a Conceptual Framework

If we think of milieu management as directional (that is, in the direction of student development) rather than merely accepting the status quo and doing the best we then can with it, we need to operate within some type of conceptual framework for student development. A number of such theories have emerged to prominence in recent years. Erik Erickson's and Jean Piaget's theories are examples of life stage or chronological models. Kohlberg's moral development and Maslow's needs toward self-actualization are examples of the hierarchical theories of human development. Blocker (1974) has devised an ecological model of student development by means of superimposing Maslow's hierarchy of needs on Erikson's framework. Using an elementary school example Blocker took Erikson's state "where the child starts to develop understanding and avoid inferiority" and observed that at the same time the child is dealing with Maslow's safety and security needs in preparation for dealing with love and esteem needs. In the light of this dual framework Blocker conceptualized an ecological system represented by the elementary school classroom that could include three ecological subsystems: (1) *the opportunity structure*, the problems the child can learn to master mixed with an optimum environmental stimulation—neither too demanding nor threatening on the one hand, not too boring on the other; (2) *the support structure*, the cognitive and affective resources in the environment for coping with stress, and (3) *the reward structure*, environmental supports such that effort expended will have a payoff toward higher self-esteem. Thus, Blocker combines two theories of human development, places them into an ecological context and comes out with a conceptual framework for utilizing the total environment in support of student development.

The critical point for us here is to emphasize the importance of college in general, and the student affairs organization in particular, in establishing a conceptual framework which forms the basis for the development of a program of milieu management as a vital supporting framework for student development (whether it be Erikson, Maslow, Chickering, or your own conceptual framework tailored to fit the goals of your college and the needs of the members of your campus community).

An example

It is in this spirit that the following conceptual framework is offered as one example of attempting to develop milieu management strategies in the college setting. With apologies to Maslow, here is one way to conceptualize the problem. Let us return to one of our basic premises, that the goals of human development are twofold, the actualization of the individual and of society, and that neither is possible without the other; thus, the relationship between the two must be symbiotic, that is, mutually growth producing.

In order to understand the nature of the symbiotic relationship between individual and group or community, it is useful to compare it with two other modal relationships that are descriptive of the way an educational institution, or an organic component of it, relates to the student. These are the homeostatic mode and the egoistic mode.

CHART II
MODAL RELATIONSHIPS OF INDIVIDUAL TO GROUP
OR COMMUNITY

Mode	Homeostatic	Egoistic		Symbiotic
Needs	Succorance	Love	Adequacy	Fulfillment
	Safety	Belonging	Esteem	Expression
	Security			
Growth				
responses	Comfort	Acceptance	Achievement	Commitment
	Contentment	Capacity for	Mastery	Actualization
	Satisfaction	love		
Defense				
responses	Dependency	Rejection	Ascendance	Escape
	Fight	Inadequacy	dominance	anarchy
	Flight	Compensation	submission	oligarchy
			Acquisition	Parasitism

Homeostatic mode. Homeostatis is the tendency of an organism to maintain itself in a state of dynamic balance or *equilibrium* of compo-nent parts that is optimum to the maintenance of life. Thus, if a person is short of water, a state of thirst ensues until a drink of water restores the balance and satisfies the thirst. In a human society such needs are often satisfied through the dependability of others, as in the case of safety needs.

Social needs such as those for affection, acceptance, love, or security are entirely dependent on a proper response from others, who are also preoccupied with meeting those same needs for themselves. Satisfac-tion of these needs can lead to feelings of *acceptance* of self and others and the capacity to love and be loved. Failure to meet these needs leads to defensive responses of *rejection* of self and others, feelings of inade-quacy, and the triggering of various *compensation* mechanisms.

Egoistic, or Power mode. In the egoistic mode the needs expressed are for *adequacy* and *esteem*. If fulfilled one has a sense of value and worth through *achievement* and *mastery*. Thwarting of these needs can lead to drives toward *ascendancy*, to do better than others, or to have power over others, perhaps to gain respect through coercion; or toward *acquisition* to acquire goods and wealth as a display of achievement, or to buy respect, status or prestige. The eogistic drive toward power is also the expression of unresolved homeostatic needs. For example, if one is hungry and food is scarce, one way to get it is by using power to intimidate, coerce, or manipulate others. Or if one feels insecure or afraid, these feelings can be overcome either by increasing one's power (*dominance*) or by becoming dependent upon one who is more powerful (*submission*).

Symbiotic mode. In a symbiotic relationship, like Carl Rogers' "basic striving," the needs expressed are for *expression* and *fulfillment*. The growth response is commitment to the larger whole, the extension of the self into the group; the self thus becomes actualized. Such terms as Maslow's "actualization" are used to describe the symbiotic goals of human development because they imply a process of expanding, growing, becoming rather than an end-point as expressed by such terms as "fulfillment," "goal attainment," "adjustment," or "maturation." Thus the symbiotic goals of human development may be conceptualized as multi-dimensional, in an expanding, unending sphere or universe, rather than as linear, where there must be a beginning and an end point, or end state. That is why the *output* of the symbiotic mode is defined as a *process. Thus, in human development theory, the ends are also the means.*

Modal Instrumentalities in the College Milieu

Chart III depicts the instrumentalities that might be found in varying degrees on a given campus that purports to be a vehicle through which students are "educated." Despite the legal closing of the *in loco parentis* era in American higher education (when the institution was viewed as a *family* and the president and other authority figures in the administrative and faculty served as *parents* to the students who were regarded as *children*), paternalism is still reflected in the attitudes and behaviors of many of those in student affairs, and certainly persists among many faculty and administrators. This parent-child relationship has two faces; that of the benevolent caring, nurturing parent, and that of the authoritarian, controlling punishing parent. The student development movement emerged in large measure as an effort to change the relationship with students from one of control to one of collaboration; from a status-based authority figure to a competency-based expert and thus, hopefully to reduce the likelihood of negative responses which are largely based on reactions to parental authority.

Increasingly the college, and particularly the large university, is being thought of as an *enterprise*, run by *entrepreneurs* in which the learner is viewed as an output or *product*. More recently, as a reflection of the rise of consumerism in the wider society, the student is becoming viewed as the *consumer*, the product becoming the act of certification at the end of the production line—graduation.

Power. The only instrumentality shown (Chart III) in which the power and control are not vested in those individuals who are at the top of a hierarchy is the *community*. Here control rests in the *membership*, who can use it to invent *processes* by which all can move toward their individual and collective goals. The leadership, and any other instrumentalities created, are responsible to a constituency who hold the ultimate power.

CHART III
MODAL EDUCATIONAL INSTRUMENTALITIES

Mode	Family	Agency	Guild	Enterprise	Community
Control	Parent	Professional	Master	Entrepreneur	Membership
Relationship	Child	Client	Apprentice	Consumer	Constituent
Output	Nurturance	Service	Credentials	Product	Process
Response	Growth	Adjustment	Skill	Skill	Symbiosis
Goal	Maturity	Well-being	Competence	Competence	Democracy
End	Independence	Independence	Independence	?	Interdependence
Negative responses	Dependence	Dependence	Dependence	Dependence	Flight to
	Rebellion	Avoidance	Rebellion	Rebellion	anarchy
	Flight	Apathy	Flight	Slavery	oligarchy
			Apathy		Parasitism
Milieu Management strategies	Consultation	Consultation	Consultation	Consultation	
	Training	Training	Training	Training	
	Primary groups	Proaction Outreach	Consumer advocacy	Community development	
	Temporary systems	Client participation	Consumer participation	Organizational development	
		Organizational development	Organizational development		

The consumer in a managed society. From what I have said thus far it should be clear that I am troubled by what seems to be to be an increasing drift toward a society of consumers whose lives are managed by enterprises. Consider for a moment the way we live—in condominiums which provide all the comforts, including managed diversions, entertainment, and social activities. But the consumer *has* become increasingly effective in influencing the enterpreneural power structure *in order to get what they want.* Thus the rise of consumer groups of all kinds for many purposes. These consumer needs are primarily homeostatic and egoistic—for better, safer products, more conveniences, a more pleasant environment, better services. The consumer is concerned with power only to the extent that those who have it give them what they want. The consumer lives in the here and now. The consumer values goods, gadgets, and experiences that can provide instant gratification.

Big Brother? Aside from the Big Brother issue is the broader question of the ethics of MM. Is milieu management in reality nothing more than manipulation? Is it in a sense directed toward bringing about behavior change through the manipulation of the environment?

Let us first define manipulation as a deliberate attempt to change behavior of others *without their knowledge and consent* regardless of whether such behavior change is good or ill. In a symbiotic academic community, which by definition must be committed to a democratic philosophy, whatever power the milieu manager possesses is not an expression of coercion or manipulation, but is an expression of the common will through the exercise of power derived from the community. There can be no manipulation unless there is an abuse of power in which the milieu manager acts contrary to the wishes of the community. Thus, the *child,* the *apprentice,* the *client,* or the *consumer* revolts, flees, protests, or counter manipulates, because unlike the constituent, they do not have the built-in power to reverse the situation.

This is not to suggest that the PSAO as milieu manager should not use legitimate administrative power to help create an actualizing environment. It means ethical use of power with the full knowledge, urging, or consent of those in the milieu.

MM Strategies

A number of milieu management strategies become obvious when viewing Charts II and III. If the direction of MM, congruent with the goals of student development, is to create an environment in which the general movement of the milieu is in the direction of a symbiotic community, then the employment of such strategies as consultation skills, organization development methodologies, and various kinds of training become appropriate for most areas, with other specific concerns, such as helping the masters move more in the direction of student-centered teaching and a learning partnership or shared journey, being applied as needed. However, first things first. The following steps are suggested.

1. *Data Collection.* What information is available from within and outside the milieu? What additional data do we need to gather? Banning (1974) has reminded us there is a wealth of rarely used and often readily available data all over the campus that need only be gathered in one place and systematically organized and interpreted. Examples are the storehouse of information on students in admissions and records offices, office of institutional research, various administrative offices, from academic deans, the campus engineer, architect, planner, police, the environmental health and safety officer, from faculty research studies, from the library, and so on.

Hundreds of institutions provided the data base for the ACE studies of entering college freshmen over a period of several years. Each institution was given the national norms on dozens of demographic, personal, and attitudinal variables along with a print-out of data for the local school. Only a handful of institutions utilized this gold mine of data. There are other well known instruments such as the CCI and the institutional Goals Inventory that can provide the milieu management team with a picture of what the campus is like along certain variables selected.

2. *Interested people.* Included in the data collection process is the identification to people from the faculty, students, staff, administration, interested citizens, families, government, and other areas who are concerned with aspects of the physical, social, cultural, psychological, and personal environments—from just plain interested persons who want to help, to experts in environmental psychology, community psychology, human development, ecology, organization and community development, and various related areas of research and technology. Such a group should be gathered and their resources brought to bear on various strategies for changing the milieu into a place in which actualization might be more possible.

3. *A base of operations.* A place on campus should be identified in which data can be stored and processed and from which the people can organize to function in the milieu. If there is a center for student or human development, that would be a logical base. Or it could be an expansion of an officer of institutional research and development, or of environmental health and safety. It is easier to expand an existing operation than to start a new one.

4. *Improving Community Governance.* In an incisive analysis of the present state of governance in higher education, Millett (1974) has observed that there are signs the new community governance model—the move toward more egalitarian representation of faculty, students, and administration in the affairs of the institution—appears to be weakening. The students, having gained new personal and social freedoms, seem less interested in the broader issues of governance. All involved are discovering that the deliberations of legislation take vast amounts of time, and many are questioning whether the cost in time and energy is worth the effort. Millet thinks the faculty, having enjoyed formulating institutional policies, are now reluctant to join with the rest of the university to legislate on academic matters where heretofore they had enjoyed considerable autonomy. The prior system of governance, often referred to as an organized anarchy, failed during the past decade on the institutional policy front, but has worked well to serve the vested interests of departmental fiefdoms.

Although one may agree on the surface with the logic of Millet's analysis, the problem appears to have deeper roots—the pervasive influence of the *consumer syndrome* on the attitudes and values of members of the academic community. It is acceptance of the attitude that the work should be done by someone else, that the final responsibility rests with someone else, that the commitment of the participant in governance does not go beyond the decision making stage, and that commitment to action, of carrying out the will of the majority is up to someone else. It is the idea that governance is somehow directed to affect the other guy, not me. Hence the faculty are glad to get involved in matters other than instruction and research, but are highly reluctant to have others involved with their own vested interests.

The problem for the milieu manager then is first one of education and training, and second, building interlocking relationships between and among governance units within the milieu.

John Blackburn has observed that in development of a community there must be a transcendent value upon which commitment can be based. This is a value that is over-arching, held in common by everyone in the community even though values on other issues may differ widely. Such a value is not likely to be found at a large complex institution. The MM should focus instead on the smaller, discrete communities that do exist within the institution, concentrate community building efforts on them, and then try to build a system of interrelated communities as a means to move toward a community of the larger whole.

One of the critical ingredients for the development of commitment to a democratic community is the capacity of the system of governance to find room for the participation of all members of the community in one way or another. We know that participation in the processes helps solidify commitment to the goals. It is amazing how narrow and simplistic is the concept of governance in the minds of many persons who think of governance as legislation—as parliamentary procedures, voting and making laws. In a democratic society governance includes all those processes within an organization that move it toward its goals. These processes can be categorized into three types: those having to do with the establishment of *goals*, with *policies*, and with *procedures*. Goals are contained in the basic documents of the community—the social contract, the constitution, the charter. Policies are the moral, philosophical, conceptual framework that express the lines of action to be taken toward the achievement of the goals. Procedures are the ways and means, the methods to be used.

There are four levels of participation in community governance: 1. *Conceptualization*, the generating of ideas, development of goals, rationale, philosophy; 2. *Authorization*, the decision making processes, the formal acts of the policy making or law making body that spell out what is to be done and who is authorized to do it on behalf of the community; 3. *Implementation*, the execution or carrying out of what is authorized by the community; and 4. *Evaluation*, the collection and analysis of data that tells the community whether its objective has been achieved, whether effectively or ineffectively, and whether it was accomplished within the established policy framework. Members of the community should be afforded the opportunity to participate in any of these levels of governance. The interests of the symbiotic community are furthered by the efforts of the MM to facilitate this process through programs of training to help members function more effectively at any level of participation, through systems linkage between self-governing groups within the larger community, and through organizational development consultation with governing units as organizations.

5. *Who is involved?* Everyone in the campus community should be involved in the creation and development of a symbiotic community— faculty, students, staff, administrators, librarians, maintenance workers, cooks, janitors, craftsmen. It is time to think of the community as a whole, not merely a place that is for students to develop and faculty to teach and do research. This means thinking of a health service for all, not just for students, a library for all, counseling for all, life planning programs for all, organization development, and human development training for all. The MM must have the authority to impact all components of the campus, to have a significant role in the staff and human development of *all* employees.

6. *The physical environment.* By this is meant 1) places to interact, work, talk or play; 2) places to watch, listen, sense, or emote; places to be alone for privacy, peace, solitude, study, or meditation. Environmental psychologists and engineers have learned much about the uses and interrelationships of space, the effects of light, humidity, noise, and temperature. Planning, reconstruction, and management of the physical environment, including traffic flow and walk patterns, movement, and esthetics should be a concern of the milieu manager.

Finally, we are now coming to a stage in our own development as professionals concerned with helping other human beings live out their lives toward actualization, when we must realize that it takes more than focus on the individual, the group, or even the community to create optimal conditions for human development; it requires the marshalling of all forces in the environment.

References

Banning, J. H., Kaiser, L. An Ecological Perspective and Model for Campus Design. *Personnel and Guidance Journal, 52,* 1974, 370–375.

Blocher, D. H. toward an Ecology of Student Development. *Personnel and Guidance Journal, 52* 1974, 360–369.

Crookston, B. B. An Organizational Model for Student Development. NASPA Journal, *10*, 1972, 3–13.

Crookston, B. B. Education for Human Development. In Warnath, C. F. and Associates, *New Directions for College Counselors*. San Francisco: Jossey-Bass, 1973, Ch. 2, 47–65.

Crookston, B. B. and G. C. Atkyns. *A Study of Student Affairs: The Principal Student Affairs Officer, the Functions, the Organization at American Colleges and Universities*. The University of Connecticut Research Foundation, 1974, pp. 58.

Crookston, B. B. Student Personnel—All Hail and Farewell! 1975, Unpublished manuscript.

Miller, T. K. and others. *A Student Development Model for Student Affairs in Tomorrow's Higher Education*. The American College Personnel Association, 1974.

Millett, John. Governance and Leadership in Higher Education. *Management Forum, 3*, December, 1974.

A Student Development Model for Student Affairs in Tomorrow's Higher Education

Summary of the T.H.E. Project

The *Tomorrow's Higher Education (T.H.E.) Project was conceived by the American College Personnel Association in 1968 as a planned response to the rapid and extensive changes expected in higher education in the years ahead. Phase I was implemented for purposes of defining the nature of learning and identifying the fundamental goals and premises of higher education. The Brown* monograph entitled Student Development in Tomorrow's Higher Education: A Return to the Academy *is published to this end.*

Phase II was designed as the model building part of the T.H.E. Project for the purpose of developing a new operational model for student affairs professionals. While student development is viewed as being the responsibility of the full academic community, attention in the following statement is focused on the role of student affairs in tomorrow's higher education. This statement is an outgrowth of T.H.E. Phase II Model Building Conference held June 4–8, 1974, at the University of Georgia. Conference participants were: John Blackburn, University of Denver; Robert D. Brown, University of Nebraska; Richard B. Caple, University of Missouri; Everett M. Chandler, California Polytechnic State University; Don G. Creamer, El Centro College; Burns B. Crookston, University of Connecticut; K. Patricia Cross, Educational Testing Service; W. Harold Grant, Auburn University; Melvene D. Hardee, Florida State University; and Theodore K. Miller, University of Georgia, Chairperson. In addition a process team of University of Georgia students and staff worked with the resource participants. They were Roger G. Bryant, Kenneth L. Ender, Barry L. Jackson, Martha C. McBride, Fred B. Newton, and Judith S. Prince, Process Team Chairperson.

416

Introduction to the T.H.E. Philosophy

Higher education in America is a dynamic institution which, by its very nature, is constantly in a process of change as is the society from which it derives. As our nation has evolved for nearly two hundred years through the agrarian and industrial phases to the present technological era, our educational system has made steady progress from a predominantly elitist toward a predominantly egalitarian system aimed at the development of an educated and enlightened citizenry.

At the present time, we are experiencing the most rapid and dramatic changes in our history, which will demand an ever increasing tempo of activity and response from higher education. In recent years, post-secondary education's needs for renewal and reformation have generated universities without walls (campus free colleges), community colleges, cluster colleges, credit by examination, continuing education units, external degree programs, off-campus experiential semesters, study abroad programs, upward bound programs, and change in liberal arts education as well as an increasing concern for student development. The directions which current change in higher education will ultimately take, however, are not yet clear.

The traditional approach to student affairs has been generally reactive in nature, rather than proactive. If we are to influence the directions to be taken in the future, we must anticipate change and help individuals and groups shape change, not merely adjust to it. Therefore, a statement of our purpose and the creation of an operational model to achieve that purpose is imperative. Such a model, stated in meaningful terms, will facilitate the development of a "proactive" approach which will better direct the efficient use of our professional resources for promoting more fully developed persons within the context of higher education in a world of accelerating change.

The essence of the Tomorrow's Higher Education Project is an attempt to reconceptualize college student affairs work in a way that will serve to provide a measure of creative input from our profession toward the shaping of higher education for the future. By reconceptualization we mean systematic review, reconstruction, and change in the fundamental conceptions about the specific roles, functions, methods and procedures that will characterize our future professional practice.

The T.H.E. Project emphasizes student development. Our need as a profession is to continue developing skills, competencies and knowledge which, when joined in a collaborative effort with others in post-secondary education, can lead to the achievement of the goal of facilitating student development. The role of the student affairs staff is to initiate, facilitate, and encourage actions which will unite the community toward the accomplishment of student development goals.

The Rationale for Student Development

Student development, in the higher-education context, is the application of human development concepts in the post-secondary setting. Human development is a patterned, orderly lifelong process leading to the growth of self-determination and self-direction, which results in more effective behavior.

The theoretical base of the Tomorrow's Higher Education model for student development can be described as eclectic. A synthesis of constructs from several hypotheses about the developmental process, including humanism, life stages and developmental tasks, and behaviorism, suggested the structure for the model and operational definitions for each function. Humanistic theories, such as those proposed by Maslow and Rogers, stress that each individual has within himself or herself the potential to become self-actualized or fully functioning and that growth will occur naturally toward that full potential in an environment conducive to such growth. Developmental-stage theories, such as those presented by Erikson, Havighurst, Blocher, Piaget, Kolberg, and Perry, divide growth into life stages for descriptive purposes. Each life stage is characterized by concurrent and interrelated developmental tasks, defined as the major learnings, adjustments, and achievements facing all individuals in a given society which must be mastered for the continuation of optimal development. Behaviorism attempts to describe human developmental processes by linking the response of organisms to stimuli in the environment; therefore, planning and programming with respect to the environmental conditions in which individuals behave and learn is emphasized. Because the functions identified as important for fostering student development are not tied to any one theory, they can be applied from various theoretical frameworks.

The concept of student development presented herein affirms that in post-secondary education cognitive mastery of knowledge should be integrated with the development of persons along such dimensions as cultural awareness, development of a value system, self-awareness, interpersonal skills, and community responsibility. Self-determination and self-direction can best result when both cognitive and affective development are considered essential to the educational missions of post-secondary institutions.

Student Development Dimensions: Who, When and Where

While the concept of developmental tasks applies equally to infancy and old age, student development focuses upon the developmental tasks encountered by students in post-secondary educational settings, which now must be defined to include late adolescence through adulthood. The focus of student development programming is directed primarily toward students as individuals, in groups, and in organizations, who affiliate themselves as developing learners within any post-secondary institution, whether they be adolescents or mature adults.

If the focus is on students only, however, the goals of student development cannot be fully accomplished. Since every aspect of the higher education environment influences the developmental climate of students, it is imperative that the development of all individuals in the academic community be considered. Therefore, the view of student development in higher education must be broadened to accommodate students, faculty, and staff—all of whom are involved in the process of learning and in the resolution of developmental tasks covering all phases of development.

The developing person is limited neither to a given population nor to a given time frame. The viable student development program takes students wherever they are, developmentally, at the moment and facilitates growth for the future. Since human development is continuous and extends throughout life, institutional responsibilities to students do not end when the academic course of study has been completed. Rather, individuals must be prepared to continue their development in meaningful ways beyond the initial college experience.

Student development is incorporated into and throughout the total institution and, to the extent that students are involved, into the larger community. Wherever students involve themselves and whatever they experience is appropriately the concern of the student development program. This implies that the student's milieu is a significant factor in development and includes both place and time not scheduled by the institution.

Student Development Functions and Staff Competencies in the Student Development Model

The T.H.E. Model calls for a move away from a status-based staffing approach toward a competency-based approach. Functions necessary to create a setting for optimal student and institutional growth are *goal setting, assessment,* and *strategies for student development,* three specific strategies being teaching, consultation, and milieu management. The contribution of the student affairs staff to the creation of an environment in which the student's development is facilitated will depend on the extent to which they systematically possess knowledge and expertise in these functions. The process of student development, therefore, as well as the content, represents a primary area of concern for the student affairs professional desiring to become a student development specialist.

I. Goal Setting

Goal setting involves collaboration between students, student affairs professionals, and faculty for determining the specific behaviors toward which the student wishes to strive. The first step in the setting of goals is to stage the general outcome expected from the resolution of developmental tasks. The focus here is not on the developmental process but on the expected outcomes of that process. The second step is the determination of *specific objectives* consistent with the overall goal. Both goals and objectives are based on sound human development theory and value judgments.

For the student affairs professional, goal setting requires skill in teaching students how to establish general goals and write specific objectives. The prime skill is to focus attention on the student and to interact in ways which will assure that the student takes responsibility for the decisions involved in the goal-setting process.

The primary function served by goal setting within the student developmental process is to establish guidelines for planned development. Through self-determined goals, students are more likely to become responsible for their own learning. By establishing short, intermediate, and long-range goals, students can assess progress in development and student affairs professionals can assess the effectiveness of their approaches.

II. Assessment

Assessment is the determination of the student's present developmental level through techniques such as behavior observation, instrumentation, and self-report. Assessment should focus on academic accomplishments and the broad range of human development tasks and related behavior, including intellectual, personal-social, aesthetic, cultural, and even psycho-motor dimensions.

For the student affairs professional, assessment requires skill in both test and non-test techniques as well as an understanding of the potentialities and limitations of any data collected. In the context of student development, assessment must be designed *with* students rather than for or about them; therefore, students should participate directly in the assessment process. Only data which can be of direct assistance in increasing student self-understanding should be collected. Although not all staff members will specialize in assessment activity, all need to be familiar with its importance to students and its place within the student development program.

As a result of the assessment process the student, in collaboration with student affairs staff and faculty, can better formulate specific personal objectives and identify appropriate behavioral change strategies to be utilized in attainment of those objectives. Likewise, through assessment procedures, the professional staff and faculty can better identify the strengths and weaknesses existent in programming and curricular endeavors.

III. Strategies for Student Development

The strategy or strategies for change selected for use by students must be based on goals which have been collaboratively determined and on the student's current level of development as assessed. The strategies include instruction, consultation, and milieu management.

Instruction refers to any interaction between student and teacher in which learning takes place and includes the more formalized teaching function applied to the achievement of a student's developmental objectives. This strategy combines knowledge and practice as the primary means to facilitate student development.

The teaching approach has potential to "academically legitimize" many valuable out-of-class developmental experiences by making them available to all students and by giving them academic recognition. Some developmental goals common to many students, such as learning how to make decisions, lend themselves very well to systematic teaching approaches. Instruction represents a way of accomplishing these legitimate learning goals via a more formalized teacher-learner relationship rather than indirectly. Integration of developmental goals with ongoing academic programs is desirable as well as the establishment of new curricula, when necessary, designed to give academic credit for structured and unstructured experiences that foster affective as well as cognitive growth.

Application of instructional strategies might include

1. Cooperation with or formulation of a department of human relations: student affairs professionals and academic faculty would teach classes concerned with developmental tasks related to human relations, value clarification, personal and group decision-making processes, and human sexuality.
2. Practicum experiences in human development: student affairs professionals would offer practical experience opportunities con-

cerned with development of self-awareness, interpersonal relationships, effective leadership, and decision-making processes—all offered for academic credit.

3. Individual courses: student affairs professionals would offer individualized developmental courses, continuing orientation courses, weekend workshops, paraprofessional helper training, and career planning programs.

Any human developmental task which lends itself to a teaching approach would be considered appropriate for inclusion within the framework of the instruction strategy for student development.

Consultation represents the utilization of knowledge, technology, and expertise toward achieving a desired objective through counseling, modeling, and similar processes. Inherent in this strategy is the concept that the primary means to self-direction is the acceptance of personal responsibility for one's own development. The role of the student development consultant should include influencing program direction and facilitating action; but it must be remembered that the client, whether student or colleague, must control the decisions and be responsible for the consequences resulting from those decisions.

The consultant should be an expert in the process and content of human development to be sought out as a resource aid to facilitate the decision-making process. Advising, counseling, and collaborative skills are used by the consultant to provide direction for individuals, groups, and organizations in order to facilitate student self-responsibility and self-direction. Two types of consultation in creating an environment are (1) consultation with resource persons, such as faculty, student affairs staff, or administrators and (2) direct consultations with individuals, groups, or organizations seeking help. Examples of consultation methods are

1. Consultation agency or student development center: staffed by experts in research, assessment, group behavior, human development, management, and counseling and others who make themselves available to consult with all members of the campus community.

2. Project teams: staff, faculty, and students with necessary competencies join together to complete a specified task such as planning a learning assistance program or a course for residence hall assistants.

3. Professional staff development: program for faculty and staff to in-

crease their capacity to deal effectively with a wide range of students or to facilitate the introduction of developmental task goals into current curriculum offerings of student activities programs.

4. Direct consultation with students: assistance provided to a residence hall community when a hall council or floor government is being established.

In effect, the consultant facilitates development in others through both indirect and direct contact approaches.

Milieu management is a form of intervention that may be more complex than either instruction or consultation. This change strategy calls for marshalling all pertinent resources of the campus community in an attempt to shape the institutional environments in ways which will facilitate desired change and maximize student development. Solid understanding of campus ecology, management theory, social systems, and the behavioral sciences is basic to the implementation of milieu management programs. A major role of the student affairs professional is one of coordinating and integrating activities to establish a developmental milieu designed to facilitate change toward achieving the desired goals of student self-direction, community maintenance, and an enlightened, democratic citizenry. Understanding of human development processes and the influence of the environment upon those processes is essential as is collaboration among the various institutional constituencies if successful implementation is to be achieved. Examples of milieu management include

1. Development of residence community groups based on common interests or goals which the members wish to explore or achieve (e.g., establishment of an intentional democratic community).

2. Establishment of programs designed to offer students opportunity to meet, mingle, and work together with peers on selected campus or community projects.

3. Implementation of a tutorial program or other student self-help programs designed to involve students in the helping process with others.

Since development is a function of the interaction processes between the individual and the environment, milieu management is an effective and productive way to change behavior through intervention with the total environment as well as directly with the student. The goal of milieu management is to coordinate all facets of an institution so that they contribute to student development.

Tomorrow's Higher Education in Action

Evaluating Student Development Processes and Outcomes

Constant and rigorous evaluation should be an integral part of the Tomorrow's Higher Education student development model. Collection and interpretation of information should be accomplished in two areas: individuals should be helped to monitor their progress toward achievement of personal goals; programs should be evaluated to determine the extent to which they optimize the opportunity for participants to achieve desired outcomes. If individuals systematically assess their movement toward specified goals and objectives, continued development is facilitated. The attainment of predetermined goals by individuals can be assessed for the purpose of evaluating a developmental program, with the quality of the program determined by its influence upon participant outcomes.

Evaluation should begin with an examination of how well the goals and objectives of programs relate to the participant's goals and objectives and how well these are being achieved. To be meaningful, evaluation must be based on pre-established criteria. It is essential, with few exceptions, that both process and outcome criteria be an integral part of the planned student development program. Only as the student and others involved in developmental planning objectively articulate the desired behavioral outcomes and procedures to achieve them can appropriate evaluative measures be employed.

Many suitable techniques (such as instrumentation, self-report, or behavioral observation) which can aid in determination of the degree of progress toward the goal(s), may be utilized. Objective quantitative research and subjective self-survey are acceptable forms of evaluation.

Evaluation offers the best means for clarifying both individual and program objectives and therefore provides a sound basis for modification and future planning. As accountability consciousness grows, the need for evaluating both student development processes and outcomes becomes imperative.

Establishment of Student Development Programs

Applying student development principles in practice does not necessarily call for a total reorganization of the student affairs structure within an institution, although application of the essential elements may lead to new and different associations and alliances within the academic community. There are at least four basic principles which need to be considered when establishing a student development program.

1. Collaboration, both formal and informal in nature, between student affairs staff and faculty is essential to the success of the student development program.

The collaborative relationship may be quite simple and informal or it may be quite complex and formal. It may involve faculty in residence hall or orientation programs and student affairs professionals in teaching or co-teaching academic courses. Collaboration implies that all facets of the academic community work closely and cooperatively concerning the facilitation of student growth.

2. The degree of commitment of the institution to student development is in direct proportion to the number of collaborative relationships (links) established between the student affairs staff and the faculty.

The more interaction and collaborative planning and programming in existence at a given institution, the more likely the student is to be exposed to and have opportunity for development in a fuller sense. Institutions which are truly committed to the concept of student development will invariably exhibit a climate of mutual cooperation throughout.

3. The flexibility and efficiency of the student affairs staff is increased by the degree in which each staff member has minimal competency in all change processes and excellence in at least one.

Success in any program is largely dependent upon the ability of the individuals involved to implement the necessary means to the desired end. The greater the ability of the institution to mobilize staff and faculty possessing competencies and skills essential to achieving the task at hand, the greater the capacity of the institution to achieve its educational mission. Staff development programs designed to upgrade student development competencies are particularly desirable and necessary to continued success.

4. The success of a student development program is not necessarily dependent on the institution's formal structure. Informal linkages which cross formal structures to achieve common goals may be equally successful.

Freedom to cross over the imaginary lines of demarcation and develop new and different linkages within the academic community usually results in creative student development programming. Facilitating cooperative endeavors of an informal nature which may blossom into comprehensive programs or which can be withdrawn represents a most effective way to utilize human resources. This is not to say that support from the top administrative levels is not extremely important. It does suggest, however, that much of value can result from informal interactions within the institution.

Available institutional resources, then, rather than formal organizational structures, determine the most desirable framework with which to structure the student development program. As student affairs professionals, faculty, and students work in mutually cooperative ways; and as they develop skills in all the student development functions, the formal lines between members of the academic community begin to evaporate and more of a team approach tends to emerge wherein the full staff represent a resource pool for student development programming. As this begins to occur, a more fully coordinated and effective program for student development will result.

Summary

The goal of the Tomorrow's Higher Education Project is to reconceptualize student affairs work in a way that will provide a measure of creative input from the student affairs profession toward the shaping of a post-secondary education for the future. Student development must be the keystone of future programs, and Phase II of T.H.E. presents a viable operational model to incorporate student development into and throughout the institution.

The competencies necessary to create a setting for optimal student growth are goal setting, assessment, and three strategies for student development: instruction, consultation, and milieu management. The success of the student development program is based on the extent to which there is collaboration, both formal and informal, between students, student affairs staff, and faculty.

As members of the academic community both learn to understand the stages of development and related developmental tasks through which those in post-secondary institutions are passing and develop competency in the functions necessary to implement the student development model, a learning environment which maximizes the integration of the student's cognitive development with the development of the whole personality can be created.

Student Personnel—All Hail and Farewell!

Burns B. Crookston

In the recent literature the following terms have been used concurrently and at times interchangeably: student personnel, student affairs, personnel work, student development, and human development. The assumption that these terms refer to the same thing is symptomatic of the confusion that has been rampant in our field for many years, particularly the past decade. An examination of the literature and convention programs over the past several years suggests three schools of thought on the subject of terminology: (a) those who cling to the old student personnel point of view will argue that all the above terms are descriptive of student personnel work, the more glamorous terms of student development and human development being at best merely stylish window dressing and at worst a passing fad; (b) those who insist there are important differences, that the terms have distinct, if not separate meanings, and that to continue glossing over them will only compound the confusion that exists not only among the professionals in the field but also within the public they serve; and (c) those who insist what we call ourselves is irrelevant, that there is a need for what we do and the proof of the pudding is how well we do our job, regardless of what it is called.

My position supports the second view: There are important distinctions that must be made, not only for our own peace of mind but also for the benefit of faculty, administrators, parents, students, and public. The major premises to be developed here are (a) that *student personnel work* as historically defined is no longer a viable concept; (b) that *student affairs* should be used to describe an area, sector, or administrative subdivision; (c) that *student development* should be used to describe the underlying philosophy of the field and the operating concepts therein, and (d) that the nomenclature of the campus has already made the above a reality; therefore, the professional literature and professional associations should adjust in usage and nomenclature respectively.

Student Personnel Work

For more than a half century we have lived with the term *student personnel work*, a descriptive anomaly that has seldom been clearly understood by faculty, administrators, alumni, parents, or even students. The word *personnel*, a military term borrowed from the French which refers to manpower, as distinguished from *material*, which refers to equipment, was first used at Northwestern in 1919 by a former World War I army officer, Clarence S. Yoakum, to describe a newly organized placement bureau (Cowley 1936). The rapid expansion of vocational guidance, testing, and placement activities in colleges and universities that took place in the decade of the twenties was accompanied by the parallel establishment of *personnel offices* or *personnel bureaus* to describe not only the place on campus in which these functions were exercised but also the functions themselves. By the end of a decade the term *student personnel work* had been expanded to describe a new "extra class domain" (Cowley 1936; Lloyd-Jones 1929, 1934) that included virtually all noninstructional activities of the college. Thus we had taken a bureaucratic term quite properly used initially to describe placement, testing, and vocational guidance functions and made it a generic term for all activities, programs and services outside the classroom, laboratory, and library that were in any way connected with developing the student. We then added to this conglomeration an educational philosophy undergirding what we called the "student personnel point of view" and said we were "educating" the students. There is little evidence that very many people outside the field have become believers.

An Educational Philosophy? During as time when existentialism had yet to make its impact on higher education, Taylor (1952) had delineated three generally accepted philosophies: rationalism, neo-humanism, and instrumentalism. To the rationalist the sole aim of education is the *development* of intellect and reason. Neo-humanism, while recognizing the primacy of cultivating the mind, assumes a dualism of mind and body, reason and emotion, thought and action, instrumentalism emphasizes the full and creative development of the whole person.

In relating educational philosophies to student personnel work, Lloyd-Jones (1952) observed that under rationalism there was little use for student personnel work save discipline and remedial services. It was at the neo-humanist institutions where student personnel work showed its greatest growth. Even Cowley, who has been given credit for coining the term *holism* to describe education fo the *whole* person, while espousing instrumentalism, actually practiced neo-humanism. He was careful to define student personnel work as *extracurricular*. The faculty, assured that student personnel workers had no intention of invading the sacred groves of academe, allowed or encouraged student personnel people to proceed with the development of often elaborate programs, services, and activities to develop the student outside the classroom. It appears no mere coincidence, therefore, that the philosophical statements of student personnel work during that growth period, the most notable being the *Student Personnel Point of View* (Report of a Conference on the Philosophy and Development of Student Personnel Work (1937), were clearly neo-humanist, thus giving free rein to the establishment of a separate administrative subdivision with a line to the president often coordinate to the academic sector advocated by Lloyd-Jones (1934) and Cowley (1936).

Under instrumentalism, espoused by Clothier and others as early as 1931, student personnel work would serve as an integral component of the total education effort of the institution. And here we come to the crux of the matter. Although writers in the student personnel field during the late forties, fifties, and early sixties extolled the virtues of instrumentalism as a concept, like Cowley twenty years earlier, they were, with few exceptions, content to develop the student *outside* the classroom. Not only was the practice of neo-humanism less threatening to the student personnel worker, in reality there was little choice. Rationalism prevailed at most institutions. Those who were concerned with the matters of the mind held the power, which they were reluctant to share with student personnel workers. From the standpoint of the student personnel worker, implementation of instrumentalism might also signify the end of a laboriously gained separate administrative domain.

Attempts at Bridge Building. As the separatist student personnel programs and services grew, sometimes into large, complex bureaucracies, serious communication problems developed within, as well as with other sectors in the college. The thrust of the movement that had gained strength outside the instructional program now sought stronger ties with the academy. Attempts to build bridges between student personnel and the academy, particularly around strengthening general education (Blaesser 1949; Brouwer 1949; Hardee 1955), led to a broader definition in the literature of that period. Student personnel work now included those processes and functions that helped build curricula, improve methods of instruction, and develop leadership programs (Arbuckle 1953; Barry & Wolf 1957; Blaesser & Crookston 1960; Wrenn, 1951). Student personnel work no longer merely *supplemented* the academic program, it was *complementary* to it. The student personnel worker had become an "educator" collaborating with the classroom teacher toward the development of the student as a whole person (Lloyd-Jones 1953; Williamson 1961), holistic in ideal, yet still dualistic in practice. Williamson (1961, 1963), having endured three decades of frustration with faculty rejection of student personnel work, during which the latter had moved from "ancillary" to "supplementary" to "complementary" but never central to the educational enterprise, insisted his holistic out-of-the-classroom student personnel worker was now an "educator" concerned with matters intellectual as well as social, civic, and emotional. The emergence of the concept of student development in the sixties came out of the recognition that such out-of-class education would never be fully effective until it became incorporated into the total philosophical and educational fabric of the institution.

Student Affairs

For a half century we have tried to convince both ourselves and our public, within and without education, that personnel work meant what we wanted it to mean, rather than what the dictionary said and the public understood. Unfortunately, it has never found its way into any language save our own private jargon. And now there has even been a decrease in the use of the term *personnel* in the nomenclature of our own sector of the campus. There is evidence that such titles as *student affairs*, *student relations*, *student life*, and *student services* emerged as expressions of a need to find more descriptive terms (Crookston 1974). In a recent study (Crookston & Atkyns 1974) of a stratified, representative national sample of 627 four-year colleges and universities, only 12.1 percent used *student personnel* in the generic title of the area and only 2.8 percent of the principal officers used *personnel* in their own title. Conversely, the legitimation of the term *student affairs* to describe a major administrative subdivision or sector had become clearly predominant. In the same study 52.3 percent of the institutions called the sector the division, department, or office of student affairs. The most commonly used title for the principal officer was vice president, dean, director, or coordinator of student, college, or university affairs.

The Crookston-Atkyns study also confirms the establishment of *student affairs* as a major administrative subdivision on the same level, in relation to the president, as academic affairs, business affairs, and other principal areas such as development or public affairs at 86 percent of the institutions. Not only has the student affairs sector as a major subdivision increased nationally when compared with a study conducted in 1962 (Ayers, Tripp & Russel 1966) but its scope has been greatly expanded. Out of a list of 81 functions known to exist in the student affairs sector at one place or another, the present study showed there are 37 functions that are the responsibility of student affairs at over half the institutions. These include management functions and academically related programs and services as well as all those programs, functions, and services usually included in the old student personnel list.

An Operating Definition. Regardless of its merit as a descriptive term, student affairs is now firmly established as a major administrative subdivision in American higher education. But let us not lead ourselves into another nomenclature dilemma. Student affairs is not a philosophy, theory, or concept; it is an area, sector, or administrative subdivision within which there are people, programs, functions, and services, many, if not all, of which contribute to the development of students as whole persons. Within this definition of student affairs, the following functions are identified: (a) all teaching, counseling, consulting, evaluation, and research functions related to or labeled as student development that are either institutionally assigned to student affairs or that function in collaboration with the academic sector; (b) all administrative or para-academic functions assigned to student affairs, such as discipline, scholastic standards, admissions, registration, orientation, records, and student leaves of absence; (c) all other programs and services provided for students by professional or paraprofessional staff that fit into the conventional historic definition of the functions of student personnel work; (d) all activities, programs, and functions generated by, run by, or controlled by students, or run by students under the control of the institution (even when there is no direct administrative control, there is an implicit coordinate or consultative responsibility in student affairs); and (e) all management functions assigned, including housing, college unions, food services, bookstore, and other auxiliary services. Also emerging is *milieu management*, the marshalling of all forces in the educational environment toward the creation of conditions most propitious for student development (Miller et al. 1974).

Student Development

Space does not permit a delineation of the dramatic parade of interlocking and interacting events and circumstances of the past decade that gave rise to the insurgence of *student development* in the terminology of the field. As already intimated, student development is not a new concept; it is a return to holism reinforced with the unerring vision of hindsight. Freed at last from the necessity of exercising the benevolent control of the parent and from adherence to the remedial model of counseling, professionals in our field, within a time-frame of only a few years, have found themselves free to relate to students not on the basis of status, but competency; not reactively, but proactively.

Behind the clamor of demonstrations and disruptions, along with changes in student affairs, some rather dramatic changes were also taking place within many classrooms. Existentialism, the focusing inward on the self, the belief that existence precedes one's essence, and that the individual must take responsibility for one's life, has had great impact. As the examining of one's life becomes academically legitimate, the pedagogical focus must necessarily turn from the subject to the student.

As the new legally defined adult students assume increased intiative and responsibility for their learning, the teacher must acquire more versatility on role responses. The result has been new developmentally oriented courses using teaching approaches that focus on the student's application of knowledge to their own growth and development as persons able to cope in a world of accelerating change. This means classroom teachers, like the student development professionals, must be capable of working effectively within a developmental frame; facilitating, collaborating, consulting (Crookston 1973). Thus, the chasm that has so long separated "teaching" in the classroom and "educating" outside appears to have narrowed to bridgeable proportions on a number of campuses. Such teachers and staff members are both talking the language and using the methodology of student development. Could this mean the dawn of a new era of holism in practice as well as in theory? Certainly the increased viability of student affairs as coordinate to academic affairs in the policy-making arena of the college can strengthen the oods. But time alone can tell.

Definitions. Student development has been defined as the application of the philosophy and principles of human development in the educational setting (Crookston 1972a; Miller and others 1974). Human development refers to the knowledge, conditions, and processes that contribute both to the growth, development, and fulfillment of the individual throughout life as a realized person and effective, productive citizen, and to the growth and development of society. Education for human development is the creation of a humane learning environment within which learners, teachers, and social systems interact and utilize developmental tasks for personal growth and societal betterment. The teaching of human developoment includes any experience in which a teacher interacts with learners as individuals or in groups that contributes to individual, group, or community growth and development and that can be evaluated (Crookston 1972a, 1972b, 1973).

While the above definitions argue that human development is the generic descriptive term for the field, for our purpose there is the difficulty that human development is too encompassing. It includes those processes that affect the development of persons in the whole of life— in any setting, be it school, work, family, group, community, or society at large, and at any age in any circumstance. On the other hand, student development by definition must imply a developmental process limited to an educational setting; it is, therefore, the more preferable term to describe our particular field. While student development suggests that only students are to be developed, this difficulty can be surmounted by the suggestion that all those in the educational setting by definition are "students" at one time or another, depending on the nature of the task and the type and quality of the interaction or transaction involved.

Proposed Nomenclature

Our analysis leads to the following conclusions and proposals: (a) *Student personnel work* should be given its due and retired into history. Efforts should be made in the professional literature and in other communications not to use the term to describe contemporary programs, services, or concepts. Although it is legitimate to use the term in its proper definition to refer to specific functions such as placement, it is recommended that a ten-year moratorium be placed on any such public use of the term, after which presumably there should be no mistake as to its proper meaning and usage, (b) *Student affairs* should be used to describe the sector or administrative subdivision on campus within which there are people, programs, functions, and services, many, if not all, of which contribute to student development. (c) *Student development* should be used to describe the concept, philosophy, underlying theories, and methodologies utilized in the many settings in which student development occurs. (d) Professional associations should change their names accordingly. The following are recommended: (a) Change American Personnel and Guidance Association to Association of Human Development Professions. This adds one word (professions) to a proposal already made by Ivey (1970). The recent addition of the Public Offender Counselor Association highlights the character of the present APGA that reflects the wide spectrum of concern that extends beyond the educational institution into the whole of life. An association of professions concerned with many aspects of human development is both apt and appealing. (b) Changing American College Personnel Association to the Association for College Student Development is under current consideration and should be supported. Most other organizations within APGA now appear functionally descriptive. The long controversy around the use of the term *guidance* is recognized but cannot be dealt with here. (c) Change the names of Personnel and Guidance Journal, Journal of College Student Personnel, and *NASPA Journal* to eliminate *personnel* and make appropriate rewording. The latter two come easy: *Journal of College Student Development* and *Journal of Student Affairs Administration.* The former requires additional consideration. Of equal importance is editorial consistency in the use of terminology. (d) Change National Association of Student Personnel Administrators to National Association of Student Affairs Administrators. There are those within NASPA who would like to change the name to National Association of Student Development Administrators. This would be a mistake because it would confuse a concept with a territory, the same confusion that now exists in their present title with tne term *personnel.* Despite the double entendre, student affairs, like academic affairs, has become the accepted term for our sector. Calling the sector *student development* is bound to raise unnecessarily the territorial hackles of academicians who can rightfully claim that student development is also their proper business, a claim with which we should all most heartily agree.

Finally, perhaps all of the above might persuade those in our academic colleges who are responsible for the training of professionals in our field to do something about changing their archaic course titles and degrees, many of which suggest we are still training student personnel workers to function in the 1950s.

"Student Personnel—All Hail and Farewell!" was edited by Carolyn Palmer, *administrative assistant for staff development in the Housing Division of the University of Illinois.*

References

Arbuckle, D. S. *Student personnel services in higher education.* New York: McGraw-Hill, 1953.

Ayers, A. R.; Tripp, P. A.; & Russel, J. H. *Student services administration in higher education.* Washington, D.C.: U.S. Department of Health, Education & Welfare, 1966.

Barry, R., & Wolf, B. *Modern issues in guidance-personnel work.* New York: Teachers College Press, 1957.

Blaesser, W. W. The future of student personnel work in higher education. In J. G. Fowlkes (Ed.), *Higher education for American society.* Madison: University of Wisconsin Press, 1949.

Blaesser, W. W., & Crookston, B. B. Student personnel work—College and university. *Encyclopedia of Educational Research* (Third Edition), 1960, 1414–1427.

Brouwer, P. J. *Student personnel services in general education.* Washington, D.C.: American Council on Education, 1949.

Clothier, R. C., et al. College personnel principles and functions. *Personnel Journal,* 1931, *10,* 11.

Cowley, W. H. The nature of student personnel work. *Educational Record,* April 1936. 3–27.

Crookston, B. B. A developmental view of academic advising as teaching. *Journal of College Student Personnel,* 1972, *13,* 12–17. (a)

Crookston, B. B. An organizational model for student development. *NASPA Journal,* 1972, *10,* 3–13. (b)

Crookston, B. B. Education for human development. In C. F. Warnath (Ed.), *New directions for college counselors.* San Francisco: Jossey-Bass, 1973. Pp. 47–64.

Crookston, B. B., & Atkyns, G. C. *A study of student affairs: The principal student affairs officer, the functions, the organization at American colleges and universities, 1967–1972. A preliminary summary report.* Storrs, Conn.: University of Connecticut Research Foundation, 1974.

Hardee, M. E. (Ed.) *Counseling and guidance in general education.* Yonkers-on-Hudson, N.Y.: World, 1955.

Ivey, A. E. The association for human development. A revitalized APGA. *Personnel and Guidance Journal,* 1970, *48,* 527–532.

Lloyd-Jones, E. *Student Personnel Work at Northwestern University.* New York: Harper & Brothers, 1929.

Lloyd-Jones, E. Personnel administration. *Journal of Higher Education,* March 1934, *5,* 141–147.

Lloyd-Jones, E. Personnel work and general education. In N. B. Henry (Ed.), *General education* (Fifty-First Yearbook, Part I). Chicago: University of Chicago, National Society for the Study of Education, 1952. Pp. 214–229.

Lloyd-Jones, E. Changing concepts of student personnel work. In E. Lloyd-Jones & M. R. Smith (Eds.), *Student personnel work as deeper teaching.* New York: Harper, 1954. Pp. 1–14.

Miller, T. K., et al. *A student development model for student affairs in tomorrow's higher education.* Washington, D.C.: American College Personnel Association, 1974.

Report of a Conference on the Philosophy and Development of Student Personnel Work in College and University. *The Student personnel point of view* (American Council on Education Studies). Washington, D.C.: ACE, 1937.

Taylor, H. The philosophical foundation of general education. In N. B. Henry (Ed.), *General education* (Fifty-First Yearbook, Part I). Chicago: University of Chicago, National Society for the Study of Education, 1952. Pp. 20–45.

Williamson, E. G. *Student personnel services in colleges and universities.* New York: McGraw-Hill, 1961.

Williamson, E. G. Commentary. In E. Lloyd-Jones & E. M. Westervelt (Eds.), *Behavioral science and guidance: Proposals and perspectives.* New York: Columbia University, Teachers College, Bureau of Publications, 1963. Pp. 54–59.

Wrenn, C. G. *Student personnel work in college,* New York: Ronald Press, 1951.

V

In Conclusion

A Rationale

The decision to select materials was based on an awareness of the history of the College Student Personnel field and the context of higher education. With that in mind, source documents basic to the growth of the profession have been collected, organized and preserved in one volume. Material selected for inclusion in this volume represents professional journal articles, Committee, Commission and Task Force reports.

Consistency in selection of articles, regardless of authorship, was maintained by choosing only those manuscripts contributing to the basic philosophy, ideals and values that formed the identity of the developing profession. Articles were not included that primarily described a specialty function such as financial aid, even though many exemplary and definitive articles were available.

We considered it important to rescue early manuscripts from oblivion such as Yoakum's (1919) in which he used his military personnel experience to call for a systematic approach to student personnel services in higher education. A major criterion for selection of articles and manuscripts was to assure a balance of contributions from practitioners, college student personnel commissions and preparation program faculty.

It is interesting to note that many of the ideas and views expressed by the early authors, such as Clothier and Bradshaw surface again in the 1937 American Council on Education committee report which was a collaborative effort of scholars associated with student personnel work. Their definition of the Student Personnel Point of View and the 1949 revision illustrates agreement among preparation program faculty and practitioners as they considered the essence of their new field.

441

Articles written after 1976 were not included because of a lack of consensus about which articles will bear the test of time and will, in the future, be considered important landmarks of our professional literature.

The Higher Education Context and the Profession

From Harvard in 1626 until the early 1800's the American system of higher education consisted of small church-related institutions, staffed by clerical faculty offering a classical liberal arts curriculum to their all white male students. These young men were preparing for ministerial and other professional roles in the New World. Reflecting the values of the early Colonists, mission statements of these institutions stressed religious and moral character development of students. Although historians suggest that the student personnel movement has its roots in the years between 1870 and 1916, Cowley (1949) reminds us that:

> personnel work . . . what might be called Alma Maternal ministrations to students had characterized the universities of the Middle Ages . . . that what has come to be called personnel work had been in operation for at least seven hundred years. . . .

The appointments of L. B. Hopkins and LeBaron Russel Briggs at Harvard in 1870 as Dean of the College and Dean of Men respectively are generally considered the first administrative recognition afforded student personnel responsibilities.

Changes occurred in American higher education during the 1800's as a result of significant societal events. These events altered the course of our educational system and facilitated the emergence of student personnel work. The secularization of institutions, the increase in size and diversity of the student population resulted from the following factors: Oberlin's decision to admit women, the elective and broadened curriculum initiated by the Land Grant Act, and the thirty year period known as the Germanic influence. These contributed to a new model for higher education. In addition, the application of scientific psychology to the study of behavior through the advances made by Cattell, Thorndike and Scott and in guidance with the work of Paterson, helped shape the new personnel movement. American institutions, previously concerned with the religious welfare of students and later with their intellectual development, began to view and value the student as a whole person.

A formal graduate preparation program was established at Teachers College Columbia University in 1916 to prepare future practitioners/administrators.

Common beliefs, values and operating principles of student personnel work were described in the 1937 and 1949 Student Personnel Point of View. These early student personnel pioneers, Deans of Students, Men, and Women brought to their new responsibilities backgrounds in sociology, educational psychology, counseling and psychology. They focused their efforts on the study of the college student and served in the areas of academic advising, discipline, vocational guidance and placement.

Following World War II and the G.I. Bill, student enrollments on college and university campuses swelled and the functional specialty areas within student personnel grew in response to increased need. Commitments to the ideals of democracy and holism marked the decades of the 1940's and 1950's. Goals for professional practitioners had evolved from serving *in loco parentis* to personalizing and humanizing the educational experience by serving in an avuncular relationship to students. With the student activist movement of the 1960's, the behavioral excesses of some students modified their relationships with student affairs staff members. As the field struggled with an identity crisis brought about by an emphasis on accountability, economic retrenchment, and student consumerism, the future role of college student personnel was the subject of several task forces. During 1972 two new documents, *Student Development Services in Higher Education* published by COSPA and *Student Development in Tomorrow's Higher Education: A Return to the Academy* published under the auspices of ACPA were added to the field's literature.

Individual differences, as advocated in the 1937 and 1949 statements, continued to undergird the new perspective proposed for the field. An orientation focusing on the application of psychosocial and cognitive developmental theories to describe human growth characterized the new philosophy. Professional roles focused on three functions: administration, consultation and instruction. Recommended skills and competencies needed to carry out these functions were goal setting, needs assessment and change strategies. Intentional change was the motivation behind professional practice with the goal being human growth and development applied to all members of the academic community. College student personnel professionals came to be viewed as colleagues with students and faculty. It was recommended that faculty be thought of as partners of the college student personnel professionals as they collaborate for the attainment of the common goal of higher education, student development.

As we look ahead to the year 2000, questions about the future role of the college student personnel field are being debated. Will higher education continue to endorse student development as a goal? Will we ever, in the words of earlier writers, succeed in making the field unnecessary? Will we continue to find in our midst scholars and practitioners who can articulate our unique contributions to higher education?

Study Questions

1. Identify and describe the evolution of the common elements, concepts and assumptions found in the early pieces of literature that contributed to the development of the 1937 and 1949 American Council on Education Statements.
2. Compare the 1937 ACE Statement and the 1949 ACE Statement. How does the viewpoint presented change?
3. Contrast the philosophical assumptions and concepts described by Cowley, Williamson, Parker and Crookston.
4. Using the SPPV as a starting point, develop the chronological sequence of major ideas and values that led to the creation of *The Future of Student Affairs* by Miller and Prince. Your response should contain an analysis of *Student Development Services in Post Secondary Education* and the T.H.E. Project, Phase II, *A Student Development Model for Student Affairs in Tomorrow's Higher Education*.
5. To what extent do you believe Blaesser was accurate or inaccurate in his forecasting of the future of college student personnel?
6. Why did Esther Lloyd-Jones argue for the separation of student personnel administration and student personnel work?
7. Mueller discusses problems associated with counseling women students in 1949. In what ways are her comments reflected in contemporary practice in student affairs?
8. Define each of the following terms and place them in the appropriate historical context: student personnel work, student personnel point of view, student affairs, student development, student personnel educator and student development specialist.

445

9. Compare and discuss the issues of significance found in the ACPA Presidential Addresses.
10. Research is generally considered to be an important aspect of the responsibility assumed by a student affairs practitioner. What evidence can you find to support this view?
11. How has the perception of the average college student, held by the college student personnel/development practitioners changed over the years?
12. Throughout the years 1919 to 1976 the roles and function of the chief student affairs officer have changed dramatically. Identify the changes and suggest a rationale for each change.
13. What particular issues or concerns appear to confront the college student personnel/development profession rather consistently?
14. Identify the ways in which the college student personnel/development profession adjusts or modifies its functions and values as a result of societal conditions. Were the modifications appropriate and why?
15. What statements or viewpoints have been presented by individuals that suggest the nature of the relationship that should exist between (1) the college student and the institution and (2) the student affairs staff and faculty?

Source List

American Council on Education. *The student personnel point of view.* American Council on Education Studies, Series 1, Vol. 1, No. 3. Washington, D.C.: American Council on Education, 1937.

American Council on Education, Committee on Student Personnel Work. (E. G. Williamson, Chmn.) *The Student personnel point of view.* (rev. ed.) American Council on Education Studies, Series 6, No. 13. Washington, D.C.: American Council on Education, 1949.

Berdie, Ralph F. Student Personnel Work: Definition and Redefinition, *Journal of College Student Personnel,* May 1966, 7(3), 131–136.

Blaesser, W. W. The future of student personnel work in higher education, In J. G. Fowlkes (Eds.), *Higher Education for American Society.* University Press, 1948.

Bradshaw, F. F. The scope and aim of a personnel program. *The Educational Record,* January 1936, 120–128.

Chandler, E. M. Student affairs administration in transition. *Journal of College Student Personnel,* September 1973, 14(5), 392–398.

Clothier, R. C. College personnel principles and functions. *The Personnel Journal,* 1931, 10, 9–17.

Commission of Professional Development of COSPA. Student development services in post secondary education. *Journal of College Student Personnel,* November 1975, 16(6), 524–528.

Cowley, W. H. Reflections of a troublesome but hopeful Rip Van Winkle. *Journal of College Student Personnel,* December 1964, 6(2).

Cowley, W. H. Student personnel services in retrospect and prospect. *School and Society,* January 19, 1957, 19–22.

Cowley, W. H. The nature of student personnel work. *Educational Record,* April 1936, 3–27.

Cowley, W. H. and Waller, W. A study of student life. *Journal of Higher Education,* Vol. 6, March 1935, 132–142.

Crookston, B. B. An organizational model for student development. *NASPA Journal,* July 1972, 10(1), 3–13.

Crookston, B. B. Milieu management. *NASPA Journal,* 1975, 13(1), 44–55.

447

Crookston, B. B. Student personnel—all hail and farewell. *Personnel and Guidance Journal*, September 1976, 55(1), 26–29.

Crookston, B. B. and Blaesser, W. W. An approach to planned change in a college setting. *The Personnel and Guidance Journal*, March 1962, 40(7), 610–616.

Dewey, M. E. The student personnel worker of 1980. *NAWDC Journal*, Winter 1972, 35(2), 59–64.

Greenleaf, E. A. How others see us . . . *Journal of College Student Personnel*, July 1968, 9(4), 225–231.

Hardee, M. D. Perception and perfection. *Journal of College Student Personnel*, June 1963, IV(4), 194–204.

Harvey, T. R. Some future directions for student personnel administration. *Journal of College Student Personnel*, July 1974, 15(4), 243–247.

Hopkins, E. H. The essentials of a student personnel program. *Educational and Psychological Measurement*, Autumn 1948, 8(III), 430–450.

Hurst, J. C. and Ivey, A. E. Toward a radicalization of student personnel. *Journal of College Student Personnel*, 1971, 12(3), 165–168.

Ivey, A. E. and Morrill, W. H. Confrontation, communication and encounter: A conceptual framework for student development. *NASPA Journal*, 1970, 71, 226–234.

Kirk, B. A. Identity crisis—1965. *Journal of College Student Personnel*, Vol. 6, 4, 1965, 194–199.

Lewis, C. L. College student personnel: A current estimate. *Journal of College Student Personnel*, January 1973, 14(1), 5–9.

Lloyd-Jones, E. Personnel administration. *Journal of Higher Education*, March 1934, 5(3), 141–147.

Mueller, K. H. Problems in counseling women. In E. G. Williamson (Eds.), *Trends in Student Personnel Work* (Part XIII: Personnel Problems of Women). University of Minnesota Press, 1949.

Mueller, K. H. Three dilemmas of the student personnel profession and their resolution. *NAWDC Journal*, Winter 1966, 29(2), 81–91.

Parker, C. A. Student development: What does it mean? *Journal of College Student Personnel*, July 1974, 15(4), 248–256.

Penney, J. F. (1969). Student personnel work: A profession stillborn. *The Personnel and Guidance Journal*, 47(10), 958–962.

Shaffer, R. H. An emerging role of student personnel—contributing to organizational effectiveness. *Journal of College Student Personnel*, September 1973, 14(5), 386–391.

Shaffer, R. H. Student personnel problems requiring a campus wide approach. *Journal of College Student Personnel*, 1961, Vol. 3, 2, 60–65.

T.H.E. Phase II Model Building Conference. A student development model for student affairs in tomorrow's higher education. *Journal of College Student Personnel*, July 1975, Vol. 16, No. 4, pp. 334–341.

Tripp, P. A. Student personnel workers: Student development experts of the future. *NAWDC Journal*, Spring 1968, 142–144.

Trueblood, D. L. ACPA President's message: The college student personnel leader of the future is an educator. *Journal of College Student Personnel*, 1964, V(3), 186–188.

Williamson, E. G. Some unresolved problems in student personnel work. *NASPA Journal*, 1967, 5, 91–96.

Wrenn, C. G. The fault dear Brutus . . . *Educational and Psychological Measurement*, Autumn 1949, 9(3), 360–378.

Yoakum, C. S. Plan for a personnel bureau in educational institutions. *School and Society*, May 10, 1919, IX(228), 556–559.

Above articles reprinted with permission